PENGUIN BOOKS

THE POLITICAL ANIMAL

Jeremy Paxman was born in Yorkshire. He is a journalist, best known for his work presenting *Newsnight* and *University Challenge*. Four of his previous books, *Friends in High Places*, *Fish, Fishing and the Meaning of Life*, *The English* and *The Political Animal* are published in Penguin.

The Political Animal

An Anatomy

JEREMY PAXMAN

PENGUIN BOOKS

PENGUIN BOOKS

Published by the Penguin Group
Penguin Books Ltd, 80 Strand, London WC2R ORL, England
Penguin Putnam Inc., 375 Hudson Street, New York, New York 10014, USA
Penguin Books Australia Ltd, 250 Camberwell Road,
Camberwell, Victoria 3124, Australia
Penguin Books Canada Ltd, 10 Alcorn Avenue, Toronto, Ontario, Canada M4V 3B2
Penguin Books India (P) Ltd, 11 Community Centre,
Panchsheel Park, New Delhi – 110 017, India
Penguin Books (NZ) Ltd, Cnr Rosedale and Airborne Roads,
Albany, Auckland, New Zealand
Penguin Books (South Africa) (Pty) Ltd, 24 Sturdee Avenue,
Rosebank 2196, South Africa

Penguin Books Ltd, Registered Offices: 80 Strand, London WC2R ORL, England

www.penguin.com

Published by Michael Joseph 2002
Published in Penguin Books 2003
1

Grateful acknowledgement is made to the Master and Fellows of University College,
Oxford, for permission to quote from the letters of Clement Attlee, and to Secker &
Warburg for extracts from Lucille Iremonger's *The Fiery Chariot*.

Every effort has been made to contact copyright-holders. Any error or omission will be
made good in subsequent editions.

The moral right of the author has been asserted

Typeset by Rowland Phototypesetting Ltd, Bury St Edmunds, Suffolk
Printed in England by Clays Ltd, St Ives plc

Pour encourager les autres . . .

Contents

Preface

Imagine the scene. A school speech day. In the hall, row after row of school blazers, their occupants caught in a maelstrom of hope and hormones, acne and apprehension. Behind them, their parents, aunts, uncles and a few bored younger brothers and sisters. On the stage, the headmaster and the chairman of the governors listen approvingly as the visiting speaker, one of the biggest names in British politics, reaches the climax of his address.

'Sad to think', he says, 'that in the days of Winston Churchill and Theodore [*sic*] Roosevelt,★ people didn't consider "service" was a dirty word. And loving your country was taken for granted.' The man speaks with passion; he loves this sort of audience. He tears off his frameless glasses and peers down into the ranks of teenagers. 'I hope', he roars at them, 'I see in this audience a future Prime Minister. I hope I see future cabinet ministers. I hope in this audience I see young people who will stand up and say "I want to serve my country" and not have others around them sniggering and laughing because they don't understand service and they don't love their country.'

It has the feel of a performance which has been given many times before, with overdramatic pauses and studied rhetorical flourishes: he is a rotten actor. This is ironic, since his whole life has been an act, based on a script he has written himself, which has given him a seat in the House of Commons, considerable wealth, deputy chairmanship of one of the biggest parties in British politics, a place in the House of Lords and the endorsement of his current party leader, who describes him as a figure of 'probity and integrity'. This audience, like most of those he addresses, long ago suspended any disbelief. He has another trope. 'I get five or six calls a day asking me to go on television. You know

★ Teddy Roosevelt had been dead twenty years by the time Churchill became Prime Minister. Perhaps he means Franklin D. Roosevelt. Anyway, the point is clear enough.

what I do? I say no to all of them. Why should I go on television to be beaten up by some ill-mannered lout who's never given any public service? Do you know what I say, ladies and gentlemen?' – and here he stabs the air with his finger – 'I say when that interviewer stands for office, when he gives some public service, then *I'll* interview *him*.'

He pauses, waiting for the applause. It always comes. His stage irritation seems to reflect a real frustration that those in what he calls 'public service' (he means politicians, rather than nurses, teachers or people who raise money to relieve world poverty) are denied the respect they deserve, sneered at, laughed at, or – unkindest of all – ignored by the British people, who seem at best indifferent to the charms or importance of politics. The louts in the television studios have all the fun and none of the responsibility. Fewer and fewer people bother even to vote.

The speaker seems genuinely to care about the state of public life in Britain. I care too. In an ideal world, of course, we wouldn't have any politicians at all. As Tom Paine remarked in the eighteenth century, 'Government, even in its best state, is but a necessary evil.' Politicians exist because we disagree. All societies need to decide how to protect themselves, how to organize themselves, how to share out their resources and the alternative to force of argument is force of fists. The creation of politics is, therefore, a proof of civilization. So, although the existence of politics may be a mark of human frailty, politics itself matters. And it matters that politics is practised by good people. As in most walks of life, people go into the trade with a variety of motives, some noble, some vain. Most seem to be genuinely convinced they can make the world a better place. Some of them have done so. A small number genuinely deserve to be called great. I do not believe they are all scoundrels.

I set out in this book to answer a number of simple questions. Where do these politicians come from? Why do they do it? Why do we seem to be so disenchanted with them? And why does the experience of politics nearly always end in disillusion? This book is not really the story of the achievements of Prime Ministers and Foreign Secretaries – they write their own memoirs, some of which I have drawn upon. Nor is it about local politics, which has become a sorry shadow of its former self. It is about the experience of politics on the biggest stage available to the ambitious young man or woman, in the Houses of Parliament. It is about how the actors in this theatre get where they want to be and about what the experience does to them. Perhaps, if we can answer these questions, we can begin to understand why the rest of us feel as we do about them.

By the time I had finished the manuscript of this book, the speech-day orator had embarked on the latest chapter of his career of public service. Jeffrey Archer was serving four years in prison for perjury.

Introduction

My first encounter with one of this curious tribe came at school. I must have been about seventeen when the local MP was invited to speak to the sixth form. More likely, he invited himself: politicians like to speak to local schools because they know that today's sixth-formers are tomorrow's voters.

I thought he was mad. Not in a foaming-at-the-mouth, baying-at-the-moon way, of course. Just very, very peculiar. He wore a loud suit in a Prince of Wales check, a blue shirt with a white collar, and a carnation in his buttonhole. He may even have had a bow tie as well. This was no more than you might expect to find draped around one of the flashier bookies at Epsom racecourse. But what stood out, what positively shrieked 'look at me!', was his moustache. This vast expanse of hair (he was bald on the top of his head) spread out from his upper lip and across his cheeks like two bushes from *The Day of the Triffids* on a race to his ears. Older readers may by now have identified Gerald Nabarro, the Conservative MP for South Worcestershire, a man who drove around in a fleet of cars marked NAB 1, NAB 2 and so on.

Nabarro, son of an unsuccessful cigar merchant, had left school in a London slum at the age of thirteen, run away to sea at fourteen and then, faking his age, joined the army, where an eight-year career saw him rise to the rank of sergeant. He then rapidly made a fortune in the timber trade and decided to become a politician. Nabarro used his twenty years in the House of Commons to become a celebrity. No successful radio discussion was complete without his fruity voice thundering out fruity opinions about the need to castrate sex offenders or to repatriate immigrants. Had he been less of a show-off, he might have risen within the Conservative party, for he had a tremendous grasp of detail in energy and tax matters (why, he asked in one of his 400 questions on purchase tax, was there a 30 per cent levy on false beards and moustaches?). To his credit, he could claim to have become the first man in the twentieth century to bring four of his own backbench bills on to the statute book, including clean-air legislation. One of his legacies was to bequeath to British politics a secretary, Christine Holman, who achieved greatness a quarter of a century later as the formidable wife of the disgraced Conservative politician Neil Hamilton and as author of the *Bumper Book of Battleaxes*. I recall little of what he said that day, beyond an exchange with one of the Jewish boys in which he claimed that they were almost certainly related, since both their ancestors had come from Spain or Portugal. There were some not particularly persuasive platitudes about the damage being done to the country by the Labour government, students, drugs, pornography and pop music. But, most of all, what Nabarro seemed to offer was a recitation – in a booming voice – of saloon-bar prejudices about immigration, Europe and why it had been right to prevent black majority rule in Rhodesia. These points of view were not particularly unusual, but there was an uneasy sense that we were listening to a litany of opinions which were held more by force of habit and repetition than anything else.

At university, I joined the Labour Club, but dropped out of any active involvement after one meeting. Student politics achieved the curious feat of being self-important and trivial at the same time. Outside the Labour, Conservative and Liberal clubs, there were huge battles to be fought about Vietnam, the military junta in Greece or why the college gates were locked at midnight. But the mainstream political organizations seemed to be dominated by people who had sketched out their life-plan at the age of fifteen and left no room in it for the main interests of most of the rest of us. Their idea of a good time seemed to be cobbling together draft resolutions for the annual party conference. I did vote against Gerald Nabarro in my first General Election, but then I knew no contemporary who would have done any different. My defiance made no difference. If you had put a Conservative rosette on a moustachioed hamster it would have been elected. The only thing which would stop Nabarro was Nabarro, and in the end he did it himself. In 1971 NAB 1 was caught careering the wrong way around a roundabout in Hampshire. Since he had made himself one of the best-known men in Britain, witnesses had no trouble positively identifying Nabarro as the driver. Yet the MP had the audacity to claim that it was not he at the wheel, but his long-suffering business secretary, a woman called Margaret Mason. The jury did not understand quite how a bald head and handlebar moustache could have been attributed to a female, and the judge fined Nabarro £250. Being the sort of person he was, the MP claimed that a terrible miscarriage of justice had occurred, appealed the verdict and, remarkably, won the case. Christine Holman appeared beside him on the steps of Winchester Court, weeping with relief that her boss had won the day. But, for all his booming proclamation that 'calumny has been defeated', the strain had broken him, and he died before the 1974 elections.

By then, I had started work as a journalist in Belfast. In Northern Ireland, I came across a form of politics which had nothing much to do with Nabarro-like flamboyance. But then, it had nothing much to do with the rest of the world either. The Unionists ranged from ascendancy toffs to sinister bigots, the nationalists from machine professionals whose power was built upon an intimate knowledge of the death notices in the *Irish News* to Jesuitical fanatics whose specialist subject was the naming of parts in an Armalite rifle. It was a form of politics which could never be accused of valuing style over substance. It was all substance and no style. One of the reasons that London-based British politicians so signally failed to make any progress in Northern Ireland for so many years was that they simply could not comprehend the intensity with which sectarian political beliefs were held. It was the first time in my life that I met people my own age, or younger, who carried guns. The first time I ever saw a General Election result being declared was at Ian Paisley's count in Ballymena. He had been sent back to parliament with *a majority* of over 27,000, which was more than the entire adult population of the town where the count was held. It made his seat one of the rock-solid safest in the United Kingdom (although in the neighbouring constituency the Unionist MP had an even bigger majority, at over 35,000, the biggest in the entire United Kingdom: if you weren't a Unionist you might as well have turned your ballot paper into a paper dart). When the returning officer finished announcing Paisley's result, the big man, encased in a vast grey leather overcoat, boomed out the doxology, 'Praise God from whom all blessings flow.' The crowd closed their eyes and took it up enthusiastically. It was life, but not as we knew it.

Occasionally, I would meet the Secretary of State sent by the Labour government in London to try to bring some semblance of normal politics to the place. Merlyn Rees, a bespectacled man who looked and sounded like the best sort of headmaster, was thoughtful, compassionate and a real worrier. But too many generations had passed in the absence of real politics: between the partition of Ireland in 1922 and the outbreak of the Troubles in 1968 the British government had been content for the place to be run as a corrupt little Unionist fiefdom. Inventing genuine democratic politics was a tall order. For a brief while Rees managed to get politicians from either side of the fence working together, but it all fell apart when hard-line Unionists called a General Strike, backed by gangs of thugs on the streets, and brought the place to a standstill. Idealism drowned when the sewage farms were on the point of overflowing. Still he soldiered on trying to find a space where conventional politics could replace war, and for a while there was even a ceasefire between the IRA and the British army. But there was too much history to be accounted for and too much to be lived. When the truce collapsed and the bombings started again, the story went that Merlyn Rees had wept. It was all too believable. After a couple of years, this thoughtful man was replaced by a former miner, Roy Mason, who had, to put it mildly, a less complicated view of the world.

When I returned to England after three years in Northern Ireland, I shared a house with a friend who was hoping to become a Liberal MP. Every weekend he would be out pounding the pavements getting signatures for petitions about dog mess in the park. On Sundays, he was up to his armpits in old newspapers and discarded telephone directories, working at the Liberals' recycling dump. It did not leave much time for a social life, although there was an intriguing period when a girl in motorbike leathers hung around the house. It turned out she worked in Conservative Central Office, but the late-night yelps from my flatmate's bedroom indicated that they, at least, had worked out some sort of power-sharing arrangement. Eventually, he accumulated enough credit in the bank to be chosen as the Liberal parliamentary candidate in what he was told was one of the party's ten most winnable seats. It turned out not to be. But by then he had moved to the constituency and his friend had set about trying to get a Tory nomination somewhere. Neither ever made it to Westminster.

A couple of years later, I was living in Notting Hill, which was part of the safe-ish Conservative seat of Kensington. The MP was a gangly, backbench baronet, Sir Brandon Rhys-Williams, a grandson of Lord Curzon's mistress and son of a Liberal MP, an expert on the European Social Charter, who proclaimed his ambition to create 'a full-scale tax credit system incorporating a structure of positive personal allowances as a feature of the community tax system'. At election time he would take himself down to the Portobello Road market with a megaphone where his impeccable Old Etonian vowels would be metallically mangled while the indifferent throng tried to go about their lawful business of buying fruit and veg. Occasionally, the crowd parted and you could see a balding fellow in a three-piece tweed suit speaking to no one in particular, but with a seraphic grin on his face. He was enjoying himself.

I saw a little more of Rhys-Williams's successor. Dudley Fishburn had been a writer on the *Economist*, and never really looked any more at home among the greengrocers than Rhys-Williams had. Doubtless, like all would-be MPs at elections, he spent time sprinting up and down people's front gardens, begging for their votes, but I saw him most often in the passenger seat of a car plastered with sandwich boards, jabbering into a microphone. 'Vote for me,' he bleated at people having lunch behind plateglass windows. 'Your Conservative candidate, Deadly Fishbone.'

He left parliament around the time I moved house, and our paths did not cross again, although I did once get a letter from him, after I had written asking him to support some campaign or other. I was impressed to receive a handwritten reply, presumably scribbled one day when he was sitting in the House of Commons chamber waiting to make a speech about Endogenous Growth Theory. The only problem was that he had obviously had such difficulty balancing the paper on his knee that the thing was more or less unreadable. There have been other MPs since then, including one Conservative who solicited my vote only weeks after he had denounced me in the House of Commons as a 'socialist' and in private as a 'thoroughgoing communist'. I sent him his letter back, stapled to a copy of the relevant page of Hansard, with the words 'You must be joking' scrawled across the bottom.

Until I started reporting on British politics – at the relatively late age of thirty-five – this was just about the sum total of my experience of our politicians. Scanty though it is, it is still probably a greater familiarity than most of us have. Since then, I have met literally hundreds of politicians. Some I have come to like, others to respect, and one or two I have learned must be handled as if they are radio-active. I know that the last feeling is reciprocated by some, but there is – or ought to be – a natural tension between reporters and politicians, and I am not close to any of them. It is easier that way. The Prime Minister's wife, Cherie Booth, once accosted me at a party and accused me of believing that 'we're all crooks'. She went on to claim that journalists were 'only in it for the money' and 'not bothered about the truth'. The best I could manage in reply was to ask if she had confused us with lawyers. Quite apart from the odd use of the word 'we', the taunt was untrue. I most emphatically do not believe that they are all crooks. Or even that they are all, always, dishonest.

But they are different from us. This book is an attempt to find out why. For a long time, I was going to call it 'Why Does It Always End in Tears?' – because that, it seems to me, is the nature of the political experience. Very few politicians leave the stage happily. Prime Ministers outstay their welcome. Party leaders are sacrificed by their parties (then, as Margaret Thatcher showed, the tears can be real). Ministers rail at the difficulty of getting anything done, and then lose their jobs because Prime Ministers want to survive. MPs despair at the absence of advancement. Voters' enthusiasm turns to disenchantment. Increasing numbers of us are finding the whole process so unappealing that we simply do not bother to vote. For most of us, elections are the one time when we have some direct contact with politicians. And what a strange bunch they seem on these brief encounters, men and women overwhelmed by a sense of their own importance, energetic, driven and wholly without a sense of proportion. Getting our endorsement – the approval of people they probably haven't even met before – really does seem the most important thing in their lives.

In the most dramatic election of recent history, in 1997, there were 3,724 people attempting to get into parliament, more than at any time in British history.[1] One quarter of them were out-and-out no-hopers with no party machine behind them, ranging from the earnest – Independent No to Europe party (515 votes in Fareham) or the Anti-Abortion Euthanasia Embryo Experiments (318 votes in Oxford East) – through the over-ambitious local candidates, like the Sheffield Independent party (which got 125 votes in Sheffield), the Island Independent (848 votes on the Isle of Wight) or the People in Slough Shunning Useless Politicians candidate (277 votes), to the idiotic – the Fancy Dress party (287 votes in Dartford), the Teddy Bear Alliance (218 votes in Kensington and Chelsea), the Mongolian Barbecue Great Place to Party party (112 votes in Wimbledon) or the Black-Haired Medium-Build Caucasian Male party (71 votes in St Ives). A benign interpretation would be that these are people for whom the electoral process is a form of therapy.

By-elections, which usually take place in the middle of a parliament when the sitting MP has dropped dead, can attract vast numbers of them, like horseflies to fresh dung. Screaming Lord Sutch, who founded the Monster Raving Loony party, stood in nearly forty elections of one kind or another, advocating policies such as putting crocodiles in the River Thames, banning January and February to make winter shorter and breeding fish in the European Wine Lake, so that they emerged ready pickled. There was never the slightest danger of his being elected, although in one by-election he did poll more votes than David Owen's immensely self-important Social Democrats, which prompted the party to give itself the last rites. Before he hanged himself with a multi-coloured skipping rope in a fit of depression, Sutch had made himself a feature of British political life, his top hat and leopardskin coat a spectacle on one declaration stage after another. When Martin Bell became the first true Independent[2] to win a seat in over fifty years – trouncing Neil Hamilton in the 1997 General Election – he spent much of the night of his victory working out how to avoid delivering his acceptance speech from between the flashing metal nipples of a seven-foot transvestite, who had used the election to campaign on behalf of a Birmingham nightclub.

It would have taken an outburst of contagious insanity for the people of Tatton to have elected Miss Moneypenny the Transformer as their MP (although he/she nonetheless picked up 128 votes). But, in truth, an absolute majority of candidates, not just the frivolous fringe, were losers from the start. Most of the Conservatives, most Liberal Democrats, most of the Scottish Nationalists, most Plaid Cymru, were wasting their time. Throughout the previous decade, most Labour candidates had known – or ought to have known – that they might as well have been beating their heads against a wall. In the first-past-the-post system, even if forty-nine out of every hundred people vote for you, if someone else has the votes of the other fifty-one, you get nothing. A Conservative standing in Bootle or Merthyr Tydfil or a Labour candidate in Huntingdon or Sutton Coldfield might as well spend the campaign playing tiddlywinks. However fiercely they whistle to keep their spirits up, they will not be elected to parliament. It follows that of the 3,724 men and women who stood for election, the great majority, well over 2,000, had the political life expectancy of snowflakes in summer. They had no more chance of becoming an MP than Miss Moneypenny.

The Liberal Democrats have been complaining for years that the British system at General Elections, by which only one candidate can be chosen for each constituency, is unfair. It can certainly produce some eccentric results. In 1951, it ejected Clement Attlee's great, reforming Labour government and replaced it with Churchill's Conservatives, even though more people had voted Labour than Conservative. In February 1974, more people voted Conservative than Labour, yet Labour formed the government. If Britain were to change its electoral system so that the number of MPs reflected the number of votes cast, it would certainly be fairer and perhaps parliament would rise in public esteem. But the change could also massively enhance the power of the party machines at the expense of independent-minded candidates and loosen the bonds between an individual MP and his constituency. It would certainly greatly increase the number of Liberal Democrat MPs (though they ask us to accept that they are making this pitch not out of self-interest but from principle). It is an issue for later. What matters for now is how any man or woman survives this lottery.

The first requirement for any ambitious candidate, obviously, is self-confidence. How many ordinary people can reduce every issue in the world to two competing questions? You must then be willing to stand up in public to declare that 'There are two ways of looking at this issue: my way and my opponent's way. My way is right. Her way is wrong.' But the readiness to reduce everything to simple binary choices is not the point. Modern politicians from the major parties are given a list of right noises to make on any subject from the size of the nuclear arsenal to what ought to go into powdered milk. No, what is striking is the public certitude, the sheer brass neck, to pronounce that yours is the one and only sensible attitude for an adult to strike. Privately, many MPs have often confessed, to diaries or to intimate friends, that they find a particular cause hard to stomach, misguided or dangerous. But they cannot say so publicly. It would be suicide.

Allied to self-confidence, or the appearance of self-confidence, is a certain sort of manic persistence. Betty Boothroyd, who eventually discovered that the exuberant exhibitionism of a Tiller Girl was good training for the demands of being Speaker of the House of Commons, spent seventeen years fighting unsuccessful elections before she was at last selected for the winnable Black Country seat of West Bromwich. She supported herself by working as a House of Commons secretary for the best part of two decades. Caroline Spelman, the sugar-beet expert who was one of that small band of Conservatives who first became MPs at the 1997 election, went through twenty-seven selection interviews before she was finally chosen for a winnable seat. It has become received wisdom (at least among many female politicians) that people like Boothroyd and Spelman found the going tough because they were women. Boothroyd herself was fond of repeating the story of a woman who told her, 'Well, I'm not going to vote for you because you're unmarried, you don't know anything about life, you don't have any children and you don't know how to run a house.'[3]

Despite the fact that these criticisms were allegedly levelled *by* a woman, and could just as readily have been directed *at* a man, the story has the advantage of seeming to endorse the conviction that there is a general prejudice against women in parliament. But plenty of men have had to show a similar Stakhanovite dedication to get themselves elected to parliament. Andrew Mackinlay – one of the minority of Labour MPs who seems to believe that the House of Commons should be more than a hired claque, there only to tell the

Prime Minister how wonderful he is – trailed around the country trying to persuade local Labour parties to give him a chance. Some of the auditions for these unwinnable seats required travelling hundreds of miles to dusty meeting halls, in the knowledge that next morning he had to be back at work. At the end of the selection process, the chairwoman would emerge to announce that they had chosen someone else, with the implicit snub 'because the rest of you aren't good enough'. It takes a thick skin to cope with that level of repeated rejection. Even when finally chosen, Mackinlay had to fight and lose four elections, until, at the fifth attempt, he finally got to the House of Commons.

If the first two requirements, of self-confidence (or the appearance thereof) and dedication, are psychological, the third is physical. To be successful, you need enormous reserves of energy. Margaret Thatcher, famously, is reputed to have managed on only four or five hours' sleep each night. (Both Hitler and Napoleon were said to have been able to get by with only three hours in bed; whether either is a recommendation for sleep deprivation is another matter.) Churchill's authority over his colleagues was bolstered by the fact that he could eat and drink them under the table. If there was an 'r' in the month, he began shadow cabinet lunches with a dozen oysters, followed by roast beef and vegetables. This was succeeded by another helping of beef and vegetables, and then a big portion of apple pie and ice cream. All was washed down first with wine and then with brandy. 'I get the drink. Stafford Cripps gets the blue nose. That's life,' he told one of his colleagues.[4]

Fourth, you must be an incurable optimist. Betty Boothroyd claims that she genuinely believed she could take every one of the unwinnable seats in which she served her parliamentary apprenticeship. Self-delusion on that scale is an obvious asset. You also need to believe that if your party gains power the world really will be changed for the better. Once you are elected, the optimism will help blind you to the fact that so much of your life is a luminous waste of time. MPs are sent to Westminster to represent their constituents and there is no career structure for a backbench MP. They must make the job up as they go along, and there may come a point when opening the seventy-eighth garden fête or speaking at the ninety-third dreary dinner begins to pall. Yet to advance in the party, to stand a chance of getting a post as the most junior of ministers, you need to keep quiet and do as you're told.

Fifth, to debate successfully you must develop the ability to sift a mountain of waffle for the one nugget which will help your argument. You must be deaf to all other possible interpretations of that fact.

Sixth, to achieve anything as a minister you need unswerving loyalty, a readiness to engage in embarrassing publicity stunts, a limitless capacity for hard and often apparently pointless work and a sufficiently clear vision to keep steering towards your objective, despite the best efforts of your opponents (and your friends sometimes) and the bureaucracy to deflect you on to a convenient sandbank.

Last, you need a wife or husband who doesn't object to long separations, to coming second, to trailing around party meetings like some well-groomed spaniel, to being admired and petted but never listened to. Your children must be prepared to put up with an absent parent whose possession of the initials 'MP' makes them a juicy target for the playground bully.

There is one other occupation where many of these characteristics – the late-night stamina, the optimism, the self-confidence, the brinkmanship – are essential. Gambling. 'It's the biggest game at the biggest table in town,' was how David Ruffley, a bright and ambitious young Conservative MP, put it when I asked him why he was devoting the best years of his life to getting on in Westminster. The casino metaphor is the right one. Win an election and you gain those talismanic initials 'MP' after your name: it is curious that, however badly society as a whole may think of politicians, we tend to have much more positive attitudes towards individual members of parliament. Send a letter on the House of Commons portcullis letterhead, sign it with the initials 'MP' and you are guaranteed a reply. The local newspaper will carry your photograph every week. Every school, Rotary Club, Women's Institute, old folks' day centre and Scout Group will want you to speak to them. With a bit of luck and a fair wind, they believe, the eminence will grow. You may go on and end up a minister, with the opportunity to steer through parliament laws which can change the lives of all your fellow citizens.

And with a bit of bad luck, you lose everything. And you may lose it all through no fault of your own. There are so many possibilities.

Your party falls out of favour. Your leader is seen as remote, out of touch or inept, or is just unlucky. Your constituency boundaries are redrawn, so your majority disappears at the stroke of a bureaucrat's pen. Your husband or wife, your child or your business partner does something very stupid or criminal. The list goes on. Every MP who has lost a seat has a hard-luck story in which he or she is the unwitting, undeserving victim.

The politician for whom it all goes wrong has nothing much to look forward to. For all the stories about people slumbering their lives away on the backbenches, since 1945 the average lifespan of a career in parliament has been just over fifteen years.[5] In the great upheaval of the 1997 General Election, 260 new MPs were elected to parliament, which meant redundancy for a very large number of people. This showed, more dramatically than at most elections (it was the biggest shake-up of the House of Commons since 1945), how limited a politician's job is. Those who found themselves looking for work soon discovered how few useful skills they had, how long they had been out of the job market, and how much they had lost touch with new styles and technologies. Some had simply no idea how to go about getting a new job. Others who blithely assumed that they would be able to walk into a boardroom somewhere discovered that the vote in Britain breaks down in such a way that there is a good chance that an MP looking for work will have represented a party whom half of the population cordially detest: why should any employer wish to hire someone who arrives trailing such a clattering load of offensive baggage? Small wonder that politicians who leave the world of politics voluntarily are such a rare breed.

There is, perhaps, a deeper reason, too. What do any of us want in life? Once the essential needs of food, drink and shelter have been met, the demands become less tangible, but only slightly less urgent. Everyone would like to be loved, for sure. We would all like to have some significance to others. Being elected an MP offers significance. How many would voluntarily surrender it? You begin to understand the older MPs who linger on in the House of Commons far beyond the time when they were any use to anyone. But they too are gamblers, if more like blue-haired old biddies lined up hour after hour at rows of one-armed bandits, than the younger MPs playing the roulette wheel or chemin-de-fer. No gambler places his stake believing he's going to lose, and somewhere in the back of the mind of every politician is the conviction that one day his or her hour will come.

For most of us, political decision-making, even active political involvement, is something we delegate to others. We ask mechanics to mend our cars, send for computer experts when our software fails and wear clothes which can be cleaned only by taking them somewhere else to be dunked in chemicals we couldn't name. The same happens with political decisions. What is curious is not that we are content to delegate to others the hard business of taking decisions, but that we choose to give authority over our lives to people who so many of the population seem to think are a bunch of charlatans.

In much of the popular mind, politicians are all the same. They're a bunch of egotistical, lying narcissists who sold their souls long ago and would auction their children tomorrow if they thought it would advance their career. They are selfish, manipulative, scheming, venal. The only feelings they care about are their own. They set out to climb the greasy pole so long ago that they had lost contact with reality by the time they were in their twenties. You cannot trust a word any politician says and if you shake hands with them, you ought to count your fingers afterwards. They are not people you would want your son or daughter to marry.

Some politicians will even play a game in which they seem to accept the judgement at face value. It is their way of acknowledging that, as a breed, they have an image problem. And yet if you spend any time with politicians you will find examples to justify every one of those adjectives. And several not mentioned, like sleazy, stupid or sex-obsessed. The most damning critic of a politician is another politician. I have lost count of the number of people who have been described by their comrades – on a completely off-the-record basis, of course – as 'corrupt', 'bonkers' or 'totally off his trolley'. Very occasionally, these remarks slip out in public, like John Major's observation that when he saw his independent-minded Eurosceptic colleague Richard Body, 'I hear the sound of white coats flapping.' Rather wetly, Major later tried to explain that he was merely pointing up Body's idiosyncrasy.

There is, simply, no way of reconciling the taxi-driver/saloon-bar wisdom with the way that so many politicians would like to see themselves. Their preferred adjectives would be idealistic, noble, selfless. They would like to be thought of as not so much in politics as in something called 'public life', in which they are 'public servants'. From this perspective, they are not our rulers: the 'masters' are the people and the politicians are merely doing our bidding. The soldiers of this selfless army have been called to the colours by a passion to right wrongs, to fight injustice and to leave the world a better place than they found it. Personal advantage is the last thing on their mind and they could be earning much more money, doing a lot less work, somewhere else. Which they would certainly be doing were they not sacrificing themselves for an ungrateful nation. How can these two images be reconciled? Each is simultaneously true and untrue, unnecessarily cruel and absurdly generous. The House of Commons contains ascetics and dreamers as well as pompous incompetents and greedy opportunists. In fact, it probably contains a higher proportion of idealists and Roundheads than mere statistical sampling would predict.

No sensitive person can read the history of the Labour party and fail to be moved by the heroic determination of its founders to improve the lives of working people. The 1945 Labour government, the creator of the Welfare State, was packed with people who had a passion to build the new Jerusalem. The Thatcher governments were just as fierce about unpicking the post-war consensus to 'set the individual free'. And every parliament contains the single-issue fanatics, who want to reform abortion laws, ban animal experiments, preserve rights of way or get public funds to make contact with extra-terrestrials, not because they have been told to do so, or because they think it will pay dividends at election time, but because, for whatever reason, they happen, passionately, to believe in their point of view.

Throughout the research for this book, I was struck repeatedly by the relevance of Enoch Powell's observation about the great 'nearly man' of late-nineteenth- and early-twentieth-century politics, Joseph Chamberlain. In his biography of Chamberlain he famously wrote that 'All political lives, unless they are cut off in midstream at a happy juncture, end in failure, because that is the nature of politics and of human affairs.'[6] There is a worldly wisdom to the words, and he was making a broader point than a comment upon the political life. But it seems to be spectacularly true of politics. He was right about Radical Joe, who was once seen as a successor to both Gladstone and Salisbury but never became Prime Minister, and whose stroke-damaged last years were an empty fulmination against the elements. But when you look at the careers of the nineteen men and one woman who did reach 10 Downing Street in the twentieth century it seems just as true of those who achieve their ambitions. With the very occasional exception, such as Sir Alec Douglas-Home, they fought all their lives to get the supreme job in British politics. Yet how many of them could be said to have left 10 Downing Street contented figures? Hardly more than one or two. For many, the culmination of a lifetime of effort was to be forced out of office, having their fingernails prised from the Prime Ministerial desk. For some, such as Ramsay MacDonald or Neville Chamberlain (Radical Joe's son), the consequence of leading their party was to live out what remained of their lives in odium. There have been the consolations of receiving an earldom and a seat in the House of Lords, a life which Disraeli described as being 'dead, but in the Elysian Fields'. It came, though, at the price of having to sit alongside people they had sent to the Lords as a way of getting rid of them. The harder they fought to avoid the waters closing over them, the sadder the figure they cut. Who was wiser, John Major who ambled off to watch cricket, or Margaret Thatcher who set up the Thatcher Foundation, to promote the values she believed had made her the country's greatest leader since Churchill?

But Enoch Powell was equally right about himself. By the age of twenty this brilliant young man had won most of the prizes open to a classical scholar at Cambridge, by twenty-two he was a fellow of Trinity College. Three years later he was a professor of Greek at Sydney University. When the Second World War began, he joined the army as a private. He emerged a brigadier. He showed the same single-minded determination in pursuing his political ambitions, and was rejected nineteen times before being chosen to fight Wolver-hampton for the Conservatives. But, famously, Powell was too

individualistic, too clever, too unworldly, too unstable, to flourish.
He finished his career a wild-eyed irrelevance as the Unionist member
for Down South on the Northern Irish border, whose main purpose
was to denounce what happened down south.

'Are you frightened of my husband?' his wife asked me when I was
sent, as a very young and inexperienced reporter, to interview him.
Yes, I replied, aware, like all of my generation, that this was the man
who had stabbed his party leader, Edward Heath, in the back in the
1974 elections, and, most notoriously, had prophesied race war in a
speech talking of 'the River Tiber foaming with much blood'. 'Oh
dear,' she said, 'everyone is. And he's such a sweetie.' And when we
came to sit down and talk, indeed he was – courteous, charming and
thoughtful. The fire had gone out of him, certainly. But perhaps he
had always been that way. Politicians, after all, are just human beings,
and few human beings are intrinsically unpleasant or dislikeable.

The sense of weariness infects the voters, too. Every politician who
makes a promise raises a hope. Election campaigns are all about
aspirations, to end unemployment, to build homes, to cut taxes, to
care better for the sick or to raise national self-esteem. Sometimes the
promises have even been honoured. Occasionally, they have been
honoured grandly. But, in the end, each government making the
pledge, whether honoured or not, gets shown the door. Oppositions,
it has been said, do not win elections. Governments lose them. It is
not that they have necessarily done anything to rile the electorate, just
that after a while we all get disillusioned and bored with them and
want a change. Even great achievements are no insurance. Having led
his country through the Second World War, Churchill found himself
resoundingly rebuffed in the 1945 election. The Attlee government,
responsible for the greatest social reforms of the twentieth century,
including the creation of the National Health Service, was bounced
out of office after only six years. Margaret Thatcher led the government which fought Britain's last imperial war, a war which was won,
against all the odds, at the other end of the earth, yet she was
defenestrated by her own party because it sensed that the electorate
was sick of her.

In the end, the experience of politics seems destined to cause
disappointment all round. For party, for politician and for voter. Why?

1. Out of the Mouths of Babes
and Sucklings . . .

Where did they all come from, this extraordinary breed? Once upon a time, they must have been normal. Can they really have sprung from their mothers' wombs full of doctrinaire certainties? Confronted by their mother with a plate of mashed banana at the age of two, did they exclaim, 'I congratulate the honourable lady on her choice of acceptable food for an infant. She will doubtless be aware of the vital importance of the banana trade to many member states of the Commonwealth. And will she join with me in protesting at the American government's attempt to force the World Trade Organization to capitulate to the interests of the American banana growers who provide such enormous donations to the Republican presidential campaign?' From some political memoirs, you might think they did.

In a strict sense, politicians are not like the rest of us. Whether they have been driven into political careers by a simple desire to represent their community in parliament or, like Margaret Thatcher, from a conviction that they alone could save their country,★ wielding power is essential. Mercifully, the proportion of people in any society who wish to tell everyone else what to do is limited. If it were not so, the country would be ungovernable. The arrangement works only because the people willing, however grudgingly, to do as they're told vastly outnumber the people who wish to order them about. Once upon a time, our leaders must have seemed normal. As babies, they bawled and mewled, they messed their nappies, and later they learned to speak and write. It was only later that they decided to make history. Was there anything in their childhoods to warn that they would turn out as they did?

It is easy enough to get misled. In the late 1980s, political journalists

★ Thatcher was quoting the eighteenth-century Prime Minister Chatham, who remarked, 'I know that I can save this country and that no one else can.' 'I must admit', she wrote in her autobiography, 'that my exhilaration came from a similar inner conviction' (*Downing Street Years*, p. 10).

became obsessed with Michael Heseltine, the man who ultimately brought down Margaret Thatcher. Heseltine, the great 'nearly man' of late-twentieth-century Conservatism, at that stage still seemed (particularly in his own eyes) to be the leader-in-waiting. Reporters wanted to know everything they could about him. An elderly aunt was tracked down and asked to reminisce about Heseltine's childhood. It turned out that she remembered him chasing cats. It wasn't much, but it was a start. Perhaps the old lady sensed the dangerous implications of what she was confessing to the inquisitive reporters, for she quickly qualified the remark. The old girl explained that 'He didn't want to be cruel, he just wanted to impose his will on them.'[1] Aha!, the journalist who tracked her down must have thought, here we have all the evidence we need of the drive to power which propelled this darling of the party on his ultimately doomed chase to 10 Downing Street. You can imagine the aunt adding the clause about why he chased cats as a way of forestalling any suggestion of sadism. But it had the reverse effect. He wanted to impose his will on them! It was the sort of hobby the young Hitler or Stalin would have gone in for: once the cats were in order, the nation would follow and then the rest of Europe. Trains would run on time from Swansea to Sevastopol. The impression stuck, and the story of Heseltine's urge to dominate the local cats is one of the few things we know of his early childhood.

There is only one flaw in the story. It is not that it is untrue. It is that it is too true. Has there been a six- or seven-year-old in history who has not tried to control the family pet, to get it to stand on its hind legs or to perform tricks? The plain fact is that most politicians have childhoods like the rest of us. The truth is that these recollections, usually garnered long after the event by biographers desperate for anything to enliven an adulthood spent in besuited backstabbing, tell us nothing much. Every family will have a similarly embarrassing tale about the childhoods of people who went on to become nurses, plumbers or Yellow Pages space-sellers.

It is true that a few of them seem to have been quite unusual children. Few could match William Pitt the Younger, Britain's youngest Prime Minister, who, by the age of thirteen, had written a five-act tragedy in iambic pentameters, called *Laurentius, King of Clarinium*. True, Enoch Powell, another classicist who claimed to have been

born a Tory, was nicknamed by his schoolteacher parents 'The Professor' for his ability at the age of three to stand on a chair and recite
the names and characteristics of the various stuffed birds dotted around
the family house.[2] But, as we've seen, Powell turned out to be too
clever for his own good.

At least Powell did not suffer from quite the degree of vanity which
his generally unadmiring son claimed had surrounded the Liberal
Prime Minister (1916–22) David Lloyd George. He once asked the
old man when he had first suspected he was a genius, to which Lloyd
George replied that he had not 'suspected' it at all. He had *known* it.
He then told a story of how, as a boy, he liked to climb a particular oak
tree and sit high up in the branches. 'Now,' he graciously explained to
his son, 'this was not the hallmark of genius, of course. Most boys in
the district liked climbing trees. But I was the only one who, when
he got up to sit on the top branch, took out a copy of *Euclid* and
began to study it. On one occasion when I did this, the singular
thought struck me, "What a remarkable fellow I am, to read *Euclid*
on top of a tree. Why am I doing this?" I asked myself. And, quick as
a flash, I answered myself, "I am special. I am astonishing. *Duw*, I
believe I am a genius." '[3] If the story is true it tells us more about LG's
self-importance than it does about the quality of his mind. Stupidity
need not be a bar to election to the House of Commons, but it is
probably an obstacle to any decent office in government. And while
there have been a handful of intellectually quite distinguished figures
at the top of government (Asquith was a prize fellow at Balliol College,
Oxford; Anthony Eden won a first in Persian and Arabic at Christ
Church, Oxford; Harold Wilson was awarded an outstanding first in
Politics, Philosophy and Economics at Jesus College, Oxford), if
anything the cleverest people in the House of Commons have
not risen to the very top. Winston Churchill, on the other hand, the
outstanding leader of the twentieth century, was described by his
form-master as the stupidest boy at Harrow. In the entire two hours
of his Latin exam to get into the school he managed to write only the
number of the first question, 'one', then to add some brackets, and
finally to hand in his answer sheet adorned with a blot and a few
smudges.[4]

Some characteristics tend to leap out at the reader of political biographies. A number of politicians do seem to have been lonely children. Jonathan Aitken, who, it is now often forgotten, was once seen as a young meteor, was diagnosed with tuberculosis at the age of three and survived only thanks to long stretches immobilized in plaster and bedridden. The loneliness of this existence was aggravated by the lengthy periods his mother spent away from home, nursing his father, a Spitfire pilot who had been shot down and severely wounded in 1942. Alan Clark, another louche luminary of 1980s Conservatism, noted in his diaries that the legacy of an unhappy childhood was that 'I am frightened of being laughed at.'[5] Jeffrey Archer, a second Conservative whose political career took the path from parliament to prison, had the same problem. Known at school as 'The Mekon' (after the extra-terrestrial in the *Eagle* comic) or 'The Pune' (because of his puny appearance), he was ruthlessly victimized. A contemporary recalled that 'He was a loner. He didn't really have any friends. In every school or class there's one kid that's picked upon. Unluckily for him he was the sort that people took against. He was not one of the crowd. He was very badly disliked . . .There was a fat boy that used to sit on him occasionally.'[6] It is almost enough to make you feel sorry for him.

But it is not just those who came to no good who had unhappy schooldays. The third Marquess of Salisbury, the last of the truly Victorian Prime Ministers and the first of the twentieth century, endured 'a boyhood of pathetic loneliness'. He had attended his mother's funeral at the age of nine, and his father was away from home much of the time, pursuing his own political ambitions. The boy grew up surrounded by forty servants at Hatfield House and utterly alone, 'intellectually and morally a hermit'.[7] Winston Churchill had an absolutely miserable time at St George's prep school in Ascot, where he was not only bullied by fellow pupils, but flogged by the head-master, a sadist by the name of Sneyd-Kynersley, who thrashed the boys so hard that their blood was said to have spattered his study walls.

Other subsequently eminent figures had miserable childhoods. George Curzon, the 'most superior person' who became Viceroy of India and Foreign Secretary, was recognized as having one of the most brilliant minds of his generation. But his early life was spent with a governess who was a sort of English Torquemada. 'She forced us', he recalled, 'to confess to lies which we had never told, to sins which we had never committed, and then punished us severely as being self-condemned.' Her punishments ranged from the physical – beatings and locking the children in darkened rooms – to the calculatedly shaming. Sometimes the young George was told to write to the butler, asking him to make a birch, so that he could be beaten. On other occasions Miss Paraman would force her victim to wear a calico petticoat and a large conical hat. He would then be made to parade himself in front of the villagers and staff with words like 'liar', 'sneak' or 'coward' scrawled upon him. So effective was his governess's tyranny that the child never summoned up the courage to tell his parents how he was being treated. 'I suppose no children well-born and well-placed', he remarked later, 'ever cried so much or so justly.'[8]

At the other end of the economic scale, David Lloyd George (despite being a self-proclaimed genius) also remembered his childhood bitterly. His mistress, Frances Stevenson, said that he had told her that if he was given the choice between dying the next day and returning to three years of age, he would infinitely prefer instant death to the tedium of childhood. He said that he looked upon the period between three and twenty 'with something akin to horror'. It was more than a question of boredom. His father had died when he was little more than a year old and Lloyd George's mother found it terribly hard to survive financially. 'He remembers', Frances Stevenson recalled, 'the look of despair which would come over her face from time to time when she did not know which way to turn to make both ends meet.'[9]

Lloyd George subsequently claimed that, coming from such a background, he could never have been anything but a radical politician, with a burning desire to change the world. Soon after becoming an MP, he joined a force of volunteers who went out hunting for Jack the Ripper in the east end of London. They failed to find him, but he returned home saying purply:

I found something worse. Something that Dante's pen alone could describe. Within a hundred yards of sanity and civilisation, a million people lived in conditions that gave the Ripper's actions a character of mercy killings. The gin houses; the doss houses; the stinking alleys and the gruesome cellars; the rickety tenements; the disorderly houses and the thieves' dens. This was London, the capital of the greatest empire the world has ever known, the centre of the richest country in the world. I set out to investigate a crime at night; I found evidence of ten thousand.[10]

Once the Liberals had been eclipsed by the Labour party, a deprived family background became indispensable to many ambitious young politicians. While much of the leadership was middle class (like Tony Crosland or Tony Blair) or even occasionally a toff (like Tony Benn), the ideal biography of a mid-twentieth-century Labour party politician has their father killed in a mining accident caused by the callous indifference of the aristocrats whose fortune is built on the sweat of the poor. Their widowed mother struggles to bring up seven children single-handedly in a back-to-back terrace until, exhausted, she dies of a curable disease when our hero is aged about thirteen. There may then be a kindly schoolteacher who takes an interest in the orphaned child, introducing them to books, paintings and, most importantly, The Struggle. A light has been lit but, because our hero has no money, there is no possibility of further education. By the middle teenage years, school has been abandoned, for money must be earned to support younger brothers and sisters. By the age of twenty, the fight for social justice is embedded irremovably in the soul.

This faith in a crusade for a better world sustained old-fashioned Labour even in the depths of despair. A few cynics might agree that, if Harold Wilson had ever had to walk to school without any boots on his feet, it was simply because he was too big for them. But when he stood up at the Labour conference and declared, 'This party is a moral crusade or it is nothing,' they applauded wildly. Even at the height of James Callaghan's catastrophic 1970s Labour government, when the country was paralysed by the Winter of Discontent, with the rubbish piled high in the streets and the dead unburied, there were still plenty in the party who seemed genuinely to believe that they were building a new Jerusalem, even if its foundations were being laid among black plastic bags.

The great nineteenth-century Conservative Prime Minister Sir Robert Peel used to tell a story about his father. Robert Peel senior was a staggeringly successful cotton magnate: by the time he was in his early thirties his Lancashire mills employed 15,000 people. With wealth came a baronetcy, a large house and a seat in the House of Commons. But his ambitions for the highest office settled on his son. Family history had it that, when the baby Peel was born, his father fell to his knees and dedicated his son to public life. At the infant's christening, he told fellow godparents that one day the boy would follow in the footsteps of the great eighteenth-century Prime Minister William Pitt. Peel himself claimed that his father once told him, 'Bob, you dog, if you are not Prime Minister some day, I'll disinherit you.'

Thus is confirmed the first rule of political success: choose your parents well. William Pitt himself was the son of a Prime Minister, who had schooled him for the office. Joseph Chamberlain, another prodigiously successful businessman (in 1874 he was able to retire on the proceeds of his screw-making empire, aged thirty-eight), had similar ambitions for his son Austen, pushing him on through Rugby School and Trinity College, Cambridge. It was a trajectory the son was incapable of sustaining on his own efforts: Austen Chamberlain grew up to share with William Hague the unhappy distinction of being the only leaders of the Conservative party in the twentieth century who did *not* become Prime Minister. When Austen was passed over for the Foreign Office in 1935, Churchill's comment was 'Poor man, he always plays the game and never wins it.' In the event, Joseph Chamberlain's dream was realized by his other son, Neville. And when that son was ejected from the premiership, his replacement was Winston Churchill, a man whose early political mission seemed to be entirely driven by a desire first to follow in his father's footsteps as an MP, and then to achieve the high office which death had denied him.

Churchill's cabinet colleague Harold Macmillan was the creature of his American mother, Nellie. She was so intensely ambitious for him to succeed that he later claimed that he owed his entire worldly success to her. When, in his late forties, Macmillan was very nearly killed in an air crash in Algiers, his first words on recovering conscious-ness were, 'Tell my mother I am alive and well.' She had planned every step of his early life and had seemed certain from the very beginning that one day he would become Prime Minister. (This is

not, of course, to say that Macmillan felt particularly close to her –
even when he had gained 10 Downing Street he admitted to a friend,
'I admired her, but never really liked her . . . She dominated me and
she still dominates me.')[11]

Some similar parental drive pushed Tony Blair. When the future
Prime Minister was eleven, his father – an active Conservative seriously searching for a seat in parliament – was hit by a stroke which
left him unable to speak. Blair described the experience as 'formative',
confessing to an interviewer that 'after his illness my father transferred
his ambitions onto his kids. It imposed a certain discipline. I felt I
couldn't let him down.'[12]

The lasting force of these early convictions is sometimes astonishing.
Even when Prime Minister, Margaret Thatcher, who idolized her
father as much as she wrote her mother out of her life story, would
still burst into tears at the memory of her father's balked career as an
alderman in her home town of Grantham. Over thirty years after the
ruling Labour group had sacked him from the post, she wept when
the subject came up in a television interview. 'Such a tragedy,' she
gulped to the astonished interviewer.[13] In many ways the true presid-
ing spirit of 1980s Britain was that of Alderman Alfred Roberts, the
small-town grocer who exercised such a profound influence over his
daughter. Thatcher explained that he gave her much more than a
simple Micawberish understanding of profit and loss.

He liked to connect the progress of our corner shop with the great complex
romance of international trade which recruited people all over the world to
ensure that a family in Grantham could have on its table rice from India,
coffee from Kenya, sugar from the West Indies and spices from five conti-
nents. Before I read a line from the great liberal economists, I knew from
my father's accounts that the free market was like a vast sensitive nervous
system . . . In effect I had been equipped at an early age with the ideal mental
outlook and tools of analysis for reconstructing an economy ravaged by state
socialism.[14]

Margaret Thatcher's was not a rich background. But in many of
the reminiscences of those who follow these family traditions there is
something so utterly self-assured, so extravagantly complacent about

their place in the world, that mere mortals just want to crawl away into a corner. A typical case is the family, represented in the House of Commons by Douglas Hogg, whose career as Conservative cabinet minister in the 1990s was notable mainly for his appearances stalking in and out of meetings of European agriculture ministers wearing a broad-brimmed black hat which made him look like a miniaturized extra from *The Good, the Bad and the Ugly*. The outfit did nothing to reassure other Europeans terrified by the prospect of British cattle infected with mad-cow disease driving the people of continental Europe insane. To understand how someone could so enjoy the disregard for the impression he was creating, you have only to reflect on the family history. There is a genetic trait which entered the Hogg dynasty with his grandmother. It shows itself in the presence of a sixth finger. Hogg's father had this extra digit (it was attached to the thumb of his right hand) amputated when he was still a baby. What could not be so easily cut away, though, was the family's unshakeable belief in its manifest destiny to rule as much of the world as possible. They have been a fearsomely clever bunch, and the men of this family never seem to have shown the desire to rebel against their fathers that many others do. When an interviewer put this point to Douglas Hogg's father, who had himself been a Conservative minister (and believed he had the capacity to lead the party and the country), his reply was breathtaking. 'We've gone on generation after generation – a long history of public service going back to the 1830s. We are extremely sophisticated people with an enormous range of intellectual weapons at our command.'[15] Modesty was not one of them.

Many of these people believe there was once a Golden Age, when what drove a political career was not ambition but something called 'service'. Another Conservative, David Maxwell Fyfe, declared that people who were cynical about politicians' motivation were, simply, wrong. 'Men who enter public life with the cold, selfish ambition of power are extraordinarily uncommon in Britain. On the other hand, the number of those who embark on a political career for selfless reasons of public service is extremely large, and is one of the least appreciated glories of our nation.'[16] Perhaps so. Or perhaps so at another time. In reality, it is one of the great myths of the Conservative party that in the not-too-distant past its benches were filled with patriotic, God-fearing soldiers, farmers and baronets whose sole aim in life was to discharge what they saw as their duty to their country and their constituents.

For the best part of 400 years, the British knew precisely who their rulers were. The political class was drawn from a tiny landed elite which, recent research has shown,[17] never numbered much more than a thousand families in England, or about 2,500 if you include the rest of the United Kingdom. As the country moved from feudalism to a form of representative democracy, the privileges attached to being a member of the aristocracy declined. Every extension of the right to vote diluted the power of the nobs, so that by the end of the nineteenth century becoming a member of the House of Commons was a much better way of securing status. It was not merely an occupation for gentlemen, but a task invested with its own especial nobility. Of course, it was not an entirely selfless trade. Membership of the House of Commons offered a frock-coated eminence and status denied to those who happened merely to be wealthy. And, for all the impact of 'new money', by the late nineteenth century some families were still producing members of the House of Commons for generation after generation. The Edgcumbe dynasty, for example, sent an almost unbroken chain of no fewer than twenty family members to represent Devon and Cornwall in parliament from 1447 right up until 1945.

Small wonder that sometimes government could seem to be almost a family business: one-tenth of cabinet members between 1868 and 1955 were themselves the sons of ministers. The administration put together by Lord Salisbury (Robert Arthur Talbot Gascoyne-Cecil) after the 1900 General Election contained so many members of his family that it was known as the 'Hotel Cecil'; the career of his Chief Secretary for Ireland is much less memorable than the quip about how he got the job: 'Bob's your uncle.' Lord Grey's Whig administration of 1830–34, which drove the Great Reform Act through parliament, included seven members of his own family. His great-great-nephew was Sir Edward Grey, later Viscount Grey of Fallodon, Foreign Secretary at the outbreak of the First World War. It was he, looking out of the Foreign Secretary's office at the dusk in St James's Park, who remarked in August 1914 that 'The lamps are going out all over Europe. We shall not see them lit again in our life.' Reading his biography, one is baffled as to why he was in public life at all: he clearly would have been much happier fly-fishing or birdwatching. An explanation is given by the Associated Press obituary on his death in 1933. 'Public life drew him, not because he had a taste for it, but because he was one of the Greys of Northumberland, a member of the great governing class of Britain.'[18]

This notion of 'public service' is full of humbug. No doubt there were some selfless individuals sacrificing themselves for the betterment of their constituents. But that was not why families like the Clives were willing to haemorrhage an average of £10,000 a year in the middle of the eighteenth century to maintain their position representing the few thousand people of Ludlow. A seat in parliament brought status and it brought practical privileges. An MP was well placed to pass laws which protected the interest of his family or class, whether it be keeping the price of corn artificially high or sanctioning the enclosure of public lands. He could also help with the divorces of friends, legitimize his bastards, fix the route of a new railway or canal or finagle commissions in the armed forces for relatives.

As the British parliament evolved into an increasingly representative chamber, there was less and less of a role for the aristocrats. Not only, obviously, did the extension of the franchise swell the number of voters, it also broadened the social base from which candidates for parliament could be drawn. During the nineteenth century, the landed class gradually stopped being divided between the Whigs and Tories, and tended to be represented only in the Tory party, 'thereby', as the historian Ellis Wasson puts it, cutting 'almost in half the number of places available in the Commons for members of the governing class'.[19] And since the gentry had tended to coalesce around conservative ideas, they were destined to lose in the proliferating number of seats all over the country which reflected the increasingly urban reality of late-nineteenth-century life. Finally, fewer and fewer families could be bothered with the idea of entering parliament, when they could have a more secure and better-rewarded life outside. A few families, like the Cecils or the Stanleys, struggled on, but by and large the tradition was dead.

That, at least, is the received wisdom.

★

No one could honestly doubt the sincerity of Tony Benn's political commitment. It cost him his seat in the House of Lords, some personal comfort and, some of his enemies say, his sanity. But Benn also came from a family with a long political history. In 1970, he helped to organize his aunt Rene's eighty-eighth birthday in the House of Commons and noted in his diary that 'she had first been inside the House of Commons in 1892, when my grandfather was elected and she was a girl of ten, and Gladstone was Prime Minister – quite remarkable'.[20] Benn's father was one of the best-known political figures of his day. As a boy Benn himself had grown up surrounded by the trappings of power, making what he described as his 'first speech' to thank the then Labour MP Oswald Mosley for tea. He had met the Prime Minister and watched the Trooping of the Colour from 10 Downing Street while still in short trousers. By the time he arrived at Oxford, Benn was keen to escape the fact that he was his father's son. At his selection interview he claimed that his father, Lord Stansgate, was an RAF officer. 'Nonsense,' said the don in front of him, mouthing 'Peer of the realm' slowly as he wrote it down. Benn's epic struggle to renounce the title which fell upon him with his father's death made him one of meritocratic democracy's most hair-shirted apostles. But even this passionate devotion could not overcome the power of genetics and family background: in 1999 his son Hilary was elected an MP for Leeds.

In the 1997 election, nineteen of those elected to the House of Commons were the children of MPs. A handful of female MPs in that parliament demonstrate the close interconnection of family and politics. Hilary Armstrong represented the very same seat in Durham that her father had held before her. The Potteries MP Llin Golding sat for the seat formerly held by her husband. Her father had been a Labour MP for thirty years. Irene Adams sat for Paisley South, another seat once held by a husband. Charlotte Atkins, the Staffordshire MP, was the daughter of the 1960s firebrand MP Ron Atkins. Estelle Morris, a former teacher destined to become Education Secretary in the second Blair term, also had an MP for a father. Dari Taylor, who won Stockton South, had grown up as the daughter of the MP for Burnley. The Crewe MP, Gwyneth Dunwoody, who by now had spent nearly a quarter of a century in the House of Commons, had been married to an MP, and had a father, Morgan Phillips, who had been General Secretary of the Labour party and a mother who had been a London councillor. Fiona Mactaggart, representing Slough, had a grandparent in parliament. Then there were the lateral relationships. The Brentford MP Ann Keen had a husband, Alan, who represented the next-door constituency of Feltham, and a sister, Sylvia Heal, who sat for Halesowen in the West Midlands. Bridget Prentice, the MP for Lewisham East, had been married to the MP for Pendle; Julie Morgan, who sat for Cardiff North, was married to the MP for Cardiff West. Angela Eagle, the member for Wallasey, had a twin sister, Maria, sitting for one of the Liverpool seats. All these were Labour politicians, but there were family connections among the Conservative women, too. Julie Kirkbride, MP for Bromsgrove, was married to the MP for Bracknell; Virginia Bottomley, the former Health Secretary, was married to the MP for West Worthing; and Ann Winterton, representing Congleton, had a husband who sat for the next-door seat of Macclesfield.

Most impressive of all was Ann Cryer, the Labour MP for Keighley. Not only had she been elected for a seat once held by her husband. She had also given birth to the MP for the east London seat of Hornchurch, John Cryer, who arrived in the Commons in the same 1997 intake as her. The young Cryer was not the first MP to follow both parents into the House of Commons,[21] but he demonstrated how not just careers but attitudes can run in families: his parents were both old-fashioned left-wingers and so was he. Nor is the pattern of family habit confined to the two big post-war parties. The Liberal party had its own Brahmins, such as the daughter of their First World War leader Herbert Henry Asquith, Lady Violet Bonham Carter, who claimed to have been discussing the finer points of party politics from the age of four. She married her father's private secretary, Maurice Bonham Carter, and produced a son who became a Liberal MP and a daughter who married a young man called Jo Grimond, who later became leader of the party. Grimond's successor as party leader, Jeremy Thorpe, had also inherited a political gene. But in his case both his father and grandfather had been Conservative MPs. What surfaced in Thorpe was not the affiliation but the flamboyant style: you could understand why the Liberal leader had a taste for campaigning by helicopter and hovercraft when you learned that his grandfather had done his electioneering by balloon.

All family backgrounds influence children, but in political families there may be dynastic ambition. For a start, there is understandable parental ambition. Chips Channon, the social diarist and MP for Southend, visited parliament as it was being rebuilt after the war, and 'looked up at the red bones – the steel girders – of the new House of Commons and wondered when my small son's voice would vibrate in it'.[22] In the event it was only a little over a decade before Paul Channon took over his father's seat. (His mother explained that he was 'a colt from a stable the electors knew.')[23] Living in a political household introduces the child to the excitement of political life early on. Because of the narrowness of most politicians' ambitions, it really can seem that the House of Commons is the only important place in Britain. Small wonder if the child of that house grows up convinced that the sole career worth having is one in which they too climb the greasy pole. The chatter which surrounds such children, with its talk of who's on the way up and who on the way out, the rivalry, intrigue, plotting and campaigning, the apparent closeness to affairs of state, to questions of peace and war, poverty and prosperity, the castles in the air as much as the low cunning, is not merely infinitely exciting. It is also not far removed from the way that adolescents naturally see the world.

There are, of course, plenty of children who rebel against and reject their parents' world: being the son or daughter of any famous person is rarely easy. But those who continue in the political trade often see themselves as finishing their parents' business or completing their mission. As we have seen, it has often been said that Winston Churchill regarded himself as fulfilling the destiny denied his father by his early death. The same was true of his predecessor as Prime Minister. As a pupil at Rugby School, Neville Chamberlain refused to have anything to do with the debating society or politics because he so hated the gloom which settled over the family home for days before his father Joseph had to make a big speech. Yet when he finally became Chancellor of the Exchequer he delivered one of the most emotional speeches ever to come from the holder of that office. The job of Chancellor is one which, it was once remarked, the British like to be performed either by a bookie or by an undertaker. Neville

Chamberlain definitely looked the sort of man who would have been at home with a coffin on his shoulder. But when, in 1932, he proposed a 'general system of protection' he did so by telling the House of Commons of the honour it gave him of 'setting the seal' on the work which his father had begun, and continued, visibly moved, that 'my father would have found it consolation for the bitterness of his disappointment if he could have foreseen that these proposals . . . would have been presented to the House of Commons in the presence of one and by the lips of the other of the two immediate successors to his name and blood'.[24]

The great majority of Labour politicians to whom I spoke while researching this book remarked that they came from politically committed families. Betty Boothroyd believed that 'It's in the blood, like coal-dust under the fingernails in mining families.' Often, children inherit their parents' prejudices about the world. Even if they come to different conclusions about how the country should be run, at the very least they come from environments in which the family is *engaged* with the world. Douglas Alexander, who entered the House of Commons in 1997, and his sister Wendy, who was elected to the first new Scottish parliament, were the children of a Church of Scotland minister and a doctor. 'We used to discuss politics over Sunday lunch, after church,' he told me. They belong to the new breed of professionals in politics, technicians comfortably at home in the new Labour party. The crusading sense which informed the old Labour party consumed entire families with its passion. Often, the party and trades unionism, with their 'all for one and one for all' sense of loyalty, seemed a part of family life. George Brown, who rose to be Foreign Secretary in the 1960s Labour government before drink sent him tumbling – both literally and metaphorically – used to boast of how deeply ingrained union sentiment was within his family in London. His father was an official in the Transport Workers Union and Brown fondly recalled his exhilaration as a teenager during the General Strike 'helping to overturn trams driven by blacklegs at the Elephant and Castle'.[25] James Callaghan was running messages for the local Labour party in Portsmouth before he was a teenager. He described himself as 'bred into the Labour Party almost as much as I was born into the chapel'.[26]

Callaghan's ministerial colleague Jennie Lee was another for whom party membership was an extension of family life. Her paternal grandfather had been a friend of Keir Hardie, the first Labour leader in the House of Commons. Her father, a miner, chaired the West Fife branch of the Independent Labour party. So deeply ingrained was the sense of political loyalty that her biographer remarked that:

the ILP was woven into every fragment of the Lees' family life: the books in the parlour glass cabinet, Paine, Marx, *The Ragged Trousered Philanthropists*; the conversations Jennie overheard between her father and grandfather as the country moved towards war, the earnest discussions with young miners refusing conscription who had received their call-up papers (James Lee had thrown his papers on the fire).[27]

Jennie Lee went on to marry the great Labour orator, Aneurin Bevan, another miner's child. Betty Boothroyd remembers as a child going to hear them both speak on Saturday mornings at Huddersfield Town Hall.

Occasionally, the political gene finds expression in opposing parties in different generations. Henry Campbell-Bannerman, who became Liberal Prime Minister in 1905, had a father who had been a prominent Scottish Conservative. It was a family history which needed some explaining. CB managed it elegantly. In his first speech to his constituents, he explained that he wouldn't apologize for being his father's son. On the contrary, he was proud of the respect in which his father was held, even by his political enemies. If there was a lesson to be drawn, he claimed, it was 'that possibly staunchness may run in the blood, that I may inherit his tenacity without inheriting the principles, and that as my father through a long public life, through good report and through evil report, in fine weather and in foul, has stuck to his party and his principles, so his son in like manner will stick to his'.[28] It worked. When Stanley Baldwin lost the 1929 General Election to Ramsay MacDonald and returned to parliament to sit on the opposition benches he was confronted by the uncomfortable sight of his own son, Oliver, sitting as a Labour MP on the benches behind MacDonald, elected as MP for Dudley. Baldwin's wife, who had previously spent much time in the gallery watching debates, found the sight of the two men on opposing sides so upsetting that she did not return to the chamber for two years.

One morning, I walked out of the tube station at Westminster and stood waiting to cross the road in front of Big Ben. I realized I was standing next to Tom Sawyer, the one-time General Secretary of the Labour party.

'What are you doing down here?' he asked.

'I'm trying to find out why people go into politics,' I replied.

'That's simple,' he said, as we waited for the lights to change. 'I never knew my father. I'm not sure my mother knew him particularly well either.' And then, without a pause, he went on, 'The party's been my father. It's always been there, to give me that pat on the back when I needed it.'

This was the most direct and powerful statement I have come across about the role that a political party can play in the life of an individual. I went home wondering how true it might be of other members of the party. Certainly, even the most superficial glance reveals that many prominent members of the Labour party have been deprived of one or other parent. Keir Hardie had been abandoned by his own natural father, a miner (or a miner carrying the can for a local doctor). Ramsay MacDonald never met his father. Ernest Bevin, the trades unionist and Labour Foreign Secretary, knew that his mother had been an Exmoor midwife (she died when he was eight years old), but never discovered who his father had been. Stafford Cripps lost his mother when he was four, Hugh Gaitskell's father died while the boy was at prep school. It is a very small snapshot. But, certainly, the most beguiling thing about the old Labour party was its moral sense. It made the movement a warm and welcoming place where anyone was embraced, regardless of their circumstances. A creed which believed in improving the lot of the most disadvantaged in society obviously had a place for those who had been emotionally disadvantaged at home. But could the experience of politics as a whole – in the Conservative party too – offer similar attractions?

Soon after meeting Tom Sawyer, I came across a book in the London Library. The author, Lucille Iremonger, was a historian married to a Conservative MP who had been commissioned to produce a book on the home lives of British Prime Ministers. But as she looked back over their careers, she noticed something very strange.[29] Deciding to confine her inquiry to the period of history she knew best, she began with Spencer Perceval, the only Prime Minister to be assassinated (so far), shot dead in the lobby of the House of Commons by a deranged bankrupt. But it was not the manner of Perceval's death which interested her. It was the fate of his parents. Perceval's father (a member of parliament) had died when Spencer was a boy of eight. As the author began to delve into the lives of other Prime Ministers, she was repeatedly struck by how many of them had suffered a similar childhood bereavement. Lord Liverpool, who succeeded Perceval in 1812, had lost his mother before he was one month old. George Canning, who followed Liverpool, had lost his father on his first birthday. Canning was succeeded by Viscount Goderich, whose father had died when the boy was four. The next Prime Minister, the Duke of Wellington, lost his father at the age of twelve. There seemed to be a pattern. Continuing further into the nineteenth century, Sir Robert Peel (Prime Minister 1834–5 and 1841–6) had been fifteen when he lost his mother. Lord Aberdeen was seven when his father died, and eleven when his mother went. Lord Rosebery (driven by the triple ambitions of marrying an heiress, owning a Derby winner and becoming Prime Minister) had been three when he lost his father. Arthur James Balfour was seven when his father died. H.H. Asquith was the same age when his father was killed after a cricketing accident. His mother Emily was virtually bedridden for much of her life, suffering from bronchitis and a weak heart.

David Lloyd George could scarcely have known his father, for he died when the boy was only seventeen months old. Others who had lost mothers included the 1846 Prime Minister Lord John Russell, who was nine at the time of his bereavement, the same age at which Lord Salisbury lost his mother. Andrew Bonar Law had lost his mother when he was two. Neville Chamberlain's mother died when the future Prime Minister was six years old. All told, of the twenty-four individuals who became Prime Minister between 1809 and 1937, no fewer than fifteen had lost one or both parents when they were children. The author found reliable statistical evidence of the 'normal' level of childhood bereavement hard to come by, but the 1921 census, which attempted to establish the numbers of widows and orphans left by the mass slaughter of the First World War, suggested that about 1 per cent of children under fifteen had suffered the death of one or both parents. Yet the figure among the Prime Ministers was *62 per cent*. This seemed such an abnormally high proportion as to shout a message.

Lucille Iremonger called her study of these bereaved politicians *The Fiery Chariot*. She had taken the title from the legend of Phaethon, the bastard son of Helios, the sun-god. According to myth, when Phaethon discovered who his father was, he set off for the east, and confronting Helios in his palace, demanded the right to drive the chariot which carried the sun. But Phaethon was too weak to control the immortal horses, and they bolted. The sun passed so close to the earth that it threatened to set it on fire. To save the world, Zeus struck Phaethon dead with a thunderbolt. His charred body fell into the River Eridanus, where his mourning sisters were turned into amber-dropping trees.

To be a perfect fit in the Phaethon complex, the candidate would need to be literally illegitimate, and few enough British Prime Ministers strictly qualify. True, Robert Walpole, the first of them (1721), was widely said to be the bastard son of a lawyer called Burrell, and Lord North bore such a striking resemblance to George III that it was commonly believed that he was his half-brother.* The theory is broader than strict illegitimacy, linking the need to achieve greatness with deprivation in childhood: the orphan quickly coming to the conclusion that 'to will is to achieve: I want, it happens'. In its most ornate form, the theory goes, the illegitimate child attempts to compensate for a sense of 'impurity' about its birth by performing an astonishing feat. The victim of the Phaethon complex is driven, needs to be seen to succeed. But the outcome of the drama is predetermined:

---

* Horace Walpole's pen portrait described him as having 'two large prominent eyes that rolled about to no purpose (for he was utterly short-sighted), a wide mouth, thick lips and an inflated visage [which] gave him the air of a blind trumpeter'. At a performance at Covent Garden one evening, he was asked, 'Who is that plain-looking woman in the box opposite?' 'That is my wife,' he replied, whereupon the embarrassed questioner tried to save himself by saying, 'No, I meant the woman next to her.' To which North cheerily replied, 'That, sir, is my daughter. We are considered to be three of the ugliest people in London.'

it will end in catastrophe. Well, perhaps. Certainly, when she came to examine the lives of the various Prime Ministers in her study, Lucille Iremonger was able to identify many of the characteristics of the Phaethon phenomenon. A childhood deprived of affection, unusual sensitivity, an outstanding mentor, extreme self-discipline, an overdeveloped religious sense, aggression and timidity, overdependence on the love of others, all featured in many of their lives.

The truest example of the Phaethon phenomenon in modern times is James Ramsay MacDonald, a genuine bastard, who became the first person to rise from the working class to become Prime Minister, and fell calamitously. MacDonald himself once told a friend that, when he was eight or nine, his mother, a servant in a farmhouse in the fishing village of Lossiemouth, had taken him for a long walk. High on a hilltop she pointed to a distant solitary ploughman at work in the valley. 'Ramsay – yon's your feyther,' she is said to have told the boy. It is believed to have been the only occasion on which he saw his father.[30] In fact, both his mother and grandmother had been abandoned women, his formidable granny having been left almost penniless with four children by a feckless baker. MacDonald's illegitimacy only once became a public issue, when the odious Horatio Bottomley (whose own parentage was a lot more questionable than he liked to pretend) published a nasty attack upon him in his rag *John Bull*. Unable to draw blood by attacking him for his 'pro-German' attitudes during the First World War, the paper was reduced in 1915 to exposing that he was not James Ramsay MacDonald, but James MacDonald Ramsay, '*the illegitimate son of a Scotch servant girl!*'[31] The first his victim knew of the attack was when he borrowed a copy of *John Bull* on a train journey from Aberdeen to Edinburgh. He spent 'hours in the most terrible mental pain'[32] as a consequence. The exposé achieved nothing – indeed plenty of people, including sworn enemies, wrote to MacDonald expressing their outrage that Bottomley should have sunk so low.

But the argument is not about the public consequences of unacknowledged parentage. It is about the personal effects. For some politicians, like Bill Clinton, the fit is almost perfect: his biological father, William Blythe, possessor of five wives and numerous illegitimate children, died before the future President was born. If one tries to extend the inquiry beyond the limits of Lucille Iremonger's investigation, a lot of British politicians do seem to have been unlucky with their parents. Of the Prime Ministers before her starting date, the second Prime Minister, the Earl of Wilmington, had been eight when his father died. Henry Pelham, the third holder of the office, and premier during the suppression of Bonnie Prince Charlie's Jacobite rebellion, had lost his mother shortly before his sixth birthday. The fourth Prime Minister, the Duke of Newcastle, was seven at the time he suffered a similar tragedy. The Earl of Bute, who followed Newcastle's second administration, lost his father before he was ten. The father of George Grenville, the seventh holder of the office, lived until his son was fourteen, but the Duke of Grafton was only five when his father died of a fever in Jamaica. His successor, Lord North, Prime Minister at the time of American independence, had lost his mother when he was two years old.

Bringing the inquiry up to date, Winston Churchill was haunted throughout his early life by the fact that his father, whom he hero-worshipped, had died in his mid-forties: his early life was lived in the baleful conviction that he would be gone by the same age. Anthony Eden lost his father as a teenager (two of his three brothers also died in the First World War). James Callaghan's father dropped dead of a heart attack when his son was nine: Callaghan's biographer describes the impact on the future Prime Minister as 'devastating'.[33] Although Margaret Thatcher failed to include her mother among her biographical details in *Who's Who*, both her parents survived until her middle age. John Major's father was already in his sixties when John was born, and died two days before his son's nineteenth birthday. Major was haunted by the old man's failing powers for years. In his autobiography, he recalls how, as a small boy, he had watched him fall off a chair because he couldn't see to screw in a lightbulb. 'Irrationally, but in the way a small boy can, I felt responsible for this,' he recalled.[34] The moment of his father's death was the point at which Major decided he had to stop being a failure himself.

Major's successor, Tony Blair, had lost his mother as a young man, but it was the serious stroke which hit his father at the age of forty that had the most profound influence. Blair was eleven at the time.

Amateur psychology is an easy and dangerous thing. What should we make of this scattering of bereavements and abandonments? Did the fact that Mao was regularly whipped by his father, Stalin beaten by his alcoholic father or Hitler tormented at home help turn them into the monsters they later became? Is it significant that Hitler, Stalin and Saddam Hussein all idolized their mothers? Freud observed that 'A man who has been the indisputable favourite of his mother keeps for life the feelings of a conqueror, that confidence of success that often induces real success.'[35] Peripheral self-publicists like Jeffrey Archer have jumped on the bandwagon. His conman father died while Jeffrey was still at school: the author later told a newspaper that 'I didn't realize it at the time, but I think losing my father triggered off my self-motivation, made me realize "Now you're on your own mate." '[36] John Alderdice, who trained and practised as a psychother-apist before he went into Northern Irish politics, comments that 'A common reaction to bereavement is to try to make reparation, to make good the loss. This is often accompanied by an identification with the person who died, an attempt to be the person who died, as a way of keeping them alive. Many politicians seem to have depressive personalities and need a level of manic over-activity to survive. It means that they tend to react to events rather than reflect on them.'

After her examination of the lives of sixteen British leaders, Lucille Iremonger wondered how an advertisement for the job of Prime Minister would read, if the post was ever to be open to general competition. She dreamed up the following:

The successful candidate will have lost one or more parents in childhood, though he may be an admitted or suspected bastard. He will suffer from other crippling handicaps, whether physical (such as a stammer, poor health or marked unprepossessingness of manner and appearance), or material (such as poverty), or psychological (such as having a brother near to him in age on whom fortune will have showered gifts ostentatiously denied to him, material, intellectual and physical). He will not necessarily be highly intelli-gent, or a brilliant orator, and may well be surpassed in both respects, and many others, by many of his parliamentary colleagues. He will be of a hypersensitive nature and will suffer from incapacitating psychosomatic illnesses, often at times of greatest stress. He will remain throughout his life isolated from his fellow men, nauseated by their junketings, and exhausted by their relaxations. He will have been miserably unhappy at his school, and possibly so much that he will never be able to bring himself to revisit it after leaving. His antipathy to sport, particularly team games, will be lifelong. His few friends will be orphaned or deprived, like himself, and he may well be married to an orphan who will be very like him in nature. He will have been subjected to the intellectual, moral and spiritual domination of a disciplinarian mentor, whose commands he will in effect obey to the end of his days. Throughout his life he will maintain a regime of austerity, bordering on asceticism, outward forms notwithstanding, and often increasing in severity with time. Whether he is a believer or not, he will have a deeply committed interest in religion. He will be subject to fits of prostrating depression. He will, if bereaved, be so desolated by grief as to render him totally incapable of maintaining his grip on life for a period, will immediately seek to resign from public life, and will suffer from its after-effects forever. He may be of a marked natural timidity and shyness, for which he will so over-compensate as to present on occasions an extremely aggressive front. He will possibly be peculiarly suspicious and credulous about magic and the supernatural, and will take an extensive interest in fiery phenomena and storms. He will be haunted eternally by a compulsive and obsessive need for total love and adoration and support from another, and will continue to seek it until death, disregarding all else, even, on occasions, the security of state secrets, in his pursuit of it or its shadow, and probably writing a million words to wives, mistresses or sisters, in his search. He will manifest a periodic recklessness, whether in love or other affairs, of a suicidal nature. He will be a devotee of Sir Walter Scott.[37]

On a broader basis than the sixteen characters she chose for analysis, we could quibble with all sorts of aspects of this. Recent Prime Ministers have grasped at Anthony Trollope, rather than Sir Walter Scott, when asked to name their favourite author. It is hard to imagine tenants of Downing Street such as James Callaghan or Tony Blair having reckless love affairs, and John Major's enthusiasm for cricket is hardly an endorsement of the idea that they all desert team sports. The Duke of Wellington may have hated Eton and refused to contribute to its rebuilding fund, but Gladstone 'considered himself bound to do anything' for the place, and so on. One fact, however, cannot be changed: there were fifty-one Prime Ministers from Sir Robert

Walpole to Tony Blair. Twenty-eight of them were the children of MPs, suggesting the importance of either genes or environment. But twenty-four – almost half of the total number – had lost their fathers before they reached the age of twenty-one.[38]

Every adult is the creature of their upbringing, the child father to the man. What marks out politicians as different from the rest of us is not that they become politically conscious of the things that are good and bad about the world: that is the natural instinct of any reasonably intelligent adolescent. Their distinguishing characteristic is not sensitivity to the world, but the belief that they, personally, can change it. They become not merely politically conscious but politically ambitious. And furthermore they come to the conclusion that they can change the world through what they say in the marbled halls of a thousand local council chambers or parliaments in Westminster, Edinburgh, Cardiff or Strasbourg.

The classic example of youthful purpose is the photograph of the eight-year-old Harold Wilson. His father had taken the boy on a sightseeing trip to London, where the child posed in his cap, shorts, knee-socks and double-breasted tweed blazer on the doorstep of 10 Downing Street. Wilson's parliamentary colleague Ian Mikardo later remarked gloomily that 'Harold was ruined by the bloody picture of him outside No. 10. He had to make it come true.'[39] Wilson's biographer plays down the significance of the photo, remarking, reasonably enough, that 'many children are photographed outside famous buildings, without necessarily seeking to live in them'.[40] But two years later, when he had been taken to Australia to visit his uncle – also called Harold – who was a National Labour party member of the state legislature, Wilson's ambition was plain. On the ship back to England, the ten-year-old told his father, 'I am going to be a Member of Parliament when I grow up. I am going to be Prime Minister.'[41] When, finally, he had reached the top of the greasy pole, the woman Wilson appointed his Transport Minister, Barbara Castle, was able to best him on early political gestures. She claimed that she wrote her first election address at the age of six. 'Dear citizuns!' (*sic*), it read. 'Vote for me and I will give you houses.'[42]

Not all of those who subsequently became our rulers were quite as determined quite as early. Other times, there is some teenage epiphany. The Labour leader Clement Attlee's first political gesture was to take part in a march to the centre of Hertford, in protest at the refusal of the headmaster of Haileybury to grant them a school holiday to celebrate the relief of Ladysmith in the Boer War. Attlee's successor, Hugh Gaitskell, used to claim that he first became aware of the social chasm in British life at the age of twelve, late in his career at the Dragon prep school in Oxford. A friend's father asked him what he was going to do when he left the school the following year. When Gaitskell told him that the plan was for him to go to Winchester, the man exclaimed, 'You don't know how lucky you are – only one boy in ten thousand has the chance of an education like that.'[43] Gaitskell dated the beginnings of his political feelings from the conversation.

John Prescott, who would become Tony Blair's deputy, was also awakened politically at school. His father had promised him a new bicycle if he passed the eleven-plus exam for the local grammar school. Prescott didn't manage it. Not only did he not get the bicycle, he had the added humiliation of seeing both his brother and sister succeed where he had failed. As if this was not humiliation enough, he wrote a love letter to a girl in his class who was going on to the grammar school. She sent it back with the spelling mistakes corrected. 'That summed up the division,' he recalled. 'The message was that suddenly you are less than they are.'[44] No further explanation is necessary for his subsequent political convictions.

In John Prescott's case, early anger did nothing to diminish an enormous sense of social responsibility. Two years later, at the age of thirteen, he travelled with his parents to Brighton to compete in a bizarre competition to find 'The Most Typical Family in Britain'. The local press had them down as sure-fire winners, but in the event they finished as runners-up, and came home with a cheque for £50. But the future Deputy Prime Minister took his responsibilities for domestic harmony seriously. At about the same age, he went down to the local police station to turn in his father. 'My dad's a magistrate,' he said, 'and I've seen him kissing another woman.'[45]

Edward Heath, who succeeded where Prescott failed, winning a scholarship to grammar school, showed his talent for politics by standing as a Conservative in the school elections and successfully opposing a replication of the infamous Oxford Union motion that 'This House will under no circumstances fight for king and country.' At Oxford, the motion had been carried resoundingly and caused a national scandal. At Chatham, Heath defeated it convincingly. John Major's educational career, in south London, was less stellar. Although he passed the eleven-plus, his life was more devoted to sport and to breeding rabbits and mice than anything else. His political ambitions were sparked, he claimed, at the age of sixteen, when the local (Labour) MP met him at a church fête and organized a visit to Westminster. Major was smitten. 'I fell in love with the House of Commons the first time I saw it, sitting in the gallery watching the committee stage of the 1956 budget. Harold Macmillan, the Chancellor of the Exchequer, briefly came into the Chamber, and after that I knew I wanted to get into the House of Commons, and that I wanted to be chancellor.'[46]

There is an almost religious tone about some of these early observations: it is as if the impressionable young mind is looking in on some rite in which figures like the Chancellor of the Exchequer, the Leader of the Opposition, even the Speaker, perform priestly roles. Although the business of politics is an intensely earthly trade, it is noticeable that religious belief seems to be much higher among members of the House of Commons than in the country at large. There is even a scattering of one-time religious novices in the place. Robin Cook, Tony Blair's first Foreign Secretary, had originally planned to become a minister of religion. And the election of 2001 brought into the House of Commons an ordained Church of England vicar (Chris Bryant, representing the solidly Labour Welsh mining area of Rhondda), an ordained Catholic priest (David Cairns, representing Greenock and Inverclyde) and a former monk (Paul Goodman, whose personal odyssey had taken him from a Jewish childhood, through two years in a monastery, via the *Catholic Herald* and the *Sunday Telegraph*, to representing High Wycombe). It is a curious coincidence that the first three Speakers of the devolved assemblies in Scotland, Wales and Northern Ireland were all sons of nonconformist ministers. The impulse to save humanity can take several expressions and reflects Anthony Trollope's rosy-eyed view of an MP's life that 'to serve one's country without pay is the grandest work that a man can do'.[47] The bit about unpaid labour has not been true since 1911, when MPs began to receive a salary. But no one goes into politics to make money. At least, they don't do so in Britain. What, then, are the early indications of a future in politics? Almost every politician is, in their own estimation of themselves at least, an embryonic great person. Some of the physical prerequisites – good health, a relatively tranquil domestic life – they are either born with or acquire by good fortune. But what is most baffling is their boundless self-confidence, their unshakeable belief in themselves.

This self-belief is the greatest obstacle to any honest understanding of why politicians do what they do. For self-confidence is so often the enemy of self-knowledge that most politicians are utterly unreliable witnesses: when it comes to attempting to explain what it was that drew them into politics, you can hardly believe a word they say. Occasionally, a politician's diary will wonder what it is all for, like an exhausted swimmer washing up on a beach. The 1992 General Election was, we were told (yet again), to be the moment when the Liberal Democrats would stage their breakthrough from the periphery into the main ground of politics. But, for all the confident predictions, the number of people voting Liberal Democrat actually went down. The party leader, Paddy Ashdown, appeared at a press conference at which the implausible claim was made that the night had been a triumph. He then went home to commiserate with those of his MPs who had lost their seats. When he telephoned one of the defeated MPs, Geraint Howells, Howells was in tears. Ashdown was sufficiently moved by the conversation to exclaim in his diary, 'God, what a terrible game this is! Why on earth do we do it?'[48] It is, you might feel, the most important question a politician could ask themselves. Go on, Paddy, do please tell us. PLEASE. We want know. Why *do* you do it? But the moment of anxiety and introspection has passed. The very next sentences run, 'In the evening Jane and I walked across the fields with Kate and Luke to the Cat Head, then back again after a couple of beers. A glorious evening. How beautiful the Somerset countryside is.' So that's all right then.

The usual answer to the question which briefly flashed across Paddy Ashdown's mind may be expressed in a single word. Power. The businessman wants to create profits. The nurse wants to cure the sick.

The politician wants power, so that he or she can control the world around them. Aneurin Bevan, Britain's greatest post-war orator, provided his own analysis in simple terms. 'A young miner in a South Wales colliery, my concern was with the one practical question: Where does power lie in this particular state of Great Britain, and how can it be attained by workers? . . . It was no abstract question for us. The circumstances of our lives made it a burning, luminous, mark of interrogation. Where was power and which was the road to it?'[49] Perhaps Bevan was being honest, or as honest as he could be. It has a stark plausibility. His record is impressive. To rise from colliery assistant (from which he was invalided out because of eye disease) to creating the National Health Service is remarkable. Even so, he was disappointed, for achieving office tied him up in endless attempts to reconcile idealism and reality.

No doubt there are still some politicians who join the circus with a similar zeal. Perhaps surprisingly, Alec Douglas-Home claimed to have been encouraged into public life by Lloyd George's urging a new generation to look at things through new eyes.[50] But, for most, a moral urge to power can only – at best – be part of the drive to succeed. In a relatively affluent country, most people do not live in abject poverty, merely in gradations of comfort or discomfort. It is said that we are all middle class now. It is not true. But it is nearly enough true to explain how passion has evaporated from politics. The contrast with earlier periods is striking. Growing up in a Bradford household where the only household appliances were a carpet sweeper and a 'dolly tub' for the family washing and where her father encouraged her never to join in school choruses of 'Land of Hope and Glory', Barbara Castle was perhaps destined to become a radical. People like her set out to change the world. They anticipated a fight, were proud to be thought dangerous and expected to be unpopular.

What we are really talking about, when politicians preview their lives, is ambition. It is true that, by their own accounts, there comes a point when some of them seem to have risen above so base a motive as the desire to get on. But even within those who sit in the grandiose rooms of the Foreign Office or the Treasury the worm continues to eat. Even in 10 Downing Street it is still alive. The most publicly venerated politician of the twentieth century, Winston Churchill, is also, perhaps, the most ambitious and untrustworthy of the lot. His life as a young man was driven by an absolutely ruthless determination to promote the noble cause of Winston Spencer Churchill. More modest souls would never have embarked upon the adventures which consumed his early life, because they would have lacked the necessary presumptuousness. Whether he was taking part in the last great cavalry charge in British military history, at the Battle of Omdurman, or filing newspaper dispatches on battles in Cuba or on the North-west Frontier, his overriding concern was himself. A more conceited, self-seeking young man would have been hard to find. When his reports of the British attempts to pacify Afghanistan appeared in the *Daily Telegraph* he was incandescent. They had been printed without mentioning his name. It wouldn't do. He had written them, he told his mother, 'with design, a design which took form, as the correspondence advanced, of bringing my personality before the electorate. I had hoped that some political advantage might have accrued.'[51] While on assignment he was working on *Savrola*, the one novel of his literary career. When his aunt Leonie asked him why he was bothering with it, he replied, '*Il faut vivre.* I hope later on to produce something really good. You know I have unbounded faith in myself.'[52]

The simply dashing young hero of Churchill's novel is exhausted by his political struggle in Laurania.

Was it worth it? The struggle, the labour, the constant rush of affairs, the sacrifice of so many things that make life easy, or pleasant – for what? A people's good! That, he could not disguise from himself, was rather the direction than the cause of his efforts. Ambition was the motive force, and he was powerless to resist it. He could appreciate the delights of an artist, a life devoted to the search for beauty, or of sport, the keenest pleasure that leaves no sting behind. To live in dreamy quiet and philosophic calm in some beautiful garden, far from the noise of men and with every diversion that art and intellect could suggest, was, he felt, a more agreeable picture. And yet he knew that he could not endure it. 'Vehement, high and daring' was his cast of mind. The life he lived was the only one he could ever live: he must go on to the end.[53]

Here, in cold print, is the secret of Churchill's political happiness. He had, even at the age of twenty-three, successfully identified his own happiness with that of his people to the point where the two could not be disentangled.

There is no more important clue to why politicians do it. Successful politicians have arrived at the happy synthesis where they associate their own advancement with the advancement of their country. Once you have identified your own interest as being synonymous with the interests of the country, the question of ruthlessness never arises: any act you commit is done for a greater good.

One of Churchill's many biographers describes him as the last of the great Whig aristocrats, who regarded himself as a natural ruler.[54] If this was really the case, he must have found the twentieth century intensely frustrating: to achieve this birthright, he needed to deploy endless cunning. During his political career he changed sides repeatedly. Each switch of party loyalty was accompanied by the usual pieties deployed by turncoats. All have believed they were bigger than the party to which they belonged. Only in Churchill's case did it ultimately turn out to be true, and for that he could thank Adolf Hitler. Michael Foot, whose achievements as an orator and writer outshone his unhappy time as leader of the Labour party, had it about right when he said that, far from being the prophet who brooded on the affairs of humankind with a superior detachment, Churchill 'was frequently the very opposite. He was always the opportunist, the buccaneer, searching for the enemy of the moment. The enemy was by turns the Liberals, the Tories, the Germans, the Russians, the British workers, the Indians, the Germans and the Russians again, and the socialists at home.' Foot went on to quote an essay written about Churchill at the beginning of the *First* World War, which caught the man's character. 'Brilliantly as he preaches, he is the man of action simply, the soldier of fortune who lives for adventure, loves the fight more than the cause, more even than his ambition and his life. He has one purpose – to be in the firing line, the battles either of war or peace.'[55] Aneurin Bevan remarked simply that he was a man suffering from 'petrified adolescence'.

Churchill had in spades the qualities which other politicians have in lesser suits, which is what brought him the ultimate glory. But most seem to see themselves as adventurers. Theirs is a Dick Whittington journey which will take them from obscurity to high office, where they will make brave and wise decisions for the benefit of the nation, until they retire, garlanded with honour, knighthood or peerage, to bask in the affectionate respect of the people whose lives they have enhanced. Small wonder that parliament is filled with people preoccupied with their own image and who see the business of politics as being about who's up, who's down, who's in, who's out. In such an environment, as the Conservative MP Christopher Hollis remarked half a century ago, 'What brings a man to the top is not superior ability but – much more often – an intense desire for success, that extra little ounce of ambition that is not quite sane.'[56]

But what is the purpose of this slightly deranged ambition? To what end, the life-plan which runs from GCSE and A Level, university, through a good marriage, good job, fine children, to MP, Minister and Prime Minister? When John Major came to reflect on what had brought him from Brixton to Westminster, he remembered the name of a now long-forgotten novel based on Ramsay MacDonald, another Prime Minister who rose from obscurity and ended his career condemned by much of his party as a traitor. '*Fame is the Spur*,' wrote Howard Spring. He was right. Political life is stimulated by ambition, and providing ambition is not obsessive, I see nothing wrong in that. Even in these cynical days it is something to be a Member of Parliament, with those precious initials after your name.'[57] Success in all fields is driven by ambition. This usually involves being seen to be better than others. In politics, where the acclamation and failure are the most public of all, the prize on offer is *significance*. The desire is for recognition, the acknowledgement by other humans of the worth of the individual. Persuading thousands – or, in the case of party leaders, millions – of fellow human beings to give you their votes is one of the greatest forms of recognition available. As a young MP explained, 'Standing on the platform as the Returning Officer announces the results, knowing that the people have chosen you, is the greatest, warmest feeling. It makes you feel life is worth living. I have never, ever, felt more alive than when I was first elected as an MP.'

2. Getting On

It is a wet, blustery January night. The rain thrashes against leaded windows. Inside, over 400 young people have crammed themselves into a room laid out like the chamber of the House of Commons. In the Speaker's chair is a tall, confident young woman in a long black dress, flanked by two young men. In the body of the hall, hundreds are squashed up on rows of leather benches facing each other. There is standing room only in the gallery above. It is the Oxford Union's best-attended debate of the term. The motion, that 'This House believes the class system is the backbone of British society,' is one of the Union's old stand-bys, doubtless withdrawn from some dusty old manila folder, along with perennials like whether private education ought to be abolished, whether the monarchy ought to be abolished, or the circumstances under which members would fight for king and country. But, in a sense, the subject-matter is neither here nor there. The capacity crowd has come to be entertained, lured partly by the promise of James Hewitt, the caddish former lover of the Princess of Wales, the editor of the *Tatler*, the radio comic Nicholas Parsons, the cricketer Imran Khan and girl-about-town Tara Palmer-Tomkinson. In the event Imran Khan isn't there, and neither are Palmer-Tomkinson, Nicholas Parsons, the man from the *Tatler* or Hewitt, who has decided he prefers to stay on skiing in Gstaad, although his solicitor has been strong-armed into standing in for him.

The audience aren't particularly disappointed, for there are other guest speakers – the interior designer Nicky Haslam, Kate Kray, one-time wife of the east end gangster Ronnie Kray, the field-sports campaigner Penny Mortimer and the motoring journalist Jeremy Clarkson. The Union has no trouble deploying its reputation to snare Big Names to speak: three recent American presidents, the Dalai Lama, Mother Theresa and Kermit the Frog have all graced its debating hall, along with dozens of well-known home-grown politicians. Most have been heard in polite silence. Tonight, the guest speakers perform as best they can in an unforgiving atmosphere which proves, if proof were needed, the rarity of the necessary skills to perform well in the debate convention. But the anthropological interest is not so much in the guests as in the students. For a start, the participants all wear evening dress – at the very minimum, a dinner jacket for the men, and, for the bigwigs in the society, white tie and tails, some with patent-leather shoes. The proposer and opposer of the motion stand at wooden dispatch boxes, the president 'recognizes' other students who wish to speak from the floor, no two people may be on their feet at the same time, except in the brief moments when attempting to interrupt one another on points of order or information. Everyone is an 'honourable member'. The speeches of the student debaters – formal, orotund, witty in a very Oxford Union sort of way ('I'm very fond of my backbone. It's my favourite accessory') – are incomparably better suited to the mock parliamentary medium than those of any of the visitors. You could have heard the same well-modulated tones at any time in the last fifty years. What is most striking about everyone who speaks is their astonishing self-confidence. 'The Union', the president declares, 'is, and shall remain, the most respected and privi- leged platform in the world for debate and freedom of speech,' putting the UN General Assembly, the American Congress and the British parliament in their place.

Three-quarters of newly arrived students join the Oxford Union. Acknowledging that mainstream politics has lost much of its appeal, the place has reinvented itself by reducing formal debates and raising the number of 'speaker events' at which the students can improve their minds by listening to 'Mad' Frankie Fraser, one of the actresses from *Dynasty* (which must, surely, have been on television before most of them were born?) or Stuart and Dean from *Big Brother*. It also offers a nightclub, snooker tables, big-screen showings of *The Simpsons* and 'Oxford's only politically correct beauty pageant'. What former members like William Ewart Gladstone would make of it, one can only guess. But complaints that the Union is not what it was have been going on for decades. In 1976, a writer in the Oxford magazine *Isis* was lamenting that all that happened in the chamber now was 'a pointless ritual indulged in by a few deluded careerists who believe that it will get them somewhere . . . The debating chamber is now simply the stage for aspiring hacks, and not very good ones at that.'[1] 'Hacks' has been the standard Oxford term of abuse for thirty or more years for people who devote their lives to the Union. It refers to their readiness to sell their souls, to stab each other in the back to advance their careers. But the disillusion with the shallow antics of would-be politicians goes back further: nearly half a century earlier, another unsigned article in *Isis* argued much the same case, in slightly more eloquent language. The Union was, said the editorial, 'discredited and decrepit'.

The sad ghost of Asquith moves slowly through the depleted benches and remembers a time when there was a voice in the House that meant more than mediocrity, and a presence that bore some stamp of greatness, some promise of valuable wisdom. In his day, a debate was a debate, and not a succession of lisping, chattering bores, each clutching his pile of notes, inaudible, inoffensive and inane.[2]

Reports of the decline and imminent death of the Oxford Union have turned out – in the usual spirit of relations between media and politics – to be grossly overdone. Three years after that *Isis* editorial, the carrying of the motion that the Union would not under any circumstances fight for its king and country made headlines around the world, being seen as evidence of the collapse of moral fibre in Britain, rather than the commitment to world peace which its pro-posers had intended. And a long list of subsequently famous national politicians were to learn their speechifying there in the years to come. Michael Foot became the youngest president of the Oxford Union, in 1933. (Foot, incidentally, is another case of public life running in families: his father was the Liberal MP Isaac Foot, his brothers ('the Feet') Dingle and John were also presidents of the Oxford Union, a third brother, Hugh, was president of the Cambridge Union. In the next generation, the great radical journalist Paul Foot was elected president of the Oxford Union in 1961.) When Edward Heath was elected president in November 1938, the *Sunday Express* ran a feature entitled 'Jobbing Builder's Son Is an Oxford Star'. (Heath was less than happy with the report: he felt his father deserved a grander title than 'jobbing builder', and they called Heath himself 'Richard' throughout. He subsequently consoled himself with the thought that it had been a useful introduction to the ways of the media.) Future Labour cabinet ministers such as Roy Jenkins and Tony Benn made their names there. The 'Hon. A.N. Wedgwood Benn', another president, was reported by *Tatler* to have 'an easy eloquence and display of wit which should make *Hansard* a joy to read in years to come'.[3] But it was his fellow Union hack and future Labour cabinet colleague Anthony Crosland who delivered the most memorable line of their time at Oxford: when Benn intervened in one of Crosland's speeches to say it was important for Labour undergraduates to discard the taint of intellectualism, Crosland crushed him with the reply that 'in order for the honourable gentleman to discard the taint of intellectualism it was first necessary for him to acquire it'.[4]

The sheer intensity of the desire to be a Union bigwig can be rather shocking, even, looking back on it, for the person with the ambition. Reflecting on a life which had encompassed jobs as Chancellor of the Exchequer, Home Secretary and President of the European Commission, Roy Jenkins admitted that 'I have often been shocked, looking back, to think that in June 1940 I was almost as cast down by defeat for the presidency of the Oxford Union as by the fall of France.'[5] The Oxbridge Unions amply demonstrate the truth of the observation attributed to Henry Kissinger that student politics are the most vicious politics of all, precisely because the stakes are so small. To the uninitiated – which includes 99.9 per cent of the population – it is simply incomprehensible that anyone could want the job of president of the Union badly enough to spend the necessary hours plotting and scheming, the weekly attendance at one fatuous debate after another, the attention-seeking speeches from the floor, the subsequent sacrifice of hours on the river, in the pub or library, to preparation of speeches which will change not a single fact of existence. Yet since 1823 it has obsessed young men and (only since 1963) women, who sometimes sound as if winning office at the Union was the most important thing in their lives. Michael Heseltine was not the first and will not be the last student to be caught tapping his glass at dinner and muttering 'Order, order,' dreaming of the day when he would become president of the Union, 'because it's the first step to being Prime Minister'.[6] The cannier operators, like Edward Heath, who had told his admissions tutor at Balliol that he wanted to be a professional politician, bide their time. He wrote to his former headmaster that he 'spent the term [his first] sitting at the feet of the great men of the day, so that next term I may speak a bit better'.[7]

Those who reinterpret the Victorian belief that becoming president of the Union occupies 'the brief interval which must intervene between Eton and the Cabinet'[8] have to campaign for office without canvassing, in the process acquiring plenty of experience in the sort of backstairs intrigue which will be necessary if they are to beat their colleagues to Downing Street. The Conservative cabinet minister William Waldegrave looked back on his days in the Oxford Conservative Association with gratitude. 'The politics', he said, 'made Tammany Hall look naïve; the battles were *never* about politics but always about personalities; the training, in short, was not too bad.'[9] Jeremy Thorpe, about whom there were persistent rumours of skulduggery in his successful campaign for the presidency of the Oxford Union, was at least honest. 'I enjoyed politicking enormously – the Machiavellian aspect. If you were *determined* to achieve an office, some of the Union Set thought this muck politics – offside. I didn't. I'm not English. I'm three-quarters Celt. And I'm bi-lingual: I speak American as well as English.'[10]

There are, it is true, other things you learn. Unlike votes in the House of Commons, where members of parliament simply do as they are told by the party whips, to win a debate in the Oxford Union you do have to persuade people to your point of view. Being active in the Oxford or Cambridge Union also gives the opportunity to meet proper, grown-up politicians, who may be able to help your career later. The days are long gone when a political meteor like F.E. Smith might move from presidency of the Union to a role in frontbench politics and still return to the place to watch – and to intervene in – debates. But the habit is long established that the parties watch the Oxford and Cambridge Unions as Premier League talent spotters sit in the wind-lashed stands of non-league clubs.

The shades of past glory lengthen over the years. The Oxford Union has given Britain five Prime Ministers, four party leaders, and a couple of dozen cabinet ministers. All, in their time, were Union hacks. Their portraits, and those of other alumni, like Benazir Bhutto, hang on the walls. It speaks volumes that when the Palace of Westminster was bombed in the Second World War, the Oxford Union wrote to the House of Commons offering its dispatch boxes as a replacement for those which had been lost.[11] The society's historian comments that 'For the Union's leading members, this would have been the most natural gesture in the world; as far as many of them were concerned, they were to all intents and purposes members of the House of Commons already.'[12] When Edward Heath translated his success in the Union to a seat in parliament he wasn't awestruck, like many new MPs, because 'when I first went to the House of Commons, in 1950, I felt I was coming home'.[13]

While this may doubtless have been a help to the young man on the make, it does nothing to raise the regard in which parliament is held. The style of the Oxford Union (and its counterpart at Cambridge) – adversarial, clever, rather pleased with itself – keeps alive a style of discussion in the House of Commons which is increasingly out of touch with the real world. At a time when the only people who saw what happened in the chamber of the House of Commons were those who took the trouble to attend, it did not matter so much if the conventions belonged to some antiquated rhetorical nursery school. But when the entire country can watch parliament on television it is another matter. If it is hard to escape the impression that what matters in the Oxford Union is clever-cleverness, that is because what really matters in the Oxford Union is clever-cleverness. It does not do to be too earnest. The problem is not that the hacks lack talent: most are highly intelligent, dedicated and able. Accomplished young Tories aspire, often justifiably, for what they call the 'quadruple', to be president of the Union, president of the Conservative Association, president of the Junior Common Room, and to get a first in their degree. William Hague did it. Yet his fate – as already noted, to be the first Conservative leader since Austen Chamberlain not to become Prime Minister – demonstrates what is wrong with the Oxford training. It had helped Hague to become a remarkably effective debater. Week after week at Prime Minister's Questions he would knock spots off Tony Blair, who had also been at Oxford but had spurned the Union as a place for hacks. Yet effective performance in the chamber of the House of Commons was no guarantee at all of popularity outside. If anything, when television makes the proceedings of Westminster seem so transparent, the tricks and self-confidence of the

Oxford Union just make the politician seem odder than ever. It is not the idiom in which most of the rest of humanity lives its life.

If success were to be measured by the number of members, the outstanding political organization in Britain over the last half-century has been the Labour party. In 1979, it proudly claimed to have over 7 million members. The Conservatives, by contrast, kept their membership figures secret, although it was generally accepted that at the time they had something over a million people on their books. Yet in the election that year the Labour party spiralled to defeat. The plain truth was that many of the people they had listed as 'members' had not bothered to vote for them.

The Conservative party made sport of the fact that Labour claimed as members people who were nothing more than members of trades unions and other organizations which had pledged allegiance to the party. Conservative party membership figures, by contrast, represented real individuals who had made a personal decision to join the party out of conviction. This too was a fiction. The post-war Conservative party did, genuinely, have the largest number of individual members. But that was not quite the same as saying that most people had joined the party because they wanted to get politically involved. The Unique Selling Point of the Young Conservatives, for example, was that they threw a cloak of respectability over the sort of fumblings which are uppermost in every teenager's mind. Julian Critchley joined the Hampstead Young Conservatives at eighteen because 'I had nothing better to do ... There were, as my mother put it, "so many nice girls", Pams, Susans, Marions, hairdressers and shop assistants, trim but respectable.' The Hampstead YCs had to pay the price of listening occasionally to Geoffrey Finsberg, the local star. But in exchange they got plenty of tennis, dancing and frustratingly chaste goodnight kisses.[14]

From 1949 until the 1960s, the Young Conservatives organized week-long gatherings at Butlins holiday camps. Under the tantalizing banner 'Mix Politics with Pleasure!', the 1958 programme offered the 'Lads and Lasses' all sorts of delights, ranging from tea dances and a Holiday Lovelies competition to whist drives and a Demonstration of Hypnotic Phenomena. This last doubtless got them in the mood for the speeches which followed from people such as Anthony Eden and Lord Woolton. In some years, mock parliaments were held. But the other attractions, from the brochures preserved in the Conservative party archive, included an ankle competition and a Holiday Princess of the Week contest ('also some fun for the lads') in 1950, a Young Conservative Crazy Gang Night ('featuring some of our craziest Young Conservatives') in 1955, and a demonstration of judo by the Harrogate Judokwai in 1958. The 1964 conference culminated in a Miss Young Conservative Contest, which even has its own file in the archive. The contestants were expected to parade around the hall twice, dressed in 'an evening dress, either full or cocktail length', and then to answer some questions. These ran as follows:

1. How old are you?
2. Are you an active Young Conservative?
3. How strong is your branch?
4. If you were a member of parliament what would you like to see done?
5. Do you like the Beatles?
6. Who is your favourite politician?
7. What do you think makes young people decide to vote for a political party?[15]

The woman who survived this terrifying inquisition most impressively was a 21-year-old zoologist called Gillian Smees.

For those too young for beauty contests, the Conservative party had other organizations, like the Junior Imperial League, which ran from 1906 to 1945, whose members were commonly known as 'Imps', and the Young Britons, which lasted until 1963. The Young Britons produced literature such as:

THE COMMUNIST MOVEMENT

★★★

HOW IT SEEKS

TO SUBVERT

BRITISH

CHILDREN

The Communist menace was kept at bay by Young Britons busying themselves in wholesome activities like making models in plasticine of the relief of Lucknow during the Indian Mutiny, organizing Inter-Dominion Relay Races, and putting on red, white and blue head-dresses, so they could form a collective Union flag.

For relaxation, there was edifying literature. One of their cautionary tales, 'A New Jack the Giant Killer', told the story of Jack's introduction, by a bad gnome called Discontent, to the land of Socialism. The staff at the Bodleian Library in Oxford, where this gem resides in the trove of Conservative party archives, had decided to photocopy the thing backwards with left and right pages transposed, which made the experience of reading it slightly surreal. Not that the tale lacked weirdness of its own. Jack, the son of a farmer, meets Discontent as he sits under a tree after his day's work. Discontent looks just like any other worker, except that he has 'a mean face, small piggy eyes and a bit of hump on his back', which ought to have alerted Jack to the fact that he was, in fact, a gnome. But Jack is a gullible lad and listens as the ugly, evil fellow explains to the labourers that in the land of Socialism workers like them own everything. The next thing he knows, Jack is working on an assembly line in this Worker's Paradise. It is misery.

Those who struggled through to page eleven of the pamphlet will have discovered that Jack was, astonishingly, just dreaming. When he wakes and describes his dream, his fellow workers nod knowingly. Jack, who once slew a giant, will now have to be on guard for Discontent and his brother Ignorance. 'They are far more dangerous than your old giants,' they tell him, 'for Discontent and Ignorance bring ruin and misery wherever they go. You'll have to fight them for us, to keep this land of ours safe, happy, and prosperous.'[16]

Who could resist a challenge like that?

Some people who have subsequently become politicians have consciously avoided teenage and student politics. Tony Blair preferred to play in a rock band, Ugly Rumours, his bass guitarist recalling 'long hair with the rather severe fringe – a slightly medieval look about him, a sort of Three Musketeers thing – a T-shirt that can only be described as "hoop necked" and possibly even "trumpet sleeved", which revealed a large acreage of rippling bare torso, and beyond that the obligatory purple loons, topped off with the Cuban-heeled cowboy boots.'[17] He is not the first party leader to have preferred other activities at university. When he was at Oxford, Alec Douglas-Home was more interested in his membership of something called the Aspidistra Society, 'which required members to destroy immediately any aspidistra encountered, and post the evidence to all other members'.[18] Anthony Eden preferred the Uffizi and the Asiatic Societies to the Union. Clement Attlee admitted that although he did attend the occasional debate at the Oxford Union, 'I . . . was much too shy to try to speak there.'[19] His successor as leader, Hugh Gaitskell, was also uninterested in politics when a student. He explained that 'We were in revolt all right – against Victorianism, Puritanism, stuffiness of any kind, but most of us weren't sufficiently bitter – or perhaps sufficiently serious – to be angry young men . . . We were, therefore, suspicious of general ideas, especially when these involved some mystical, collective, common good. We preferred the happiness of the individual as the only acceptable social aim.'[20]

And there are plenty of examples of subsequently famous politicians who believed one thing as students and something else when they became active in politics. Clement Attlee admitted to being a Conservative at university, becoming a socialist only after moving to live in the east end of London. Another Labour leader, Harold Wilson, served as treasurer of the Oxford University Liberal Club. Roy Jenkins, who left the Labour party in the 1980s to form the Social Democratic Party, had done the same thing forty years earlier, when he left the University Labour Club to begin the Democratic Socialist Club. But these are exceptions. For the most part, the attitudes struck at university are attitudes which stick. Increasingly, mainstream political life is dominated by people who took to it at university. Although Blair himself had preferred prancing around with Ugly Rumours, after the 2001 election his cabinet was packed with former student hacks. His Foreign Secretary, Jack Straw, all heavy-rimmed glasses, dark hair and flailing arms, had been president of the National Union of Students. Charles Clarke, whom Blair made party chairman, had been all beard and shoulder-length fair hair thirty years earlier, another leader of the National Union of Students. The Chancellor of the Exchequer, Gordon Brown, had been elected Rector of Edinburgh University while still a student, in a campaign promoted by nubile students calling themselves 'Brown's Sugars'. Blair's Home Secretary, David Blunkett, had been so precocious that he was already a Labour councillor in Sheffield at twenty-two. By the same age, his Northern Ireland Secretary, John Reid, was vice chairman of the Scottish National Union of Students, having previously been president of the student association at Stirling University. The Leader of the House of Commons, Robin Cook, had run the Labour Club at Edinburgh University, before going on to chair the Scottish Association of Labour Students. When Alistair Darling was appointed Secretary for Work and Pensions, the Aberdeen *Evening Express* proudly reported that he had once been president of the city's university student union. The Scottish Secretary, Helen Liddell, had been campaigning for the Labour party since the age of eleven. Although she claimed to find university politics 'effete', she had reached the semi-finals of the national student debating competition (her predecessor as Secretary of State for Scotland, Donald Dewar, had enjoyed teasing her by pointing out that he had reached the finals of the competition, along with the former Labour leader, John Smith). The Trade Secretary, Patricia Hewitt, had been active in student politics at Cambridge, the Education Secretary, Estelle Morris, at Warwick, the Transport Secretary, Stephen Byers, at Liverpool Polytechnic.

By the start of the twenty-first century, just about the only remnant of an earlier tradition of political engagement was the Deputy Prime Minister, John Prescott. Still smarting from his failure to get into grammar school, Prescott managed finally to make his way to Ruskin College, the trades-union-sponsored establishment in Oxford set up at the turn of the twentieth century to give those who had been denied an education a second chance. His tutor remembered a young man most like another, albeit fictional, Oxford student. 'My student seemed a very incarnation of Jude the Obscure,' he recalled, 'with a tremendous appetite for learning, fiercely independent opinions and a determination, like the tragic hero of Hardy's novel, to crack the secret of knowledge.'[21] Prescott's eagerness to learn harks back to a noble history in the Labour party of poor men and women who fought their way to power through self-discipline and self-education.

From Keir Hardie, the party's first leader, onwards, prominent Labour politicians have risen to the top without the benefit of higher education. Aneurin Bevan, one of the towering figures of the twentieth-century party, was cursed with a brutal elementary school headmaster, who persuaded him that, even had it been available, secondary education was a waste of time ('Any fool can see that two and two make four,' he said much later, 'but it takes a real capacity to stretch it to five, or better still, six or seven').[22] Ernest Bevin, another of the greatest twentieth-century politicians, had started work as a farm labourer by the time he was eleven. For these sort of people, the only education available was through classes offered by organizations like the Plebs League or the Workers' Educational Association after work, or, for a select few, at places like the Labour College in London (which Bevan attended and thought a waste of time). Others forged their political careers through the chapel: Bevin became a Sunday-school teacher and then a preacher in the Baptist church in Bristol. It would be hard to exaggerate the importance of nonconformism in the development of the Labour party's sense of moral purpose.

For most of those who rose through the party in this way, the true seat of learning was the local Labour party organization. Perhaps they glamorize it when they recall long evenings in which university graduates and milkmen would sit over pints of beer and argue the rights and wrongs of unilateral disarmament or whether Clause Four of the party constitution really committed Labour to nationalizing the means of production, or was just a vague aspiration to pacify the left. But the local party organizations could be astonishingly intense places, riven by factions and dominated by ambitious people whose working lives were almost entirely secondary to their political activities. For such passionately argumentative places, these constituency organizations often chose surprisingly docile candidates for parliament. Union officials who had outlived their usefulness among shipworkers on Clydeside or miners in Yorkshire would be offered the chance to become the local MP. Seizing, or being coerced into, a new career in their fifties or beyond, many would arrive in London, conclude they were out of their depth, install themselves in a congenial bar and hardly leave it.

Now, parliament has become a middle-class institution. The old

Yorkshire mining constituency of Don Valley, for example, was represented in parliament for generations by one-time manual workers. At the 1997 election it returned Caroline Flint, the first woman, the first non-manual worker, probably even the first non-Yorkshireman, to represent it. Her predecessor had been a lorry-driver, sponsored by the National Union of Mineworkers. Ms Flint was educated in west London, went on to the University of East Anglia, and then worked as a local authority equal opportunities officer. She is typical of a group of people who see political life as an extension of the 'caring professions'. She cannot imagine circumstances under which she would rebel against the Labour whips, and is so new Labour and media-savvy that she even proposed to her partner (who worked for her in the constituency) by fax, a fact which was duly printed in the newspapers.

By the time the Labour party in Don Valley came to choose Caroline Flint (crucially, by the new system of one member, one vote, rather than the committee meeting over a few beers), there was only one working pit left in the area. The British middle class has been steadily growing for years, and looks set to continue growing. The class issues across which British politics divides are less and less stark. But the more that politics becomes the preserve of a particular social group, the more it is vulnerable to those whose only ambition is to go into it because they seek the status they think attaches to being an MP. The idealists still exist. But they are joined by increasing numbers who seem much less interested in doing the job of an MP than in *being* an MP. You can see them any day in the House of Commons, men and women who ask questions not because they want to find anything out but to draw attention to themselves, issuing press releases, endlessly drafting Early Day Motions congratulating Marmite on lasting a hundred years.

A qualitative change takes place when politics is essentially a game played between people who all agree on the boundaries of what is possible. All student politics is part serious, part play-acting, like some children's game. For all their intensity, the passions are comical, and most comical when most seriously meant. In general, the left is saddled with earnestness. Saving the world is no laughing matter. An ambition to leave it alone, or wreck it, is another thing altogether. The difficulty is that, with the passion extracted from it, politics can become no more than a playground for shallow people. When Neil Hamilton ran his campaign to become president of the student union at Aberystwyth (part of the University of Wales) he promised in his manifesto that 'the constitutional pedants, the ledgerbook minds, will be resolutely crushed beneath the iron heel of a victorious people marching on the road to destiny.' He appeared at the hustings in a black cape, black trousers with riding boots and a white jacket crossed with a red sash, and accompanied by several 'bodyguards'. If elected, he promised to abolish parliament and suppress the working class. Although this ambitious programme was not enough to win him the presidency, he was able to advance his political agenda through editorship of the student newspaper, which he renamed *The Feudal Times and Reactionary Herald* (a title borrowed from the Way of the World column in the *Daily Telegraph*), complete with a Reich-style eagle on its masthead. He also sent the names of left-wing student 'subversives' to the Education Secretary, Margaret Thatcher.[23] Scarcely more than ten years later, he was Conservative MP for one of the safest seats in England.

It is hard to imagine a comic-book right-winger like Hamilton ever contemplating joining any other party currently represented in parliament. But others do occasionally change sides. In the first Blair government, the Conservative MPs Peter Temple-Morris and Shaun Woodward both decided they were in the wrong party and crossed the floor to the Labour benches. Temple-Morris had always been what Mrs Thatcher dismissed as a wringingly 'wet' Tory. But Woodward had been Director of Communications for the Conservative High Command for the first two years of John Major's government and had entered parliament in 1997 by running a campaign which did down Tony Blair and new Labour. Now, within the space of one parliament, he seemed to think that Blair was the new messiah. Within six months of the second Blair government taking office, Paul Marsden decided that he, too, had made a terrible mistake, and abandoned his former colleagues for the Liberal Democrats. All three belong in a procession which extends back through the defectors from the Labour party who founded the SDP, through Ramsay MacDonald's creation of National Labour in the 1930s, and the splits in the Liberal party in the 1900s and 1920s. After studying the attempts of defectors to justify their actions, the historian Peter Clarke decided there was a pretty standard speech they delivered, the notes for which went something like this: '– deep regret at sad moment – strong ties to the party in which brought up – lifetime of service, proud of achievements – great leaders of yesterday, Gladstone/Keir Hardie/Attlee, etc. – but now would turn in their graves – betrayal of finest traditions – *I have not changed, the party has changed* – heavy heart, sleepless nights, no alternative, etc.'[24] It is a good summary, and anyone who spends a decade or two with half an ear on parliament can expect to hear it at least once. As Clarke points out, it is usually followed, soon afterwards, by a venomous attack on the defector's old colleagues.

If it was simply a question of changing support for a football club it would be another matter. As it is, the decisions that politicians make affect all of us, and to suppose that an elected representative can suddenly wake up one morning and decide that he or she has been wrong, and that people won't object when told that they too were wrong – wrong to follow their instincts, wrong to agonize about whether, this time, the party was really worth supporting, wrong to believe the candidate's promises – is more than naive. It is stupid. There is a price for political conviction. It is paid in stuffing envelopes, handing out leaflets, knocking on doors and offering to help old ladies to the polling station. This passionate engagement with public affairs when contemporaries were playing or following sport, going dancing or rebuilding old cars is not an alternative hobby. It is an alternative life.

Just down the road from the Oxford Union lived the psychiatrist Anthony Storr, who counted a number of politicians among his clients. Shortly before he died I asked him whether he had any idea what drove them. He thought about it for a moment and delivered himself of the withering verdict that 'They all have an irresistible urge to be recognized and applauded, while, unfortunately, having no discernible talent.' He has a point: which brilliant young student, told they could become one of the country's greatest eye surgeons, or even commercial lawyers, would give it up for a life in which the rewards are so unpredictable? The pay is worse than they might expect at the top of other professions, the exposure is more or less constant and the legacy most will leave behind is negligible. Most of us are second-rate, so it is not necessarily any great insult to point out that politics is largely practised by second-raters. Take two political partnerships. If, in 1976, anyone had suggested that Tony Blair (a struggling, newly qualified barrister) or Gordon Brown (a lecturer at Glasgow College of Technology) or even John Major (a not very significant figure at Standard Chartered Bank) or Norman Lamont (an asset manager at Rothschilds not expected to make the main board) would one day be running the country, they would have been laughed out of the room. That they achieved so much reflects the curious combination of drive, dedication, gambling skills and sheer luck that characterizes the political trade. To succeed requires a set of skills, of which by far the most important is resolution. In that sense, it is not unlike a vocation for the priesthood. But, crucially, it lacks the saving grace of submission to a greater authority. After seeing them at close quarters, Anthony Storr had concluded that 'One or two of the politicians I met were virtual psychopaths. Anything – even if it was a wife or children – which got in the way of their advancement was just dispensed with.' He was, frankly, baffled, and despairingly asked John Freeman, a former Labour MP, later ambassador to Washington, 'Are they all mad?' Freeman replied, 'They all have a beetle gnawing at their insides.'

Most of us do not choose to become politicians, and for very sensible reasons. The job is inherently insecure: you may fail to win a seat, you may be deselected by the local party, or the Boundary Commission, which determines the size and shape of parliamentary constituencies, may redraw the map and, with a stroke of the pen, remove your majority. The job requires a degree of schizophrenia if you are to have any success in combining a life in the constituency opening fêtes and sorting out housing benefit problems with the role of a legislator at Westminster, where you will have to do exactly what the party managers tell you to do. For much of the week you will also probably be separated from husband or wife, who may have little taste for spending the intervening weekends at an endless round of turgid constituency functions.

Philip Norton, an academic who has devoted his life to studying the political process, decided he would rather be an observer than a participant after realizing that advancement had nothing to do with merit: he knew what he spoke about because he had sat on the selection committee which had chosen Jeffrey Archer as a Conservative candidate. When, later, he was asked by the then party leader, William Hague, to investigate ways of improving the calibre of people going into political life, he took evidence from the banker Sir Nicholas Goodison.

'How could more mature people be encouraged to take up politics?' he asked.

'I suppose', he was told, 'that when someone was in their mid-forties and realized they weren't going anywhere in their career, they might consider changing direction.'

'You mean we could attract low-flyers?'

'I suppose I do.'

3. Getting In

And now here is a former president of the Oxford Union campaigning to get into parliament. He wears a filthy, dark-blue moleskin suit, which seems to belong to someone an entirely different shape. His white shirt is frayed right around the collar, held together with a tie which might once have held up the trousers of a Wiltshire blacksmith. He seems to be wearing his hair back to front. His conversation is peppered with words like 'gadzooks', 'ripping' and 'top hole'. Asked to name the members of his party's shadow cabinet (he cannot), he exclaims, 'What a girlie swot question!'

It is 1921, Bertie Wooster running for parliament, with Jeeves lost somewhere along the way. But, no, this Wodehousian invention is a candidate in the General Election of June 2001. Boris Johnson (the son, incidentally, of a Conservative member of the European parliament) is standing as the Tory candidate for Henley-on-Thames. Johnson is too intelligent a man to believe there is any chance of his not winning the seat, and too intelligent, too, for the 1920s schoolboy mannerism to be anything but cultivated. Perhaps it has something to do with the fact that his grandfather was Interior Minister in imperial Turkey. He has had a stellar career – King's Scholar at Eton, Brackenbury scholar at Balliol, Oxford's most worldly college, president of the Union, and a lightning rise through journalism to become a columnist on the *Daily Telegraph* and editor of the *Spectator*. He has been 'blooded' in an unwinnable Labour seat in Wales, where he acquired five words of Welsh: 'Vote Tory' and 'fish and chips'. This time, he knows he will be home and dry. But why would anyone want to give up something at which they were so successful in order to become a politician? Why surrender the chance to throw rotten tomatoes to be on the receiving end? 'I want to put something back. I don't want to set myself up above politicians, to laugh at them, to sneer at them, to bash them about.' There was something inherently admirable about this ambition, which almost stifled my response. But it came out anyway. 'Oh come off it!' I exclaimed.

'Well, that's 70 per cent of it.'

And the other 30 per cent?

'Complete egomania.'

I told him I thought he'd got the proportions the wrong way round. But a career in journalism enabled him to recognize the weakness of my rejoinder straight away. Plenty of other journalists have made a similar journey since the Second World War, from distinguished Conservatives such as Iain Macleod (the *Spectator*), Edward Heath (the *Church Times*) and Nigel Lawson (the *Spectator*) to Labour illuminati such as Richard Crossman (the *New Statesman*) and Michael Foot (*Tribune*). All justified their decisions in similar terms: that journalism may have been more fun than life as a backbench politician, but it lacked the moral legitimacy that came from being actively engaged instead of standing on the sidelines. (In the event, Boris Johnson managed to eat his cake and to have it, since he hung on to his jobs editing the *Spectator* and writing a column in the *Daily Telegraph* – sitting in the House of Commons one day and 'bashing up' politicians the next.)

And here Johnson is on a bright, blue-skyed morning, working a leafy avenue of detached £700,000 houses where the Jaguars (his) and the Mercedes estates (hers) seem to be delivered with the gravel for the drive.

'Hello, er, sorry, I'm Boris Johnson, your Conservative candidate in the election.' The words come out in a strange throaty mutter, because his forehead is pointing at the ground and all that the potential voter can see is a haystack of blond hair. He is either being incredibly rude, or he is hugely embarrassed at the necessity of asking for their support, like an old-fashioned aristocrat's distaste for discussing money. His four helpers from the local constituency association, all grey hair, golf-club blazers and Tory rosettes, guide him from one front door to another in his disagreeable task. He is completely hopeless, stuttering, confused, shambling. But it is not exactly an onerous task getting their support: Henley is the sort of place where they'd vote a mule into parliament if it promised to kick in the right direction.

'Count on my vote? You certainly can, providing you'll get us out of Europe and bring back corporal and capital punishment,' says a not particularly unusual customer. 'Give those guttersnipes who broke the station windows a good thrashing and they won't do it again,' says a man with a nose the size of a cauliflower. Another says her only reservation is that Boris's columns in the *Telegraph* have too many jokes for her taste. In the entire campaign, the closest he comes to actual hostility is when he is told he ought to return to a chip shop half a mile away. There are people there keen to meet him. He trudges back through the streets and enters the shop with the words 'I'm Boris Johnson, I'm told you'd like to meet me.' 'No we wouldn't,' comes the reply.

One of Boris's blazers told me that the Labour candidate lived near by, and added, 'You should see the state of her house. If that's how she looks after her own property, how would she look after the rest of us?' Intrigued, I pay her a call. Her house didn't seem any different from any other on the executive-style housing estate half a mile away. Perhaps the blazer objected to the evidence that she was a working woman with children. She smilingly invites me in for a coffee to explain the strategy.

Or she would have explained the strategy, had there been one. The fact staring Janet Matthews in the face was that the returning officer's declaration on election night was not going to be an invitation to give up her job in Henley-on-Thames's public library. I wondered why she was bothering. 'I just felt we needed a local candidate, to show that Labour people do live in areas like this, so people don't think it's a foregone conclusion. Michael Heseltine [the retiring MP] was a useless constituency representative. He turned up for the wine-and-cheese evenings, and the Conservative dinner-dances. But he ignored the rest of the people. He hardly even held surgeries. I want to be a constituency MP for everyone.'

It is a noble ambition. But, in these parts, to be Labour is to be permanently hobbling about, covered in electoral bruises. She had just spoken at a pensioners' meeting organized by Age Concern. At the end, a smiling old widow approached her with the words, 'You know, dear, I agree with every single word you said. But my husband would turn in his grave if I didn't vote Conservative.'

Mrs Matthews had already failed in elections to the district and county councils. And now she faced an opponent who had the awful weapon of 'celebrity'. Week after week the pages of the *Henley Standard* carried pictures of Boris Johnson at one function or another, while she might as well not have existed. The state of the local Labour party wasn't much help. In theory, there were 500 members. But great numbers of them gave up labouring ages ago: at forty-five Mrs Matthews now often found herself much the youngest person at meetings. The idea of appointing a 'youth officer' who met the requirement of being under twenty-eight was risible. She had been unable even to find enough people to stuff envelopes for election literature.

Janet Matthews is precisely the sort of person – sensible, compassionate and involved – who would benefit any healthy democracy. But getting into parliament in a town like this, against a candidate like that, was a transparently doomed venture. I pointed it out, as gently as I could. She smiled.

'A lot of people say, "Well, you're very brave." But that's not it. I'm not brave. I *want* to do it. I'd like to win. I'd *love* to win.' It was unnecessary to say more. She had defeat written all over her. Which was a shame since healthy societies need people like her, mothers who become school governors because they're concerned enough to try to make things better. But she knew she'd taken on a hopeless mission. Apart from anything else, why, on a beautiful, bright May afternoon a fortnight before polling day, wasn't she out canvassing?[1]

When the previous MP, Michael Heseltine, realized that his career was not going to follow the trajectory he had sketched out for himself at Oxford, from president of the Union to Prime Minister, he threw in the towel. The local Conservative organization was inundated with applications from aspiring successors. Being the twentieth most safe Conservative seat in the country had something to do with it: if the Conservatives were ever to lose the place, they would have been reduced to half the strength of the Liberal Democrats. Two hundred and ten applications were eventually reduced to Boris.

Johnson's killer blow at the selection meeting had been to play the idiot savant. Asked whether he believed in more private sector involvement in the National Health Service, he recounted his most recent experience of the NHS. His wife had been giving birth, and, after many hours at her bedside, Johnson was peckish. A nurse came by, with a couple of slices of toast. The new mother was asleep in the maternity ward. Johnson wolfed down both slices. When his wife awoke, tired and hungry, she asked for toast, only to be told that her husband had eaten her allotted supplies. He had been unable to procure any more. 'You find the person who is i/c toast, and you ask for some more, and there isn't any more, of course, Mr Chairman, because you have had your ration, and when you move to open your wallet, you find that this is no good either. You can't pay for things on the NHS. It's a universal service free at the point of delivery, delivery being the operative word, Mr Chairman, ha, ha, ha.'[2] A ripple of laughter follows the discovery of the pun. And so on. And so on. 'If the private sector can sort out the toast shortage, I think it's a thoroughly good thing,' said the would-be MP. He got the nomination by thirteen votes, out of well over a hundred.

These local committees have far more power than they recognize. For not only are they choosing a person to represent the constituency at Westminster. They are also moulding the parliamentary party. And it is on the appearance of the party in parliament that the voters will make up their minds at the next election. So when the local constituency group gets together to pick someone to represent the area, it is determining the future face – and fate – of the party.

The most cavalier selection meeting of recent history must have been that of Iain Macleod, in the General Election of 1945. Macleod, who later rose to become Conservative Chancellor of the Exchequer, had confined his student political career to a single speech at the Cambridge Union. The rest of the time he read poetry, played rugby and gambled. But his obsessive gambling gives a clue to his aptitude for the political life. (When he started work he was able to earn ten times his salary at the bridge table.) After the war, he was on leave in the Outer Hebrides when the election was called. There was no Conservative organization in the islands, so Macleod and his father called an inaugural meeting of a non-existent organization, at which Macleod senior (who was in fact a Liberal) appointed himself chairman. The meeting then adopted his son as the official candidate. There were no challengers for the post, since father and son were the only two people in the room. Macleod had a lot of cousins in the Western Isles, but even so managed to come last in the poll.[3]

Proving the rule that self-confidence is the absolute prerequisite of political advancement, Macleod got himself a job at the Conservative Research Department. (A stint as a party researcher has since become a well-worn path to parliament.) He took lodgings with his bridge partner, a doctor whose patients included the chairman of the Enfield Conservative Association. Hearing from his partner that the Tories were looking for a new candidate, Macleod simply phoned the chairman asking to be considered. When told the party already had forty-seven names to consider, he simply replied, 'Then forty-eight won't matter.'[4] Macleod was selected. A couple of years later, he learned that the boundaries of the constituency had been redrawn, removing its Labour majority at the stroke of a pen, and his parliamentary career was off. He hadn't even been on the list of approved candidates kept by Central Office. (Nor was John Major when he first stood for parliament.)

For much of the twentieth century, in much of the country, getting a Tory seat was a matter of cash as much as confidence. The spirit which led the British parliament to reform itself in the nineteenth century, to get rid of the idea that you could buy your way into parliament, hadn't really sunk in, as Duff Cooper discovered when he became one of the final three hopefuls for the seat of Stroud in Gloucestershire in 1924. Expecting tight cross-examination about legislation passing through parliament, he revised avidly. He also did plenty of homework on agriculture, about which he knew nothing. Instead, he found that the six or seven men and women on the selection committee merely wished to know three things from him. They asked about his health. Then they asked him about his religion, or rather they made sure that he wasn't a Roman Catholic. And finally, they wanted to know how much money he could give the local Conservative Association. Cooper made a quick calculation and offered to pay £300 a year, which was three-quarters of his parliamentary salary. 'They were very polite,' he recalled, 'and as I travelled back to London that evening I thought, with characteristic optimism, as I looked out of the carriage window, how well I should get to know that journey in the days to come. I did not have long to cherish the illusion, nor did I ever make the same journey again. Two days later I learned that an older, possibly wiser and certainly much richer candidate had been selected.'[5]

It is no misrepresentation to say that some MPs literally bought their seats in parliament. In the 1930s, when Quintin Hogg fought his way on to the Conservative party list of approved candidates, he was told that he would never become a Tory MP without contributing at least £400 a year to local party funds. In financial terms, this truly made a parliamentary career a zero-sum game: £400 was precisely what an MP was paid. The custom had a long history. Standing for Southport in 1886, George Curzon was asked to cough up for three-quarters of the election expenses, and to pay the local association £50 every year. The practice persisted even until after the Second World War: in 1947, Edward Heath was asked to pay £100 a year into local party funds, a sum which was well beyond him.[6]

Tory candidates are no longer expected to pay for the local association's wine-and-cheese evenings. But they must negotiate a familiar obstacle course. There will be the difficult question of ambition, to begin with. If, like Michael Heseltine, they plan to become Prime Minister, the committee may throw them out straight away, on the grounds that they won't have time or interest enough to look after the constituency. On the other hand, there may well be people on the committee who would like to bask in reflected glory by being on first-name terms with a cabinet minister, or perhaps even a Prime Minister. In 1947, Edward Heath was turned down by one selection committee because he was too ambitious, and then by another, at Rochester and Chatham, because, they told him, they were looking for someone who might become a cabinet minister. The chairman informed the future Prime Minister, 'I am afraid that we do not think you will ever hold office of any kind.'[7]

There will be expectations that the candidate will live in the constituency. This may be less of an ordeal for an ambitious politician hoping to represent Exmoor or the Lake District than for someone of similar temperament aspiring to represent Skelmersdale or Toxteth. But all know that to progress they need to be in London. George Walden, who abandoned a highly promising career in the diplomatic service for the chance to represent Buckingham, avoided the danger of too much contact with his constituents by answering the question, 'Will you live here?' with 'I will have a house in the constituency,' which was strictly true but not the same thing at all.[8] Few could nowadays expect to get away with the reply William Anstruther-Gray gave to his selection committee when asked the same question. 'I will hunt over it,' he said.

The ambitious Conservative or Labour politician appearing before the selection committee has already passed through a vetting procedure in which party headquarters has tried to make sure he or she is at least a member of the party, and can be expected to perform more or less adequately. The days when Jim Prior was driving his tractor through Norfolk and was asked why he didn't stand for Lowestoft are gone. Summoned to some meeting hall full of local members, the candidate will then have to give the performance of their life. To have any chance of success, they will have spent the weeks beforehand immersed in the history and culture of the place. They will have read the back-issues of the local paper for the past year. They will have spent endless evenings and weekends driving around, trying simply to get a feel for the area.

The style of these meetings revealed the very different preoccupations of the parties. At Labour selection meetings, there used to be much catechizing of the candidate, to make sure he or she was ideologically pure. Where did the candidate stand on the compulsory nationalization of major industries, whether ripe for it or not? Did he or she believe in punitive rates of tax for the rich? Would he or she promise not to accept a peerage on retirement and thus perpetuate the indefensible institution of the House of Lords? Conservative selection meetings have had less doctrinal interests, apart from whether the candidate was sound on touchstone issues like hanging. Nowadays, a candidate can expect to be interrogated for their attitudes to the European Union.

Boris Johnson's selling points to the selection committee – his innate Toryism, his intelligence, his sense of humour, his celebrity – were obvious. But his greatest asset was sex. Boris had the critical Y chromosome. With a few exceptions, it has been a great deal harder for a woman to be selected by one of these committees than for the possessor of a pair of testicles to be chosen. In 1945, Barbara Castle was able to get herself on to the shortlist for Blackburn, the seat she was to represent for over thirty years, only because women in the local party rebelled on discovering that every person on the original list was a man. When, much to everyone's surprise, she won the nomination, she was instructed that she should stop using her maiden name (Barbara Betts) at once and become Mrs Barbara Castle.[9] Admittedly, the earlier experience of her Labour comrade Jennie Lee was altogether different. She had been asked to stand in North Lanark as a direct consequence of her fiery performance at the 1927 ILP conference. An eyewitness recalled that 'a young, dark girl took the rostrum, a puckish figure with a mop of thick black hair thrown impatiently aside, brown eyes flashing, body and arms moving in rapid gestures, words pouring from her mouth in Scottish accent and vigorous phrases'.[10] It sounds such a memorable performance that it reinforces, rather than undermines, the argument that women were obliged to perform better than men in order to advance.

If the problem for women in the old Labour party was the difficulty of persuading a room full of men with pipes and flat caps, in the Conservative party the difficulty was the discovery of the limits of sisterhood. It is true that the Conservatives gave Britain its first woman Prime Minister. But when she had tried for the Tory nomination at Beckenham Margaret Thatcher had been rejected outright because of her sex. Even when chosen for Finchley, from which she would become one of the best-known politicians in the world, the local newspaper reported that she analysed the dangerous situation in the Middle East 'with the skill of a housewife measuring ingredients in a familiar recipe, [and] pinpointed Nasser as the fly in the mixing-bowl'.[11] Give that reporter a pay rise.

Seeing Doreen Miller sitting in her office in Marylebone, in a check jacket and grey skirt, listening to her missionary enthusiasm, it is no trouble at all to imagine her in the House of Commons. She is energetic. She is an instinctive Conservative (she wept real tears as the bill to abolish the voting rights of hereditary peers passed through parliament). Yet she has never been either a councillor or an MP. Perhaps it was because she started too late. The party grandee who first interviewed her for the candidates' list told her that he had been one of seven people at Oxford who had wanted to get into parliament.

They simply looked up all the MPs in parliament who were over seventy and then divided up their seats between them. When the MPs died or retired, they attacked their constituencies like fighter pilots. Every one of them now sat on the green benches. Doreen Miller, by contrast, had spent the first twenty years of her working life bringing up her children and building her business.

Still, she sailed through the initial selection by Central Office and got herself on to the list of people judged suitable to be interviewed by individual constituency associations. She energetically set about trying to find a seat. Time and again she would hear of a constituency looking for a Conservative candidate. Off would go the letter. And back would come the rejection note. Undaunted, she ploughed on. In all, she applied to over 140 constituencies. That is getting on for a quarter of the seats in the House of Commons. Only one-tenth of them bothered even to talk to her. But when she did get an interview she must have impressed, because in thirteen of the fourteen seats she made it on to the shortlist. And then her troubles began again.

For a start, there was the fact that she was usually the only woman on the shortlist. So, instead of representing half the electorate, she seemed to belong to some strange, obscure sect. And she found the other candidates brimming with an alarming bombastic self-confidence. They frightened her. 'When I saw how fierce they were, I just kept consoling myself with the thought that, whatever they had got, I was a good wife and good mother.'

But the biggest problem of all was the other wives and mothers.

'The local associations were dominated by women. You could see them sitting there thinking, "I didn't escape from the kitchen sink. Why should you?"'

Soon she was getting the strong impression that what these middle-aged women were looking for wasn't another middle-aged woman, but someone who would make a nice son-in-law.[12]

'I'm quite sure that if any of my three sons had been standing against me at a selection meeting, he'd have got the job. Apart from the son-in-law factor, he'd have been younger and a lot more malleable.' One aspiring female MP after another tells the same story of the critical importance of sex. How, they are asked, can they look after their children properly if they are away at Westminster? What did their husbands think of the idea? (At some selection meetings, husbands have had to explain that it is not they but their wives who are the candidates.) In one case, the candidate was asked what her husband would do for sex if she was away at Westminster all week. It was not so much that the party had no place for women as that it had far too precise an idea of what their place was. It was in the kitchen, where they could exercise their ambitions by making cakes for constituency fund-raisers. After the Tories' crushing defeat in the 2001 election, Kenneth Clarke, running for the leadership, declared that the party needed to reach out to 'the women – and the Welsh'. That said it all. Even the woman appointed as 'vice-chairman with responsibility for women' remarked that 'The Conservative party is simply not a place where a younger woman – and I mean women under something like 60 – can feel at home.'[13]

Kenneth Clarke has a point. When the Labour party went through its dark night of the soul in the late 1980s it acknowledged that, if it was ever to return to power, one of the many things it had to do was to raise the number of its female MPs. It decreed that 'Within ten years, after three general elections, half the parliamentary party will be women.' Before the 1997 election, Labour headquarters ruled that for various winnable seats, where the sitting MP was retiring or where the smallest swing in the vote was needed for the party to win the contest, the shortlists should be made up entirely of women. Although subsequently judged illegal (on the understandable grounds that because it banned half the population from consideration it fell foul of the Sex Discrimination Act), the policy had the result the party wanted. In the 1997 election, thirty-five of the newly elected female politicians arrived at Westminster by way of a selection process which excluded half the population. As soon as he could gather them all together in London, Tony Blair summoned the press to Church House and posed among them for the photographers. It was a fair enough boast: the number of women in parliament had doubled, and most of them – 101 – were Labour MPs. The Liberal Democrats – who numbered only five women among their fifty-two MPs even after the next election, in 2001 – repeatedly rejected the idea of women-only shortlists because they considered them 'illiberal'. Perhaps so. But in the new parliaments that began life in Cardiff and

Edinburgh in 1999, which had insisted upon selection arrangements whereby constituencies were obliged to choose both male and female candidates, about 40 per cent of the legislators were women.[14] Despite all the efforts of the Labour party, the national parliament in London entered the twenty-first century with fewer than a fifth of its members women. The proportion was lower than it was in Mozambique, Rwanda or Turkmenistan. Even North Korea did better.

But it goes further than sexual discrimination. Because membership of political organizations is such a minority pursuit, selection committees are necessarily atypical. By selecting largely the same type of men, these local associations actively seek out people who are unrepresentative of society as a whole. It is at its worst in the Conservative party. As it surveyed the wreckage of its second successive election defeat in 2001, wiser heads understood that the way it chose its candidates had much to do with why it was no longer the formidable machine it had once been. In an increasingly diverse country, the Conservative party was saddled with a bunch of people in parliament who looked and sounded much the same. Their grey-suited uniformity just made them appear to have less and less to do with the rest of the population. Conforming to the demands of a selection process in the hands of an ageing, unrepresentative gaggle of blazers and twinsets, they inevitably ended up looking, as one despairing party member put it, 'soulless, selfish and smug',[15] coldly conformist figures who fitted in with the party but not with the country.

The business of choosing an MP may be taken out of the hands of the minority who can attend selection meetings by giving all members of the local party a vote, but this too has drawbacks. When Dale Campbell-Savours was chosen as its candidate by the Labour party at Workington in Cumbria in the 1970s, there were sixty-one people at his selection meeting. When he retired at the 2001 election his successor was chosen under new rules designed to stop activists controlling the process: all 750 members of the local party were entitled to a say. The inevitable consequence was that they chose someone they knew, a former teacher, council leader and member of the European parliament. It is another indication of the way in which politics has become professionalized.

★

There is a certain type of politician who will reply to the question 'Who is your favourite author?' so predictably that you know what they will say before they open their mouths. There will be a few preliminaries about how they have too little time to read much these days. And then the name of Anthony Trollope will fall from their lips.

Trollope may not be the most highly regarded of nineteenth-century novelists. But he has the sort of dark-suited, big-bottomed manner that appeals to men of affairs. When a Trollope Society Lecture was instituted, the first person to deliver it was Roy Jenkins, one-time Chancellor of the Exchequer, Home Secretary and President of the European Commission and a man never knowingly overestimated or under-lunched. In the following years, a succession of figures who have reached the top of the tree have given the Society the benefit of their critical appreciations of the man – Conservative cabinet ministers such as Enoch Powell, John Biffen, David Young and John Wakeham, Brussels bigwigs such as Christopher Tugendhat, editors of *The Times* such as William Rees-Mogg and Simon Jenkins, Governors of the Bank of England such as Robin Leigh-Pemberton, from the academically distinguished (Lord Blake) to the shameless (Jeffrey Archer). Within a year of losing his job as Prime Minister, John Major was giving the annual lecture, using the opportunity to attack the tabloid press by comparing its editors to Trollope's repulsive creation Quintus Slide, editor of the *People's Banner*. If the roll-call has a predominantly Tory flavour that is a reflection of the nature of the times and the fact that, until the Labour party discovered red roses and grey suits in the 1990s, most of its politicians were required to pretend that their favourite bedside book was Robert Tressell's tale of 'twelve months in hell', *The Ragged Trousered Philanthropists*. Yet Liberal Democrats such as one-time party chairman Richard Holme and deputy leader Alan Beith have been happy to be associated with the Society. And when Donald Dewar, Labour's bookish First Minister in Scotland, died, the author invoked at his memorial in the Scottish Parliament was Trollope.

Why should Anthony Trollope be the politicians' novelist of choice? One reason may be that some of his novels, for example, *Phineas Finn*, are set in the world of politics. But even those which take place in smart London society or in the cloisters of provincial cathedrals bristle with the sort of intrigue, scheming and bitchiness which characterize political life at Westminster. So many of them are tales of men on the make. Acutely aware of the way every waking hour of their own lives can be filled with 'stuff' of one kind or another, politicians may also appreciate Trollope's sheer industry – up before breakfast knocking out his fiction at the rate of a thousand words an hour, before setting off for a day's work in the Post Office.

But the politicians can derive comfort, too, from the fact that Trollope took them seriously. 'I have always thought that to sit in the British Parliament should be the highest object of ambition to every educated Englishman,' he wrote in his autobiography. 'I do not by this mean to suggest that every educated Englishman should set before himself a seat in Parliament as a probable or even possible career; but that the man in Parliament has reached a higher position than the man out . . . that of all studies the study of politics is the one in which a man may make himself most useful to his fellow-creatures, – and that of all lives, public political life is capable of the greatest efforts.'[16]

It was a long time before Trollope felt able to answer this noble call personally. He was fifty-three and had quit the Post Office, angry at having been passed over for promotion. It was, by his own admission, a bit late to be starting a new career. Charles Dickens, who held politicians in healthily low regard, simply couldn't understand why a successful writer should choose to debase himself, to waste his time and energies soliciting the goodwill of the voters of a place in which he was certain to get hammered. 'Anthony's ambition', he wrote in a letter, 'is inscrutable to me. Still, it is the ambition of many men and the honester the man who entertains it, the better for the rest of us, I suppose.'[17]

Yet Trollope could hardly be accused of total naivety about the snakepit he was fighting to enter. *Phineas Finn* had told the story of a young Irish barrister's career as an MP, and the price to be paid if you stuck to your principles. The story was still running as a serial in *St Paul's* magazine when, in 1868, the author was given the chance to test his belief in the dignity of political life by standing for parliament as a Liberal for the Yorkshire seat of Beverley. It was not, he knew, the ideal seat – he had had his eye on a constituency in Essex, which a hunting friend had hinted he might be able to swing for him. He had no connection with Beverley and the place was solidly Tory.

The town was a byword for corruption. There had been a clean election a few years previously, in 1854, but, as *The Times* commented, it 'was quite an accident'. The rest of the time, things followed a predictable pattern. The chief Conservative MP also happened to be the town's main employer. When it came to municipal elections, the Tory agent sat in the Golden Ball pub handing out money to prospective voters, and the town's publicans were paid by the party to serve free beer to those who voted Conservative. The 1867 Reform Act which had enfranchised much of the male working class might as well not have been passed: a local working man summarized the situation pithily: 'the working classes look upon the privilege of the vote only as a means to obtain money'.[18] A Liberal politician had cautioned the novelist that he would spend a lot of money, and stood no chance.

However much he may have celebrated political life in his fiction, Trollope found the business of trying to get elected 'the most wretched fortnight of my manhood'. The few consolations of his time in Beverley, like the occasion when he was seen sneaking out of town in high leather boots and red coat for a day's fox-hunting while his loyal party workers slaved away, did nothing to mitigate the humiliation of being obliged to trail himself around the town, soliciting the good opinion of the electors. The novelist, who once saw a picture of himself and said it looked 'like a dog about to bite', found that the business of canvassing brought forth nothing but self-loathing. 'Perhaps nothing more disagreeable, more squalid, more revolting to the senses, more opposed to personal dignity, can be conceived,' he wrote in the last of his Palliser novels.

The same words have to be repeated over and over again in the cottages, hovels and lodgings of poor men and women who only understand that the time has come round in which they are to be flattered instead of being the flatterers . . . Some guide, philosopher, and friend, who accompanies him . . . has calculated on his behalf that he ought to make twenty such visitations an hour, and to call on two hundred constituents in the course of a day. As

he is always falling behind in his number, he is always being driven on . . .
till he comes to hate the poor creatures to whom he is forced to address
himself, with a most cordial hatred.[19]

Finally, on 16 November, the four candidates for the two seats in
parliament stood on the hustings in pouring rain in the town's Market
Square. Each man made a speech, 'during which various members of
the audience amused themselves by lobbing occasional cobblestones
and lumps of wood at them. The two Tories left the stage, after which
the mayor called for a show of hands and declared that the Liberals,
Trollope and Maxwell, had been elected. The Tories immediately
protested that many of those who had put up their hands weren't
even electors, and demanded another vote the next day. This time,
their machine swung properly into action, and by mid-morning, with
the pubs pumping free beer into voters, things were going their way.
By close of play, as the Tory machine settled the bills of complaisant
publicans, the mayor declared the seats won by the Tories. Having
spent £400, Trollope came bottom of the poll.

The author claimed that his humiliation was like 'water off a
duck's back', and told a friend that he would 'have another fly at it
somewhere, some day'.[20] But he never did. He had the consolation
of seeing a Royal Commission set up to investigate malpractice in the
election, and the satisfaction that Beverley was disenfranchised as a
result. His discomfort shows that he wasn't a real politician. He may
genuinely have believed that sitting in parliament was 'the grandest
work that a man can do'. But he lacked that vital spark which made
it possible. Some proper politicians find the banalities of campaigning
tiresome. None enjoys losing. But most seem to adore the business of
knocking on doors and endlessly repeating the same lines.

The truth is, though, that in any election most are destined to lose,
however brilliantly they may campaign. They cannot swim against
the tide, and if the electors are sick of their party, their party will
lose. Reconciling yourself to defeat requires profound psychological
fortitude, and the chasm between theory and practice is deep. 'No
part of the education of a politician is more indispensable than the
fighting of elections,' Winston Churchill wrote.

Here you come into contact with all sorts of people and every current of national life. You feel the Constitution at work in its primary processes. Dignity may suffer, the superfine gloss is soon worn away; nice particularisms and special private policies are scraped off; much has to be accepted with a shrug, a sigh or a smile; but at any rate in the end one knows a good deal about what happens and why.[21]

He was able to test this theory when, in 1923, he fought a seat in Leicester. It would be only a few months before Labour formed their first government, under Ramsay MacDonald, and the canvass returns were brought to him at the dinner table just before polling day. 'He had had a very hard evening,' one of those present recalled, 'and looked very tired. He said nothing for a few moments, then he looked at us. "So, they don't want me. Very well: one day they will want me," he said almost truculently. He drew up his chair and resumed his dinner.'[22]

But there are limits to stoicism. In someone as acutely conscious as Churchill of the possibility of early death, the workings of the constitution were a waste of time. Seven years later he was reflecting that:

I have fought up to the present fourteen contested elections, which take about one month of one's life apiece. It is melancholy when one reflects upon our brief span, to think that no less than fourteen months of life have been passed in this wearing clatter. By-elections, of which I have had five, are even worse than ordinary elections, because all the cranks and faddists of the country and all their associates and all the sponging 'uplift' organisations fasten upon the wretched candidate. If he is a supporter of the administration, all the woes of the world, all the shortcomings of human society in addition, are laid upon him, and he is vociferously urged to say what he is going to do about them.[23]

Fighting campaigns which are doomed to fail has two benefits. It gives would-be politicians the chance to learn all about campaigning: provided they don't actually drive down the vote, they can be said to have 'won their spurs'. At the same time it provides the party with a supply of cannon fodder for the many seats it has no chance of winning. That is the theory at least. Too much of a lost cause is something else. Josiah Wedgwood, of the famous pottery family, became an MP in 1906. Wedgwood's selection experience does not seem to have been particularly gruelling: he sat for thirty-six years as MP for Newcastle under Lyme, first as a Liberal, then for the Labour party and then as a loosely affiliated semi-independent. But, after a lifetime of watching ambitious people trying to make their way, he had these cautionary words about the experience of trying to secure a winnable seat.

The youthful aspirant, fresh from a presidency of the Cambridge Union, suffused with desire to serve his country and save the world, encounters the Party Secretary. The Party Secretary has 200 hopeless seats to offer and talks heartily of 'winning his spurs'. Every four years he goes down to a fresh constituency with never a chance to win. Age creeps upon him, bitterness corrodes his youth, and he solaces his soul with the aphorism: he who is not a misanthrope at forty can never have loved mankind.[24]

Cyril Thornton set out to win a seat in the British parliament in May 2001. He was not a product of any party machine, had gone through no strange selection ritual, owed no favours, had been obliged to make no unrealizable promises. His motivation was pure. His country was in peril and only he could save it. Cometh the hour, cometh the man, and Mr Thornton, ex-Indian army, was that man. First he would take the Sussex seat of Wealden in the General Election. Then the rest of the country would follow. When I arrived at his immaculately tidy bungalow on the edge of the town of Uckfield, Thornton, a tall, lean and bald man, had assembled the massed ranks of the Pensioners Coalition. They consisted of Cyril and his wife, Audrey.

To be fair, he had been in contact with another disgruntled pensioner in the north-west of England, who was standing on the same ticket, so the Pensioners Coalition was bigger than one family. There were two families involved. Here, in his armchair in the corner of the sitting room, he puffed on his pipe and planned a revolution.

The Sussex Weald is all small towns and villages, 99 per cent white, gravel-drived, car-owning, the sort of place Disgusted of Tunbridge Wells would move to if he found Tunbridge Wells a bit too bustling.

It is so solidly Conservative that the Labour party won not a single ward in the local council elections. It is also the place where A.A. Milne invented that great fantasist, Winnie the Pooh. Thornton, who is standing for parliament at the age of eighty-four, sounds as though he has a similarly slim grasp on reality.

'I've never started a fight I couldn't win. Never in my life,' he says in a curiously Indian-accented bass. 'I really believe I will win. In fact *I know* I'll win.'

Audrey bustles out to refill the teapot and reappears with a plate of perfectly square ham-and-cheese sandwiches, Sancho Panza to his Don Quixote.

Cyril Thornton's campaign leaflet is headlined:

DO YOU TRUST LABOUR ★ CONSERVATIVE ★ LIBERAL
DEMOCRAT POLITICIANS? IF YOU DO NOT
VOTE FOR CYRIL THORNTON
WIDELY EXPERIENCED — BATTLE-TESTED

Over the following seven pages, Thornton explains how pensioners have been conned by successive governments and defrauded of legitimate pension increases. He promises immediate rises of £12 a week for all. There will be government grants to install electric stairlifts, to supply electric scooters so pensioners can go shopping, and to provide free home visits by chiropodists. One hundred and sixty-five seats in the House of Commons will be reserved for pensioners on the ground that they make up a quarter of the population. But he is not a single-issue fanatic: there is more to life than bunions and surgical stockings. He is against globalization ('Nothing that can be made at home will be imported') and would renationalize the railways, withdraw from the European Union, shut down immigration, reform the constitution and legalize drugs. 'Drug barons, traffickers in drugs and human beings, convicted rapists, serial killers, paedophiles, corrupt politicians and public servants will have all their assets seized and be exiled for life and kept incommunicado in Outer Hebrides camps, where they will be free to make their own regimes and lifestyles in islands that are mined and provisioned by helicopters.' It is the sort of manifesto that *Daily Telegraph* leader-writers have erotic dreams about.

Thornton's claim to be 'battle-tested' is based on his experience in a Maharatta regiment in the Indian army. After a career in the Indian customs and excise, he moved to Britain in 1962, where his CV included working in the Bank of England, administering pension schemes and, at the age of fifty-nine, entering the music industry, where he wrote a sentimental monologue, recited by Peter Barkworth, entitled 'Sleep Well My Son'. He is not a wealthy man, and running an election campaign is not cheap. His explanation is that 'I've raised six children and I can only wear one suit at a time.' And, luckily, the previous summer, he had bet a thousand pounds on George W. Bush winning the American presidential election at odds of fifteen to one.

As Audrey returns with another pot of tea, he sucks on his pipe and explains his strategy. 'First, you have to demoralize the enemy. Then you have to have sound policies, and then tell people what you're going to do and how you're going to pay for it. There's an old Sanskrit saying: It's not men who make events. It's events that make men.'

I tentatively point out that this is one of the safest Conservative seats in the country: even in the meltdown of the 1997 election it still returned the astonishingly smooth Geoffrey Johnson Smith to parliament with a majority of over 14,000. Pigs are more likely to fly than the Conservatives are to lose the place.

'Aha! But Mr Johnson Smith is retiring. The Tories have got to get their new man elected.'

Yes, but the bloke they've chosen to inherit this plum, Charles Hendry, a former public relations man, is the professional politician incarnate. He's collected local loyalties the way some people collect air miles: vice chairman of Battersea Conservatives in London at twenty-two, candidate in Clackmannan in central Scotland in 1983, then protesting loyalty to Derbyshire at Mansfield, in 1987. At least he didn't have to travel far for the 1992 election when he must have been thrilled to win the High Peak constituency. In parliament, William Hague could spot a chap on the make, and chose him as his Parliamentary Private Secretary, or factotum-cum-informant, the first step on the ladder to power. When tragedy struck in the Tory wipeout at the 1997 election, Hendry took down his battered suitcase and set off on the search which ended with him becoming a loyal son of

Sussex. In this sort of place, he would have to grow a further two heads and be caught in bed with the Archbishop of Canterbury's entire family – and family pets – to lose the seat of Wealden.

I had seen Hendry at a rally in a Brighton hotel room the previous week, where William Hague had turned up to bang what was left of his drum. To warm up the grey-haired Conservative supporters Michael Portillo had come on stage, and tried to wind them into a frenzy with appeals to 'Stamp your feet if you've stuck a leaflet through a letterbox.' They did the best they could, although they'd have preferred to be asked to do something less common, like quietly tinkling their jewellery. Portillo's ring-mastering culminated with a parade across the stage of the party's candidates in the region, like some counter-beauty contest. Twenty or so figures, all but one of them men in dark suits, then marched across the stage in pairs waving at the crowd, who did their best to seem excited. 'And the next MP for Wealden, Charles Hendry!' Portillo had cried, but they were all identically dressed so it was hard to tell whom he was talking about. The only recognizable figure was the enormous hulk of Nicholas Soames, struggling not to look embarrassed, making the stage quake with his mighty footfall as he strode across. I wondered what on earth his grandfather Winston Churchill would have made of it all, and by then Hendry was gone.

Yet old Cyril Thornton's conviction that he will unseat his enemy in this pinstriped army is unshakeable. In his *basso profundo* he dismisses sympathy at his departure into the bourne from which no traveller returns with a passionate, 'This is *not* a joke. I tell people who say they'll support me, "*Don't* get involved if you're not big enough to sit behind a ministerial desk."'

Behind a ministerial desk? What planet is he on? Never in the history of modern British politics has an organization been cooked up in someone's front room in Uckfield and swept into the government departments of Whitehall. Yet he seems perfectly sane. He has made plans for his parliamentary salary, keeping £6,000 a year for travel expenses and giving the rest to the constituency.

But, I pointed out, you're eighty-four.

'I am. And all my arteries are blocked. I shouldn't be alive at all. Do I sit in the corner and feel sorry for myself? Damn that.'

But running for parliament?

'It's simple self-interest. I want to die in a country at peace with itself and free. I want to bequeath it to my children and if possible to share it with everyone.'

It was so artlessly, unselfconsciously said that I believed him. I think he might even have believed it himself. For the next few weeks, a series of home-produced press releases dropped on my mat. The Pensioner Coalition was developing policies on every subject under the sun. Thornton could sort out the Balkans. He could take Britain out of Europe. He was bringing a lawsuit against the Commission for Racial Equality. Occasionally, there were handwritten additions. 'I have sent out 40,000 copies of my manifesto. But we are off-limits to press, radio and TV' . . . 'the country is teetering on the brink of an abyss' . . . 'Blair, Hague and Kennedy are all paid-up members of an elite political class. All three are political pigmies with no experience of the world.' His only media exposure seemed to be a report of a meeting at the Community Hall in the *Hailsham Gazette* in which Cyril had said, 'We elderly people, whether we like it or not, will have to take over the running of the country. Pensioners will have to accept that responsibility.'[25] A bandwagon was rolling. Big-time.

Yet when the returning officer stood up to declare the results of the 2001 general election for Wealden, Cyril Thornton had piled up 453 votes. He was a mere 25,826 behind Charles Hendry. In Manchester, a model called Jordan (real name Katie Price) had also stood as an independent. Sponsored by a tabloid newspaper and with no manifesto beyond what were claimed to be the most stupendous breasts in Britain, she polled nearly twice as many votes as Thornton.

For a few months after the election, Cyril Thornton continued to send me press releases, on subjects ranging from the threat of fundamentalist Islamic terrorism to his unsatisfactory experience of the National Health Service while waiting for treatment at the Princess Royal Hospital in Haywards Heath. I called him up a few months after his defeat. Had he been disappointed?

'Not at all. I see Tony Blair is being forced to take up one idea of mine after another. Mark my words, soon he'll be forced to implement all my policies. And by the way, we have a little apartment in Portugal. Do come and stay. It has two bedrooms. The only disadvantage is that there's only one loo. But not everyone wants to go at the same time.'

Cyril Thornton's candidacy was only one of 2,659 attempts to get into parliament which failed in the summer of 2001. They ran from the apparently rational to the ravingly eccentric, through Cornish nationalists, environmentalists, communists, fascists, pacifists, anti-abortionists, withdrawers from the European Union, residents groups, spiritual healers, religious organizations, legalizers of drugs, imprisoners of sodomites and expellers of foreigners, to the Jam Wrestling Alliance, the Church of the Militant Elvis and an unemployed computer operator holding the world record for lying in a bath of baked beans. While standing for election was not necessarily financially expensive – a £150 fee to register their parties, and a further £500 to stand as a candidate – it had been costly of time. As a result, many, perhaps most, of the fringe candidates were either unemployed or retired.

Periodically, some busybody affecting concern for the dignity of the constitution will suggest that having so many self-publicists and nutcases standing for parliament somehow undermines the democratic process. Something really should be done to make it more difficult for them to stand. While this would have the advantage of rendering life simpler for the returning officers at elections, it would cut across a fundamental principle of democracy, that anyone may seek the right to legislate. It would make elections even more the property of the great party machines, and the way they behave is one of the reasons so many people find politics so unappetizing. It would also make life a lot duller. Apart from Screaming Lord Sutch, the most durable of the post-war fringe candidates was Lieutenant Commander Bill Boakes, who stood in thirty-one parliamentary elections, as leader of the Land, Sea and Air, Road Safety, Democratic Monarchist, White Resident and Women's party, a platform which, one way or another, ought to have guaranteed the votes of much of the country. Nor was he short of practical policies, which included relocating London Airport to the middle of Bodmin Moor. Tragically, he was never given a chance in parliament and a political career dedicated to road safety ended when he was knocked down and died in a traffic accident.

★

The juggernauts which crush independent spirits such as Cyril Thornton are mighty beasts. Thornton belongs to the era of Clement Attlee (whom he vaguely resembles physically). When Attlee led the Labour party to victory in the first election immediately after the Second World War, he campaigned across the country in his family car, with Mrs Attlee at the wheel. 'While his wife drives,' wrote the *Daily Mirror*, 'Mr Attlee puts on his glasses, rests on a brown and green folk-weave cushion, and does the crossword puzzles . . . If their car is held up at a level crossing Mrs Attlee gets out her knitting – a pair of grey socks.'[26]★ Attlee's obliviousness to image was so pronounced that one is tempted to think it must have been conscious, like John Major's use of a soapbox in the 1992 election, to point up the brassy noisiness of the Labour machine. Likewise, Attlee's homely style showed up Churchill's purple progress around the country: the British people do not like to be taken for granted and don't care for arrogance.[27] The biggest mistake made by the Labour party in its unsuccessful campaign in the 1992 election was to stage a rally in Sheffield, at which the would-be Prime Minister, Neil Kinnock, jumped about on stage like some over-caffeinated warm-up man, while members of the shadow cabinet sauntered on to be presented as the next government. It was so much an exercise in hubris that the British people inevitably decided that they would be no such thing. Privately, Kinnock knew the Sheffield rally had been a big mistake (as, astonishingly, did almost everyone involved – after the event). But he was powerless to prevent it. The idea of a party leader left, like Attlee, to his own devices in an election campaign is now unthinkable. He or she will be cocooned inside a giant ball of glass carried by hundreds of party workers. Nothing untoward will be allowed to happen. Spontaneity? No thanks. Who knows what might happen if the voters were to get involved in the carefully choreographed meetings designed to convince credulous television viewers that there is a real campaign going on?

By the time that the parties have paid for the billboards, the advertisements, the helicopter rides for the leader and his entourage

★ His campaigning style cannot have been quite as restful as the image suggests, however. His wife was known as one of the worst drivers in Britain. At one point, the road-safety campaigner Commander Boakes tried to have her prosecuted.

and the rest, the costs of these campaigns can spiral. Getting elected in 1997 cost the Labour party £26 million. Losing cost the Conservatives £28 million. In the next election, in 2001, the bills had been brought under some control, but even so, the Labour and Conservative parties spent around £12 million each on their campaigns. The Liberal Democrats disclosed that their campaign bus required 1,700 bananas, 244 packets of Jaffa Cakes, 200 gallons of mineral water and 4,600 cans of Diet Coke.

The result of the 2001 Tory campaign was to increase the party's total of MPs by one. It spent nearly a million pounds campaigning in Scotland. The net product was to win the seat of Galloway and Upper Nithsdale, which, opposition parties pointed out, must have made the new MP the most expensive member of parliament in history. At least it was an improvement on the 1997 election, where 4.5 million Conservative voters rewarded the vast spending by not voting for them: the number of Conservative MPs was cut in half. Those who worry that British democracy is being undermined by money and marketing can take some comfort from the electorate's refusal to be bought. Had the Conservatives spent three or four times as much money in either election, they could not have changed the outcome. In 1997, in government, the party was visibly rotten. In 2001, after four years of missed opportunity in opposition, it simply did not look like a credible alternative government.

It is one of the polite fictions of the British political class that the voters make up their minds how to vote after close scrutiny of the party manifestos. In fact, the only people who study them are other politicians and a few political journalists.[28] Even many of the candidates haven't read them. For party leaders, they can be an unnecessary nuisance, because they give a yardstick by which to judge performance. Margaret Thatcher produced the most curious argument against them. 'If the elector suspects the politician of making promises simply to get his vote, he despises him, but if the promises are not forthcoming, he may reject him. I believe that parties and elections are about more than rival lists of miscellaneous promises – indeed if they were not, democracy would scarcely be worth preserving.'[29] This is a remarkable position, simultaneously naive and knowing. Of course elections are about more than manifestos. But a manifesto, a promise of what the party will do if elected is a contract by which the performance of the winning party can be judged. This immediately puts the government of the day at a disadvantage, as it has a record by which it can be judged, whereas no one holds the Opposition to account for things they said they would do if they had been elected last time. Just about every single government that has taken office since the end of the Second World War has made the British people the same promise. Vote for us, and we will all get richer. But a higher rate of economic growth was one thing they could not deliver. Thinking back over his lengthy career in politics, Roy Jenkins remarked that:

The more the secret of higher productivity and a dynamic economy eluded us, the more the search dominated each election campaign. But not, on the part of politicians, in a mood of questioning humility. The opposition party of the day always believed it had the philosopher's stone. Elect us, they – including me – said, and the economy will bound forward. Quite often they were elected, but the economy did nothing of the sort. The result was a widening gap between promise and performance.[30]

And as the gap grew, so too did public distrust of politics and politicians.

One simply cannot now imagine a conversation taking place in any party headquarters of the kind that took place between the Conservative leader Andrew Bonar Law and one of his advisers, in 1922.

BONAR LAW: They tell me that we have to have what is called a slogan. What do we have for this election?
ADVISER: Well, I know the country is feeling that they don't want to be buggered about.
BONAR LAW: The sentiment is sound . . . let us call it 'Tranquillity'.[31]

It sounds ludicrous, but it fits a tradition of Conservative slogans before the party discovered the Saatchi brothers' advertising agency. In 1929 Stanley Baldwin ran on the zippy, 'Safety First. Stanley Baldwin: The Man You Can Trust'. Thirty years later, in the 'You've never had it so good' days of Harold Macmillan's leadership, the party released posters of the new family car being washed by its happy owners, and of a family around the dining table with a television set in the background. 'Life's better under the Conservatives,' ran the caption. 'Don't let Labour ruin it.'*

The Labour pitch has been the mirror-image: smash the tranquillity, go for change. The 1964 Labour manifesto, written in the 'cleans right round the bend' language of the advertising executives who were now getting heavily involved in election campaigns, could as easily have been stuffed through letterboxes in 1945 or 1997.

A New Britain . . .

The country needs fresh and virile leadership.

Labour is ready. Poised to swing its plans into instant operation. Impatient to apply the New thinking that will end the chaos and sterility.

'New' – as in 'New Britain' – sometimes allied to 'Hope' (1983), is a favourite Labour word for their campaigns. 'Tomorrow' – as in 'A Better Tomorrow for Wales' or 'Tomorrow Scotland' (1970) – has been more of a Conservative word, despite the party's consistent promise of a better past. 'Win' – as in 'Scotland will win' or 'Wales will win' (1987), though not, so far, 'Britain will win' – forms part of Labour slogans. In the event, of course, in 1987 Labour had another ten years in the wilderness still to come, by which time they had moved on to 'It's time for a change' and 'Things can only get better'. There is a lot of use of the word 'action' in Conservative propaganda – as in 'Actions not Words' (1966) – and plenty of promises to 'Put Britain First' (1974) – where else would a national government put it? Liberal manifestos have a habit of looking like pamphlets handed out by revivalist Churches, ranging from the baffling 'What a Life!' (1970) to the cuddly, at the time of their alliance with the Social Democrats, 'Working Together' (1987). They really ought to be set to music by a vicar with a pair of sandals and a guitar.

* The slogan was appropriated (or misappropriated) in the 1960s by the Oxford University Conservative Association, which devised a poster showing a heavily made-up girl leering at the camera, with the slogan 'Life's better under a Conservative'.

Manifestos and campaigns give the voter the opportunity merely to compare the promises. But, since seismic changes in public mood take place a great deal less frequently than do elections (in the last sixty years they have occurred with the elections of Clement Attlee, Margaret Thatcher and Tony Blair), many elections are destined to be more matters of style than anything else. Hence, the party headquarters' obsession with control. Modern campaign strategy is in the hands of a group of people, some of them elected politicians, others – advertising men, pollsters, public relations executives – who would rather draw a much bigger salary and whose contact with the general public is as personally involved as that of a biologist with a slide of frogspawn. Sometimes the result is to make it seem as if the campaign is being fought in some parallel universe. It looks like Britain. It sometimes even sounds like Britain. But it seems to be peopled with cleverly constructed products of artificial intelligence.

The Labour campaign for re-election in 2001 was launched not, as generally happens, by the Prime Minister announcing in Downing Street that he had asked the Queen to dissolve parliament, but on the stage at a school in south London. At St Saviour's and St Olave's school in Southwark the Prime Minister was serenaded on to the stage by a choir singing 'I who make the skies of light, I will make the darkness bright. Here I am.' He then stood beneath stained-glass windows proclaiming 'Heirs of the Past, Makers of the Future', took off his jacket (this astonishing feat earned him a round of applause) and told the assembled teenagers – all of whom were too young to vote – the date of the election. Even some party members retched at the shamelessness of it all. For the launch of the Labour election manifesto, the party paraded its leadership in an exhibition hall in Birmingham, surrounded by a hand-picked group of nurses, teachers and old soldiers.

The Labour party was not, of course, the sole offender. Both Conservative and Liberal Democrat campaigns were similarly organized for the benefit of the television cameras. It was just that they carried them off less well and people cared less about them, since the outcome was a foregone conclusion. When the Liberal Democrats' Charles Kennedy visited some Highland Games near Inverness during the campaign, the television pictures showed him sitting in the grandstand, apparently watching the racing, caber-tossing and bagpiping. In fact, he watched precious little of the competition: he had arrived, exchanged words with a group of children ('Do you know my dad?'), delivered a prepared quip for the television cameras (the true but hardly earth-shattering 'William Hague is desperate') and stayed in the stands long enough only for the cameras to record his presence. And after spending an entire day campaigning with the Conservative leader William Hague, the presenter of *Channel Four News*, Jon Snow, calculated that the total amount of time spent with members of the 'public' was a mere forty minutes.

There was a time, and not so long ago, when politicians spoke at public meetings. Quintin Hogg would denounce opponents as anything from jellyfish to Mafiosi, break his walking stick over a portrait of Harold Wilson, or shake his fist at hecklers, while calling them 'loudmouth morons'.[32] Genuine public meetings involving the party leaders scarcely happen any more: the parties make sure that any members of the public are there strictly by invitation. That is why the occasional genuine exchange between prominent politician and voter can be so electrifying. The two moments which stood out in the election of 2001 came when members of the public penetrated the cordon sanitaire erected around the leaders and real life intervened. In Birmingham, as the Prime Minister arrived to visit a hospital, a woman broke from the crowd and harangued him about the way that her cancer-stricken partner had been treated inside the hospital. On and on she went, while Tony Blair stood looking sheepish, concerned, irritated. In four minutes, the Prime Minister could only mutter that he was trying to do something. 'No you're not,' Sharon Storer shot back at him, before turning on her heel and storming off. Ms Storer did not have the faintest idea how the National Health Service could be improved, since, she told me later, she was against tax increases, had no suggestions about where the government might save money elsewhere, and rejected any idea of personal insurance. But her intervention was exhilarating, because in an age when campaigns are fought through the mass media that sort of thing, the genuine exchange between political leader and member of the public, is simply not supposed to happen.

The bus containing Blair's deputy, John Prescott, pulled into the drab seaside town of Rhyll, north Wales, that evening. The crowd which greeted him, angry at the government's indifference to the plight of the countryside, badly hit by the fallout from the foot-and-mouth crisis, was not what the campaign managers had ordered. As he walked towards the theatre where he was to speak, an egg sailed out of the crowd and hit him. Throwing eggs at politicians seeking election is a venerable British political tradition. But Prescott, a former merchant navy steward, had a famously short fuse to complement his brutal approach to the English language.* Instantaneously, his left fist lashed out, hitting the protester on the side of the head. The egg-thrower, who possessed one of the worst haircuts ever to appear on international television, wasn't the sort of chap to turn the other cheek – or ear. He leaped upon the Deputy Prime Minister and the two men fell scuffling over a wall.

These two incidents provided the only real life of the 2001 election campaign, which was the dullest in recent memory. It seems hard to believe that the hordes of pollsters, image consultants and television producers, the frenetic chase around the country and the constant exposure of one stunt after another can really have made for an election duller than that in which Mr and Mrs Attlee trundled around the country in their family saloon, he with his crossword, she with her knitting. But it is true. The reason is not hard to find. In between filling in his crossword, Attlee was fighting for 'the establishment of a Socialist Commonwealth of Great Britain', as the Labour manifesto promised. The contrast with modern elections is not merely that it is hard to imagine Cherie Blair knitting, but that the more fuss campaigns make, the less they have to say. The fleets of buses, the chartered trains, the camera crews and satellite dishes, the cascades of balloons, the soaring campaign theme songs, are deployed in the service of more and more similar objectives. No one seeks the creation of a

---

* At a visit to a catering college in Falmouth the previous week he had been presented with a giant loaf of bread. The transcript of his speech reads as follows: 'Well last time I came they gave me the biggest Cornish pasty I ever had and I ran six weeks of the election that time and we did a very good result and I've got bread and water this time – a little less, but frugal like Gordon Brown – that's why we've got a good economy so thank you very much can we have a picture taken with you now?'

socialist commonwealth any more. With the end of ideological conflict, instead of being offered a choice of philosophies the voters
were merely being offered a choice of managers. When Attlee faced
Churchill in 1945, some 73 per cent of the electorate turned out to
vote. When they clashed again in 1950 and 1951, the proportion rose
even higher, to well over 80 per cent. Yet, in the 2001 election, the
number voting fell to below 60 per cent for the first time since the
election held in December 1918. Curiously, the turnout was highest
in places where people found it hardest to get to the polling stations,
like Brecon or Galloway, while in parts of inner-city Liverpool,
Manchester or Leeds, where polling stations were within walking
distance, half – even, in one constituency, two-thirds – of those who
could have voted simply didn't bother to do so. There is a way of
construing this indifference as a good thing. It might, conceivably, be
the sign of a healthy society: people who are relatively happy with
their lot may not feel impelled to go out and vote. It might, perhaps,
reflect a recognition of the declining powers of the national parliament. But what it clearly demonstrates is the paradox that those who
are most dependent on the state seem to have the least engagement
with it.

4. New Boys and Girls

And so, after the cheering has died away, when the toasts have been drunk, after the run on the banks' reserves of false sympathy, after the instantly forgotten speeches of thanks and the mean-spirited booing from supporters of the bad losers, after, perhaps, the TV trucks have de-rigged and returned to base, after the vote-counters have left the town hall to its rancid fug, after the ballot papers they so meticulously sorted into piles of political preference have been taken away under lock and key, after the weeks of smiling, exhortations, promises and foot-weary begging, the victorious candidate goes to bed. He wakes a few hours later, with fuzzy tongue, in the lodgings which have been home for the campaign. The marked ballot papers, twenty-four hours ago livid with his future, are now so much rubbish.

Some seem to find this morning-after feeling distinctly queasy-making, like an ill-judged one-night stand. If they have been successful in a seat that party headquarters had not expected them to win, they are stuck with it for the next four or five years. In the meantime, the facts they have learned by heart about the importance of the fish-oil extraction industry to the local economy acquire a new force: now they will have to live among the fish-oil factories. The defeated candidates will say a probably genuine thank-you to the local party workers who have devoted themselves to the fruitless attempt to get the candidate into parliament for the last few weeks. In return, they may do the candidate the courtesy of saying what a good fight he put up. Then, with feelings of mutual relief, the activists will return to their everyday jobs or to pruning their retirement roses, while the candidates slink off to their real homes by the first available train or car.

By comparison with the task facing the successful candidate, that is the easy part. Famously, there is no job description for the role of a member of parliament. If such a thing could ever be drawn up it might weed out some of the borderline personalities who make it into the House of Commons. All that is certain is that in a representative democracy, they are now a representative. What that means, they must discover or make up as they go along. There is, of course, the immediate boost to the self-esteem of having earned the right to put those magical initials 'MP' after their name. It is quite clear from talking to politicians that, even in these diminished times, the status conferred by this title really matters to them. Nothing stills the gnawing of self-doubt better than the simple business of winning. There is something else, too. As one of the grandest politicians of the last thirty years put it, 'Even after all the scandals and the public cynicism, it's still quite something. *C'est une bonne adresse.*' In trying to explain the pleasures of the job, the same politician came up with the devastatingly simple explanation, 'You cannot overestimate the sheer pleasure of the sound of your own voice.'

But the speaking part is the obvious bit. Everyone knows that politicians stand up in the House of Commons and deliver speeches. The rest of it – whether to serve on committees, how to help constituents while fending off the nutters, how to rise up the greasy pole, whether to devote yourself to the business of government or the business of parliament, even where to find an office, has to be made up as you go along. Because there are over 650 MPs, but only enough room on the leather benches in the chamber of the House of Commons for about 420 to sit down, just finding a place from which you will be able to deliver the oratory which will give you such pleasure is no mean task.

And the sheer physical presence of the Houses of Parliament presents the first challenge. This is one of the most recognizable buildings in the world, up there with the Taj Mahal, emblem at once of a nation and of an idea. The White House and the French Assemblée Nationale are also political buildings. But neither carries the sheer weight of history that presses down on the stones of Westminster.

Technically, the place doesn't even truly belong to the people. Westminster is a royal palace, as much as Buckingham Palace or Windsor Castle. For anyone who has ever spent any time in the American Senate or House of Representatives, the difference is almost palpable. The Palace of Westminster does not set the citizen at ease. It was not designed to do so. When a member of the public goes to

the Palace of Westminster, the first thing the duty policeman wants
to know is what he or she is doing there. Palace protocol assumes the
citizen has the right of access to their MP (if he or she chooses to see
them) and, if space permits, the right to witness debates. But the voter
is – literally – a stranger, sitting in the Strangers' Gallery.[1] From here
they will be able to gaze down on debates whose style is, to say the
least, opaque. If they are particularly fortunate they may even witness
the point at which members of parliament vote on an issue, when the
chamber will ring to the Speaker declaring, 'The Question put that
the bill now be read a second time. As many as are of that opinion say
"Aye,"' which is followed by a bellowing of the word 'Aye', followed
by more bellowing of the word 'No', and the Speaker shouting, 'The
Question put forthwith, pursuant to Standing Order Number 63.' It
might as well be spoken in ancient Greek. Suddenly, the handful of
MPs in the room is swamped by dozens, perhaps hundreds, of men
and women who seem to emerge from the woodwork, to vote in
debates they have not attended and on matters they may not even
understand. The elector can wonder whether he's been deposited at
some secret station on the London Underground which exists in a
parallel universe.

The newly elected members may arrive at Westminster as ignorant
as anyone else. The danger is that the more they learn of the curious
ways of parliament, the further they become estranged from the
people they purport to represent. At first, the contrast with the
moment of election could not be starker. The politician leaves
the declaration as the chosen son or daughter of Wigton or Clee-
thorpes. He or she arrives at the great Gothic pile on the north bank
of the River Thames not as the Messiah but as – at best – a nervous
chorister. The religious metaphor is appropriate. The Houses of
Parliament have a distinctly and deliberately churchy feel to them. It
is partly the high vaulted ceilings and the tiled floors, the way the
sunlight breaks through leaded windows, the pew-like benches, the
carved wood and stone, the mosaic images of the patron saints of
England, Scotland, Wales and Ireland in the Central Lobby. But it is
more. The British parliament sits at Westminster rather than anywhere
else because it was here that Edward the Confessor chose to build a
new abbey. The Palace of Westminster, the seat of government,

developed as an adjunct, as the main royal residence, until Henry VIII decided to live at Whitehall. The first permanent meeting place of the House of Commons, provided by Henry's son Edward VI, was the king's former private chapel, St Stephen's, in which the Speaker's chair was installed in front of the altar (this is said to be the reason that MPs are expected to bow to the Speaker). But it is more even than the impossibility of separating the secular from the religious. The real reason the Palace of Westminster as a whole feels so much like a church is that – like a church or cathedral – this is a building whose form expresses more than the functions performed within it. The Houses of Parliament are the place in which the laws of the country have been made for centuries. Yet they also somehow have come to embody the peculiar feisty yet fusty spirit of British democracy.

For anyone with the slightest tingling appreciation of history, to arrive here, knowing that it was in Westminster Hall that Simon de Montfort held his parliament in 1265,[2] that this was where Thomas More, Guy Fawkes, King Charles I and Warren Hastings were put on trial, where Oliver Cromwell swore his oath as Lord Protector, where dead kings and queens and statesmen have lain in state, can be a humbling experience. 'I have never lost my awe for the institution of Parliament or the majesty of the building,' John Major wrote at the end of his failed political career. 'It has history in every nook and cranny, and the shades of the past can easily be conjured up even though its purpose is to prepare the future. The place half glances over its shoulder at what has been.'[3] A half-glance is an underestimate. Had it not been such an intrinsically conservative building, perhaps he would have found it a great deal easier to persuade his party to follow him on the journey he was trying to undertake into a European political union.

It requires a particularly strong radicalism, arrogance or force of character not to be intimidated by the stones of the place. David Lloyd George found Westminster imposing externally, but 'crabbed, small and suffocating' inside.[4] The words are accurate: the place is gloomy, dark, cramped and impractical. But what most people see is not the building so much as what the Palace represents. Aneurin Bevan, the Welsh miner's son, arrived there in 1929, in his early thirties, but already a veteran of the class struggle. He recognized that 'If the new member gets there too late in life he is already trailing a pretty considerable past of his own, making him heavy-footed and cautious. When to this is added the visible penumbra of six centuries of receding legislators, he feels weighted to the ground. Often he never gets to his feet again.'[5] You could make the reverse argument just as easily: a young person may be more readily intimidated and more likely to be shaped by the institution they have joined.

But Bevan's most telling point about the physical setting in which British politics takes place was more precise. What Westminster exuded was not so much a shared national version of history as a political interpretation of it. The statues of long-dead statesmen in the place could be interpreted in religious terms. 'Here he is, a tribune of the people, coming to make his voice heard in the seats of power. Instead, it seems he is expected to worship; and the most conservative of all religions – ancestor worship. The first thing he should bear in mind is that these were not his ancestors. His forebears had no part in the past, the accumulated dust of which muffles his own footfalls. His forefathers were tending sheep or ploughing the land, or serving the statesmen whose names he sees written on the walls around him . . .'[6] Bevan concluded that the rituals of this strange religion were deliberately designed to undermine the conviction politician, 'an elaborate conspiracy to prevent the real clash of opinion which exists outside from finding an appropriate echo within its walls'. The point is overblown, perhaps. But it is a genuinely political one, not a question of class background. When John Major arrived at Westminster, despite his lack of familiarity with gentlemen's clubs, he felt at home straight away, 'as happy as Bunter in a bakery'.[7]

Those who succumb to the charms of Westminster soon lose all ability to see the Palace as outsiders might look upon it. David Maxwell Fyfe, who rose to become a Conservative Home Secretary and Lord Chancellor in the 1950s, provides one of the most rose-tinted pictures in his immensely self-important memoirs, *Political Adventure*.

To enter the House of Commons is not merely to enter a political institution, it is the coming upon a new world, complex, hazardous, inconstant, demanding, and perpetually fascinating. This pride and pleasure never faded throughout the twenty years I sat in the Commons . . . There is something about the Commons which is timeless; its collective wisdom, which is almost uncanny, playing on the characters of individuals has something to do with it. All the tricks and artifices of the hustings, all the tedious verbal paraphernalia of party politics, wither and expire in this atmosphere. A man who is not proud to be there has no right to be there.[8]

Enoch Powell, another Conservative, spent over thirty years in the place, and his biographer comments that 'His love of institutions was fully realised in the Commons, where procedure is everything, and he could conduct his relations with others on the basis of time-honoured conventions, rules and regulations. Month by month, he grew more attached to the Commons and could imagine no life other than as an MP.'[9]

It was not ever thus, and it need not always have been thus, despite what the politicians like to believe, for the Palace of Westminster has shown an unlucky tendency to burn down throughout its history. The most critical fire came on the evening of 16 October 1834, the consequence of a decision to modernize the way in which the government recorded its income. Astonishingly, until then it had still been registering its receipts with 'tally sticks' – notched pieces of wood which were split in two, so both parties had a record of the amount paid. The radical 1834 decision to move over to pen and paper led to the mountain of tally sticks being used as firewood. Sparks from one of the stoves in which they were being burned set fire to nearby wooden panels. It was at about seven that evening that people on the streets outside first noticed flames coming from the building. Soon crowds had begun to gather (they included the artists Constable and Turner, the latter of whom found the sight awesome enough to form the basis of a brilliant oil painting). The fire brigade was summoned, but an unusually low tide that evening meant the firefighters found it difficult to pump water out of the Thames. By the early hours of the morning, the flames had gutted the place. Eyewitnesses described a melancholy sight the next day, with the ruins of the building glowing a ghostly red in the hot embers where once had stood the chamber of British democracy. All that was left was the medieval great hall, built by William Rufus.

The destruction of such an emblematic building was, of course, a terrible event. But it also might have been an opportunity. The old Palace had, after all, been the embodiment of the corrupt regime which existed before the Great Reform Act of 1832, when access to the initials 'MP' was confined to a tiny social class and depended more upon whom you knew and what you could afford than anything else. The most notorious abuses of the democratic process were the 'pocket boroughs', such as the two seats at Thirsk, which had been controlled by the Frankland family for over 140 years without their ever having the inconvenience of anyone standing against their candidate. The 1832 Act, which extended the vote to middle-class adult males and abolished the rotten boroughs, was a characteristically British version of the revolutionary spirit which had swept France at the end of the eighteenth century. Which is to say it was a great deal less radical than the expression 'Great' Reform Act might have suggested: working men and women could forget any thought of a role in choosing the legislature. But the Act was the biggest change to hit parliament since the waters closed over Oliver Cromwell. A political class less invested with the spirit of ancestor worship which Bevan identified might have seen the fire as an act of God, delivered to provide a new building which would express in stone and wood the principles of a more modern state.

Instead, two years after the Great Reform Act, the politicians demanded more of the same. They insisted upon a replacement parliamentary building in what was considered to be the 'national' style, which was decreed to be 'Gothic or Elizabethan', thereby proving yet again that politicians are quite the worst possible people ever to make aesthetic judgements about anything. What they wanted was not a visionary, open building which proclaimed a belief in a democratic future, but a monument which looked back to medieval times. The designs from Charles Barry and Augustus Pugin fitted their intentions perfectly. These two highly conservative figures (Pugin seems at times genuinely to have believed the medieval world superior to the century in which he found himself living) produced an ornate building which glorified the politicians and largely excluded the public. Most of all, it applauded neither the people nor their elected representatives, but the unelected monarchy, whose property the place had originally been and which was provided with its own Royal

Entrance, Royal Staircase, Robing Room, Royal Gallery and Prince's Chamber. Outside, most of the decorative statues celebrated kings and queens instead of politicians or public. The building expressed the pecking order. At the top was the monarchy. Second in importance was the House of Lords. And, next, well below, there was the rabble in the House of Commons.

This pecking order survived through the twentieth century in the ceremonial aspects of life in parliament. When the Queen 'opens' parliament, she rides there in some splendour from Buckingham Palace, where one of the more dispensable government whips has been left as a hostage, in case she should not return. She enters the Palace of Westminster surrounded by heralds rejoicing in names like the Rouge Dragon Pursuivant, Portcullis Pursuivant, Maltravers Herald Extraordinary, and the Norroy and Ulster King of Arms. She is greeted by more people whose democratic endorsement is less than crystal clear, like the Earl Marshal, the Lord High Chancellor and the Lord Great Chamberlain. She sits on a gilded throne in the House of Lords, facing dozens and dozens of peers in warm red robes, here and there the occasional tiara. Black Rod (usually a retired senior soldier or sailor) is sent clipping off in his gaiters to 'command' the House of Commons to get itself down to the Lords to listen. There is a little ritual about the door being shut in his face, but then the Commons obeys. The Queen reads out her speech explaining what legislation will be introduced in the coming months – it has been written for her by the government – while the elected lawmakers stand crammed together in the entrance to the chamber. It is all like something out of a fairytale.

Less than a century after Barry and Pugin's vast edifice was completed, Adolf Hitler gave the British a second chance to reconsider whether this type of building was any longer the most appropriate for a modern democracy. The German bombs which destroyed the House of Commons in May 1941 left nothing much standing but the outer walls: this time the firefighters concentrated their efforts on saving the medieval hall. Rebuilding would have to wait until the war was over, but in the meantime a committee was to be appointed to draw up plans, and parliament as a whole debated the question. In the spirit of dogged determination which saw the British through the Second

World War, Winston Churchill simply said, 'I cannot conceive that anyone would wish to make the slightest structural alterations in the House of Commons other than perhaps some improvement in ventilation.' Churchill had spent forty years in the House, but this was more than a simple expression of affection or innate conservatism.

In his most telling observation about architecture, Churchill told the House of Commons, 'We shape our buildings, and afterwards our buildings shape us.'[10] His argument was that the particular character of British democracy was directly influenced by the environment in which political debate took place. Charles Barry's design for the chamber of the House of Commons had deliberately echoed the shape of its former meeting place, St Stephen's Chapel. Churchill understood that what he was proposing 'would sound odd to foreign ears', but so be it. He insisted that the new chamber should be 'oblong and not semicircular'. Furthermore, 'it should not be big enough to contain all its members at once without overcrowding' and 'there should be no question of every member having a separate seat reserved for him . . . We attach immense importance to the survival of parliamentary democracy. In this country it is one of our war aims. We wish to see our Parliament a strong, easy, flexible instrument of free debate. For this purpose, a small chamber and a sense of intimacy are indispensable.'[11]

Scarcely a voice was raised in disagreement. Even normally rebellious Labour MPs spoke of the old House of Commons having been more than stones, 'a sentient place'. Expressing a different perspective which continues to find voice to this day, Nancy Astor, the first woman to take her seat in the House of Commons, disagreed. Like many female MPs since, she argued that having the place arranged with benches of politicians facing each other 'almost like dogs on a leash' inevitably made for confrontation. She wanted a circular chamber. No one supported her, although the leader of the Independent Labour party, James Maxton, always his own man, did think that MPs were being altogether too unambitious. He liked the idea of a brand-new parliament thrown up somewhere outside London 'in good English parkland', equipped with first-class road, rail and air transport links. This was promptly derided by a Cornish MP as 'a sort of Potters Bar Canberra'. The rest of the House of Commons showed themselves as much in the grip of necropolitan passion as their nineteenth-century predecessors. As for the idea that parliament might discuss legislation in some horseshoe arrangement of seats, it had been 'the death warrant of parliamentary democracy on the continent'. If the French had only been blessed with a rectangular chamber, one MP remarked, 'the effect on democracy in France might have been far different'.[12]

And so it was that, nine years after the House of Commons chamber had been destroyed by enemy action, in 1950 MPs took possession of a Gothic replica, a pastiche of a pastiche, homage to a homage. It seemed the most natural thing in the world. One of the very few dissenting voices, the architectural critic of *Country Life*, delivered himself of the withering verdict that 'We are a sentimental people, and thus deficient in aesthetic judgement.'[13] The desire not to change anything at the behest of the Nazis was an understandable one: it would have seemed a form of defeatism. But its consequence was to leave the British with a parliamentary building designed for another age entirely. That day in 1950 MPs gathered to inaugurate the rebuilt House of Commons with both Conservative and Labour in black morning coats. In prayers led by the chaplain, they thanked God for the new old building.

Everything about the place seems to proclaim its remoteness from the citizens of Britain. The policemen and the white-tied and tail-coated messengers have that superiority that you imagine on the faces of the grander sort of butlers. They immediately make you feel you've trodden in something on the way in.

Which is quite possible, since anyone wanting to visit the Palace of Westminster (and the vast majority of the British people will never go near it) may have spent hours standing around on the pavement outside. Those visiting by appointment, for a guided tour given by their local MP – schoolgroups, party members, delegations from the local branch of the Women's Institute – tend to have a subdued, well-scrubbed Sunday-best air about them. Those hoping to watch one of the setpieces of parliament, such as Prime Minister's Questions (anoraks and guidebooks instead of jackets and ties) may have been queuing for ages outside in the rain, for demand is heavy and space miserly. If they arrive in time for the start of the parliamentary day (five hours or so later than the start of everyone else's working day), they may find themselves sitting on a bench in the echoing Central Lobby. 'Stand up and move forward!' the policeman shouts in a voice that brooks no disobedience. The citizens do as they are told, clutching their belongings and shuffling into a little huddle in the middle of the Lobby. Several of the older women visiting their MPs seem to have put on their best hats for the occasion. The cry 'Hats – off – strangers!' from the policeman has them fumbling. (If the sitting of the House finishes after midnight, it is the policemen who must take off their helmets as the Speaker passes. No one can quite remember why.) The Speaker's Procession clip-clops its way down the corridor to the Lobby, a faintly Ruritanian file of mace-bearer, Speaker and the little House of Commons chaplain bobbing on behind. The disdainful policemen part the citizenry, and the trio disappear through the doors into the chamber.

The newly elected MP gets here elated, triumphant, ambitious and confused. When Tony Benn first arrived at the House of Commons, after a 1950 by-election, he was twenty-five. Newspapers sent photo-graphers down to capture the moment when the latest scion of the political dynasty took his seat. The new boy was pictured shaking hands with a blasé Westminster policeman. The following day, when Benn arrived for a day's work at the House, the policeman failed to recognize him and shooed him away. (Visiting him at Westminster, his young wife was obliged to go through the same performance as every other member of the public, filling in a green card, to be carried on her person at all times. On one occasion, under 'Object of visit', she wrote 'A kiss'.)[14] The policemen have mellowed a little since then. Now they are supplied with a list of the names of each new MP and, provided the politicians introduce themselves, their egos are immediately gratified by being ushered past the long lines of visitors, bypassing security screens and metal detectors.

The sense of triumph may not last long. Sometimes it barely survives the walk from the street to the Central Lobby. The new MP may have campaigned to get here as a member of a party, but he or she is alone at Westminster. As long as the party is campaigning for govern-ment it will teach prospective MPs how to work a room, how to handle a media interview, how to draft a press release. Until very recently, once they got elected, it didn't even tell them to get a computer, or how many staff they needed. Many newly elected MPs were afraid to ask their colleagues, because to do so would have been to show their weakness. Nowadays, many new MPs are given short induction courses, to help them find their way around the building, with its fourteen restaurants and seven bars. But after that they are on their own. The euphoria can easily give way to frustration, often lasting for years, or even for an entire parliamentary career. The options are to succumb to the embrace of the party and accept that the only way you are going to increase your salary or status is to try to climb the ministerial ladder, to settle for obscurity, or to become 'a House of Commons character'. Julian Critchley admitted that for the unambitious what parliament provided was not a bad life. 'The Palace is kept uncomfortably warm; somewhere in the bowels is a boiler, taken from a battleship, and, while the House is sitting at least, the alcohol flows freely,' he wrote.

In recent years MPs have been given offices – the more senior have a room to themselves, with a sofa and an armchair. We are discouraged from plugging in percolators. Nevertheless, given a camp bed, the use of a telephone at the tax-payers' expense, light and heat and unlimited supplies of stationery, it is little wonder that on arrival, some of us, at least, are rarely seen or heard of again. And we have the best library in London where nice old things drop off while reading the *Spectator* only to wake to the sight of girls up ladders. There is a chained copy of *Private Eye* and a tendency among some of the stricter library girls not to permit novels to be supplied to Members. But even that proscription can be avoided. If it were not for the continual arrival of the post, life would be complete.[15]

You can see where the reputation as 'the best gentleman's club in London' came from. Critchley went on to give an example of the prevailing maleness of the place. 'I once asked an aged Knight of the Shires, who was somewhat silent, whether, after a lifetime spent at Westminster, he would make any changes to the fabric of the Palace. Only one, he said. He would place photographs of women MPs in their underwear along the escalator which carries MPs up from their underground car park.'[16]

As in everything, timing, over which the individual politician has almost no control, is critical. Although every party fights every election publicly claiming to scent victory, the plain fact is that some elections are better lost, and others are better won by a modest majority. If the Conservatives had won the 1929 election, they would have had to face the economic crisis which did for Ramsay MacDonald. If they had won the elections in 1945 and 1964 they would have had to deal with the woes which were stored up for Attlee and Wilson. And if only the Conservatives had not dumped Margaret Thatcher and squeezed themselves a fourth successive term in 1992, the whole humiliating débâcle of the European Exchange Rate Mechanism would have been left to Labour. The sight of a Labour Chancellor of the Exchequer standing battered and blinking in the glare of television lights outside the Treasury as he threw in the towel would have confirmed every Conservative scare story about the inability of social-ist governments to manage the economy: there is every chance the Tories would have been back in power at the next election. On the other side of the coin, however much a landslide may have done for the morale of the Labour party in 1997, to be one of a parliamentary party of 419 did not do much for the ambitions of individual back-benchers. For the individual to shine, he or she really needs to belong to a party which has formed a government but doesn't have too big a majority in parliament.

It is part of the folklore of the House of Commons that all that the newly elected politician can expect in the way of accommodation is a locker, a coathook in the Members' Cloakroom, and a piece of pink ribbon from which to hang his sword. Until 2000, the lockers weren't even numbered consecutively. Getting an office, even one to share, so the legend goes, is a project on a par with Theseus' attempts to navigate his way through the labyrinth to slay the Minotaur. The memoirs of ageing politicians are replete with accounts of how they managed for years to consider affairs of state while perching on a radiator at the side of a Westminster corridor: they must all have developed the most appalling haemorrhoids. It is not that the stories are untrue – as late as 1966, fewer than half of MPs even had their own desk and filing cabinet, and the pink ribbons are still there – so much so that they tend to foster an unreal image of parliamentary life.

Before the evolution of the citizen-as-consumer and the arrival of computers, part-time MPs probably did not need much more than a desk, a blotter and access to a telephone. The grander members of parliament, like the Home and Foreign Secretaries, Leaders of the Opposition and so on, have always had imposing offices in Westminster, with panelled walls and gilded ceilings. The whips, whose job it is to enforce discipline, have their own offices. Cabinet and junior ministers cluster together.

But, until very recently, for many MPs an office was not merely a luxury. It was a hallucination. On the old English principle that anything worth doing in life is worth doing for the love of it, it was simply judged unnecessary. Just as being a member of parliament was not a full-time job, so there was no need for any Westminster politician to be provided with much more than a broom-cupboard from which to operate. The lowliest American member of Congress – and many of them were very lowly indeed – was frequently astonished to see the miserable working conditions of British members of parliament. In a perverse way, many British politicians took pride in the sheer rottenness of their surroundings, because it meant they were relatively untainted by the trappings of power. Some even exulted in it, left-wing MPs on grounds of conscience, right-wingers because it fitted their belief that the country was best governed by gentlemen amateurs.

Today the new MP, who is usually neither a gentleman nor an amateur, has higher expectations. He or she will be issued with three security passes, guaranteeing the researchers and secretaries they hire access to the Palace; although the House of Commons administrators are not quite clear how it's done, they are convinced that many MPs comfortably exceed the limit. When it comes to offices, they will soon discover the power of the whips, who enforce party discipline like prefects at a Victorian public school: the nicest offices – like those high up above Speaker's House, with magnificent views up and down the Thames – are given out as rewards or inducements. The process is remarkably inefficient. After the 1997 election the whips kept some government backbenchers waiting seven weeks before they deigned to give them offices. Getting a phone connected could take weeks, too.

To occupy those offices the whips have not handed out, the MPs must persuade an immensely polite, mild-mannered late-middle-aged lady (the school matron) in the office of the serjeant-at-arms, the functionary who carries the golden mace in the Speaker's procession and performs the role of school bursar. Longer-standing MPs have attributed their gradual rise from dog-kennel office to something more substantial to the fact that they have wooed matron with potted plants. The truth is that many of them are terrified of her: not so long ago, one MP was heard telling another in the car park that matron had told him to take down some shelves he had put up in his office. 'But I got one over on her,' he crowed. 'I didn't do it for a whole week.'

The convention that MPs were not professionals belongs in the nineteenth century, when most of the population was excluded from parliamentary politics. Until the early 1900s, MPs were not even paid a salary, it being assumed that any gentleman could support himself while he was sorting out the country's affairs. The arrangement obviously discriminated against anyone who needed to earn a living, and throughout the nineteenth century various radical organizations had attempted to change the law, always without success. But the creation of the Labour party, and the arrival in parliament of people who needed wages simply to eat, made some sort of pay essential. In 1911, MPs decided to give themselves their first salary (although they were careful to call it an allowance). It was set at £400 a year, approximately equivalent to £25,000 today. MPs rubbed along happily enough, until the first post-war Labour government, when the new regime immediately raised their pay, to £1,000. In an age of austerity, where food and clothing was rationed, it had the unmistakable whiff of politicians getting their snouts in the trough. One of the new MPs returned in the 1945 landslide was Barbara Castle, elected to represent the cotton town of Blackburn. She fully supported the pay rise, but soon discovered it did not play well on the doorsteps of Lancashire. 'I was heckled about it,' she recalled. 'I remember a particularly horrible woman who kept bawling at me. So eventually I shouted back "So you'd like just to be represented by rich people, would you?"'

In truth, £1,000 was more than adequate, but hardly enough to live like a lord. By the 1960s, the salary had been raised to over

£3,000, and MPs were also being paid expenses, along with free first-class rail travel, free telephone calls, and a strict daily ration of twenty-four large sheets of House of Commons writing paper, twenty-four small sheets of the same, and the appropriate number of envelopes. During the 1970s, with the country gripped by inflation, the salary doubled. Being a lawmaker also means that a politician is engaged in one of the few collective activities in which those taking part can decide their own salaries. Since then, as their job has become more and more a full-time one, they have lost no opportunity to raise their own salaries. During the 1980s the salary doubled again. In 1996, MPs raised their pay from £34,000 to £43,000, an increase of 26 per cent. Hoping to forestall future embarrassments, pay was henceforth to be linked to that of senior civil servants, and increased every year in line with inflation. But, three years later, the organization to whom MPs had delegated the task of assessing their worth decided they had fallen behind again, and recommended another pay rise. By 2002 they were earning £55,000 a year. In addition, there were allowances, for employing staff of up to £70,000 a year, another £18,000 in 'incidental expenses' for running an office, £20,000 to meet the living expenses of MPs from outside inner London, a mileage allowance for their cars of £1 for every two miles (and an allowance for cycling of seven pence per mile), free rail travel for themselves and their families and a 'resettlement grant' for those who retired or lost their seats of at least half the annual salary. Ministers who lost their jobs were entitled to continue drawing their ministerial salary for three months, and former Prime Ministers were paid £70,000 a year for the rest of their lives. Everyone was entitled to a pension based on their final salary and length of service.[17]

Throughout the 1990s, the complaint persisted that MPs were not being given the facilities they needed to discharge their responsibilities. Since the Palace of Westminster had been designed for another age, MPs started farming themselves out to other buildings in the area, along the Embankment, across College Green, in the old police headquarters at what had been Scotland Yard. Yet the Speaker was still saying that Westminster 'lacks the full number of offices we need now to carry out our duties'.[18] So parliament marked the new millennium by opening yet more accommodation for MPs. Looking like an inverted cow's udder, Portcullis House was, per head, the most expensive office block ever thrown up in Britain. Having one of the best views in London, adorned with potted fig trees from Florida and linked to the Palace of Westminster by a bomb-proof underground passageway, it was about as lavishly fitted out as any building ever built with public money.

The more parliament has diminished in its status and functions, the better have its facilities become. At the time when Britain ran much of the world, members of parliament managed with little or no staff and scribbled letters to anxious constituents (if they wrote to them at all) in the House of Commons library or while sitting in the chamber. Now, when its legislators scarcely even make the laws of their own country, almost all are equipped with telecoms, secretaries and researchers. In any other business, a policy of greater investment for lower real productivity would be a certain route to oblivion. It has occurred in the case of parliament because MPs have developed such a very different idea of what they are supposed to be doing. We are no longer sending people to parliament to sit on the green leather benches and wisely consider affairs of state, before coming to a measured judgement. And the less effectively the House of Commons does the job of holding governments to account, the better pleased will the governments be. Luckily for government, as we shall discover, we are sending people to Westminster who see their job very differently from the way their predecessors once saw it.

'They've become a bunch of arse-crawling social workers,' is the way the one-time Conservative cabinet minister Norman Tebbit puts it. And, as the job has changed, so has the type of person who performs it. They are going into politics younger and more biddable, and fewer and fewer of them have had much of a life outside politics. It is not that British political life has suddenly become professionalized – what were Gladstone, Disraeli or Churchill if not professionals? – but that virtually the entire membership of the House of Commons think of themselves as career politicians. 'When I went into it, the Commons used to be the sort of place where Tom would know about farming, Bill about steel-making, Fred about retailing, because those were the family businesses,' recalled Edward du Cann. 'There used to be a man in the Commons called Jennings. He was a very nondescript fellow.

But if ever there was a defence debate, everyone would crowd into the chamber to listen to him. You see, he knew what he was talking about.' This almost textbook recollection of a Golden Age has a partisan feel to it – the Labour benches had people who had been miners, seamen or doctors on them – but it encapsulates a belief that the sort of people going into politics has changed. Certainly, if such people rose to speak in the chamber today, many MPs, if they listened at all, would do so from the televisions in their offices while they dealt with letters from constituents about leaking drains. But the most unsettling sense is that the specialism has gone, for specialism requires application and experience. It is a lot easier just to make a lot of noise. In which other job could you expect to be taken seriously on subjects about which you know nothing?

This has not been a sudden transformation. The last gentleman amateur to lead a major party was Sir Alec Douglas-Home. When he retired after losing the 1964 election, Sir John Colville, who had served in the private offices of Chamberlain, Churchill and Attlee, wrote him a note. 'This is a severely professional age,' he told the ex-Prime Minister. 'There will probably never again be men who are prepared to subject themselves to all the indignities, disappointments and ingratitudes of public life merely because they want to serve their country. If, as I suspect, you are the last of that breed, this week is a sad one in our history.'[19] Half-a-dozen years later, when people such as Kenneth Clarke and Michael Howard were beginning to make their way in the Conservative party, Humphry Berkeley had noticed the change. Where once the Tory benches had held people such as Sir Harry Legge-Bourke ('a gentle, honourable man, incapable, I would judge, of telling an untruth, totally without personal ambition, who sees his membership of parliament as an act of public service'), now they were increasingly occupied by young men on the make. 'He and those such as him are being replaced by human efficiency machines, constructed for utility, rather than grace. They reel off figures to anybody who is prepared to listen – these statistics frequently include the size of their own parliamentary majorities. They have not learned the art of conversation. They appear to communicate by conducting a series of interviews with each other . . . For them the House of Commons is a stepping-stone to the glittering prizes of office and power.'[20] The man or woman who saw politics not as service nor – like Bevan – as crusade, but as a career, had soon taken root everywhere.

Not only does the existence of what is effectively now a separate political *sect* make it harder to reconnect the process with the people, it hardens the intellectual arteries of everyone involved. With a tiny number of exceptions, to advance in one of the parties you now have to strike an attitude at the age of eighteen or twenty and remain true to it for the rest of your active life. Aside from religious orders, it is hard to think of another area of human endeavour where what is most prized is the fact that you have never changed your mind. The high commands of political parties which lose office generally take the opportunity to redesign and reorganize themselves, in the hope of becoming more attractive to the voter. But the infantry are required to stay loyal to the colours. To go to your grave boasting that you have never wavered in the beliefs you held sixty years earlier is to confess that you have learned nothing from experience. And if we required such consistency from the Church, it would still be arguing, with Bishop Wilberforce, that Genesis provided a more accurate version of the origin of species than the theory of natural selection.

If you look at Northern Ireland, you can see how very much the nature of MPs has changed. Ulster Unionism was driven by a belief that rule from Dublin was the same thing as rule by the Pope in Rome, given the undue influence accorded to the Catholic Church in the Irish Free State. The Unionist machine persuaded the Protestant majority that in order to have influence with the British government they needed to send imposing people (they tended to be upper-middle-class males) to London. In 1959 there were twelve constituencies in Northern Ireland. Every one was represented by a Unionist. Their leader in parliament, Sir David Campbell, had spent his career in the colonial service, ending up as Lieutenant Governor of Malta. Another was a former district officer in Tanganyika. Of their colleagues, one, 'Pud' Grosvenor (Fermanagh and South Tyrone), was heir to the richest dukedom in Britain, eight of the group had been at public school, three at Campbell College in Belfast alone. Four of them were lawyers, and only two came from comparatively modest backgrounds. Forty years later, the number of Northern Irish seats in parliament had been increased to eighteen, thirteen of which were held by Unionists. By now, the belief that 'united we stand, divided we fall' had taken a knock, and three different varieties of unionism were represented in parliament. Very few of the MPs indeed could be said to have had much of a life before taking up a formal political career (exceptions being one former heating contractor who boasted of being chair of the all-party plumbing group, and a former sales manager who listed among his accomplishments the chairmanship of the all-party denture service group). Ian Paisley, a man whose entire life had been consumed by the struggle with 'the whore of Babylon', was unusual only in the vehemence of his conviction. By 1999 his sidekick, Peter Robinson, had already sat at Westminster for twenty years, and at the next election would see his wife elected to join him there. Among nationalists and republicans holding the remaining seats the professionalization of politics was even more pronounced: SDLP politicians were veterans of the old civil rights struggle, while politics in one form or other had occupied the entire adult life of both Sinn Fein MPs of that parliament, Gerry Adams and Martin McGuinness. These people may not be typical of the average British member of parliament. But they share with them the characteristic that they are, increasingly, people who have done nothing else. Their enemies claim they would be unemployable elsewhere.

Gerry Adams and Martin McGuinness are unusual, too, in having got into parliament despite (indeed, because of) a notorious youth. In mainstream politics, the fear of revelations of past excess can severely limit the field of potential candidates. During his short-lived and ill-advised attempt to become mayor of London, Jeffrey Archer spoke at a meeting at London University. From the back of the hall he was persistently barracked by a young man telling him the Tories knew nothing about transport policies for ordinary Londoners. Archer rounded on him, saying, 'If you think transport's bad, why don't you go into politics and do something about it?' To which the young man replied, 'Jeffrey, if the press ever got hold of what I've been up to in the last three years, I wouldn't last five minutes.' And all around the room, heads nodded, agreeing, 'Yeah, me too.' The truth is that the people who have the most energy and ideas are precisely the people who are most likely to have some skeleton in a cupboard somewhere.

The difficulty lies with the public's comfortable hypocrisy, in saying they want politicians who are in touch with the real world, while simultaneously expecting them to have lived monkish lives.

It would be unfair to blame the Labour party exclusively for the general colourlessness of the House of Commons: it was in the Thatcher years, after the Conservatives had reformed their selection procedures, that the procession of die-cast careerists pushed aside the people who had seen something of the world. But the party which has done most to change the way it chooses its aspirant members of parliament is the Labour party. In 1999, it began to require aspiring MPs to be screened by party headquarters. Candidates were obliged to attend training weekends, to submit standardized CVs, and to be interviewed by a panel which included at least one member of parliament. The intention, according to a senior party figure, was to 'weed out the charlatans' who might have somehow sneaked through the old selection system in which constituencies chose their own representatives. He was frank about what this meant. People who 'appeared not to have a pragmatic line on policy disagreements' or could 'not avoid sounding divisive and combative if disagreeing with party policy', or who 'showed an unpreparedness to listen to the whips' would be eradicated.[21] In theory, the final choice of candidate remained the responsibility of the local constituency. But headquarters also made it harder for constituency radicals to deselect MPs they felt were too slavishly obedient to London. And when the Conservative MP Shaun Woodward suddenly defected to Labour, officials simply called up MPs with safe seats and offered them inducements to stand down. When, eventually, the safe seat of St Helen's became available, they ensured that the immensely popular local council leader, Marie Rimmer, was excluded from the shortlist.

The consequence of all these changes has been to ensure that the Labour benches in parliament are increasingly peopled by ambitious, biddable professionals. For many, their MP's salary is the most they have ever earned. It would be surprising if this material comfort had no effect upon how ready they are to defy the party machine. Even after five or six years away from their previous job, how many people would be willing to take a chance on being able to pick it up again if the party decided it no longer needed them?

Between 1918 and 1935, an average of seven out of every ten Labour MPs came from a working-class background. By the time of the Labour landslide in 1945, that proportion had dropped to under half, but four out of every ten still described themselves as 'workers': Attlee's cabinet alone included six former miners. In the post-war years, the numbers who could honestly call themselves anything of the sort gradually waned. By the time of the 1997 election, 45 per cent of the parliamentary party came from a professional background, and only 13 per cent now chose to call themselves 'workers'. Labour MPs now tend to be drawn increasingly from the Welfare State salariat – teachers, lecturers, health service bureaucrats – rather than from the working class. The number of former working men and women in the 2001 parliamentary Labour party was down to fifty-one, or 12 per cent; in his election address that year, one Labour candidate had been reduced to boasting of his coalminer *grandfather*.[22] Of course, many of the old-fashioned trades have vanished, with the demolished steelworks, the sealed-up mineshafts and the rusting former car-plants. But it is noticeable that what has replaced the traditional Labour politicians is not the person who works in a call-centre or assembly-plant. Their place has been taken by someone who does not belong to their class at all: after the 1997 election, there were more Labour MPs who had attended public schools than had had manual jobs. The characteristic Labour MP has now either worked as a political professional – as a special adviser in a think-tank (or somewhere); as a college lecturer or a civil servant perhaps – where every single payment into their bank account has come directly from the taxpayer. Half of the entire new intake of MPs in the 2001 election had had some sort of professional political background, as a researcher to an existing MP, as a special adviser to a minister, or as a trade union official.

It is noticeable, too, that most of the toffs scarcely seem to bother any more. In 1959, there were seventy-six Etonians in the House of Commons. By the 2001 election, the figure had fallen to fourteen Conservative MPs, two Labour and two Liberal Democrats. Parliamentary salaries are much better than they once were, but a talented person entering politics will never be particularly well paid by comparison with many of his or her similarly ambitious contemporaries.

The Victorian constitutionalist Walter Bagehot (who stood for parliament three times, and failed on each occasion) thought that what we wanted in parliament were 'sensible men of substantial means'. Bagehot's comment, along with his disdain for the masses, belongs to the days before Britain became a true democracy. But it still helps if you don't have to worry about money. One very grand Conservative MP told me his accountant had calculated that 'My time in politics has cost me £2 million. I make no complaint. But you can see why some people might be put off.'

For all the air-conditioning and fibre-optic cables which have somehow been chiselled into the nineteenth-century stonework to meet the demands of this professional class, the cliché remains true that newly elected MPs often feel they have arrived at some awful *Decline and Fall*-era minor boys' public school.[23] Newly arrived women MPs who have spent their professional careers in education can be slightly more precise. Of the 1997 intake, Diana Organ, the new MP for the Forest of Dean and a former special-needs teacher, thought the place was 'a real cross between an Oxford college and a girls' boarding school'.[24] The member for Milton Keynes South West, Dr Phyllis Starkey, who had been a fellow of Somerville College, Oxford, felt it was 'a bit like being at nursery school on the first day . . . because you felt so small'.[25]

   The analogy is overworked. But that does not mean it is untrue. The similarity goes beyond initial impressions. Newcomers will have to learn the odd school customs – that rubbing the left foot of the statue of Churchill in the Members' Lobby before delivering a speech is supposed to bring good luck, or that any MP may demand a pinch from the loaded snuffbox kept by the doorkeeper's chair – to assimilate the pettifogging rules which decree whether or not a man may take his jacket off or chew a mint, and to master the extraordinary linguistic contortions necessary if they are to formulate a question, an amendment or a draft piece of legislation. They will be expected to learn the sort of subtle assessments which distinguish relationships in school peer-groups. They will be expected to acquiesce in the generally held view that so-and-so, who is full of original ideas, is actually a 'bore' or an 'irrelevance', while someone else, who spends a lot of time jumping up to spout predictable banalities on every possible occasion, is 'a House of Commons character'. As one honest MP put it to me, he spent his first six months at Westminster wondering how on earth he had got to the place, and the next six months wondering how his colleagues had ever got there.

Being a politician is an odd job. No other form of employment is quite as all-consuming: neither at work nor at home can you escape from the fact that you are a member of parliament. And, cut off from the normal nine-to-five, locked up with 650 others also leading the same unusual life, no wonder they start to act like the inmates of a boarding school. Harold Nicolson, who went into politics after thirty years as a diplomat, noticed the echoes of his puberty at once.

One recognises the same preference for 'character' (which is the House-master's phrase for 'convenient conformity') as against the imagination or independence (which are classed as symptoms of the 'crank' or 'freak'). There is an identical laugh a little too loudly at the headmaster's jokes; the same propensity towards herd-giggling when any untoward incident occurs; the same overt desire to address the Captain of Cricket by his Christian name.

The echoes became loudest at the end of the parliamentary term (the official word is itself revealing).

The sense of impending release, the imminence of other and gentler standards of social behaviour, the approaching interruption of our communal existence, create an atmosphere of comradely vivacity. Old animosities are discarded with our school clothes; the shout of derision, the obviously averted eye, give place to polite enquiries regarding the approaching holidays . . . even the head prefect has discarded his flowing tails in favour of a neat green suit. Amity abounds.[26]

Nicolson's son Nigel arrived in the House of Commons after a by-election in Bournemouth East in 1952 and found the spirit unchanged. As he waited to swear his oath of allegiance to the Crown, the former Labour Chancellor of the Exchequer Hugh Dalton whispered in his ear, 'In a few minutes you will walk behind the

Speaker's chair into the obscurity from which you should never have emerged.'[27]

It is all reminiscent of the threats of the school bully. To establish himself, the ambitious politician still needs to be able, if not to carry the House of Commons with him, then, at the absolute least, not to lose it. Many nineteenth-century aristocrats, it is said, like Lord George Bentinck, thought addressing the House of Commons beneath them, 'an occupation like taking one's children to the sea-side – an occupation which marked one as one of the middle class'.[28] The twenty-first-century politician, being middle class to the core, has no such luxury. By parliamentary convention, the new MP speaks glowingly about his constituency and warmly (if possible) about his predecessor, while the House of Commons listens in polite silence. Yet the terror-inducing qualities of the audience and the resonance of the debating chamber can paralyse. Richard Brinsley Sheridan, who became one of the great political orators of the eighteenth century (one of his speeches lasted an astonishing five hours and forty minutes), was so petrified by his maiden speech that he was counselled to abandon politics and stick to writing plays. Edward Gibbon, whose scholarship and elegant style made his *Decline and Fall of the Roman Empire* one of the greatest historical narratives of all time, spent twelve years in the House of Commons without making a single speech. 'The great speakers', he explained, 'filled me with despair, the bad ones with terror.' The young Winston Churchill survived the ordeal only because his next-door neighbour provided him with an opening joke.

Those who get through the experience apparently unharmed can find that the conventions of parliament draw the sting of anything they have to say. There is a well-known account of a nameless MP's maiden speech which has all the hallmarks of a Westminster story (that is, it is almost true and almost funny). He is said to have delivered his maiden speech and then to have retired, exhausted and triumphant, to the tea room. An elderly colleague complimented him with the words, 'My boy, that was a Rolls-Royce of a speech!' It was later pointed out to him that the old buffer said the same thing to every new MP, and that what he meant was that it was well oiled, almost inaudible and had gone on for a very, very long time.[29] And even when the compliments are kindly meant, the habits of the House of

Commons seem designed to extract all passion. Aneurin Bevan's description of the working-man MP, arriving at Westminster fired up with the injustices visited upon the people who elected him, explains how this happens:

He delivers himself therefore with great force and, he hopes and fears, with considerable provocativeness. When his opponent arises to reply, he expects to hear an equally strong and uncompromising answer. His opponent does nothing of the sort. In strict conformity with parliamentary tradition, he congratulates the new Member upon a most successful maiden speech and expresses the urbane hope that the House will have frequent opportunities of hearing him in the future. The Members present endorse this quite insincere sentiment with murmurs of approval. With that, his opponent pays no more heed to him but goes on to deliver the speech he had intended to make. After remaining in his seat a little longer, the new Member crawls out of the House with feelings of deep relief at having got it over, mingled with a paralysing sense of frustration. The stone he thought he had thrown turned out to be a sponge.[30]

The new MP must learn the rules. He must understand that if he wishes to take part in a debate he may have to sit in the chamber of the House of Commons for hours (during which time he may well hear every single point he had been planning to make made by someone else), hoping somehow to catch the Speaker's eye. He may not eat or drink while there, may not read the newspaper, may not even carry a briefcase. If he finally gets called to speak, he must be careful to avoid words the Speaker may object to, such as coward, git, guttersnipe, hooligan or rat. He must not find it strange that, for a piece of legislation to become law, it must be endorsed in Norman French. In a dramatic concession to the imminent arrival of the twenty-first century, in 1998 MPs were absolved of the need to put on a collapsible top hat in order to make a point of order during a division.

Most of all, there is the terrible problem of the audience. With a few exceptions – resignation speeches, for example, when there is a good chance that the resentment which has been simmering away for years will finally boil over – MPs do not go to the chamber of the House of Commons to listen. They go to talk. This makes

Westminster quite unlike almost any other platform on which a politician might be asked to speak. At a public meeting the audience have generally come to hear the speech. Great parliamentary characters, well-known orators and party leaders can still usually count on a curious audience inside parliament. But the rest of the time the chamber is filled with people who are there because they want to make a speech themselves. It therefore follows that anyone else speaking is merely getting in the way. They do not want to listen. They want others to sit down and listen to them. The schoolyard atmosphere means that collective bullying is just part of daily behaviour. The best description of the sort of climate this creates dates from 1836. Written by 'one of no party', it will be instantly recognizable to anyone who has spent a few hours watching parliamentary debates.

'I rise, Sir, (Ironical cheers, mingled with all sorts of zoological sounds), I rise, Sir, for the purpose of stating that I have ('Oh! oh!' 'Bah!' and sounds resembling the bleating of a sheep, mingled with loud laughter). Hon. gentlemen may endeavour to put me down by their unmannerly interruptions, but I have a duty to perform to my con—(Ironical cheers, loud coughing, sneezing, and yawning extended to an incredible length, followed by bursts of laughter). I say, Sir, I have constituents who on this occasion expect that I—(Cries of 'Should sit down,' and shouts of laughter). They expect, Sir, that on a question of such importance ('O-o-a-a-u-' and loud laughter, followed by cries of 'Order! order!' from the Speaker). I tell honourable gentlemen who choose to conduct themselves in such a way, that I am not to be put down by—(Groans, coughs, sneezings, hems, and various animal sounds, some of which closely imitated the yelping of a dog, and the squeaking of a pig, interspersed with peals of laughter). I appeal—('Cock-e-leeri-o-co!' The imitation, in this case, of the crowing of a cock was so remarkably good, that not even the most staid and orderly members in the house could preserve their gravity. The laughter which followed drowned the Speaker's cries of 'Order! order!') I say, Sir, this is most unbecoming conduct on the part of an assembly calling itself de—('Bow-wow-wow,' and bursts of laughter). Sir, may I ask, have honourable gentlemen who can—('Mew-mew,' and renewed laughter). Sir, I claim the protection of the Chair. (The Speaker here again rose and called out 'Order! order!' in a loud and angry tone, on which the uproar in some measure subsided.) If honourable gentlemen will only allow me to make one observation, I will not trespass further on their attention, but sit down at once. (This was followed by the most tremendous cheering in earnest.) I only beg to say, Sir, that I think this is a most dangerous and unconstitutional measure, and will therefore vote against it.' The honourable gentleman then resumed his seat amidst deafening applause.[31]

It must take a very thick skin to emerge from that sort of barracking with any dignity intact.

The safest thing is to get the protection of the party: this at least ensures that there is one set of benches which is not making farmyard noises. With any luck, they may even cheer you on. The problem here is that so often the appearance of collegiality on government or opposition benches is a sham. One new MP after another confirms the old story that in parliament your worst enemies aren't sitting on the benches opposite: they're alongside or behind you. The best way to get the respect of the party is to earn it, either by having a recognized authority on the subject on which you speak, or – and this comes much more easily to anyone who has learned the tricks of the debating societies at the old universities – by being an accomplished speechifier. This has nothing whatever to do with having any knowledge or expertise. Indeed, any knowledge beyond the bare essentials may be a disadvantage, because it will cloud the vision and obscure the terribly simple solutions which are so obvious to anyone with the perspective of ignorance.

If the politician has neither great expertise nor particularly adroit debating skills, he or she can turn to the party managers for support. Their help comes at a price. The new MP will already have discovered that all the best offices for backbenchers have been allocated by the whips as rewards for those who have proved their reliability. The best thing he or she can do to ensure good treatment is to be amenable: any illusions the eager new member of parliament may have about his or her unique contribution to democracy will soon be dashed. Unless the government has the narrowest of majorities, opposition MPs can achieve little. And the life of a mule harnessed to a wheel can have more excitement to it than that of the government backbencher in parliament. The novitiate will soon discover that his or her party has a set of expectations which manage the unappetizing combination of being both low and stringent. To be considered a loyalist, they will be required to show up in the chamber of the House at all hours of the day and night within eight minutes of the division bell sounding, and to be shooed into the 'Aye' or 'No' lobby like so many drowsy sheep. They will be given helpful questions to ask of the Prime Minister and his cabinet colleagues, and told when they should demonstrate support for a policy announcement or a 'spontaneous' intervention. They will be told when to remain silent, whatever their conscience may tell them.

Sometimes they receive their instructions in unsolicited letters. A couple sit on my desk. One, from the MP for Hastings, Michael Foster, serving as the Parliamentary Private Secretary to the Attorney General and Solicitor General, has a plaintive tone to it. 'Dear Colleague,' it reads, 'The Law Officers' "slot" for Oral Questions is not always well attended.' (This is something of an understatement: the 'always' is redundant.) To deal with the problem, 'I am currently revising our List of those colleagues who would be willing to ask Questions of the Solicitor General,' adding, for the benefit of those who can't think quite how they might take up this invitation, that 'We can . . . provide you with suggested areas of questioning.' What Mr Foster is asking his colleagues to do is to turn question time from a way of holding the department to account into an opportunity for free publicity. The second letter is from the MP for Cambridge, Anne Campbell, who was working as Parliamentary Private Secretary at the Department of Trade and Industry. Ms Campbell is ceaselessly crying for parliament to be made to work better. Her private letter is more businesslike. 'Dear Colleague. This Thursday, (27 July), is tabling day for DTI questions for answer on 2 November. I would be very grateful if you would consider tabling one of the suggested questions enclosed.' There follows a list of twenty-nine possible questions, five on what the government is doing to promote small businesses, four on the manufacturing and textile industries, eight on E-commerce, nine on science policy and three on 'Hi-tech business'. A typically incisive contribution asks, 'What steps are being taken to keep Britain at the forefront of scientific advances?'

Ms Campbell evidently did not get takers for all her suggested fearless interrogations. But, on the appointed day, the MP for Colne Valley, Kali Mountford, told the minister how impressed local mill owners had been by the quality of government help they had received for the textile industry. Sally Keeble, who had won Northampton North in the previous election, asked about help for small businesses ('excellent progress' was being made). David Kidney, who had won Stafford, threw a patsy question about the probable benefits to industry of trading in the euro. A fourth freshman MP, the Merseysider Claire Curtis-Thomas, tireless campaigner for improved baby-changing facilities at Westminster, asked what the government was doing to promote a better public understanding of science (loads, of course). Her fellow Merseyside first-timer, Louise Ellman, wanted to know to whom the Particle Physics and Astronomy Research Council was accountable. A sixth new member, the former social worker Steve McCabe, MP for one of the Birmingham seats, invited the minister to condemn people protesting against the high cost of fuel.

Why do they collude in this pantomime? Many will not consider it an insult to their intelligence to be used as some sort of speak-your-weight machine for the government because they genuinely believe in what the government is trying to achieve: after all, they promised the voters that a change of regime would make life better. Some perhaps have a real interest in the subject of their question. Others may simply want to be noticed: the Labour majority was so huge that, four years after the election, veteran members of the press gallery were still gazing down on the massed ranks of Labour politicians and playing 'Name That MP!' Still more, doubtless, were glad simply of the chance to demonstrate their unswerving loyalty, in the hope that it might help their chances of advancement.

Almost all of this passes without the rest of the public noticing. The complaint is made – repeatedly – that politics has moved away from the chamber of the House of Commons, out into the radio and television studios and the columns of the newspapers. With a few exceptions, policy announcements are no longer made to the few dozen MPs scattered around the green leather benches. They are made on the radio to millions of listening voters. This, the MPs say, is a Bad Thing, since it deprives them of the opportunity to hold the government to account in the cockpit of democracy. They have yet to explain why this process can be done only in a converted chapel under rules of conduct, some of which date back to the sixteenth century.

But the core of the problem of public confidence is to do with parliament itself. The trouble with letting television cameras into the Commons is that they have done their job too well. The party machines collude in something called 'doughnutting', a fraud on the public in which every spokesman is seen to be surrounded by half-a-dozen other politicians, to take advantage of the tight regulations which restrict how the television companies may show the House. The impression is thereby given that MPs are all busily about their business when, in fact, the rest of the chamber may be almost empty. But even this petty deception cannot obscure the simple fact, which television has made plain, that the place is full of obscure procedures, arcane language and excruciating tedium. It places too much emphasis on debating-society point-scoring and too little on detailed analysis. The farmyard noises which signify approval or scorn make the business of democracy seem cheap. It is over a century since Curzon described the Commons as 'the playground of jesters and the paradise of bores',[32] and it has not noticeably improved in the meantime.

But, however tiresome they may find the Palace of Westminster, there is one place where they are really taken seriously.

5. Look at Me!

It is three o'clock on a dark November afternoon. The rain is bone-numbingly cold and the cows on the hillside across the valley have huddled together in the corner of a field for warmth. This side of the valley is uncultivated, has been ever since it was a medieval hunting ground for deer. Amid the dripping, blasted oak trees, a man in an extraordinary blond wig is holding aloft a spade. The rain lashes across the hillside and is turning the hairpiece into some surreal golden candyfloss helmet, plastered to the sides of his skull. Nothing is happening.

The man under the rug shakes a little earth off the spade and asks another man if he has a camera. He grins. The camera flashes. The wigged one puts down the spade and picks up an oak sapling. He smiles again. The camera flashes. Then he holds both spade and sapling aloft, and once more the camera flashes. Then he pretends to dig the ground and the flashlight pierces the waterlogged gloom for a fourth time. By now, with his yellow hair, orange face and sodden aquamarine cotton jumper, the man is starting to look like an aerial view of the island in the middle of a Caribbean lagoon.

The weather is another matter. It is quite astonishingly cold, cold enough to have any sensible person sheltering indoors, nursing a cup of tea or a whisky and appreciating the steam on the windowpanes. But the object of the photographer's attention has a greater destiny. The bedraggled blond bombshell is the member of parliament for Lichfield. The man with the camera is from a local wildlife trust. Truth to tell, the MP is disappointed. He had been hoping there would have been professional photographers present. But, when he arrived, it turned out the local press had all found other things to do. So here he is, alone on a hillside but for the representatives of an organization trying to promote tree-planting, one of whom happens to have a pocket camera.

It is not enough that the sapling is planted. It must be seen to be planted. And it must be photographed, so that others can see it has been planted. And so he pleads through the rain, 'You will be sure to send the picture to the *Mercury* and the *Mail* and *Post*?'

The point of the exercise is not the worthiness of the cause – that is self-evident. No, it is that a particular individual is seen to be doing the planting. That individual, the member of parliament for the city which gave the world Joseph Addison, David Garrick, Samuel Johnson, Erasmus Darwin and Elias Ashmole – founder of Oxford's wondrous Ashmolean Museum ('the greatest virtuoso and curioso that ever was known') – is the curiosity on the hillside, Michael Fabricant. He has represented the city since the 1992 General Election. 'Lichfield. I *love* this place,' he gushes.

Michael Fabricant's day in his constituency had started at ten minutes to ten in the morning, when he arrived in the lobby of a local bank, took off his tweed jacket, blue shirt and patterned tie, and borrowed a T-shirt. He then climbed aboard an exercise bicycle and pedalled for fifteen minutes, while two photographers from local newspapers snapped away. This particular day, he might have been in the House of Commons arguing one of the great ethical issues of the hour, the rights and wrongs of research upon human embryos. Yet here he is, in Lichfield, sitting on an exercise bicycle.

'I'm doing thirty miles an hour!' he exclaims for the inevitable newspaper photographer. No, you're not: the thirty miles is the distance the bicycle is estimated to have 'travelled' since someone started riding it long before you arrived. People drift in and out of the bank, fresh from the stalls outside in the marketplace selling cut-price blankets and net curtains. 'What's this all about?' asks one. 'It's a marathon for Children in Need,' says the bank manager. Another photographer arrives and Fabricant smiles obligingly: whatever else he may or not do for Lichfield, the city is represented by a man who knows how to send out a press release. He does not hear the woman laden with shopping who has come in to use the cash machine when she asks, 'And who's *he*?'

On and on he puffs, for the allotted fifteen minutes, his permanently tanned face glowing like an amber traffic light. The bank staff are grateful for their MP's endorsement and the few coins which have been dropped into the bin by the bicycle. Again, no one can reasonably dispute the worthiness of the cause. That is not the point. The question is why Fabricant should choose to spend his morning sitting on an exercise bicycle in the marketplace of Lichfield instead of deliberating about where human life starts or ends.

Half an hour later, our hero is down at the headquarters of the WRVS where yet another photographer is present (how many newspapers can a smallish market town support?). Then, into a car with a couple of volunteers delivering Meals on Wheels to a succession of housebound old people. They are variously cheerful, miserable, stroke-stricken, diabetic, smelly, houseproud, forgetful or agoraphobic. Most of them are glued to day-time television cookery shows from behind the shelter of the zimmer-frames perched in front of their armchairs: the more manically the camp chefs prance around the screen, the lower the old people seem to subside into their seats. None is annoyed to see this unexpected extra delivery-man with a tinfoil meat pie and apple turnover (several confess that Meals on Wheels is their only contact with the outside world), and Fabricant is quick on the small-talk.

'Lovely parrots,' he says to an old lady with enough wrapping around her leg to have shrouded Tutankhamen.

'They're budgerigars.'

'Oh yes. Of course they are.'

He has boundless enthusiasm for everything. 'Squirrels? I *love* squirrels.' Isn't that pampas grass? 'Comes from South America, you know . . .' Isn't Lichfield a marvellous city? 'It's so undiscovered. We need a good mass murder to get the media down here.'

Michael Fabricant is well mannered. He knows about a few things. He can certainly make conversation. He is incorrigibly jovial and friendly. The question with him is something altogether more intangible. It is simply, what is an MP *for*?

Fabricant has called for catering in the House of Commons to be taken over by his local Indian restaurant (Lichfield holds the *Guinness Book of Records* title for the largest curry ever mixed), and sent out a press release claiming that he inspects all lavatory bowls to see whether they are locally made. He has sat on a few committees in Westminster, but if you took a poll among MPs about whom they considered the most impressive member of the House of Commons, Fabricant would not, to put it politely, be anywhere near the top. In Westminster, if they bother to think about him at all, they think of him as a figure of fun. Worse still, Fabricant is not merely aware of his reputation. He actively promotes it. 'It took me a long time to realize that the House of Commons chamber is a place to act in,' he told me over a beer. 'People play up in the place. And I know perfectly well that I'm one of the worst offenders.'

Why do it then?

'Because I *can*.'

'But it's just being a smart-arse,' I say.

'Yes, but the point is, I *can* be a smart-arse.' Perhaps that is enough of a justification for a man who was once memorably described as being 'a leading disc jockey in several parts of Hove'.[1] The 'Micky Fabb' days with the mobile disco, tie-dyed T-shirts and loon pants, and the exclamations to 'Shake that thing!' or 'Strut your funky stuff' are behind him now, even if the front-combed hair-weaving wig is not. Yet, here in Lichfield, he is something else. The point about all this frenetic activity (the cycling, house-visiting, sapling-planting and general gladhanding will be followed in the evening by a black-tie dinner in the Guildhall with all the local worthies) is not that it is in any sense harmful. It is just that it seems so pointless. The only measurable dividend seems to be paid in photographs in the local papers. The objective is not to be doing anything in particular, but to seem to be doing *something*, to be ubiquitous, part of the fabric of Lichfield life. On other days he will be speaking in schools, visiting local playgroups, or engaged in any one of a thousand other activities others would not have the energy for. Why, I asked him, does he do it?

'They're events where people want to see me,' he replied. And? 'I love it. There's no cinema in Lichfield. On Friday nights, the kids go out and get drunk. And sometimes when I'm walking home, they'll run up to me shouting and say, "You're Michael Fabricant. I voted for you!" I just *love* that.'

It's believable. As we walk around Lichfield, people really do exclaim, 'Hello, Michael!' as he passes. Anyone anxious about their significance in life, wondering whether their existence mattered to anyone, would find immediate consolation. The reverse side of the intense narcissism of being a politician is its appalling loneliness. The consolations are the conviviality of fellow inmates in the House of Commons (one sometimes suspects that much of the opposition to changing the working hours of parliament is simply a reflection of the fact that so many MPs have no home to go to) and the public recognition in the constituency. So, when asked what is the point of all this endless gladhanding, Fabricant gives an instant answer. 'Because I like being MP for Lichfield. In fact, *I love it.*' All the activity does have a dividend, too. In the 2001 election, he achieved a swing from Labour to Conservative well above the national average, because the people of Lichfield knew who he was. And however much of a fool he may appear to be in Westminster, here in his constituency he is *the member of parliament*, man of substance, *homme sérieux*. It is the great consolation of becoming an elected politician: be you never so great an addle-pated ninny, in your constituency you are somebody special.

In 1937, the future Labour MP Tom Driberg claimed to have overheard two MPs talking about their weekend plans.

One said, dolefully, that he had to go to his constituency.

'Oh Lord,' said the other, in sympathy, 'what an awful bore.'

'Yes,' said the first, 'and the worst of it is, I shall have to go there again next year too.'[2]

Modern MPs find this sort of anecdote simultaneously funny and baffling. The great majority of them cannot comprehend how anyone could get away with such a cavalier attitude. Most don't even have the desire to attempt it. Their commitment to constituency work is at the heart of what many of them think they came into politics for.

In historical terms, it is a recent phenomenon. When Jennie Lee arrived at Westminster she was told she had to decide whether she was going to be a socialist politician, or 'another bloody social worker'.[3] Neil Kinnock told me that Jennie Lee's husband, Aneurin Bevan, did not even hold surgeries when he sat for Tredegar. The saying was 'He comes here every summer, whether he's needed or not.' One Labour MP first elected in the 1945 Labour landslide returned to his constituency soon after parliament had begun sitting.

He arrived at the station to be greeted by the station master in his top hat, asking 'whether he would be following the previous Member in paying his annual visit at that time of year'.[4] But no modern MP has had the sheer, glorious contempt of the eighteenth-century member for Southampton, Anthony Henley. Henley had inherited a manor and a small fortune, and was described by a neighbour as 'a man noted for his impudence and immorality'. Parliamentary records do not have him down as voting at all for his first six years as an MP, until, in 1733, the Southampton corporation wrote to ask him to oppose the impending excise bill, which would cost them money. Henley had evidently decided he had had enough of constituency pressures. He wrote back a letter which appeared in the *Weekly Register*:

> Gentlemen,
>
> I received yours and am surprised at your insolence in troubling me about the excise. You know what I very well know, that I bought you.
>
> And I know well what perhaps you think I don't know, that you are now selling yourselves to somebody else.
>
> And I know what you don't know, that I am buying another borough.
>
> May God's curse light on you all.
>
> May your houses be as open and as common to all excise officers as your wives and daughters were to me when I stood for your scoundrel corporation.[5]

The spirit of Henley lives on in a handful of (mainly Conservative) politicians: contempt for his constituents shines through in Alan Clark's *Diaries*, and his perceived indifference was said to be the explanation for Michael Portillo's loss of his Enfield seat in the 1997 election. But most of Henley's successors are a more assiduous bunch. Not for them the question of why any talented person would want to spend their weekend afternoons in Watford Conservative Club read-ing out the bingo numbers. The vast majority of the infusion of new politicians who entered parliament in the 1997 landslide claimed their most important role was 'to be a good constituency member'.[6] One wonders if they realize what is involved, for the demands are incessant.

Bob Marshall-Andrews, the squat, fruity-voiced MP for Medway, was once asked, at the age of fifty-five, if he would abseil down the outside of an office block. Andrew Mackinlay, who became MP for Thurrock in the 1992 election, turns out for Scout Gang Shows, Operatic Society talent competitions, and more or less anything else he's asked to attend or judge. Mackinlay aspires only to do what he can for Thurrock and to bring some life back into the House of Commons. Even so he admits that 'Because I go, they invite me back next year. But by then, of course, I've picked up a whole lot more events, and each year they also invite you back. And pretty soon the diary is crammed. I'm not complaining. It's not unpleasant. It's just that you have no time to think.' The contrast is with Gladstone. His diaries, which he kept from the age of fifteen until he was eighty-five, recorded what he read each day. In total, he is estimated to have consumed nearly 20,000 books and pamphlets, on everything from philosophy and theology to science and poetry. Even many comparatively junior political figures today seem scarcely to read beyond the headlines on the front pages of the daily newspapers.

Retired MPs from earlier generations look at this hectic constituency activity with horror. 'I went to Westminster because I wanted to play a part in big issues, like changing society and the defence of the realm. I see my successor thinks he's there as some sort of local councillor,' one of them told me. Indeed, the constituency aspects of the job had assumed such significance in their lives that the Speaker confessed to fearing they were so busy attending to their constituents that they were unable to discharge their task of holding the government to account. This was, of course, not something that troubled the Blair government greatly, which, on the principle that the devil makes work for idle hands, encouraged many of its own backbenchers to spend one week in six away from Westminster in the constituency.[7]

There have always been politicians, usually on the Labour side, who took their constituency responsibilities seriously. Barbara Castle recognized that one of the reasons she held Blackburn through ten General Elections was that between times she would knock on people's doors and say, 'Hello, I'm Barbara Castle, your MP. What can I do for you?' Leaving an appeal to voters until election time runs the danger of being accused − justifiably in some cases − of being interested in local people only when wanting something from them. The constant knocking on doors runs the risk only of being pickled in tea. Yet, in the parliament which ran from 1959 to 1964, less than one-third of MPs listed addresses in their constituencies in *Who's Who*. One Tory MP for a Lancashire seat had addresses in London, Yorkshire and Iraq.[8] No thoroughly modern politician would take a similar risk. For the last twenty years, most MPs have been spending most of their weekends in the constituency.

In the 1940s and 1950s, MPs were reckoned to be receiving two or three letters each day, to which they could easily reply in longhand. But in the 1960s everything changed; the volume of mail trebled, and the proportion of MPs holding surgeries in their constituencies grew from 60 per cent to 90.[9] By 1986, MPs were being sent over 6 million letters a year, perhaps half of them from constituents, an average of thirty letters a day for each MP.[10] What had been a total weekly parliamentary mailbag of 10,000 letters a week in 1964 had risen to 40,000 by 1997. After the election that year, some MPs were claiming to have mailboxes bulging with between 100 and 200 letters each day.[11] There is, of course, simply no way of responding personally to that number of letters if one is to do anything else worthwhile in parliament.

'Let me show you my in-tray,' a Conservative backbencher boasted one morning. Then he reached under his desk and produced a metal wastepaper basket. 'That's it! Only place for it! Makes life so much simpler.' He glowed with pride. 'The truth is, most of my colleagues here just let themselves get terrorized by it.' He paused for a moment. 'We *are* talking off the record, aren't we?' To be fair to the MP, whose wish to remain anonymous I must respect, he did add that any personal letter directly from an individual constituent got a personal reply the same day: his argument was that most of the mail sent to MPs was general stuff – organized write-ins by people trying to secure his support for some campaign or other, or complaints which he could do nothing about, or which were none of his business. 'There are few subjects on earth on which more bullshit is talked', he went on, 'than the constituency mailbag.' He has a point. But it takes a few years in parliament – and a very healthy majority – to see it.

★

It is raining in Bermondsey. This is the sort of place where it seems to be always raining. Grey skies, endless streets of gimcrack terraced houses and vast, cheaply built housing estates, peppered with video shops, pawnbrokers and charity shops. In the day room of a little block of sheltered housing for the elderly, a couple of dozen local people are sitting at formica-topped tables, waiting to see their MP. They are male and female, children and the very old, white, black and Asian. They all have the lined-before-their-time faces of the poor.

If you leave out the small strip of ritzy, river-front flats which have been knocked out at vast cost for the benefit of the City money-brokers, it's a fair summary to say that Bermondsey is inner-city deprivation personified. The constituency has more people living in council housing than anywhere else in England. In the old political map of Britain, it was as bovinely Labour as anywhere in the country. And that was the Labour party's undoing. Bermondsey was one of the party's pocket boroughs, the sort of place it could take for granted, and in 1983 that thoughtlessness cost the party the seat. The sitting MP, Bob Mellish, a big old party bruiser, resigned and the constituency party, assuming the place was theirs for ever, chose as its candidate Peter Tatchell, portrayed in the media as an outrageous, gay Australian. In the battle which followed, the Liberal candidate, Simon Hughes, won by a country mile. Since then, every week Hughes has held a surgery somewhere in the constituency, where people can bring him their problems. This Saturday morning people will tell him their worries about their health, their housing, their social security benefits, their children's education, their fear of racial attack. For these people, the member of parliament represents the last hope in the fight between the individual and Them, the forces of the state, the Benefits Agency, the prison service, the educational system, gangsters, bullies, the people who decide who can live where. The term 'surgery' is well chosen. The electors go to the MP because something has gone wrong. And they pray he can prescribe some wonder drug.

Their MP arrives in his trademark vehicle, a broken-down old London taxi which would certainly not pass any Hackney Carriage Office inspection, full, as it is, of old umbrellas, House of Commons Order Papers and, oddly, a pile of gravel. In any division into Roundheads and Cavaliers, Hughes is a Roundhead – educated, thoughtful, church-going and, in the yah-boo world of Westminster, seen as altogether a bit too serious and prim. This morning, he is wearing a check open-neck shirt and is full of boundless energy. He switches the radio to a soft rock station and invites the first customer into his surgery. She is a woman whose brother is in prison on remand. The prison doctor has discovered he is suffering from stomach cancer and she wants him to be released because the prison hospital wing is entirely occupied by men trying to come off drugs. The woman is worn down, distressed and at the end of her tether.

'Here's what I'll do. I'll find out when the trial will be, I'll talk to the prison governor. The police will want a second opinion about his cancer, of course. But I'll find out what the national guidelines are on people being released on compassionate grounds – someone will have to put up a surety: do you have any money?'

She does not, but thinks that money can be found.

'OK. I'll get back to you in a week. If I don't, you ring me.'

Then there is a couple living on housing benefit who believe they are owed forty pounds. Oh, and the roof of their council maisonette leaks. He promises a visit from a local councillor.

Then, as the radio plays 'All I want to do is have some fun', there is a woman whose ten-year-old daughter has had a knife pulled on her by a school bully. She has reported the incident to the head-teacher and to the police, but the threats continue. He promises to talk to the school and to the police. 'Here's my phone number, call me if it happens again.'

Several other constituents come to complain that their children have been rejected by the secondary schools they had been hoping to attend. Hughes explains, repeatedly, what the schools are entitled to do in choosing their pupils and what hopes there may be of making a successful appeal. He or one of his colleagues will come with them to the appeal, if they wish.

Then, as the Eagles play 'Take It Easy', another mother tells of how her son has had his head jammed through a set of railings near the school and a knife stuck to his throat. The family cannot stand the racial attacks any more and are moving out (the area has a highly mobile population – a quarter of them will have moved on before the next election). She wants Hughes to help her get transferred to work in a Job Centre in Essex. Hughes not only offers to intercede, but tells her he can find a couple of tenants for her flat while she's moving.

A Pakistani woman explains in fractured English that she wants to be rehoused because she has noisy neighbours. Hughes deftly discovers that she is suffering from depression, asks which Day Centre she attends, and says that, if she can produce letters from her doctor, psychiatric nurse and head of the Centre, he will ask the council to see if they can find her another flat. Next is a mother who moved house eight months ago and has been unable to find her daughter a school place: he promises to send her a full list of all the vacancies at all the schools in the area, both inside and outside the borough. She is followed by an intensely ambitious Nigerian couple upset that their son has been turned down by London Nautical School, where his elder brothers had done well. Hughes offers to find out how close he came to being accepted and to accompany them to the appeal hearing.

Finally, a woman of about sixty and a leggy, glamorous model of about thirty walk in. It turns out they are the mother and girlfriend of one of the men who smashed their way into the Millennium Dome to try to steal the world's biggest diamond. They're upset that he's being held as a high-security Category A prisoner. The prison authorities had even stopped him telephoning his dying grandfather. They are worldly enough to realize that the MP can't get him released ('I mean, I know he's been a naughty boy, Simon,' says his mother), but can the MP do anything to get him recategorized in prison?

The session had been scheduled to run from nine in the morning to twelve noon. The catalogue of misfortune finally ends after 1.30. In the days when Hughes held his advice sessions in the evenings, they often wouldn't end until 1.30 or later the next morning. It has been a pretty normal sort of session for March. No one had broken down in tears as sometimes happens, there was nothing like the young man in another constituency whose father and uncle had killed themselves, who had attempted suicide himself, who the council had decided wasn't a priority case for housing and who was living in the back of an old car. The MP had spent hours making him repeat, 'I am a significant person.'

Hughes, who decided he was a Liberal at fifteen, has one of the

heaviest case-loads of any MP. He has many of the characteristics of
the nobler clergy, having deliberately chosen to live in the inner city
and working as a youth leader before becoming an MP. He admits
that 'Faith principles give a much more coherent starting point than
any political party.' None of the problems which has been brought to
him this morning is really a political one, it is just that the politician
(in other places or other times it might have been the parish priest) is
the advocate of last resort.

This sort of approach to politics – small scale, local and personal –
is a Liberal Democrat speciality. It has obvious attractions to any
organization which has seen the dangers of complacency for other
parties. It is blindingly clear why the notion of MP as hired gun
appeals to those who struggled – and failed – to find their way through
the bureaucracy that bears down on the lives of the poor. It is equally
obvious why it appeals to someone like Simon Hughes, who once
contemplated a career in the Church. Whether behaving like some
unlicensed superior Citizens' Advice Bureau, in areas where the MP
has no strict competence, is the best use of a legislator is a different
question.

There is another approach. Eric Forth, an Elvis Presley fan who
represents the commuter heaven of Bromley, personifies it. A lean
Glaswegian once described as not having L-O-V-E and H-A-T-E
tattooed on his knuckles 'because he was looking for something
ruder',[12] Forth should have been arrested years ago for offences against
style. (Today he is wearing a violently tailored pinstripe suit, a blue
shirt with a white collar, an extraordinary scarlet and yellow tie, a
gold watch chain and assorted costume jewellery.) He is one of the
biggest bruisers in the House of Commons, a reputation earned by a
one-man guerrilla campaign to ambush pieces of legislation he does
not like, his weapon being an encyclopaedic knowledge of the details
of parliamentary procedure. But he also has a bitterly perceptive view
of the degree to which politicians are the authors of their own
misfortunes. 'The truth is, MPs have collaborated in this idea of
themselves as local councillors. I used to hold surgeries. Did them for
years in my old constituency and concluded they were a complete
waste of time, quite apart from the danger of women walking in and
taking all their clothes off or something. Now, I advertise a "surgery

hotline", with the number of my office in the House of Commons. Someone rings and says, "I want to speak to my MP," and I say, "You're speaking to him," and if I haven't sorted out their problem in fifteen minutes, I promise them a home visit. I'd be amazed if I did more than three or four home visits in a year.' There speaks a man who is either remarkably successful or represents a safe Tory seat.

It is probably true that many of the problems with which MPs deal ought to be someone else's responsibility, but then, it is because they have nowhere else to turn that constituents sit for hours in pubs and community centres on Saturday mornings, waiting to pour out their woes to a sympathetic ear. Many are lost causes, the majority being problems outside the MP's competence, some are barking mad (several MPs have noticed that the volume of mail they receive in green ink rises and falls with the phases of the moon, reaching its peak when the moon is full). But to abandon constituency surgeries altogether requires the sort of confidence that comes only from twenty years at Westminster, for it is noticeable that MPs are at their most active on behalf of their constituents during their first term in the House of Commons.

There are many good arguments for MPs holding surgeries. They force politicians into contact with the real and surreal things that happen to all of us. (One of the Independent MP Martin Bell's earliest constituency surgeries brought an elderly couple seeking advice about damage caused by a falling cow landing on the roof of their car.) It is the one time when the pieties uttered about being 'servants of the people' can acquire true force: the Labour MP Tom Swain was once found smiling at a note of a telephone message from a constituent. It read 'Please ring re broken grate.'[13] Enforced contact with the public at such sessions also gives an understanding of how well or badly legislation is working and how government agencies are treating the citizen. When Tristan Garel-Jones retired from the House of Commons, the one and only thing he missed about politics was the constituency work, because 'If you're ever tempted to be frivolous about homelessness or racial discrimination or something, then having met a victim or two in your constituency makes you count to one hundred before opening your mouth.' And constituency surgeries provide one of the very few opportunities for a politician to achieve something: at least, at the end of their careers, they can look back and see that they sorted out some genuine problems.

The cry 'Well, I'm going to see my MP about this,' and the implied threat to the obstructive bureaucrat that the politician will descend upon them, like some demon headmaster, gives comfort both to the aggrieved elector and to the elected. Sometimes it works: a letter on House of Commons notepaper, with the portcullis device, still carries the resonance to make jobsworths justify themselves. But politicians cannot perform like some good fairy in a pantomime. Nor should they: the rules for the allocation of public housing, education or health ought to be drawn up fairly, rather than depend upon who can beg, borrow or steal the most impressive megaphone. Often, the only comfort the politician can offer is a shoulder to cry upon. There is an additional complication, in that so much of the work of the state has been removed from the civil service, which was at least accountable to ministers, and transferred to 'agencies': in such cases, all the MP can do is to write to the boss to ask that the case be dealt with properly. But the example of the Child Support Agency, the organization set up to force absent fathers to pay for the upkeep of their children, suggests they might have spent their time better. Once the Agency had been established, MPs suddenly found their surgeries flooded with angry or distraught fathers, upset at the heavy-handed way unelected administrators were asking them for money. The problem was not with the principle of child support, upon which parliament largely agreed. It was that the legislation it passed was so badly written, so full of holes, that mistakes, inefficiencies and injustices were inevitable. If MPs had spent more time scrutinizing the bill they'd have had to spend a lot less time trying to clear up the mess afterwards.

But constituency work has one other, less tangible, yet significant benefit. John Butcher, a junior trade minister in the 1980s, was once at a meeting with his European counterparts in Brussels. As the gathering broke up on a Friday night, his French counterpart was chauffeured away to spend the weekend at her apartment in central Paris. Butcher had to travel to Coventry, where, the next morning, he would have to explain to a woman at the end of her tether why he had failed to get her a new council house. 'Two-thirds of my constituency complaints were nonsense or hopeless, from people who were beyond help, deluded or dimwitted. But the remaining one-third were people with genuine grievances or problems, and they *really needed* my help.' And here in his constituency the politician who likes to believe he is the master of his own destiny can be harangued by a man in a string vest with third-degree halitosis, saying 'YOU'RE MY MP,' as if he owns him. Both recognize that, in a sense, he does.

The politician's concern is not, of course, entirely disinterested. In a constituency of, say, 70,000 voters, there may be 20,000 households. At election time there are about four hours in the working day when it is reasonable, and possibly worth while, to call on the inhabitants of most of those houses: the rest of the day, they will be asleep, at work, having breakfast or supper, bathing the children or getting ready for bed. Let us assume that the politician is skilful enough to give the impression of having listened to their problems, and has enough charisma to make an impression within the space of two and a half minutes. He can, therefore, canvass perhaps twenty-four houses in one hour, or one hundred a day. In the three weeks of the election campaign, the best the candidate could hope to achieve – assuming no loonies, no time-wasters, no invitations for cups of tea, no time spent walking from neighbourhood to neighbourhood – would be to visit perhaps one in twenty of the households in the constituency. Holding advice sessions is one way of getting the message out that the MP is working away for his constituents.

It is also a way of making contact with people in the constituency who are not political associates. The darkest secret is that some MPs simply cannot stand the people they rely upon to get them elected. One spoke frankly about his activists. 'They all have an attitude problem. They hate the world. They hate each other. By the time you finish the selection process, you've already got a good section of the local party, who supported the other candidates, thinking you're useless. Pretty soon, most of them end up hating you. That's how it is: the MP's there to be hated. And the longer you're in parliament, the more people you upset, so they hate you more. The fact is, they're barmy. Who in their right mind would pound the pavements handing out leaflets?'

The answer to this question is, fewer and fewer of us. Joining a political party is only for very unusual people. Ring the Conservative party headquarters to ask 'What's the latest fiction on the total number of your members?', and a cheerful young woman with a posh voice will laugh and tell you that 'The current figure is about 330,000.' In Camilla's mother's day, the answer would have been 'Over a million.' In her grandmother's era the figure would have been even higher. At one point in the 1950s, when membership was seen as a real asset to the ambitious business person, the party claimed over 3 million. The Young Conservatives, with 150,000 members, boasted that they were 'the largest political youth movement in the free world'. For decades, the Labour party maintained totally bogus membership figures, by including members of trades unions. In terms of individual member-ship, in the early 1950s, it too could claim to have a million adherents, a figure which gently declined through the later 1950s and 1960s and went into freefall with the Callaghan government, the Winter of Discontent, and the rise of Margaret Thatcher.

It is hard to escape the feeling that, whatever boasts the parties may make about their membership, the leadership really thinks of them as nothing but a nuisance. At the highest levels, indifference to their feelings is nothing new. 'I have the greatest respect for the Conserva-tive Party Conference,' said Arthur Balfour in 1909, 'but I would no more consult it on a matter of high policy than I would my valet.'[14] What had changed by the end of the century was that it had become received wisdom that elections could be won by effectively managed, centrally controlled campaigns. These campaigns required money and organization rather than mass membership. Why should either of the big parties waste time and energy recruiting members when they needed only to touch a Hong Kong or Indian business tycoon, a Greek shipping magnate or a Formula One racing boss for a million?

The time that the size of the membership really seems to matter to leaders is when they are in opposition and seeking endorsement. Most recent big-time politicians have made fools of themselves by promising to arrest this decline in membership. When William Hague inherited the Conservative party, in the aftermath of the 1997 election defeat, he pledged himself to 'double the size of the party within two years', with the slogan 'a million for the millennium'. Not only was the maths dodgy (one million would have meant nearly trebling the membership), so was the prediction. By the time the two years had passed, membership had actually fallen, as older Conservatives died and could not be replaced. The party did its best to hide the truth, but, in the opinion of those who had studied membership closely, the party was in worse shape than at any time since the First World War. Labour were jubilant. Memories are short in politics, but had anyone chosen to carp, they might also have reminded Tony Blair that, in his first party conference speech as leader, in 1994, he had committed himself to 'the creation of a genuine mass membership party', which his deputy, John Prescott, translated into 'Let's start talking and stop implementing this membership drive.' The audience got the point anyway, and, as supporters recognized that Blair needed an increase in membership in order to validate the changes he was making to the party, subscriptions started to rise. Once the party had won power, membership started to sink again. It is hard to resist the feeling that, once they were in government, the leaders felt they had other things to worry about.

Perhaps the mass-membership party is dead in an age of the citizen-as-consumer. There do seem to be moments when a political organization appears to meet a need. In the early 1980s the Social Democratic party emerged from nowhere to sign up over 50,000 members, until it fell apart. With the longer-established parties, the figures do suggest that more people will join if they believe there is a realistic chance of their party wielding power. That would be another explanation for why Labour party membership rose steadily through the 1990s, peaked after the 1997 victory, and then began to drop. Having reached 400,000 before the 1997 election, by the 2001 vote for the second Labour term the total had fallen to 310,000, and the following year to 280,000. (At the same time, in early 2002, the Liberal Democrats were claiming 76,000 members.) The total membership of the three main national parties was, therefore, under 700,000 people. At the same time, English Heritage had 400,000 members, the Royal Society for the Protection of Birds over 1 million and the National Trust nearly 3 million. It is not that people have lost their political instincts so much as that they do not find expression through conventional party politics.

British political parties have managed the remarkable achievement of modernizing in such a way that joining them seems a dated thing to do. As society has become more atomized, individuals have redirected their energies into campaigns which have much more narrowly focused ambitions than a generalized prospectus for the salvation of the broader community in which they live. At the time of the 2001 General Election, Amnesty International and Greenpeace between them had more members than any of the political parties. This disengagement from old-fashioned party politics was most acute among the young, whom the Labour party freely admitted it was failing to attract. The consequence is that those people who do belong to political parties are, by definition, unusual. This might not matter very much if their activities were confined to pounding the pavement at election-time. But their power goes wider. As we have seen, they choose the candidate who will try to get elected for the constituency. Effectively, therefore, they have picked every single member of the House of Commons. Under the influence of a belief in 'party demo-cracy', the members are also allowed a significant, sometimes decisive, voice in who will lead the party, thereby determining who will become Prime Minister. Unusual they may be. Unimportant they are not.

The lucky politician will rub along happily with his local members: after all, they all belong to the same party. But the spectre of dislike or even deselection means that many MPs are at least a little bit frightened of their local party. 'The rule of thumb', one of them told me, 'is that, at any one time, one in three of them is out to get you. It may be because they never thought you were much good in the first place. It may be something as earth-shattering as the fact that you failed to turn up to their Pea and Pie supper. And because we have this reselection pantomime, every local butcher or solicitor gets his day in the sun when they have to be listened to.' And, as every political party covers a spectrum of views, there is a good chance that at some point or other the politician is going to find that the members expect a commitment – it may be on anything from relations with the rest of Europe to capital punishment – that cannot be given. The politician then relies upon the argument most elegantly put by Edmund Burke in a speech to the voters of Bristol over 200 years ago.

'Parliament is not a *congress* of ambassadors from different and hostile interests,' he told them, 'but . . . a deliberative assembly of *one* nation, with *one* interest, that of the whole . . . You choose a member indeed; but when you have chosen him, he is not a member of Bristol, but he is a member of *parliament*.'[15] Under this classic formulation, the MP is elected not merely to make the prejudices of his electors law, but to sit as their representative, using personal judgement to decide how to vote on the issues of the day, loyal to something larger and more intangible.

The fortunate ones will be pretty much left in peace by the local party. All will be expected to show their faces at fund-raising events, social occasions and annual dinners. Here they may be able to get away with telling a few anecdotes about their time at Westminster, retail a bit of gossip, make a joke or two at the Opposition's expense, and then escape into the night. Faced with their activists, more sensitive souls despair. George Walden, Conservative MP for Buckingham for thirteen years through the 1980s and 1990s, found that the experience turned his stomach. What the members wanted was not originality but platitudes about Britain 'standing tall in the world'. 'If you want your audience to listen to what you have to say,' he decided, 'you can only say what has been said already. They do not want new music, they want music they know. Stray one note off the score and they go instantly deaf on you. So just close your ears to the abjectness of what you are saying, spit it out and be done.'[16]

And here is the final objection to the fact that politics has become so much the property of a small clique. It kills the language. The banality of sentiment, the endless repetition of flat phrases from which all meaning was wrung out years ago, is the sea in which the activists swim. The speaker churns out the familiar words because he or she believes that everyone understands them. They seem, like coins which have passed through a thousand pockets, to have an agreed value. The truth is that they have a sheen, but no significance. George Orwell noticed it sixty years ago, when discussing the language of politicians in wartime.

When one watches some tired hack on the platform mechanically repeating the familiar phrases – *bestial atrocities, iron heel, bloodstained tyranny, free peoples of the world, stand shoulder to shoulder* – one often has a curious feeling that one is not watching a live human being but some kind of dummy . . . A speaker who uses that kind of phraseology has gone some distance towards turning himself into a machine. The appropriate noises are coming out of his larynx, but his brain is not involved as it would be if he was choosing the words for himself.[17]

Perhaps the most remarkable aspect of Orwell's observation is not that it is so accurate, but that the identical empty clichés have proved so durable. When terrorists flew hijacked aircraft into the World Trade Center and the Pentagon, the British Prime Minister stuck his hand in the bran-tub of banalities and came out with precisely the same phrases ('free peoples of the world', 'stand shoulder to shoulder' and so on). Clichés are useful because they lack ambiguity. But Orwell concluded that 'Political language – and with variations this is true of all political parties from Conservatives to Anarchists – is designed to make lies sound truthful and murder respectable, and to give the appearance of solidity to pure wind.'[18]

The place to listen to this wind, and for the inquiring anthropologist to observe *en masse* the unusual beings who join political parties, is the annual conference. These gatherings – part revivalist gospel meeting, part boozy party, part ineffably tedious evening class – have taken place in end-of-season holiday resorts for generations. What their purpose was depended upon who you were and where you stood in the party hierarchy. For Conservatives of almost all stations they have been occasions for long dresses, costume jewellery, hair lacquer and gins-and-tonic, where the local MP entertained his loyal workers and the Leader graced the constituency agents' ball. For the zealots in the Labour party, they were a means of trying to keep the leadership true to the principles of socialism. For the Labour leadership, they were a way of trying to convince the membership that they had not betrayed the party's principles in the hope of getting elected or retaining office. Throughout the 1950s there were regular, titanic clashes between left and right which seemed to be tussles for the very soul of the party. For Liberals and Liberal Democrats, despite David Steel's extraordinary instruction to 'Go back to your constituencies and prepare for government' in 1981 (at the next election the party returned precisely seventeen MPs to Westminster), conference has been a place to wonder whimsically about what would happen if they ruled the world and everyone knitted their own muesli. Until very recently, the casual visitor felt out of place at all of them.

It is only those outside the conference halls who made those inside seem balanced. Throughout the 1990s, a thin Mancunian could be found standing on the pavement outside the conference hall. He used to travel from Blackpool to Bournemouth to Brighton accompanied by a giant expanding bicycle, which eventually reached a length of almost twenty feet and served as a mobile billboard. He used it to hang a placard proclaiming that 'SMOKING KILLS 2,000 BRITONS EVERY WEEK'. No one paid him much attention as they strode purposefully into the conference hall, yet day after day, rain, shine and howling gale, he stood on the pavement. I once asked him where he lived and he told me, 'In dustbin liners.' For nine years his registered address was 'The Doorstep, the Daily Mirror', where he had taken up residence after Robert Maxwell reneged on a promise to ban tobacco advertising in his papers. He lived, he told me, on a diet of baked beans and onions. By the autumn of 2000, now greying at the temples, but still in his old blue anorak and open-toed sandals, he had abandoned the bicycle for a guitar. Anyone who showed the slightest hesitation was treated to three verses about how evil the Labour party had been to exempt Formula One racing from the ban on tobacco advertising. But he is wasting his time if he thinks that lobbying the party conference will make much difference to party policy.

The truth is, the annual party conferences are empty vessels. The Conservatives have at least had the honesty to admit for decades that their gatherings have no power at all to make policy. You have only to sit through one thundering ovation for a call to bring back the birch or the rope and to castrate sex offenders, to watch the thrilled, gleeful reception which greets such speakers, and to note the polite indifference of the party leadership to realize that the whole thing is a sort of ideological dumbshow. As long ago as 1949, Sir David Maxwell Fyfe, the man given the job of reforming the party organization, wrote, in tones oddly reminiscent of European totalitarianism, 'The Leader is served by the party's various policy committees, and these in their turn are influenced by the views of the party as revealed in the various resolutions at the party conference . . . But endorsements and pronouncements are the prerogative and responsibility of the Leader.'[19] It is worthy of Mussolini. What a contrast with the Labour party, which has always protested its 'democratic' credentials! Clement Attlee explained the principle. 'The Labour Party conference lays down the policy of the party, and issues instructions which must be carried out by the Executive, the affiliated organisations and its representatives in Parliament and on local authorities.'[20] Because it had such a crucial role in determining policy, the annual conference produced reverberations which shook Blackpool, Margate, Scarborough or wherever the gathering was taking place. It was at conference that Aneurin Bevan produced his 'The language of priorities is the religion of socialism' (Blackpool, 1949) and his two most scathing comments on attempts to commit the country to unilateral nuclear disarmament, 'You call that statesmanship? I call it an emotional spasm' and 'If you carry this resolution, you will send Britain's Foreign Secretary naked into the conference chamber' (both at Brighton in 1957). His rival in the party, Hugh Gaitskell, made his commitment to 'fight, fight and fight again to save the party we love' at Scarborough in 1960.

But, as part of the process of making the party electable, in 1997 the vital task of determining policy, and thereby deciding what the party stood for, was taken away from the National Executive chosen by conference and given to a so-called Policy Forum. At which point, Labour conferences became as empty of policymaking importance as Conservative ones have almost always been. It is not that the conferences have no value nowadays. It is just that their value has changed. They still give activists a chance to sit up arguing and drinking until four in the morning. They are a way of assessing the party's *Zeitgeist*. But nothing the delegates say will make the blindest bit of difference if the leadership doesn't agree.

For the annual gatherings of all the major parties have been turned from political into commercial events. At a characteristic conference of the party in power, fewer than one in ten of the 20,000 attending may be there as party delegates. The remaining 18,000 are lobbyists, advertisers, business people, reporters, technicians and general hangers-on. The great days of important debate are long gone. Of the 2001 Labour conference, party officials were privately frank. 'It's about making some money,' one said. What started out not many years ago as a series of trestle tables laid out in the corridors around the conference hall, trying to drum up support to fight world poverty, injustice or destruction of the environment, has now become a series of advertising arcades, paid for by companies selling junk food, importing nuclear waste or selling arms. For £3,500 MegaGlobal Inc. could buy a table at a dinner to be addressed by the Leader, for £4,000 they could have their name on the videoscreen showing the Leader's speech, for £10,000 they could sponsor a question-and-answer session with the Education Secretary. At the 2001 conference, the hamburger chain McDonald's splashed out £15,000 sponsoring a reception, to be attended by the Leader, celebrating a hundred years of 'socialist' conferences. The taxpayer was left to pick up the cost of policing this vital part of the democratic process.

The Leader's Speech is designed by the party managers as the highpoint of the conference. He has to galvanize his troops, to persuade them that he knows where he is going, that their unpaid effort is worth while, that the party has more giants to slay. The Leader is the embodiment of the party, his face the one on the posters they will put up in their front windows and shove through a thousand letterboxes. The Leader is the flesh-and-blood proof that in a mass-media age politics is, finally, about personalities. The great lie about the Speech is that it is about party policy. It is not. Certainly, it has to play adequately within the conference hall. But, as long as he isn't incoherently drunk or paralysed by stage fright, the audience will all leap to their feet at the end and applaud ecstatically.

A full hour before the speech is due to be delivered, party delegates are queuing outside the hall for a good seat. At Labour conferences the public address system is usually playing some ancient rock number like 'Let's work together'. Both parties once used the final afternoon to present awards to stalwarts who had spent the best years of their lives in the service of the party. When it reinvented itself in the 1990s the Labour party relegated this procession of arthritic men and women to a time of day when it was less likely to be broadcast to the nation. The Conservatives, however, continued to hand out huge silver cups to constituency associations before the Leader's Speech, harking back to an earlier age. One or two other items of business also survive. The conference chairman – usually a prosperous businessman with knife-edge creases in his suit – must be thanked. This involves the recitation of his steady rise from pork-pie sales rep to managing director of a chain of motorway service stations. The chairman belies his record of sound judgement with a reply in which he makes the previous few days sound as if they have been a series of discussions between Socrates and his disciples. Phrases such as 'fascinating debate' and 'stimulating discussion' fall from his lips, suggesting that he has spent the last few days somewhere else. Then there is an appeal for money, sometimes carried out by a comedian whose gift for fantasy included in the last conference before the party's comprehensive humiliation in the 2001 election the claim that 'We're on the eve of something magical here.'

At Tory rallies in the Thatcher era, stewards thoughtfully left a Red Ensign or Union Flag on each seat for the delegates to wave when, swept up in a tide of uncontrollable enthusiasm for the Leader, they could express themselves only by jumping to their feet, repeatedly singing the first verse of 'Land of Hope and Glory', and swooning for a smile. In the years after the disaster of 1997, the flags gradually disappeared, along with the self-confidence. Today only a handful of representatives have flags to wave, and they tend to be the sort of people who look as if they spend the rest of the year dressed up as pearly kings and queens. Besides, much of the audience appear to need mechanical assistance to get to their feet.

Half an hour before the Leader is due to speak, there is not one empty seat in the place, and aisles and sides are packed too. The ministerial, or shadow ministerial, team are lined up like school-children in rank after rank, usually slightly off to one side, a bridge between the Leader and his party. The ambitious conceal any shame they may feel at being there simply to provide approving cutaway shots for the television crews. Had they had their microphones better placed at one recent Labour conference, the television producers would have caught one senior minister beginning a whispered chorus of 'The wheels on the bus go round and round, round and round, round and round,' before getting a whispered 'shush' from colleagues.

The lights are dimmed, a video appears on the giant screens. It is filled with images of a grateful nation and the Leader looking purposeful, statesmanlike, benevolent. Graphics roll, reciting the party's achievements or promises. Finally, the lights come up again and, to a battery of flashing cameras, the Leader appears. Mrs Leader and acolytes may follow. The Leader basks in the orchestrated applause and waves to the audience. He looks as if he is pleased by the enthusiasm. But he knows he deserves it: the key impression the image-makers want to convey is self-confidence.

Now the speech begins. There will be jokes. Some of them may even be funny. There will be recitations of achievements. There will be ringing declarations of ambition. There will be denunciations of opponents. There may be a soaring passage which does not appear in the printed version given to the press two minutes before the speech began – television and newspapers will later report that this was where the Leader 'spoke from the heart', implying that, in this speech which has been weeks in preparation, the key piece of oratory hadn't been thought about until the Leader got to his feet.

Oratory is not the right word. Successful speakers at party conferences have largely discarded the rousing vision, the cloudy imagery and the rhetorical resonance of even twenty years ago: they do not suit the small screen. Television is a medium of impressions and more intimate tone. So the speech is an awkward hybrid, part talk, part declamation. It is a tottering tower built upon false opposites, the world reduced to simple, binary choices. The Leader is a man of the people, for the many not the few, for freedom not tyranny, for justice not injustice, for wealth not poverty, for the future not the past, for full stomachs not empty ones. On and on it goes. It is not in Fidel Castro's league, where harangues could last seven or eight hours. But it can sometimes seem that way, fifty minutes of hortatory moralism in which clichés collide with each other, the best so seductive that even the most uninvolved might come to believe that the world really is so easily improved. At the end, however indifferent the performance, the audience will rise to their feet, clap and cheer and smile. In the euphoria which now overtakes the conference, the Leader's Wife appears again. She has to be well turned out, but in an unostentatious style. She may, like Cherie Blair, be a successful person in her own right, but, for now, she is there only to look adoring, happy and inspired, afternoon arm-candy. The rest of the platform party will be on their feet, applauding as if the Leader has just come down from the mountaintop with news that war and hunger will be banished from the world and all those present will share next week's rollover lottery jackpot. The Leader and his Wife will wave to the crowd, kiss each other affectionately, occasionally spotting a non-existent friend in the euphoric crowd below them. They will appear to point to the person, as if saying, 'Great! So you're one of the Chosen People, too!'

After a couple of minutes smiling and waving they may then leave the platform to stroll among the delegates, who show no sign of flagging in their enthusiasm, despite sore hands, the thunderous din and the sheer pointlessness of continued handclapping. The Leader and his Wife clutch outstretched hands and smile endless smiles. Television and press photographers now deploy shoulders and elbows to maximum effect, desperate for the shot which will show best the people trying to touch the hem of the Leader's coat: it is not wise to be weak, old or infirm in the scrum which rolls around him. Finally, reluctantly escaping the roiling sea of adoring admirers, the Leader will reach a door and a handful of heavies will block the access of anyone who wants to follow. It all looks ecstatic, purposeful and energetic. And every bit of it is a sham.

The whole thing has been planned, down to the last detail. The speech is not written by the Leader but by a team which may run into dozens. It has been rehearsed and rehearsed and, if the rehearsal isn't enough, it's scrolling through on a transparent 'sincerity machine'. The Leader's closest aides are there in the hall to lead the applause. Even the opening wave to the crowd and the spontaneous plunge into the devoted masses have been walked through the previous night in a closed conference hall. The minimum length of the 'spontaneous' standing ovation was decided before the speech began, because, if there are rivals for the leadership who have spoken earlier, there must be no suggestion of waning popularity: at the Labour conference in September 2000 both Gordon Brown and Tony Blair received standing ovations which lasted precisely four minutes and twenty-nine seconds.

6. Busy Doing Nothing

How are we to decide whether the man or woman we send to parliament is earning their keep? Most of their valuable work for constituents will go unreported and unnoticed by anyone except those who benefit. Newspapers across the land carry reports week after week of what the local MP has said or done. These are, though, not quite what they seem, and are often based upon press releases the politician may not even have seen. Even letters to the editor may have been drafted by party headquarters, with spaces left blank for the MP's secretary or researcher to fill in the name of the constituency. As for reports of what the politician has said, these really ought to carry health warnings. Any news release which says, 'John Brown condemned the government and said that he would fight to his last breath for extra money for his constituents,' without saying quite precisely where and when he said it, probably means he said it in the bath.

More troublesome local newspapers may set out to check up on their member of parliament by finding out how often they have voted in the House of Commons. But voting records merely show that an MP was present when the House held a division: they may just have dashed out from their office when the bell sounded. The electronic version of Hansard makes it possible to discover whether an MP has spoken in a debate, or been struck by the terror which reduced Edward Gibbon to twelve years of silence. But, without much closer investigation, it is impossible to distinguish between the well-researched, thoughtful speech and the cheap, point-scoring jibe. Perhaps the MP claims to have submitted a record number of written questions. But they may all have been written on the same half-dozen days of the year. Standing up and asking questions may merely indicate they've been lucky in a ballot. Perhaps the politician claims to be busy sitting on a select committee, 'scrutinizing government policy'. But attendance there is no pointer to their having had anything useful to say, and they may anyway have left after half an hour to attend to 'constituency business'.

And then there is the Early Day Motion. This can be confidently tabled by any MP in the certain knowledge that it will never be debated in the House of Commons. The number can run to thousands in each session of parliament. Many attempt to draw attention to serious issues like slavery in north Africa, or the trade in endangered species. Others are preposterous. In the 2001–2 session the House of Commons was invited to congratulate Peterhead Academy on winning the Scottish heat of the 2002 Rock Challenge, to applaud the proprietors of the White Horse Hotel in Strichen, Aberdeenshire, on being named UK Vegetarian Food Pub of the Year, to agree that much modern art is 'pretentious, self-indulgent, craftless tat', to express 'its great sadness at the death of Marjan, the Kabul Zoo Lion', to view with concern the sacking of Mike 'The Mouth' Elliot by Century Radio, to deplore the closure of the Wrexham Lager Beer Company, to congratulate the organizers of the Kent Show, Aberavon rugby club and Arsenal, Fraserburgh, Birmingham City, Partick Thistle, Queen of the South, Yeovil Town and Luton Town football clubs, to admire Young's Brewery for providing the only draught beer permanently available in the Strangers' Bar, to applaud Mr Creemy for winning a silver medal at the national ice-cream championships, to condemn the sale of Putney Post Office, to criticize a new biography of James Watt, to praise compost heaps, a monument to carthorses in Liverpool and the dog which won the Cruft's championship, to salute the Old Smithy Tea Room in South Shields and Rachel's Dairy in Ceredigion and to 'lighten up and tune in' to a forthcoming gig by Arthur Lee, founder of the American rock band Love. All were prepared, printed and set out on the parliamentary website, at public expense.

There is nothing intrinsically wrong with elected politicians spending their time dreaming up inane causes for others to endorse. But it does tend to raise some questions about what an MP is really for. Jobs which are advertised in the newspapers carry a clear idea of what is involved. Gardeners tend gardens, car mechanics fix cars, finance directors direct finance. But one elected politician after another has remarked that there is no job description for an MP. Leaving aside the constituency work, which most consider important, what are they to use parliament for? The ambitious politician (and none of them is without ambition) can decide that, since it is usually governments which make laws, the way to change the world is to get into government. If his or her party is in opposition this may involve years of unrewarded and often unrewarding toil sitting on backbench committees, a spell as dogsbody to a frontbench spokesman, followed, if they are lucky, by a call from the leadership to become a junior spokesman on something or other. Even then, the party may lose the next election, in which case the best they can hope for is to become a frontbench spokesman on something or other, and more years of carping at government policy.

It isn't necessarily all that much better for the newly elected MP of a governing party. To stand a chance of getting even the most junior of jobs, you must prove to the party managers that you can be trusted. This requires unswerving loyalty to the leader's line at all times, even if it means biting your tongue. Then, when someone somewhere high up in the government falls sick, falls from grace, or just falls out of favour there are endless hours sitting by the telephone, hoping that as someone has been bumped up into the cabinet to replace them, and their place has been taken by someone lower down the hierarchy, and so on, eventually the call will come for you to become parliamentary private secretary to the minister responsible for haddock quotas.

For all the vanity involved, no politician joins the game because they want to make the world worse. But, to make it a better place, you need power. So there are very few indeed who do not at least consider this path to the stars in the early stages of their careers. When the reality dawns upon them – that at any one time there is room for fewer than a couple of dozen around the cabinet table – they may consider the second possibility open to an MP. This is simply to try to discharge the House of Commons' job of holding the government to account, by keeping the closest of eyes on the laws it plans to impose upon the people MPs have been elected to represent. Since this will best be done by the exercise of a spiky independence, in choosing this career they will probably be cutting themselves off from the chance of a job in government. If that does not deter them, they can look forward to a worthwhile if unglamorous lifetime of service on committees, asking awkward questions or pursuing campaigns.

Their model here might be the Labour MP Tam Dalyell, forty years as MP for West Lothian/Linlithgow and never a job in government. The fact that he started his political life as a Conservative (at Cambridge, he was president of the Conservative Association) gives an early indication of his independence of mind. His brief spell as a Labour spokesman (under Michael Foot) was terminated when he took up one of his numerous crusades, this time over the British operation to recapture the Falkland Islands after their invasion by Argentina. There followed obsessional campaign after obsessional campaign – to withdraw British troops from Northern Ireland, to prove that Margaret Thatcher had lied about the sinking of the Argentine battleship, the *General Belgrano*, to prevent the creation of a Scottish parliament, to rehabilitate the Libyan dictator Colonel Gadaffy, or to prevent the 1991 Gulf War. His technique of deploying dozens of obscure questions, the answers to which might knit together in his mind into evidence of a conspiracy, was often baffling to outsiders. The secret, he said, was 'not to mind being a bore' on a subject. When he rose to speak in the House of Commons, in his appalling suits and unkempt grey hair, other MPs groaned inwardly. Dalyell, received wisdom went, was wearisome. And probably mad. But he was unembarrassable and they heard him out because they respected the fact that he could get under ministers' skins. Dalyell was successful in some of his campaigns, just bewildering in others. But he was always his own man. Of course, it probably helps if you're an Old Etonian, and a baronet, with an ancestral home in the Borders (The Binns), with peacocks on the lawn. But he wanted nothing from the party leadership, and so it had no hold over him.

Or thirdly, the new MP may just decide that the House of Commons is a pleasant enough place to pass a few years, and be content with a life of quiet indolence. Nigel Nicolson lost his position on the Conservative benches when his Bournemouth party ran out of patience with his liberal line on capital punishment and his opposition to Anthony Eden's attempt to recapture the Suez Canal in 1956. After leaving the House, it struck him that his time there had simply flown by, what with listening to debates or ministerial questions, taking part in a committee or two, entertaining visitors on the terrace by the Thames, or sitting gossiping in the Smoking Room until it was time to amble off home. And all the time constituents would start their letters with the words, 'I hesitate to trouble you when I know that you are so tremendously busy.' He decided that 'There is no place where a man can occupy himself more intensively or usefully, and no place where he can hold down his job by doing so little.'[1]

This is very much the view of parliament as some sort of gentleman's club, but it is not the impression given by most modern MPs. I have lost count of the number who have complained to me that they have no time to themselves. This non-stop activity can have pretty disastrous consequences for politicians' families (see Chapter 8), but the real difficulty, the corrosive, undermining anxiety about this life on a hamster's wheel, is that there is simply no relationship between activity and achievement. A mechanic can look at a car he has repaired, a plumber can bask in the satisfaction of an unblocked drain. With the occasional exception – a constituent rehoused, a benefit problem settled – the ordinary MP has no way of demonstrating that all this bustle in constituency and Commons has got them anywhere. In theory, we are almost at the point when we could dispense with a parliament altogether. The technology exists to make it possible for the will of the people on every subject under the sun to be expressed through direct electronic voting in referendums. Most politicians are against the idea. The arrangement would make much – but not all – of their life's work unnecessary, of course. But it is hard to resist the conclusion that their opposition is based also upon a fear of what the people of Britain might say if they were allowed a direct hand in shaping the laws of the land. Holding instant votes on issues such as whether to restore capital punishment would produce a raft of laws which the political class of the country would find objectionable. In which case, since politicians do not necessarily consider themselves there to express the views of their electors, what are they there for?

Nigel Nicolson's answer forty years ago was that parliament 'is composed of men and women professionally equipped to digest an enormous variety of facts and opinions fed to them from above and below, from Ministers and from their constituents, and no alimentary canal can be a substitute for a stomach'.[2] It would be hard to find a more concise justification for parliament's existence. One of the many hypocrisies in criticism of politicians is that the public would make a better job of it. But the truth is that most people do not like making the simple either/or choices to which all political decision-making is reduced: we recognize that life is more complicated than that.

At times of national crisis, however, the House of Commons can still appear to rise to the occasion. The three hours on Saturday morning, 3 April 1982, when it discussed the Argentinian capture of the Falkland Islands, was one such occasion. At times like these, the place can still seem to distil national anxieties and hopes. Reading the transcript of the debate, the stunned unanimity of the House of Commons is striking. But to compare such an event with the record of a truly great parliamentary occasion, such as the Norway debate in May 1940, is to realize how the House of Commons has shrivelled. Admittedly, the earlier debate took place in more momentous times: the sudden, shocking end of the Phoney War, the horrifying proof of the German capacity for lightning invasion and the first British disaster. The security of Great Britain itself was at stake, rather than the way of life of 1,800 sheep-farmers at the other end of the world, in a group of islands the Foreign Office had been anxious to get rid of for years. Margaret Thatcher, the Prime Minister, was untested in battle, and the military reputation of the Leader of the Opposition, Michael Foot, was as a protester for disarmament.

But it was not simply that charged times make for charged politics. The 1940 motion upon which MPs voted, calling for the adjournment of the House, looked innocuous enough. Neville Chamberlain opened the two-day debate an exhausted man. The British expeditionary force he had dispatched to German-occupied Norway had been deployed with scandalous lack of planning and support. It was soon forced into a humiliating retreat and withdrawal. After praising the valour of the servicemen involved, Chamberlain came to his own responsibility for the humiliation with a terrible world-weariness. 'Ministers', he said, 'must expect to be blamed for everything.' This brought forth cries of 'They missed the bus!', turning back on the Prime Minister his own complacent claim a few days before the invasion of Norway, that 'Hitler has missed the bus.' Chamberlain continued to try to explain away the catastrophe and to minimize the damage. 'We have to take account of the fact that we have suffered a certain loss of prestige, that a certain colour has been given to the false legend of German invincibility,' he said, but, he added, 'I think the implications of the Norwegian campaign have been seriously exaggerated.'[3] It was the best gloss he could put upon it, but it was feeble stuff.

Chamberlain had seriously misjudged the national mood, as the speeches which followed his lame opening showed. Labour's Clement Attlee was viperish. The Norway adventure had been distinguished by an absence of proper intelligence and a lack of organization, of energy and of resolution. 'People are saying that those mainly responsible for the conduct of affairs are men who have an almost uninterrupted career of failure . . . Norway follows Czechoslovakia and Poland. Everywhere, the story is "Too late." '[4] Later, Leopold Amery, the charismatic right-winger whom Chamberlain thought he might have been able to count upon (they were both Birmingham men, among other things), was even more brutal. He was a short man with a formidable mind, if usually an indifferent speaker. But this speech closed with words he borrowed from Oliver Cromwell. Pointing directly at the Prime Minister, Amery repeated Cromwell's words when he expelled the Long Parliament. 'You have sat too long here for any good you have been doing. Depart, I say, and let us have done with you. In the name of God, go.' The former Prime Minister, David Lloyd George, who had never liked Chamberlain, was equally devastating. 'He has appealed for sacrifice,' he said; '. . . I say solemnly that the Prime Minister should give an example of sacrifice because there is nothing which can contribute more to victory in this war than that he should sacrifice the seals of office.'[5]

The debate was one of the great events in modern parliamentary history. But, apart from the passion, the other striking aspect is how many of the contributors seemed to know what they were talking about. In the elaborate courtesy with which so much parliamentary invective is surrounded, the place seemed full of 'honourable and gallant' members, the words used to address military men (just as lawyers – despite any evidence to the contrary – are always 'honourable and learned'). The benches were packed with majors, colonels, captains, commanders, admirals and generals. They were men who spoke, therefore, with some authority on military matters. By general consent, the turning point in the debate had been a blustery contribution from an admiral of the fleet.

Sir Roger Keyes had represented North Portsmouth for six years. A spare figure with widely spaced eyes, dark hair parted high on his right temple, and overlarge ears, the man was something of a legend. Churchill described him as 'sprung from a long line who had fought for king and country in all the wars that Britain ever waged',[6] and the admiral could trace his forebears back as far as an ancestor who had served King John in 1203. Born on the North-west Frontier, Keyes had gone to sea as a midshipman on a frigate equipped with sails. Before he was thirty, while serving in China and supported by only thirty-two sailors, he had captured a fort which Russian and German generals, backed by up to 4,000 men, had thought impregnable. During the First World War he had commanded submarines, tried to force the Dardanelles, and, in what was regarded as the most audacious naval operation of its day, raided Zeebrugge. More than any other figure alive, he was held to embody the spirit of Horatio Nelson. Before the Norway disaster, Keyes had argued fiercely – and ineffectively – for the heavier naval involvement which might have made the operation a success. To prove his faith, although nearly sixty-seven when war broke out, he had begged to be put in command of the raid himself.

The admiral – GCB, KCB, KCVO, CB, CMG, CVO, MVO, DSO, DCL, LLD; Grand Cordon, Order of Leopold; Grand Officer of the Legion of Honour; Croix de Guerre (both French and Belgian) – had dressed carefully that morning. He arrived in the House of Commons in the full uniform of an admiral of the fleet. There was much gold braid. There were six rows of medals. And there was a steaming temper.

When Colonel Josiah Wedgwood claimed that the British navy could have protected the Norway force had it not run away to the far end of the Mediterranean to escape bombing, the admiral boiled over. 'That is a damned insult,' he roared. The Royal Navy, known as 'the silent service', had endured enough. The admiral was determined to have his say, 'because I wish to speak for some officers and men of the fighting, sea-going navy who are very unhappy'.[7] The Norway campaign was 'a shocking story of ineptitude, which I assure the House should never have been allowed to happen'. Keyes did not blame his friend, the First Lord of the Admiralty (Winston Churchill). In fact he admired Churchill and was 'longing to see proper use made of his great abilities'. For that to be possible, by implication, Chamberlain had to go.

Winston Churchill himself made a dignified speech in which he pointed out that the Prime Minister 'thought he had some friends. He certainly had a good many when things were going well.'[8] But it was hopeless. A Conservative majority of 249 was reduced to a mere 81. Chamberlain was mortally wounded. Within two days, Churchill had become Prime Minister.

Many who heard and saw the admiral's speech agreed that it was the central point in the debate, the moment at which party loyalty dissolved. In strictly political terms, Sir Roger's intervention was much less effective than that of many others: he did not make a particularly telling case, and deployed none of the rhetoric or studied aggression of many other contributors. His influence came not from what he said so much as what he represented. When an admiral of the fleet stands up in the House of Commons and speaks because, he says, he has been asked to do so by his brother officers, he is bound to be listened to. There is scarcely a figure in the contemporary House of Commons who could expect to be taken seriously if he or she claimed to speak with authority for the navy, or for most communities of interest. It is the inevitable consequence of the emergence of a professional political class. Indeed, it sometimes seems that in the modern House of Commons the less someone knows about a subject, the more likely they are to be called to speak on it. Contemporary politicians doubtless know many more of their constituents than their predecessors did. They certainly spend much more time on constituency affairs. But most do not speak as members of any section of society apart from their own party.

The life of a backbench MP has never been what you might call glamorous. Within a decade of the Norway debate – and in the midst of one of the most creative governments of the twentieth century – Christopher Hollis MP was wondering why anyone would want a parliamentary life.

The member of Parliament is at the beck and call of all men day after day from eight o'clock in the morning until twelve o'clock at night. The problems pour in upon him thick and fast without respite and from all directions. He has to give so many decisions that he can never properly give his mind to anything. He has to sacrifice his home life, his recreations and even that cultural background from which we may presume his political convictions derived, and without refreshment all political convictions must become arid and tasteless and mechanically repetitive.

Hollis, a Conservative, had followed precisely the same career trajectory as Boris Johnson was to take later – Eton, Brackenbury scholar at Balliol, president of the Union – and might therefore have at least been expected to enjoy the business of debate. But this, too, was tiresome.

In Parliament he finds an unhealthy life full of temptations, all the frustration of endless hours of bobbing up and down to catch the Speaker's eye in order in the end to mumble for a quarter of an hour to empty benches. Supposing that he has something to say, there could not well be any place where the saying of it is less likely to have effect than in the House of Commons. On the wireless he can reach millions, in the newspapers hundreds of thousands, where in the House of Commons he reaches perhaps twenty of whom the majority probably are not listening. He has to play his part in the party game, much of which the keenest of politicians must with all the will in the world often feel to be a dreary and childish farce.[9]

That was in 1949. Since then, things have got worse. The flaw in Nigel Nicolson's argument that the House of Commons acts as a national 'stomach', rather than as a simple tube which runs straight from the mouth to the backside, supposes that the House of Commons is made up of hundreds of individuals who exercise their judgement independently. It is not. The picture of a parliament made up of people of autonomous mind, deciding what was best for the nation on the basis of personal judgement, belongs in the middle of the nineteenth century.

As we have seen, before then most MPs were financially independent and at least partly independent of party. Some of them had no opposition at all in their constituencies. Many had no greater ambition than to sit in the House of Commons. Governments were formed when interests merged, often nudged along by the wishes of the king or queen. But, from Gladstone's first government onwards, political life has become increasingly the fiefdom of big party organizations. Specifically, the development of the Labour party put an end to the old habits: it was made up of collectivists who ran for election representing a party which promised to act collectively to bring collective change to society. The party had a constitution in which members made policy at the annual conference, and it expected its representatives in parliament to implement that policy. It believed in a 'mandate' – governments were elected to carry out pledges made during election campaigns. The Conservative party may never have been as tightly controlled. But it began to change too, expecting its members to do as they were told, in order that it be able to exercise the authority it had received from the electorate. In this context, to talk of the House of Commons exercising considered independent judgement is a fraud. Power in Westminster is in the hands of the party leaders, exercised through the party whips. Scarcely any MPs now decide for themselves how they will cast their votes in a Commons division: they get their instructions and they act upon them.

Of course, the party machines say that it is a two-way process, that the leadership listens to the opinions of the members. In one, crucial sense this is true. The lesson that Neville Chamberlain learned was also bitterly learned by the later conservative leaders Anthony Eden and Margaret Thatcher. In the Labour party, Jim Callaghan and Neil Kinnock learned it too. A leader can survive only if he or she has the support of the parliamentary party. Those who have risen highest have the furthest to fall. Margaret Thatcher, a woman who had stamped her personal convictions all over government, both at home and abroad, lost office without ever losing the votes of the British people. She thought she understood the reasons her government had run into such hostility in the country at large. Her insistence upon the unfair and unpopular 'community charge' to fund local government, the high interest rates caused by her former Chancellor of the Exchequer's decision to 'shadow' the Deutschmark, unease at her attitude to the rest of Europe, in which she both signed the Single

European Act and yet continued to pour acid on dreams of a greater single Europe, were all comprehensible matters of policy. They might, she believed, be set right. But she had failed to reckon with the something intangible that had gripped her parliamentary party. When the Conservatives lost Eastbourne – Eastbourne of all places – to the Liberal Democrats in a by-election, panic set in. Thatcher had planned to fight the next General Election, and thought she might then stand down a couple of years later. Now, grand party figures such as Lord Carrington began to mumble questions about whether she might think of leaving earlier, so she could go with dignity, and at a time of her own choosing. Sensing how the tide had gone out on his leader, her remarkably undramatic lieutenant, Geoffrey Howe, resigned from her government and then used the House of Commons to denounce her dramatically.

Belatedly, realizing that her time was up, Thatcher began to appear in the Commons Tea Room, canvassing support from rank-and-file MPs. But her rival Michael Heseltine had been there before her. Repeatedly. Finally, she called in the cabinet, one by one, and received the same message from almost all: personally, the minister would vote for her, but did not believe that she could win a vote of the whole parliamentary party. The game was up. 'Democracy is no respecter of persons,'[10] Margaret Thatcher wearily commented later. 'I was sick at heart,' she wrote bitterly; '. . . what grieved me was the desertion of those I had always considered friends and allies and the weasel words whereby they had transmuted their betrayal into frank advice and concern for my fate.'[11] Thus she discovered that, however much a British Prime Minister may dine with queens or dance with presidents, their destiny is in the hands of their own colleagues. It is a powerful warning against the inclination which seizes any Prime Minister with a comfortable majority to spend their days at international conferences and to regard the House of Commons as just an inconvenience and to stop listening to their own MPs.

But it is a very rare event. For the most part, the party system is one in which the commands come from the top and are obeyed at the bottom. In his book *The Charm of Politics*, Richard Crossman remarked that the modern system of centralized government, 'buttressed by a party system which limits the elector to choosing between the Cabinet and the Shadow Cabinet . . . has steadily degraded the status of the individual MP, and, most serious of all, is rapidly transferring both debate and decision from the publicity of the floor of the Commons to the secrecy of the party caucus in the committee rooms upstairs or the party headquarters outside'.[12] It has not got better since he wrote that in 1958.

According to a senior figure in the Conservative party, somewhere in central London is a safe containing a brown envelope. Inside the envelope is a photograph. It shows a well-known politician, a tireless campaigner for 'family values', in what used to be called a 'compromising position'. He is naked. There are a number of women – also naked – in the photograph. It also includes a dog. Who took the picture is unknown: it was sent anonymously to the party with no covering letter or explanation of any kind. The photograph has been taken out of the safe only once, when the MP at the centre of the picture had threatened to rebel over a piece of legislation. He was invited to the whips' office and offered a drink. Then he was tossed the envelope. He opened it, blanched, and spent the rest of his political career doing as he was told.

The whips – the term is derived from the 'whippers-in' who control packs of hounds – are the keepers of parliament's dark secrets and custodians of the baubles of public life. For the average backbencher, the whip is the street-corner thug they need to get past on their way home from school. Treat him with respect, and life will be fine. If you cross him, watch out. Occasionally, whips can get literally physical: the Conservative Derek Conway ('At my secondary modern, if someone hit you, you hit them back as hard as you could') was once seen trying bodily to pick up a fellow MP to push him into the right division lobby. David Lightbown, another Conservative whip, was notorious for his ability to use his twenty-stone weight to pin reluctant MPs to the wall. Paul Marsden, a Labour MP unhappy with the party line on anti-terrorism legislation in 2001, found himself pushed and shoved, called an 'arsehole', and then pressed by a whip against the wall, with an arm across his throat.

But usually their methods are slightly more subtle. They have favours to dispense, places on fact-finding missions to Switzerland or

Australia with accommodation in comfortable hotels, trips to places in the Indian Ocean to promote British ideas of democracy, or the chance for a backbench MP to become the Big I Am of nothing much, like being sent off to the North Atlantic Assembly, with more hotels and foreign travel on offer. Then there are honours to be splashed around. They used to follow a pattern: eleven years' service for a knighthood, seventeen for a baronetcy, perhaps a viscountcy after a few years in cabinet. Modern MPs have to wait longer for their long-service medals, and even then the gong is at the mercy of the whips. Derek Conway recalled with obvious delight the way he had dealt with a colleague who rebelled against government policy on a matter of conscience. 'He had been approved for a knighthood. It was a real pleasure putting a line through his name. And even more of a pleasure telling him.'

Where inducements or threats fail, there is an endless capacity for making life difficult. The whips determine who can leave the Westminster area and when. One woman who served in the first Blair administration was called back to vote in the House of Commons just as she was at the end of a 120-mile drive home. She obeyed the summons, drove back to Westminster and found the vote had been cancelled. Those who do as the whips desire find life is easier. Those who persist in defiance can find them utterly Machiavellian. What else the whips get up to is a mystery. By tradition, they do not give interviews, and their victims are usually afraid to speak out, not least because it makes them look weak. But in his October 2001 rebellion the Labour MP Paul Marsden took the unprecedented step of recording the dressing-down he had had from the government Chief Whip, Hilary Armstrong. Armstrong had been born and bred in the Labour party, stuffing election envelopes at the age of eight, and, as an adult, she had inherited her father's rock-solid Labour seat in Durham. Paul Marsden, the son of a Labour councillor, had won Shrewsbury from the Conservative whip Derek Conway, against all the odds, in the 1997 Labour landslide. Four years later he found himself increasingly uneasy at the way the Blair government was aligning itself with George W. Bush's military campaign in Afghanistan. In the course of trying to explain why Marsden was wrong, Armstrong said or shouted, according to Marsden, 'those that aren't with us are against us', 'war is not a matter of conscience', 'it was people like you who appeased Hitler in 1938' and 'the trouble with people like you is that you are so clever with words that us up north can't argue back'.[13] The verbal assault was followed by a whispering campaign suggesting that the cause of Marsden's anxiety about the war was simply that he was insane. A few weeks later, he defected to the Liberal Democrats.

Other victims of the whips have simply left parliament. Jenny Jones, a one-time social worker and local councillor, returned as an apparently archetypal new Labour MP for Wolverhampton in 1997, found herself shouted at and called a 'fucking cow' by one of the whips. (His management skills were rewarded in the next government reshuffle when he was appointed a Home Office minister.) Tess Kingham, another 1997 entrant, was called in by the whips after complaining that she was being instructed to vote for things she didn't believe in, and which had not even been in the party manifesto. She was told that, if she failed to do as she was told, she could expect to find her private life all over the tabloid newspapers, and that her constituency party would find resources cut off by headquarters. She quit parliament at the next election, saying the whips' behaviour was 'an affront to democracy'.[14]

The whips prefer to point to another, more benevolent side of their work. They like to claim that they are as much a counselling service for MPs as they are enforcers. MPs with money troubles who approach the whips often find a sympathetic ear, before being put in touch with a wealthy party member who will offer an interest-free loan. But the price of accepting the money is that, when told to jump, they ask only, 'How high?' The 'black book' or 'dirt book' which lists all the scuttlebutt about a party's MPs (known in the Major government as the 'Unstable List') contains details of all those in the parliamentary party with a drink problem, those who are teetering on the edge of bankruptcy, and those who are running second families in London. The parties retain sympathetic doctors – specialists in alcoholism and depression in particular – to whom members can be referred. But the slimmer the government majority, the nastier the whips become: then the list is a weapon of virtual blackmail.

Every party contains its share of obsessives, some of whom have a fragile grasp on reality. I once asked a whip how many of his MPs were 'slightly loopy'. He replied, 'Slightly? Slightly? There's no slightly about it. There are plenty who are stark staring mad. I think it's a form of autism: they can stand up in the House of Commons and make what sounds a perfectly rational speech on investment in the railways, but the moment they sit down they are completely insane again. There is a man in the House of Commons who believes – really, truly believes – that 10 Downing Street is manipulated by a witches' coven in Gloucestershire.' Another whip told me that during the Major years there was even one MP who had become so unhinged by the business of being a politician that he had retreated to a monastery: the whips' office sent a car down to collect him whenever there was a crucial vote.

Privately, the whips will try to justify their existence by saying that they offer members of the party the chance to communicate their feelings to the leadership: if enough MPs are troubled about a stance on a particular issue, the party will change course. Clearly, since governments are formed by parties, and no party – and therefore no government – can survive without a sense of collective responsibility, there needs to be some way of enforcing discipline. But the assumptions of the party leaders about the role of the individual member of parliament have changed radically. Leo Abse remembered a furious Conservative MP in the 1960s boiling over as he spoke of 'the bloody impertinence of the whips: they want me to become a junior minister'. Yet after the 1997 election, Tony Blair gathered together the unprecedented number of Labour MPs and told them, 'You are ambassadors for the party.' Anyone who took this injunction literally risked turning themselves from a constituency representative into a travelling salesman. It was only later that some of them realized that collective responsibility had no counterpart in collective decision-making.

In opposition, for example, the party had claimed that a Freedom of Information law was 'absolutely fundamental' to the reforms Labour would bring to the government of Britain. Most of the shadow cabinet had taken in a belief in open government with the first pint of beer at the student union bar. But that is exactly the sort of commitment which seems much more attractive when in opposition than it does when in government. So cynics were not surprised when there was a distinct lack of urgency about introducing legislation after the 1997 election. When, finally, a bill was laid before parliament, the 'absolutely fundamental' principles turned out to be distinctly conditional. So many exemptions had been introduced that the rights the bill offered the citizen turned out to be fewer than those enjoyed in the United States, Australia, Canada, New Zealand and the Irish Republic. Dozens of backbench MPs remained true to their beliefs, though, and fought behind the scenes and then on the floor of the House of Commons to persuade the Home Secretary to modify the bill so that it reflected more accurately the noble promises they had made while in opposition. But, when the time came to vote, the whips marched on the government's stage army and crushed dissent. All the close and reasoned argument about how the bill might be given some teeth ended with the whips shepherding Labour MPs into the division lobbies with the words, 'Government this way. Intellectual wankers that way.'

The whips are the people who make the party system work and, although they come in for their share of deserved abuse, in reality they are just a symptom of a sickness. The official handbooks tell us that Britain is a liberal democracy. The popular version of history has it that a long tussle between the monarch and the people ended in defeat for despotism and victory for representative democracy. Ever since the Glorious Revolution of 1689 and the Bill of Rights, the British people have governed themselves. But in reality, of course, what happened was that power shifted not from king to people, but from king to parliament. In practice, most of the time, power lies not with parliament but with party. Those ambitious for power will whip themselves. As Thomas Jefferson warned two centuries ago, 'whenever a man has cast a longing eye on offices, a rottenness begins in his conduct'.[15]

The opportunity for an individual MP to become a historical footnote, with his or her own pet piece of legislation on the statute book is, literally, a lottery. MPs choose a number, and then the Speaker pulls numbers out of a barrel. Eric Pickles had been entering the ballot for ten years, in much the same spirit as most people play the National Lottery – as a habit, a dream, and with no real expectation of ever being successful. But in November 2001, his luck suddenly changed. Eric Pickles, the roly-poly Yorkshireman now representing a constituency in Essex, hit the jackpot.

Pickles, who takes a close interest in food, decided to use his opportunity to try to bring in a bill which would oblige food manufacturers to put labels on their produce certifying the ingredients' origins. The legislation would not only ensure that people knew what they were eating, it might also save British farmers from being bankrupted by foreign competition. Weeks of research later, during which time he talked to farmers, food manufacturers and retailers, Pickles had his draft bill. He had even got the endorsement of the trade association representing the food and drink industry. After prayers in the chamber of the Commons, at nine-thirty one Friday morning, he stood up to introduce his legislation. Labelling of foodstuffs may not be the most earth-shattering of topics. But British farmers were convinced it was a way of trying to save domestic food production from unfair foreign competition. And it could be a matter of life and death: several MPs told of constituents who had children with such severe nut allergies that unwitting exposure might be fatal. Yet what distinguished the debate was the sheer fatuousness of most of the contributions. Pickles's exposition of the need for a bill reflected his homework. British farmers were being undermined by foreign competitors who were able to rear their animals in conditions which would be illegal in Britain. As a consequence of the competition a recent survey had revealed that average British farm incomes had fallen to £8,000 a year. A labelling system would enable the consumer to see what was what. His problem was the government had decided it wanted nothing to do with the idea. Legislation of the kind Pickles was proposing would raise enormous difficulties with the authorities at European Union headquarters in Brussels. Instead of trying to protect farmers or consumers, it decided that Eric Pickles should be driven into a siding where he could steam away to his heart's content, doing nobody any harm.

The first Chris Bryant, the recently elected MP for Rhondda, knew about the bill was when he was accosted in one of the numerous corridors of the House of Commons by a government whip. He had been chairing a student debate in one of the committee rooms and was told to get into the chamber at once. The bill needed to be 'talked out'. He sat down as the burly Yorkshireman explained the urgent need for consumers to be given sufficient information on which to make an informed choice in the supermarket. The word 'supermarket' was an invitation for the Labour operation to begin. Candy Atherton, a former party press officer, wanted to know whether Pickles had a 'reward card'. He did. Up jumped Bryant. 'I wonder whether the honourable gentleman is worried by reward cards and the fact that, generally, all supermarkets are fully aware of what food he eats week by week?' Pickles was not, and continued describing his visit to the meat counter. There he had picked up a packet of 'Wiltshire cured' bacon. Upon examination, he 'became convinced that the unfortunate pig that supplied it had not so much as seen a postcard of Wiltshire, let alone visited that fine county'.[16]

By now, he was getting into his stride. But the harrying went on. He mentioned Hansard. Bryant wanted to know when it had been commonplace for Hansard to be read at the breakfast table. Pickles wanted labels to declare where the main ingredients of processed food had come from. Bryant wanted to know whether the provenance of lemons in a lemon tart would have to be disclosed, despite the fact that they did not constitute 25 per cent of the content. Pickles mentioned 'Czechoslovakian bacon'. Bryant was anxious to point out that nowadays the country was known as the Czech Republic.

Other MPs raised other vital issues. Did the milk in 'Cornish Clotted Cream' have to come from Cornish cows? Should Yorkshire puddings, Cornish pasties, Lincolnshire or Cumberland sausages or Gloucestershire Old Spot pigs be produced only in the county of their name? And then, three hours into the debate, came Bryant's main contribution. Having been ordained as a Church of England vicar he was better equipped than most to deliver a sermon for as long as possible on a subject of which he had been until then more or less ignorant. He reminded the House of his worries about supermarket loyalty cards. He wondered why he had seen a shop selling 'out-of-date crisps – 22p'. He pondered the relative merits of using eight or eighteen lemons in a lemon tart. He told MPs of the ice-cream manufacturer in his constituency, the very Mr Creemy we met earlier in this chapter. Finally, he held forth, in remarkable detail for a man who confessed he knew nothing about food labelling, about the challenges which Britain might face under articles 226 and 227 of the Treaty of Rome. After thirty-eight minutes, he sat down again.

By parliamentary standards his had not been a particularly lengthy intervention. But, together with the efforts of other ambitious back-benchers, it was enough. The relevant minister summed up why the government thought that bringing in laws to label food in Britain would land the country in trouble with the European Union, and at half-past two, almost in mid-sentence, the debate was adjourned. The bill was dead. The House of Commons had devoted five hours to apparent discussion of a subject which affects the livelihoods and health of vast numbers of British citizens. It had been largely conducted by a tiny handful of people who knew little of what they were supposed to be talking about, and, at the end of it all, precisely nothing had been accomplished.

Pickles, a natural optimist, wasn't even particularly disappointed. He understood how parliament worked, and recognized that if the government didn't like something, there was no chance of it ever becoming law. The only satisfaction he said he had was that he caught Chris Bryant in the Hansard office later, trying to change the numbers of the articles of the Treaty of Rome on which he had seemed to hold forth so knowledgeably.

If you want a job on Hansard, reporting what has happened in the House of Commons, you first have to be capable of understanding John Prescott, the former merchant navy steward whom Tony Blair described as 'the best deputy a leader could have'. Prescott's approach to words is rather like a child's trick of shuffling cards by throwing them all up in the air. Applicants for a job on *The Official Report* (it is named after Thomas Hansard, who bought the right to report parliament from the debt-ridden William Cobbett in 1811) are given a tape of Prescott in full flow and then asked to transcribe what he was trying to say. The process illustrates an important fact about the report, that it is not a verbatim record of what was said in the chamber of the House of Commons, but what the participants wanted to say. All MPs have the right to 'check' the transcript of what they said in the hour and a half after they have finished speaking, and are entitled to 'clean up' the text, although they are not supposed to alter its sense. A recent applicant to join its staff of a hundred made perfect sense of the Prescott peroration, and was offered a job at once. He declined on principle. 'I cannot', he wrote back, 'be party to an organisation which makes politicians appear better than they are.'

Although Hansard still prints over 3,000 copies of the previous day and night's debates by seven-thirty the next morning, it is hard to discover who reads the thing. By 2001, the total number of private subscribers to this printed journal of record had fallen to just two. A copy was delivered daily to a street in Gosport in Hampshire, and another to Cadogan Square in Chelsea. The London address belonged to Sir Denis Mahon, fourth son of an Irish baronet, grandson of the Marquess of Sligo, an old boy of Eton, alumnus of Christ Church, Oxford, with a long, distinguished career as an art historian. Why on earth should he have had such an appetite for the posturings, the rhetorical tropes, the baying choruses of applause or derision, and the oppositional tedium of 650 politicians? I telephoned him. His answer made it sound as though the question had never really occurred to him.

'I like to keep up with what's happening in the world of arts and museums,' he said.

But surely there are better ways than having the entire verbal output of the House of Commons delivered to your house every day? What does he do with them all?

'I keep them, of course. I've mountains of them.'

But how can you ever find anything? Why not just look up what you want on the electronic version of Hansard on the Internet?

'I'm very old, you know,' he said. 'I'm over ninety. And I think I'm pretty mad.'

I thought about going down to Chelsea to see his enormous library. But I rather doubted I'd be able to open the door.

The majority of the small number of people (about 300,000 visits a month) who want to check what an MP said on a subject will now do so through the Internet, where the electronic Hansard appears every day. But most of the population get their information about what's happening in British politics from the newspapers, radio or television. And the reporters who impart this knowledge largely do not get it from the chamber of the House of Commons. Apart from accounts of the ritualized duels at Prime Minister's Questions, what happens inside the chamber rarely makes the front pages any longer. However well a politician may prepare a speech on any subject under the sun, the chances of it being reported to the outside world are negligible: the days when newspapers devoted pages – sometimes as much as half the news pages – to what happened inside Westminster are long gone.

'The lobby' – the list of accredited political reporters kept by the serjeant-at-arms who are allowed access to places in parliament denied to other reporters – spend much more time following up instructions from their newsdesks to chase gossip and embarrassment than their predecessors ever did. Their daily briefings from the government spokesman are at least now acknowledged to exist (twenty years ago, they would refer to the briefings given by the Leader of the House and his shadow as coming from 'blue mantle' and 'red mantle') and there are many fewer claims that something is 'authoritatively understood': now the Prime Minister's spokesman is at least acknowledged to exist. Ordinary members of parliament have reluctantly had to accept that, if there is to be an important announcement of government policy, they may be the last to know. It is a pretty well constant complaint from all sides that the media pay too little attention to what happens in parliament. But there is a perfectly good reason for the decline in parliamentary reporting. It is simply that the chamber of the House of Commons no longer matters in the way that it once did. Fifty years ago, reporters got most of their information about what the executive was doing by sitting in the press gallery and recording what ministers told parliament. Now they get fed directly by the government, in a blizzard of news conferences, on- or off-the-record briefings, press releases and interviews. Why pay any attention to parliament when the government pays it so little heed? Almost the only time when a debate in the chamber matters is when the government has a narrow majority, and it must court possible dissenters to survive. The rest of the time, members of parliament are just talking to themselves. I once asked one of them why he did it, and he said, 'I know no one gives a damn. But the only way to get on is through the party, and the party won't advance anyone who doesn't perform well in parliament.'

With the notable exception of the annual Budget statement, the floor of the House of Commons has become just about the worst possible place for a minister to make a policy announcement. Ministers prefer to appear on morning radio and television programmes to say that they cannot pre-empt what they propose to announce in the House of Commons later in the day, and then do precisely that. If there is to be an announcement about reforms to education, the Education Secretary will be filmed visiting a school. If there is to be an initiative on health, the Health Secretary will be found at a hospital. So, if the House of Commons, as politicians frequently complain, is under-reported, it is at least in part because that is how governments like it.

You can see why. The wired world prizes a different form of communication, where the emphasis is on brevity, immediacy and informality. House of Commons debate is an idiom from another age. But without a written constitution, 'procedure' is all. Of course, when governments have narrow majorities, what happens in the chamber of the House of Commons matters, because all governments have to be able to command a majority. When a decaying government is hanging on to power by its fingernails, as in the dying days of the Major government, the press gallery above the Speaker's chair will be packed with reporters, desperate to see whether tonight would be the night when a rebellion by backbenchers might trigger a vote of no-confidence. But the job of parliament should be a great deal more important than parties and leaders. Historically, the place existed not to make laws but to vote upon whether the king should be granted his request for more money. This provided the opportunity to voice grievances. Now, decisions about spending billions of pounds are made simply on a nod of the head. When a government enjoys a healthy majority, it is hard to think of a system in which parliament has less control over the taxes imposed on the citizens or over the spending planned by the government. The dice are loaded against the backbencher who wants to try to hold government to account. The minister is driven to the House of Commons, does not have to hang around before making a speech or answering a set of questions, while his private secretary sits in the box near by, armed with facts, documents and moral support. 'It's a Rolls Royce way of being a Member of Parliament, all the wheels are oiled especially for you and your life is made extremely easy,' Richard Crossman decided. 'The whole of Parliament is geared not to help back-benchers criticize Ministers, but to help Ministers overcome back-benchers.'[17] The watchdogs no longer strain at their leashes. Some perform occasional tricks, like walking on their hind legs. The rest lie about looking wistful, hoping for a biscuit.

In December 1998, Martin Bell, Britain's solitary Independent MP, stood up to speak in the House of Commons. Bell had arrived in parliament as the embodiment of public disgust at the tawdriness of political life. A respected war correspondent, whose clipped manner had fallen out of favour with a new generation of BBC managers, Bell had reinvented himself in the 1997 General Election by standing as a white knight against Neil Hamilton, whose taste for all-expenses-paid visits to the Ritz in Paris had done so much to damage the Conservatives. Bell's anti-sleaze campaign ejected Hamilton from what had been the fifth safest Conservative seat in the country. The massive popular backing for Bell − he crushed Hamilton by over 11,000 votes − was not universally reflected in Westminster, however, where many professional politicians saw him as sanctimonious, Conservatives for the damage they believed he had done their party, Labour politicians for his contempt for their fawning performances at Prime Minister's Questions. His ignorance of procedure could put him at their mercy.

Bell's speech that December evening ought to have commanded respect. He was speaking about the Anglo-American bombing of Iraq. The strikes were supposed to be a punishment for Saddam Hussein's refusal to allow international weapons inspectors free access to his military bases. But they began the day before the House of Representatives was due to decide whether Bill Clinton should be impeached for introducing Monica Lewinsky to the contents of the presidential underpants and then lying about it afterwards. A mere coincidence, claimed Tony Blair.

Because most politicians abide by the convention that you don't rock the boat when British servicemen are in action, there were very few individuals willing to question the justification for raining high explosives down on Iraq. Martin Bell was one of them. As he stood in the Commons, he denounced the entire enterprise. There was, he said, little international support for the bombing, and its consequence would be not to break the power of the Iraqi dictator, but to stiffen the resistance of his people. It was a powerful denunciation, the more so for being so rare. Julian Brazier, a military Conservative MP once memorably described as seeming to have made one parachute drop too many and landed on his head,[18] was outraged. Having delivered his speech from a position low down on the opposition benches, Bell had moved to sit on the cross-bench, directly facing the Speaker's chair. It was a reasonable place for an Independent to sit. Yet it was not technically part of the House of Commons. Brazier rose to denounce him, saying, 'I am particularly aware of the presence of the honourable member for Tatton.' The Deputy Speaker, who was supervising the debate, rose to tick him off. 'Order!' he barked. 'The honourable member for Tatton is not in the Chamber, so the honourable member should not refer to him.' Brazier ate humble pie instantly. 'I stand entirely rebuked, Mr Deputy Speaker . . . Although we can see him, I accept that he is outside the Chamber.'[19]

This is the sort of incident that leaves the public baffled. How on earth can someone be there, yet not be there? Anyone – politician, reporter or functionary – who has come to terms with this procedural nonsense soon feels a kinship with others who have done so. One veteran of the press gallery noticed that whenever he met an MP or fellow reporter on neutral ground, he was acutely conscious of a kinship uniting them. 'It is as if one said to oneself: "Here is someone with whom I appeared to have shared some long, searing experience – shipwreck for instance, or trench warfare – something which I hold in common with him, but not with my own family, or with my oldest friends and colleagues."'[20] This comradeship is all very well, but the difficulty is that while all those involved might understand why someone can be both inside the chamber of the House of Commons and outside it at the same time, the rest of the nation, able now to watch the whole thing on television, does not.

Television and radio tend to concentrate upon Prime Minister's Questions, but this is little better. It is, by a long way, the hot ticket, with the public galleries usually packed with people who have queued in the rain outside. Spectators are rarely disappointed. The place is crowded, the atmosphere excitable. There are House of Commons clerks in their wigs and gowns, the serjeant-at-arms in his white tie and tails, with his sword resting awkwardly at his side, and MPs crammed into the gangways. Three, four or at times six Hansard reporters sit in the middle of the press gallery above the Speaker's chair. Other seats in the press gallery seem to have been allocated according to some nameless Masonic ritual. 'You can't sit there! That's the *Dundee Courier*'s place!' How do I get a seat, then? 'You mean your father didn't put you down for one at birth?' asks the man from the *Daily Telegraph*.

In the flesh, the astonishing thing about the House of Commons chamber is its size; television fails utterly to convey how small it is – not to mention how indifferent most of the members are to most of the proceedings most of the time. Occasionally, when the chamber is packed for a big event like a resignation statement, the old cliché about the atmosphere being charged is justified. The rest of the time, the overwhelming impression is one of detachment. Before the Prime Minister enters the chamber, the Secretary of State for Northern Ireland is on his feet, making a statement about the tortuous progress towards replacing thirty years of violence with politics. The account in Hansard the next day will make it seem as if he was speaking to a rapt and attentive House of Commons, from which occasional figures rose to ask well-informed questions. The reality is that he speaks to a room around which are scattered a handful of people, most of whom are gossiping among themselves. No wonder they have loudspeakers built into the benches: the noise level is worthy of the worst-behaved primary school.

At one minute to three, the party leaders' spokesmen and spin doctors slide into the side galleries above the MPs, each positioned, not behind their champion but facing him, as if, Svengali-like, they can think thoughts into his head. Suddenly, there is not a seat to be had. The Prime Minister has slipped on to the government frontbench below. He exudes smiling confidence. The Leader of the Opposition chats to the shadow cabinet members on either side of him.

First we have the prepared questions and the prepared responses. The Order Paper lists numerous identical questions asking the Prime Minister if he will tell MPs what he's been doing today and will do later on. Why the interest in who he's had lunch with or whether he plans to take his wife out to dinner? The answer is that, like people who are there but not there, the questioner has not the slightest interest in what the Prime Minister is doing today. But the device enables the questioner to get in with a supplementary question, which is designed either to make him look a fool or to fawn all over him.

Having a block of parliamentary time set aside specifically for questions to the Prime Minister is a relatively recent phenomenon. In Churchill's time it was simply the custom for the Prime Minister to answer later questions on the Order Paper, the list of business for the day. Viscount Chandos sometimes had lunch with him beforehand and recalled:

He was completely relaxed. The Prime Minister's number on the Order Paper was usually in the early 40's [*sic*], and he knew with uncanny precision when he would be reached. Sometimes a bottle of champagne stood on the table, and he and I drank a glass or two of it. Once or twice during luncheon he would ring the bell for a private secretary, add to an answer or polish a phrase with a relish only equal to that with which he attacked the luncheon. At about ten minutes to three the private secretary would come in and say, 'They have reached 23.' 'Good, there's plenty of time,' and he would pour out a small noggin of old brandy. At this moment I would become rather restive and anxious lest he should be late. A quarter of an hour later 'Number 36' would be announced. 'We must go at once,' he said and, with that, shot out of the room into his car and was in his place about two or three questions before his own were reached.[21]

Chandos's recollection was that the questions 'were not usually intended to be helpful'. But even when Prime Minister's Questions began as a formal, twice-weekly event, under Harold Macmillan, it was still, essentially, a means of eliciting information about an office that had come to dominate government. There were leaders of the Opposition in the 1960s and 1970s who chose not to take the chance to ask questions because they felt there was nothing they particularly wanted to know. But in the bitterness which suffused politics in the 1980s, it increasingly became a way not to elicit information, but simply to score points.

When John Major and Neil Kinnock faced each other across the dispatch boxes, they agreed to try to return Prime Minister's Questions to something of its original information-gathering function. But, determined though they were to make it less of an adversarial knock-about, they failed, because their tribes couldn't live without the spectator sport. Pressure from both sides forced them to return to political point-scoring. Major was left thinking the whole experience was a waste of time. 'Prime Minister's Questions is a farce in its present form and ought either to be reformed and made relevant or abolished altogether,' he says. 'It started out as a serious attempt to question the Head of Government. Then it developed into an attempt by the Opposition to make the Prime Minister look inadequate, and by the Prime Minister to make the Opposition look shallow and foolish. Now, it has become a trivial spectacle that does some harm – and no good – to Parliament.'

When Tony Blair found himself answering Prime Minister's Questions, instead of asking them, he compressed the twice-weekly fifteen-minute sessions on Tuesdays and Thursdays into one thirty-minute session on Wednesdays. Blair maintained that he had not reduced the scrutiny of parliament. In a strict accountancy sense, he was right. But the effect of cutting his appearances before the House of Commons from twice a week to once was, first, to ensure there was less room for topicality, and second – and worse – to turn the event into even more of a ritual joust between himself and the Leader of the Opposition. (There was the added consequence of allowing some MPs to think that the parliamentary week ended on a Wednesday afternoon, after which they could slink off home.) William Hague or Iain Duncan Smith would arrive having spent much of the morning rehearsing with a gaggle of advisers. Each would then get to his feet and recite a collection of carefully chosen statistics, interspersed with jokes which had been written for them – Hague's staff could watch the proceedings on television and, in what looked like ventriloquism, mouth the words falling from their leader's lips – and finish off with a soundbite designed to lodge in the public memory. 'Bite' was a well-chosen description, for they were most like the sort of junk food served by some international hamburger chain, full of bright pack-aging and tasting of nothing very much. The Prime Minister would then respond, often with a 'bite' which his own staff had cooked up. And the ritual encounter would grind on and on, getting nowhere. Sometimes, it took up over half of the allotted time, which meant that the remaining hundreds of MPs who might have wished to find something out from the Prime Minister had perhaps twelve or thirteen minutes between them.

Then the Liberal Democrat leader would rise to his feet and begin, 'Has the right honourable gentleman had the chance to read the Early Day Motion on . . .' Often as not he would be drowned in hoots of derision. Of course the Prime Minister hadn't. No one had. It was a silly question, but the mockery was something else. Both Labour and Conservatives want to pretend it is still 1959, when there were only seven MPs in parliament who did not take either the Labour or Conservative whip. But after the 2001 election there were eighty, which was the largest number in almost eighty years. When Paddy Ashdown was leader he was driven half-mad by the scorn, as he admitted when he poured out his soul to his diary.

As soon as I was called by the Speaker they all started shouting. The anti-Europeans wanted to vent their wrath on somebody and I was the obvious target. I hardly said a word before Dennis Skinner shouted, 'Make way for Captain Mainwaring.' This caused everybody to fall about in mock mirth. God, I hate this place. It is puerile, pathetic and utterly useless and I long for the day (if it ever comes) when we have the power to change it completely. I left incandescent with rage but trying not to show it.[22]

On one particular afternoon, a couple of Labour backbenchers stand up to ask toadying questions about how marvellous the government is. Remarkably, the Prime Minister agrees with them. Then, a question on a genuine matter of local importance, the closure of a local brewery, is raised by the constituency MP. It means the loss of real people's real jobs. But the MP is nervous and takes refuge in his notes, then forgets that he is supposed to be asking a question, not making a point. The bullies are upon him at once, hooting, 'Speech! Speech!' and laughing in derision.

On the questions roll, while, up in the public gallery, a couple of students get to their feet and unfurl a banner denouncing human rights abuses in Turkey. This sort of thing is not supposed to happen. From the back of the gallery, attendants in white ties and black tailcoats swoop down the steep steps like demented magpies. Attempts to silence the young Kurds are hampered by the fact that, while some of the attendants are trying to wrestle them away, others are sitting on their chests. Protest slogans continue to emerge from beneath the sea of tailcoats. They manage to make a lot of noise.

Down below, the world turns as if nothing at all has happened. The questions roll on, still asking the Prime Minister to outline his activities for the day. 'Stop the killings in Turkey!' screams a girl's voice from above, while, below, the MP for Mitcham and Morden is on her feet asking the Prime Minister if he would like to come to a party she is holding that evening for a hundred teenagers who will vote for the first time at the next election.

And then, after half an hour, it is all over for another week. The protesters have been thrown out on to the street for daring to bring the horrors of Turkish torture into the Palace, and the chamber empties, as MPs scurry off to write Christmas cards to their constituents. The MP for Colchester gets to his feet to raise an urgent point of order. A website has been set up in his name. Furthermore, it has been set up by political enemies. Will the Speaker please make a ruling on the subject? The MP is not exactly a household name: his most famous campaign has been to have the game of darts acknowledged as an Olympic sport and he has found time in his hectic political schedule to spend two weeks on a vital visit to the 5,000 inhabitants of St Helena. You might think he would take Oscar Wilde's view that the only thing worse than being talked about is not being talked about. But he does not. The Speaker is disturbed and expresses 'strong disapproval'. And then, to a House of Commons which has suddenly shrunk to a few dozen MPs, the Health Secretary is making a statement about the way that mentally ill people will be treated in future. All the journalists have gone from the press gallery. Most of the politicians have vanished. Life is back to normal.

Those who have worked with the Prime Minister say that the preparation for this empty jousting may have taken him from eight in the morning until three in the afternoon, with a few breaks for meetings. He will have begun by reading the newspapers, since most of the topical questions will be related to something in that morning's editions or on that morning's radio. The first challenge is to try to guess what he might be asked about. Briefs will be called for from the relevant Whitehall departments. By lunchtime, all will have been written, and the Prime Minister will then, like some last-minute student on the eve of an exam, sit at his desk and try to cram as many facts as possible into his head. Can this really be the most effective use of his time? What is achieved by testing his memory? True, an Opposition leader who cannot cut it in Prime Minister's Questions will not command the support of his parliamentary party. But that is a world away from whether he or she will command any support in the country as a whole: William Hague regularly trounced Tony Blair at Question Time. Yet he led his party to electoral catastrophe. It is rather hard to see who, precisely, benefits from the ritual.

But you can see the attraction of becoming a member of the government. In a world in which most people live and work in hierarchies, the politician has no career structure. Unless they become a member of the government or Leader of the Opposition, or fall into a handful of other special offices, such as being Attorney General or one of the whips, they will earn the same basic salary of £55,000 whether they are a wet-behind-the-ears newcomer to the House of Commons or have sat there for twenty years. The odds on becoming Leader of the Opposition (whose salary of £120,000 is almost that of a cabinet minister, and whose office receives half a million pounds of public money a year) are perhaps three hundred to one. Once you have ruled out the no-hopers, in a reasonably balanced parliament the odds of a member of the ruling party joining the government are only three or four to one, and the chance of entering the cabinet about fifteen to one. But, to get to the starting gate for the race to ministerial office, you need to be seen by the whips to be reliable. This is nothing like the same set of skills which make for a good scrutineer.

But there is a third way for an MP to increase their (official) salary. You might become Speaker, thereby ensuring that you more than double your pay. The odds here are, theoretically, six hundred and fifty to one. In this one person is embodied the whole of the House of Commons: the Speaker is the flesh-and-blood expression of the history of British democracy. The traditional appointment ceremony, in which the chosen person is 'dragged' to the Speaker's chair, reflects the historically dangerous nature of the job: the Speaker's responsibility was to defend the House of Commons against the demands of the king. Since the first occupant of the office in the fourteenth century, seven Speakers have been beheaded.

No doubt those who aspire to the job do so for the noblest of reasons. To an outsider, they are opaque. The (in fact relatively few) hours of listening to debates are one thing. What passes for a social life is another. 'And here's my dining room,' Betty Boothroyd told me one afternoon, when I went to see her shortly before she retired as Speaker. 'The table's been laid for dinner for a delegation of forty visiting Hungarian parliamentarians.' Dinner for forty Hungarians? What would they talk about all evening? Did any of them speak English? 'I hope so,' she said, but didn't seem too worried.

The archaic process whereby MPs voted to choose her successor illuminated various other curious aspects of parliamentary life. When she was campaigning for the job, Gwyneth Dunwoody, one of the contenders, was frank. 'The trouble', she told me, 'is that everyone in this place is a total liar. They swear blind they're going to vote for you, and you know full well that they've said exactly the same thing to every other candidate who's spoken to them. They're dreadful. They'll say anything.' Dunwoody's weary realism about her parliamentary colleagues might have made her a good Speaker. She was certainly independent. But during the enormously convoluted voting process (it took seven hours) she was knocked out early on. When, finally, the votes were taken, there were many who felt a sort of reverse Darwinism had taken hold, in which the winner, Michael Martin, turned out to be one of the least qualified for the job. Some of the reasons why he and the other contenders wanted the post are not so opaque: The salary of £125,000 is on a par with that of a cabinet minister, but the position has none of the political uncertainty and requires only about three hours' work in the chamber during the days when parliament is sitting. There is an enormous apartment inside the Palace of Westminster and a peerage on retirement. Betty Boothroyd's memoirs of her time as the first woman to hold the job revealed some of the perks: the invitation to sit in the royal box at Wimbledon, the hand-stitched gloves from the Worshipful Company of Glovers, the pictures loaned from the royal collection. For some reason, she felt she needed a headdress, and bought 'a neoclassical diamond tiara made by Garrard's in 1900 . . . it had six brilliant diamond pinnacles and what the jewellers call a graduated form of anthemions (honeysuckle), each encircled with a trail of forget-me-nots'. On appointment, her successor showed his commitment to the twenty-first century by preferring trousers to tights and pantaloons while sitting in the chair.

But increasing public respect for parliament will take more than a change of clothes. It is not as if politicians don't realize they have a problem. It is just that government has shown little inclination to do anything about it. The alarming fact is that most of the enormous numbers of regulations which affect the British people are never even debated in parliament. They are invented by civil servants (many of them working for the European Union, sometimes acting on their own, sometimes acting on instructions from the Council of Ministers) and become law as 'statutory instruments', bypassing political scrutiny because they are 'secondary legislation' which can become law without debate. The abundance and mundanity of these regulations, from the Potatoes Originating in Egypt (Wales) Regulation 2002, through agreements with Lithuania about income tax, or parking regulations in Stoke-on-Trent, to the implementation of European directives on when and how British clocks may be moved forward for summer time, are extraordinary, simply for what they reveal about the extent of government interference in the lives of British citizens. In 2001 alone, over 3,000 passed into law. In a society which has become as regulated as modern Britain, there are not enough minutes in a year for parliament to debate whether it is appropriate that the stretch of the A58 from Halifax to the M62 motorway be downgraded from the status of trunk road. But it is salutary to reflect that the people we elect to parliament have nothing whatsoever to do with so many of the regulations which affect our lives.

In theory, the role of parliament is quite clear. It represents the governed. The government is formed by whoever can gather the largest number of its members to his or her cause. The rest act as a watchdog. The Public Accounts Committee, an invention of the Victorian parliament, retained a certain magisterial independence in the late twentieth century. But by the 1960s it was clear that something needed to be done to give parliament teeth. Remarkably, in light of her subsequent authoritarian reputation, Margaret Thatcher was persuaded to acquiesce in extending the role of select committees, whose job it was to 'shadow' Whitehall departments. When Richard Crossman attempted something similar in the 1960s, there had been derision in cabinet. In response to his proposal to introduce topical debates, at which ministers could explain policy, there was wailing and gnashing of teeth. 'It's asking a terrible lot of us, Prime Minister,' bleated George Brown. 'We're busy men.'[23] Minister after minister agreed with him: they were quite occupied enough already, and simply could not take on any more responsibilities, like trying to explain themselves to parliament. Crossman noted bleakly in his diary:

Most of these Ministers were individually as well as collectively committed to parliamentary reform. Yet after two years they've become Whitehall figures who've lost contact with Parliament. And of course what they're saying is pure nonsense. Ministers aren't bothered by Parliament, indeed they're hardly ever there. . . The Executive rides supreme in Britain and has minimum trouble from the legislature. Perhaps it's because Parliament is so entirely subordinate to the Executive that my colleagues were saying, 'We can't allow this Parliamentary Party to bother us.'[24]

The select committees which followed the reforms introduced by Margaret Thatcher's Leader of the House, Norman St John-Stevas, have produced a number of coruscating reports in which the incompetence, inadequacies and indolence of government have been laid bare. They are obviously sufficiently irritating for the whips to try to make sure that membership of such committees, and particularly their chairmanships, are kept out of the hands of the Awkward Squad. But it is completely counter-productive that party machines should have anything at all to do with who sits on parliamentary select committees: their job is to keep government honest, not to be its poodle. If they become packed with people who are there essentially to toe the party line they become a way of not so much digging up the truth as burying it. They are, anyway, not all they seem. In any new parliament the first job of the clerk to a select committee is to tell it what it ought to investigate. The clerk is a civil servant with, in theory, no particular axe to grind. It is he or she who writes the final report: according to one of those involved, even the report on how to reform the way the House of Commons works was written by the clerk to the committee, who received only three recommendations from the politicians. When I asked one of the clerks how he decided what the committee wanted to recommend, he replied, 'It's a case of getting away with what the committee will wear,' which is not quite the rigorous scrutiny so many fondly believe in.

There are frequent proposals to make the select committees more powerful, so that the House of Commons can keep a more effective eye on ministers. The Catch 22 is that any decision to do so lies in the hands of the government. Is it any wonder that MPs find the lure of government office irresistible?

7. Power at Last

And so our hero becomes a minister. At last, all the years of gladhanding, the endless meetings agreeing strategy and making alliances, the tedious speechifying, the even more tedious listening to other people's speeches, the hours and hours spent on the whips' instruction in the House of Commons, the ridiculing of enemy ideas which privately seemed rather sensible, the keeping silent when conscience demanded voice, the steady reconciliation of idealism to reality, the empty applause for policies not believed in, can bear fruit. Now, finally, the politician can get on with what attracted him or her to politics. There is power to be wielded. After nineteen years of what he called 'apprenticeship' in opposition, Denis Healey became Defence Secretary. As he put it later, 'I felt like a man who, after driving his Jaguar for hours behind a tractor on narrow country lanes, finally reaches the motorway.'[1]

But before getting the chance to make something happen the politician has to receive the call from the Prime Minister. To be offered a job in cabinet, the MP usually has served in the shadow cabinet, or as a junior minister in a previous government. But the final decision is the Prime Minister's alone. It is a moment when Prime Ministers have supreme power in their party and they can exercise it almost cruelly. When Anthony Eden was called in by Stanley Baldwin in 1935, Baldwin asked him who he would recommend for the job of Foreign Secretary. The 38-year-old Eden suggested recalling Austen Chamberlain, whose achievements at the Locarno Conference, which set the boundaries of western Europe after the First World War, had been rewarded with the Order of the Garter and a share of the Nobel Peace Prize. But the Prime Minister dismissed the idea, saying that Chamberlain was 'ga-ga'. Eden then proposed Lord Halifax, but Baldwin would not contemplate a Foreign Secretary who sat in the House of Lords. The Prime Minister then wearily turned to him and said, 'It looks as if it will have to be you.'[2] Not surprisingly, Eden left the interview with less than a spring in his step.

Sometimes, Prime Ministers have little choice: after the 1997 election Tony Blair was obliged to make Gordon Brown Chancellor of the Exchequer, because the entire party understood that that was the deal on which they had carved up the leadership. Very occasionally, people get appointed to one of the very big jobs in government because they cannot be denied it. Ernest Bevin, the dominant trades union leader of the twentieth century, was co-opted into Churchill's wartime government as Minister of Labour and then went straight into Attlee's government as Foreign Secretary because, as Roy Jenkins put it, 'There was no other position in the Foreign Office, unless it was that of a rather truculent liftman on the verge of retirement, which it would have been possible to imagine his filling . . . It was Secretary of State or nothing.'[3]

At other times, brilliance in the House of Commons can ensure promotion. Seven years after Bevin bundled into the Foreign Office, Iain Macleod was summoned to Downing Street by Churchill. Macleod half believed he was to be ticked off for refusing to represent the party at some boring meeting of the Council of Europe. He emerged, ashen-faced, fifteen minutes later. Churchill had heard him pull off the remarkable feat of demolishing Nye Bevan in a House of Commons debate a few weeks earlier and thereupon decided to make him Minister of Health. Macleod's wife was waiting outside in the family car. 'Please drive me to the nearest telephone box,' he said. When she asked why, he told her about the appointment and added, 'I have to take over the department and I've got no idea where it is, so I think I'd better look up the address in the telephone book.'[4]*

But most would-be ministers are condemned to an anxious wait. The gnawing worry about whether or not they will be offered a government job, with mood swinging from confident expectation to despair, is laid out in Chips Channon's diary in the spring of 1938. It is franker, more absurd and more revealing than most accounts, but the sheer nervous desperation is there in every ambitious politician.

---

* Sometimes, jobs can be lost just as arbitrarily. It was said that Lloyd George appointed Neville Chamberlain his Minister of National Service, but then took a dislike to him for 'having the wrong-shaped head', and sacked him.

In late February Channon is thinking that, although Rab Butler is a 'scholarly dry-stick', he ought to cultivate him, in hope of becoming his Parliamentary Private Secretary, the lowest rung on the ladder of government. Two days later 'by the mercy of God', he happens to come across Butler in the House of Commons and greases up to him, oozing compliments about how lucky the rest of Europe is to have him at the Foreign Office. Someone suggests to Butler that he might consider hiring Channon as his PPS and inwardly the diarist's heart leaps. He exclaims, like a love-struck teenager, 'I cannot believe it, I, Chips, at the Foreign Office. Will my star lead me there?' But, a couple of days later, he is plunged into gloom because Butler has seemed to ignore him in the Commons. The next day, hope springs again, because the Chief Whip hints that he may indeed get the job of PPS, but he must be careful not to gossip. A day after that, he has what he calls 'a temporary "sinker"' when he sees a rival MP sitting on the PPSs' bench in the chamber of the Commons. But it turns out that he has been appointed PPS to another minister, and that night – joy oh joy! The object of his emotions sidles up to him as he leaves Westminster. Would the swooning creature consider becoming Butler's PPS? 'Would I?' exclaims Channon. 'My heart throbbed, and I felt exhilarated, as I said he was voicing my life's dream . . . I, Chips, PPS – how lovely – but to the Foreign Office, is beyond belief exciting. I can hardly wait to take up my duties.'[5] In the event, this vain man ('Chips at the FO – shades of Lord Curzon, and how pleased he would be,' he writes) made more of a contribution to understanding politics through his diaries than through anything he did at the Foreign Office. But the ambience of government, even for one of its most lowly members, lived up to his expectations. 'I love my life,' he gushed in July: 'I love sauntering through the Park to the FO and meeting the PM on the way: I love the rich flowers and seeing the Horse Guards disappearing under the arch, and I like the whole atmosphere of despatch boxes, Government messengers, the whole grey and red Government racket: the hurry and animation of Downing St. How could I have ever lived any other way?'[6]

To the outsider, the big boxes covered in red leather and embossed with the initials 'ER' are the most visible trappings of office. Every night, they will arrive, stuffed with official papers for decision and signature. In time, the minister will often come to hate them for the way they crowd in on the few hours of the day, usually late at night or early in the morning, when the civil service has decreed there is no meeting to attend, no building to open, no speech to be made. But, for now, the secure communications network, government cars and drivers, the private secretaries, inner offices and outer offices, are all immensely seductive. It is like being admitted, after a lifetime of longing, to the most exclusive of clubs. The civil servants huddle about the minister far more protectively than any collection of secretaries or personal assistants in the private sector: there may be four or five people answering the phone in an outer office. But, most of all, there is the intoxicating sense of being in on something. At last, a doer, not a watcher. It is best summed up in the happy confidence of Hugh Dalton (Labour Chancellor of the Exchequer, 1945–7) at a cocktail party: 'My dear boy, what I am going to tell you is a DEATHLY secret.'[7]

To be in on the deathliest secrets of all, senior ministers must first become Privy Councillors. Most cabinet ministers are members of this hangover from the early sixteenth century, as are the leaders of the significant opposition parties.* But those who find themselves appointed to cabinet jobs may find that their first task is not to attack poverty or make the state more accountable, but to turn up at an office in Whitehall, to be taught how to bow and scrape. There, they are rehearsed in the business of kneeling while holding a bible, how then to advance a few paces, how to kiss the sovereign's hand, and how to shuffle away backwards. When Clement Attlee was sworn in as a Privy Councillor, he wrote to his brother Tom that they had all been told they must wear frock coats, which had become such obsolete items of clothing that they could only be hired. Thus to become a Privy Councillor. 'It is one of the curiosities of the British constitution that the only fee payable is one of 12/6 to Moss Bros.'[8]

---

* For an Order in Council to become law, it must be read out at a meeting of the Privy Council and acceded to by the monarch. For this to happen the Lord President of the Council must recite the title of the Order to the Queen, in order that she may say the single word 'Agreed.' This piece of mummery may often require busy members of the government to travel to the Royal Family's Scottish holiday retreat, Balmoral, a journey which can write off an entire day.

Formal dress is no longer insisted upon. But the flummery still presents left-wingers with a real problem. Three separate accounts exist of the ceremony held when the Labour government took office in October 1964. The party had been out of power for thirteen years. Its leading lights were bursting with enthusiasm, pride and ambition. But first they had to be taught how to make obeisance. Richard Crossman, the new Minister of Housing, thought that nothing 'more dull, pretentious, or plain silly has ever been invented. There we were, sixteen grown men. For over an hour we were taught how to stand up, how to kneel on one knee on a cushion, how to raise the right hand with the Bible in it, how to advance three paces towards the Queen, how to take the hand and kiss it, how to move back ten paces without falling over the stools – which had been carefully arranged so that you did fall over them. Oh dear!'[9] Tony Benn, who had been appointed Postmaster General, was not so much incredulous as furious. Naturally, he found the whole business repellent. The rehearsal was 'terribly degrading'. The oath had 'a real Mau-Mau quality'. He tried to show his contempt by chattering away throughout. He thought the officials were 'profoundly shocked' by this.[10]

After the rehearsal, they went down to the Palace for the real thing. Each travelled in his own ministerial limousine, of course. They were met, said Benn, by 'an officer in breeches, spurs, a sword and full Court dress'. At this point, indignation threatened to get the better of him. He asked his cabinet colleague Herbert Bowden, the designated Lord President of the Council, if he could be excused swearing the oath. Not if he wanted to see cabinet papers he couldn't. With bad grace, Benn gave up his protest. He conceded that others also found the process distasteful. But 'it was particularly unpleasant for me'. Nonetheless, he agreed to be humiliated 'for the sake of the party'. 'I have always wanted to be a Privy Councillor because it is the greatest honour in the parliamentary field, but when it came to it, it was terrible . . . I left the Palace boiling with indignation and feeling that this was an attempt to impose tribal magic and personal loyalty on people whose real duty was only to their electors.'[11] He salved his conscience by unburdening himself in his diary.

Richard Crossman was equally contemptuous (although two years later he would take over from Bowden as Lord President of the Council) but retained more detachment. To him, the overwhelming impression was of the utter emptiness of the occasion. 'It was two-dimensional, so thin, like a coloured illustration in *The Sphere*, not a piece of real life. It's the thinness of it that astonishes me still.'[12] Barbara Castle could at least see the humour of the occasion – the requests from the flunkeys that the Privy Councillors be sure to hand back the bible when they had finished swearing their oath upon it, because it was the only one in the Palace – and noted the Queen's 'naturalness' in this most eccentric of ceremonies. After they had negotiated their way through a sea of footstools, the Queen remarked, 'Never have I seen so many people walk backwards so far so beautifully. Poor Mrs Castle had such a long way to go.'[13]

The Queen must be bored stiff by the endless repetition of this bit of pantaloonery. Occasionally it shows. When the Liberal Democrat leader Paddy Ashdown was sworn, he thought the Queen 'reminded me of an impatient housewife in a shopping queue, sort of hopping from foot to foot'.[14] On the other hand, having seen the performance hundreds of times, she at least knows how it's supposed to be done. After the 1997 election, the newly formed Labour cabinet trooped down to Buckingham Palace to watch those who were not yet Privy Councillors swear the oath. First came those ready to swear on the bible. Then came the assorted atheists, affirmers and non-believers. Nick Brown, the new Chief Whip, shuffled forward. As the oath was read out, the Queen exclaimed, 'Stop! There's been a mistake!' Brown froze, as if he saw a lifetime of striving for office being snatched away by a woman who sat on the throne by an accident of birth. For a second, the rest of the cabinet watched as expressions of shock, disappointment and anger passed across his face. Then it turned out that the Queen had simply realized that the wrong oath was being recited.

Once the formalities have been completed, ministers set to their briefs with enthusiasm. Just as, in the long term, governments collapse from exhaustion, so, in the short term, many politicians who finally get somewhere near the top of the tree feel invigorated. Barbara Castle watched Margaret Thatcher's first performance as leader of the Conservative party at its annual conference in 1975. The party was still in opposition, but what struck her most was how astonishingly energetic she seemed. She attributed what she called 'the vitamin of power' to success. 'Success in politics does as much for a woman's looks as falling in love. It *is* falling in love – with success and power.'[15] Some successful politicians claim almost to have relaxed into the job of being a minister. Richard Crossman found that he felt better, less exhausted and more on top of things when carrying the burdens of office. When he opened his red box and saw 'that I have to decide on the boundaries of Coventry or on where to let Birmingham have its new housing land, I find these decisions easy, pleasant, and I take them in a fairly light-hearted way'.[16] Gerald Kaufman, who wrote the best guide to being a minister, based on his experience at the Department of Industry in the 1970s, might perhaps cite this as an example of 'ministerialitis', the most obvious symptom of which is 'a perceptible swelling of the head', brought on by the obsequiousness of the departmental staff and access to chauffeur-driven cars, private lifts, washrooms and the rest.[17]

There is a limit to how long this intoxication can last. The American Democrat politician and Governor of New York, Mario Cuomo, once defined what happened when a party finally gets power by saying, 'You campaign in poetry. You govern in prose.'[18] Another way of putting it might be to say that parties campaign actively, but, paradoxically, much of government is passive. The ambitious politician who makes it to the top believes that he or she has a chance to make a mark on history. And here comes the next paradox. A century ago, the government was an infrequent meddler in people's lives. In times of war, it raised taxes or levied troops, but most of the time it left people alone. Most of the population didn't even pay income tax.[19] If they built a house, the bricks they used had scarcely changed since Queen Elizabeth's charter to the Tylers and Bricklayers' Company in 1571. Various building statutes laid down the density of housing, but otherwise they were left to their own devices. The experience of two world wars accustomed the British people to an all-powerful government. The philosophy of John Maynard Keynes – that governments could guarantee people jobs by controlling public spending – made more government seem a good thing. And since 1945 the British have certainly had it. The claim that more laws have been passed in Britain since the Second World War than in the entire period between 1066 and 1945 seems entirely believable. If you examine Hansard, you discover that in 1900 the Lords and Commons discussed legislation for 112 days. By 1999 the Commons were sitting for 170 days. The number of words spoken had doubled. The volume of legislation had increased dramatically. In 1900, parliament passed 65 Acts and 995 Statutory Instruments, or pieces of subordinate legislation. In the first year of the Blair government, which had no empire to administer, parliament passed 69 Acts and over 3,000 Statutory Instruments.[20] In the twenty-first century, everyone's life is affected by government.

The newly appointed minister approaches this leviathan with a mixture of confidence and anxiety. A party which has been out of power for a long time may have no one in the leadership with any experience of government at all. Even if they have been in the shadow cabinet, and are therefore familiar with some of the issues, newly appointed ministers are still ignorant of how government operates. With politicians increasingly devoting their entire adult lives to politics, few have any knowledge of business, of farming or of life in the military, all of which may be areas they will be expected to regulate or direct. Most will not admit to as much ignorance as Alec Douglas-Home, who was foolish enough to tell a journalist from the *Observer* that when he was given an economic brief to study, he liked to have a box of matches handy, so he could move them around to help him understand what was being said. But even a clever chap such as the Labour MP Bryan Gould, who had studied economics at university, had difficulties when he was given a job in the Department of Trade:

I knew very little about the subject and was almost entirely dependent on the views of others. Worse than that, I had no means of making a proper judgement as to which view should be preferred. My predicament was common among MPs. Virtually none had enough expertise to enable them to make independent judgements. We were all suckers for the prejudices of the City analysts and academic economists with whose views we were daily regaled in the media. The level of parliamentary ignorance about economics was at times quite astonishing.[21]

It takes a particular sort of intellectual self-confidence (or arrogance) to rise above the anxiety of ignorance. The political journalist Alan Watkins tells the story of how

the late Francis Hope's mother once had a dream about Richard Crossman. She was seated in a dentist's chair and he, attired in a white coat, was about to attend to her teeth.

'Don't be so silly, Dick,' she said. 'You know you're not a dentist.'

'I know I'm not, you fool,' Crossman replied, 'but I can work it out quite easily from first principles.'[22]

To these two initial difficulties – the vast scope of government and the ignorance of those called upon to run it – must be added several more. The most frequent gripe is about the civil service. In theory, since the middle of the nineteenth century the bureaucracy which runs Britain has been a purely professional, disinterested, incorruptible organization dedicated only to serving the country thanks to the reforms introduced by Sir Stafford Northcote and Sir Charles Trevelyan. Before that, the administration of the country was in the hands of unambitious and often indolent men 'whose course', one of the service's historians wrote, 'was one of quiet and generally secluded performance of routine duties'.[23] Since then, the higher levels of the civil service have been the preserve of fearfully clever men and women who have won their jobs through competitive examination. In 1950, one of their leaders described the character of the ideal civil servant. 'He must be a practical person, yet have some of the qualities of the academic theorist; his work encourages the longest views and yet his day-to-day responsibilities are limited; he is a student of public opinion, but not a party politician.'[24]

The grandest civil servant, the Cabinet Secretary, can wield formidable influence. Each retires with a collection of photographs showing the different cabinets they have served: the only constant, in an ever-changing sea of faces, is that of the Cabinet Secretary. Famously, he (they have all been men) attends all cabinet meetings, recording what is said. As numerous senior politicians have noticed, Cabinet Secretaries prefer an idealized version, laying out what ministers might have intended to say, to a verbatim note, which most couldn't manage anyway, since they don't have shorthand. They like to cling to the perception that they are pure and disinterested. Certainly, no recent occupant of the post has had as close a relationship as the one which existed between Neville Chamberlain and his head of the civil service, Sir Horace Wilson, a passionate believer in appeasing Nazi Germany. Three months before the outbreak of war Beaverbrook complained that politics had been wiped out and parliament had become an irrelevance. 'Today, we are living under despotism by consent . . . the country is at present being ruled from the anteroom of Downing Street.'[25]

Horace Wilson's enormous and baleful influence was possible only because he identified so closely with Chamberlain, whom he addressed as 'Neville, dear'. For the most part, senior civil servants have tended more to be noted for their sinewy persuasiveness or their mental gymnastics, like the 1960s Cabinet Secretary Burke Trend, of whom it was said that he could draft the most complicated White Papers in his head. But the problem with clever minds is that they need something to occupy them. Some ministers seem much better able to understand this than others. Aneurin Bevan, creator of the Labour party's most lasting monument, the National Health Service, was one. 'He had', one of his biographers writes admiringly, 'the precious gift of being able to concentrate upon essentials and leave the details to his civil servants: he would expound to them the principles under which he wanted them to operate and then trust them to get on with it. In other words, he understood the proper roles of Minister and civil servant.'[26] The inherent disadvantage which confronts the new minister is that, while politicians come and go, the bureaucracy goes on for ever. Gerald Kaufman talked about 'its majestic imperturbability' and had no doubts about its capacity to look after itself, even if this meant obstructing the wishes of the elected government. The first question members of a department ask themselves when they learn they are to have a new minister is 'What have we got here?' 'The new minister may turn out to be rude, lazy, irascible, dirty, a drunkard or – worst of all – stupid. And they are stuck with him, particularly the Private Office, who have to live with him all the time. To begin with, they operate on the safest principle, namely that he is an imbecile.'[27] This need not always turn out to be accurate (although John Major did, rather touchingly, say that he decided to become a minister because his academic qualifications were too poor for him ever to have become a mandarin). The loyalty of the civil servant is not to any particular party or government, but to the administrative machine, and specifically to his or her part of the machine, whether it be transport or education or defence. Each department has its own ambience and its own ideas about how to do its job. Several of them are more or less permanently at war with each other. Kaufman concluded that if you wanted to be sure of getting something done to which the civil service might object, the safest way was to stop it getting caught up in the fighting between departments. If the all-powerful Treasury is being enlisted as an ally against you, talk face to face with Treasury ministers. If, after all that, they are still not on your side, you had better think of another idea.

Kaufman was undoubtedly right in his belief that, of all the White-hall departments, the Treasury is the mightiest. The Foreign Office, with its emollient diplomats and vast Victorian offices, adorned with murals of Britannia Bellatrix or Pacificatrix, may embody the belief that it once administered the greatest empire since ancient Rome. But it is the Treasury which controls the domestic imperium. The dominance is simply explained: the Treasury controls the government's income. Other departments just spend it. (The ascendancy certainly cannot be due to any great financial acumen, since under the stewardship of the Treasury, the value of sterling has steadily plummeted since the end of the Second World War, while the country has stumbled like a drunk from inflation to recession and back again. The Treasury is just as much a prisoner of the British economy as any other department of government: the days are long gone when Lloyd George could look at the job of being Chancellor of the Exchequer to the richest country on earth and wonder, 'Have you ever thought how it felt to play God?')[28]

Confronted with an insufferable new minister, the civil service can console itself with the long view: politicians are here today and gone tomorrow. If today's minister dislikes some project the civil service has cooked up, he or she will be gone in two or three years and then, with a change of government, or a ministerial reshuffle, the old projects can be taken down from the shelves, have the dust blown off them, and be presented to the new incumbent.

If there is one persistent theme in the memoirs of many one-time ministers it is a low-level drone about the determination of the civil service to get its own way. Occasionally, the whine will snap into an anguished yelp. Once inside a ministry, these accounts suggest, the politician has to be on guard not to be taken prisoner. The tricks are numerous and devious. Confronted with an idea they don't like, civil servants can organize endless meetings to delay its implementation, or persuade other government departments to object when the issue is due for discussion in cabinet. If it is likely to cost money, they may be pretty confident of Treasury support; if not, they can enlist the aid of outside pressure groups, with the inevitable result that it appears in the newspapers. Safest of all, they can keep the minister on a short leash. There is control of the minister's diary, for one thing. This means that awkward people – or people the civil servants think might be awkward – can be kept away. It also means that the empty hours can be filled with meetings, briefings, visits and news conferences. The pressure of public or private events was, Harold Wilson's press secretary thought, 'like a tide that is always coming in. If there is a gap in the Prime Minister's diary, then the civil servants will try to fill it with another official engagement.'[29]

And not just Prime Ministers: the same relentless pressure bears in on many members of the cabinet. One of Wilson's ministers, Richard Crossman, thought his civil servants were trying to drown him in paper, so that he couldn't be a nuisance.[30] 'When I get home to my house in London at about ten or eleven at night from the House of Commons, there are one, two, three, four, or even five boxes, which include not only the papers for the next day's meetings, but the decisions which I have to take that night before reaching the Ministry the next day. The first job you have to do is to prevent yourself becoming a slave of the red box.'[31] Some succeed. Many fail. Barbara Castle ended up sometimes hoping the government's opponents would get their way, simply because she had no energy left to fight her corner, she was so exhausted by the demands of ministerial life. 'I just haven't got the strength to work more than sixteen hours a day,' she despaired.[32] At the most Machiavellian level, if the private office believes there is a danger of a minister making a decision with which the civil service disagrees, the meeting can be spun out until there is simply no time for the politicians to come to any other conclusion than the one that has been prepared for them.

It is noticeable that all these complaints come from Labour politicians. But it does not mean that Conservative ministers have found the civil service entirely congenial. Among the disciples of Margaret Thatcher, it became received wisdom that the civil service was one of the main obstacles to change. When the Conservative John Redwood became Secretary for Trade and Industry, he decided that dealing with the bureaucracy was rather 'like playing multi-dimensional chess'. The overriding impulse within the civil service was to conform: the greatest condemnation which could be uttered about a particular individual within a department, he found, was that he or she was 'too independent'. The second difficulty was the belief within the service that 'for every question there has to be an answer'. The consequence was that the civil service developed an encyclopaedic approach to government. It was not so much that it actively set out to obstruct as that, after generations of heavy central government, it had so many policies for so many issues that every action had collateral consequences and was therefore best left undone. Which explains why, even when a general election brings about a profound sea-change in British politics, most policies, in most departments, do not alter.

The diaries of Tony Benn – an archive so vast that it can be described only as an obsession (he is in the habit of taking a tape recorder with him even when taking part in live television interviews) – recount his epic battles with established thinking. Once upon a time Anthony Wedgwood Benn was the youngest backbencher in Clement Attlee's government, until he was forced to leave the House of Commons on inheriting the title of Lord Stansgate. He then proclaimed his loyalty to the socialist cause by spending three years fighting to disclaim the title, eventually returning to the House of Commons as an MP for Bristol. Harold Wilson rewarded his radical convictions with the job of Postmaster General. The role was not quite as empty as it sounds to twenty-first-century ears, because the small empire he oversaw included postal services, broadcasting and telecoms, employed nearly 400,000 people and contained, in the Post Office Savings Bank, what Benn believed was the biggest bank in the world. He entered government brimming with radical zeal. The

General Post Office (as it was then called) would be revolutionized. There would be advertising on the BBC. He would create a state-owned 'Giro' bank, which would operate across post office counters. As he tells it in his diaries, Benn drove at high speed straight into a brick wall. The explanation, he felt later, was that 'the deal the civil service offers you is this: if you do what we want you to do, we will help you publicly to pretend that you're implementing the manifesto on which you were elected . . . they are always trying to steer incoming governments back into the policy of the outgoing government, minus the mistakes that the civil service thought that the outgoing government made'.[33] Time after time, Benn's brilliant ideas came to nothing. In January 1965 he was furious that his scheme for Christmas cards produced by the Post Office was being obstructed. A retired brigadier produced a report explaining the enormous difficulties which would be involved in printing 15 million cards. Benn had no idea that anything like that number was under consideration, and concluded:

This is the way the Civil Service undermines you if it doesn't want to do something. It simply produces a paper to say that a thing cannot be done. It is all so discouraging . . . The trouble with the Civil Service is that it wants a quiet life. The civil servants want to move slowly along the escalator towards their knighthood and retirement and they have no interest whatsoever in trying to develop new lines of activity.[34]

A month later he is exclaiming, 'The Civil Service is a nightmare. God knows how you can instil real excitement into it.'[35]

There is an unmistakable whiff of Mr Pooter about some of Benn's ambitious projects. His attempts to get the Queen's head taken off postage stamps and replaced with works of art or other illustrations provide the most comical tale. In this, he saw himself as a David fighting Goliath, blocked at every turn by massive obstruction from the Establishment. Back and forth the letters go, with the result we can all see on any modern postage stamp: the designs come and go, but the Queen's head always stays. Benn eventually persuaded himself that the Queen herself might even have been indifferent to the whole thing. 'The real enemies', he concluded, 'are those forces of reaction, the Tory Party, the Civil Service, the Palace flunkies and courtiers –

who use the Queen as a way of freezing out new ideas.'[36] On and on our hero soldiered, until, in June, when he thought he had got agreement that the size of the Queen's head could be reduced, he 'discovered that my instructions on stamp policy have simply not been followed . . . Unless you watch them like a hawk they simply don't do what they're told.'[37]

Benn was neither the first nor the last minister to believe that the civil service was out to get him. (When the first Labour Prime Minister, Ramsay MacDonald, arrived in Downing Street, he had even insisted on personally opening any letter addressed to him. He is also said to have been caught on one occasion looking up train times for one of his secretaries.) So the truth may be slightly different. Was it possible that Harold Wilson – one of the most devious senior politicians of modern times – had simply decided that the way to contain his most noisily radical colleague was to put him in a job where he would be marooned on sandbank after sandbank? Benn seems at one point even to accept the possibility himself. Speaking of his time at the Department of Industry, ten years later, he recalled his Permanent Secretary describing him as 'a radical minister in a non-radical government', and added, 'I was faithful to the manifesto, but the Prime Minister did not support the manifesto on which he had been elected. Therefore, you had the power of the Permanent Secretary uniting with the power of the Prime Minister who was actually unconvinced by, and felt himself to be uncommitted to, the manifesto upon which he, as well as myself, had been elected.'[38] Other members of that government, who might not have claimed such sanctity, came to much the same conclusion. David Owen was certain that civil servants conspired against Benn, because they sensed that he was out of tune with his colleagues. (The spirit of fraternal comradeship was not helped by the suspicion that Benn was saying things in discussion simply so he could record his courageous utterances in his diary.) In his (unpublished) account of the times, his future cabinet colleague Edmund Dell thought he'd hit upon the solution. 'It is now not understood really at the Department of Industry how the Benn mind works. Except perhaps to the extent that it is increasingly understood that any project, however absurd, which involves the expenditure of public money will secure Benn's support, provided it is likely to bring him some political kudos as a leader of the people.'[39]

The civil service is an easy target. Just as all mothers-in-law are humourless old nags and all Italians wave their arms about, civil servants are a lot of smoothly clever Sir Humphrey figures, intriguing in gentlemen's clubs to frustrate the aims of politicians. They will achieve this obstruction, moreover, in the most intellectually condescending way possible, which ensures that it is the minister who ends up looking the fool. But there is an alternative analysis. It is not just a question of the best approach, of whether ministers might achieve more if they decide not to go at the job like a bull in a china shop. It is the unsettling feeling that some of these politicians are simply using the civil service as an excuse for their own failure. It is possible to read these endless chronicles of political frustration differently. Alan Clark's diaries are larded with descriptions of the obstructiveness, pomposity and archaic uselessness of the inhabitants of Whitehall. An alternative interpretation of his relatively brief and distinctly undistinguished time in government might be that he left no memorial behind because he had little to offer.

Consider the relationship from the other side. The civil servants suddenly find themselves with a new boss they do not know, and who almost certainly does not know them. He or she may also be profoundly ignorant not merely of how the department works, but perhaps of the entire field – agriculture or trade, say – which it is supposed to supervise. He or she may be considerate and thoughtful, or may turn out to be an utter martinet. It is said that as a minister Quintin Hogg was so petulant that he would tear up papers officials had laboriously prepared for him in front of them, or stab his pen through documents he didn't like. When he discovered that a tape on to which he had dictated letters for typing was blank (because he had pressed the wrong button) he blamed the machine. When his government-issue pen ran out, he threw it at the wall.[40] His staff had to work out a rota for answering the buzzer which summoned them to his office, so that his vile temper could be shared out fairly. This was an extreme case, but the peculiar form of self-absorption which characterizes some politicians can make them especially ill-suited to close working relationships.

The people who join the civil service are another breed altogether.

Although by common consent the overall calibre has fallen, as bright young graduates succumb to the lure of tedious work in the City of London for astronomically better rewards, the top levels of the profession still contain plenty of clever, smooth and sophisticated figures. You do not go into the bureaucracy if you want to wield mercurial power. But, curiously, the experience of Margaret Thatcher's government, which was initially seen within the bureaucracy as something of a catastrophe, left some of them with a real taste for the smack of political leadership. Government, she showed, did not need to control telecommunications, own oil companies, avoid confrontations with the miners, placate other European governments. The mandarins may not have cared for her whirlwind style at first. But she introduced them to the pleasures of the dominatrix. Their initial lack of enthusiasm was replaced by a respect for the fact that she had a clear set of priorities. 'The great thing about Mrs Thatcher', one of them once told me, 'was that you didn't have to ask her a question to know what her answer was.'

More humdrum politicians can take months to get control of their departments, which, left to their own devices, will continue doing what they did before the election that brought a change of government. The Secretary of State cannot even choose his own Permanent Secretary, the official who runs the department. One former Secretary of State, who ran one of the bigger government departments, told me that he simply never understood what his Permanent Secretary did all day. 'As far as I could see, his main preoccupation seemed to be recommending who got knighthoods and that sort of thing.' Another said his impression overall was that the civil service was 'over-staffed and under-managed'. Worst of all, he thought, were the civil servants who had been seconded to work in business. 'They come back thinking they know how the private sector works, when the fact of the matter is that the company they've been attached to has put them somewhere out of the way, where they can't do too much damage.'

For all that, it is human nature to enjoy being associated with a winner, and the politician who seems to be going places, getting things done and attracting complimentary headlines, generally finds the bureaucracy on his side. But given a choice between the risk of getting bad headlines by doing something, and getting no headlines at all by doing nothing, the institutional preference is for a quiet life. The British civil service is pretty free of financial corruption. Its secret vice is that desire for tranquillity.

For a politician trying to get things done, the real problem with the civil service seems not so much that it is reactionary as that it limits the choices available. 'As far as I could see,' one senior cabinet minister told me, 'no one ever went to a cabinet meeting to discuss the best or even the second best policy option. Those had already been discarded by the civil servants. So, all that was ever in question was whether you went for the third, fourth or even the fifth least bad option.'

Barbara Castle, who became one of the most unpopular ministers in Harold Wilson's government, had a simple motto. Reflecting, shortly before she died in her Buckinghamshire cottage, on what had gone wrong with politics, she said that the words 'Abandon Love All Ye Who Enter Here' ought to be inscribed above the door to every ministerial office. It is an interesting point. 'It *enhances* the standing of politicians to be prepared to be unpopular,' she said. 'You're never going to get anywhere if you want everyone to love you.'

And yet being loved is what so much of contemporary politics is about. In a post-ideological age, the Labour party has built its success upon seeming safe and appealing to people who might never otherwise have voted for it. Yet you cannot achieve radical change without being willing to confront those who might be disadvantaged by it. The difficulty is that the great battles which divided the parties after the Second World War – on nationalization or nuclear weapons, for example – are finished. The Welfare State brought the state into everyone's lives, but the consequence has been that it turned ministers from lawmakers to managers. And managers of a system which is bound to fail, at least part of the time. Where, once upon a time, governments impinged very little upon people's lives, there is now scarcely an area of human behaviour which is not touched by the law. Yet, while government is all pervasive, it is not, by its nature, particularly effective: the public knows from its own experience that ministerial boasts about the superiority of British health services, education or transport systems are empty. So the opportunity which the politician thought he had to make an impact on the lives of the entire population is just as easily an opportunity for the citizenry to blame him for the failures they see all around.

In an age when politics was driven by profoundly differing convictions about how the world ought to be organized, enemies were the price of progress. But when all that is being argued about is the mechanisms by which services are delivered to the general public, there is nothing to stiffen the backbone. Politicians have to become evangelists for a system which is intrinsically incapable of delivering what is asked of it: the greatest credibility problem of modern politics is that the political process cannot answer adequately for the performance of the public sector. It follows that the wisest ministers are those who realize soonest how very little power they really have. The number of politicians who can look back on their ministerial careers and feel that they really made a significant difference to their country is small. Roy Jenkins could honestly recall his time as Home Secretary and say that he had achieved something, in endorsing the reforms to the laws on abortion and homosexuality. Margaret Thatcher emasculated the trades unions. Tony Blair gave Wales an assembly and Scotland a parliament. But quite what the Secretary of State for Culture, the three junior ministers and their aides write in their diaries each night is something of a mystery.

To try to discover how people who had devoted their lives to politics might handle the awesome complications of being put in charge of a government department whose basic challenges were not political but managerial, I wrote to Alan Milburn, MP for Darlington. Milburn, who had been brought up by a single mother in a County Durham pit village, was once part of the International Marxist Group, the British section of Trotsky's Fourth International. His entire adult life had been devoted to politics, on a journey that had taken him from hard-left agitator to Tony Blair's Secretary of State for Health. Now, he was in charge of the biggest department in government. In the days of the Cold War, the British National Health Service was described as the largest European employer after the Red Army. More recently, the Department of Health simply said it was the biggest employer in Europe. In Alan Milburn, it was presided over by a man whose entire managerial experience had been as the part-proprietor of a left-wing bookshop in Newcastle called Days of Hope, known locally as Haze of Dope. In an interview, he once testified to his entrepreneurial skills by boasting that he had 'personally developed the badge market in Tyneside'. Soon after he left the shop, the business had gone bankrupt, although whether that had been coincidence or the effect of losing the expertise of its badge-seller was unclear.[41]

My letter asked if I could spend a day with him, to see how good a preparation the badge-selling triumph had been for running an organization that employed 1.1 million people. About a month later, his head of public relations telephoned to say that he would be happy to have me 'see him in action'. It was just a case of setting a date. She would call back. A week went by. A fortnight passed. A month came and went. I called her back. She was always 'out of the office', 'in a meeting' or 'rather busy', and promising to ring. She never did. I called a further ten or twelve times, and each time encountered one or other of her assistants, who promised to leap into action. One time it was even let slip that the Health Secretary was just trying to find a suitable day when I could come in and see him leading his staff. Slowly, it began to dawn on me that I had just joined another of the famous National Health Service waiting lists. After five months of telephone calls I tried another tack. I really didn't mind whether the Health Secretary wanted to let me watch him at work or not. But it would just be good to know one way or another. Even that phone call was unreturned. I tried one last time, and finally one of his secretaries said that he would indeed be willing for me to spend a day with him. But the only convenient date would be six weeks after the manuscript of this book had to be handed in for printing. After that I began to understand why Days of Hope had never become a fixture on every high street.

How long does it take for a cabinet minister to make a difference? Probably a lot longer than most of them have got. Of the first Blair cabinet, ten ministers – getting on for half its membership – were gone four years later. Almost every year the cry goes up that the Prime Minister is planning to reshuffle his government. Mostly, these reshuffles occur in the summer, but the whispering begins in the spring, like a slow handclap in the Circus Maximus, as the audience waits impatiently for someone to be thrown to the lions. Often enough, the whispering campaign that someone is being prepared for sacrifice has been started by the very people with whom the minister shares the cabinet table. Unless stilled quickly, it can build to an unanswerable chorus, which can be silenced only by the production of a victim. Reorganizing a cabinet has big attractions for a Prime Minister, of course. It not only gives the opportunity to get rid of people who have underperformed but can also be a way of breaking dangerous alliances among potential rivals for the top job, by removing them from the cabinet, or at the very least exiling them to some unappealing job such as looking after farmers. The space made available around the cabinet table can be used to promote allies and to try to keep the government looking fresh.

The consequence of this constant change is that ministers often stay in their job long enough to be a nuisance, but not long enough to make things any better. It is common practice to move junior ministers on after a year or so in post. But at cabinet level, unless they are familiar with the subject from a conscientious period as opposition spokesman, ministers will spend much of their first year learning the job, dependent upon the permanent officials. In the second year, they may begin to make a mark. Often it is only by the third year – at which time they may well be on the way out – that they are fully in command. In some government departments, the turnover rate has been so high that you wonder whether the newly appointed Secretary of State even had time to choose a new set of office curtains before he or she was moved on. In May 2002, Tony Blair's Transport Secretary, Stephen Byers, resigned his post, confessing that he had become an embarrassment to the government. Byers had proved to be a spectacularly unlucky minister, held personally responsible both for his own errors of judgement, such as whether or not clumsy members of staff should be dismissed, and for others, such as rail accidents or air traffic control failures, which he had been powerless to prevent. His personal aloofness had made him no friends, but, by common consent, at the time he took the job the British transport system was chaotic. Byers had had precisely eleven months to attempt to sort it out before he threw in the towel. He failed.

But, if the British people were looking for an explanation of why the system was such a mess, they might have looked at the record of his predecessors. Between 1947 and 1997 there were twenty-five different politicians at the head of the Department/Ministry of Transport. This works out at an average period in office of two years. The longest anyone stayed in the job was six years (in the post-war Attlee government). A further three individuals, including figures such as the motorway apostle Ernest Marples, lasted four or five years – long enough to make an impact. But that means that in the remaining twenty-nine years there were *twenty-one* different people in charge of transport policy. The Thatcher and Major governments ate up Transport Secretaries and spat them out: in the eighteen years between 1979 and 1997, they got through eleven of them. Most major transport projects are estimated[42] to take thirteen years to plan and implement and many may take much longer. Is it any wonder that Britain has a shambolic transport system?

There is another consequence of constant reshuffles. The longer a government stays in office, the fewer competent people there are to be given jobs. It is difficult enough at the start of a fresh administration, since, although in theory the Prime Minister may appoint to the cabinet whoever he wants, on the whole he must choose elected MPs, and must also be sure to placate the prominent figures in the party who may later challenge him for his own job. This can make for a jaw-droppingly low ratio of potential candidates to places. Once the Prime Minister has excluded from consideration the clapped out, the unproven, the unreliable, the hostile, the inept and the unstable, there remains a very small group indeed. Furthermore, the single prerequisite achievement of each candidate has been their ability to persuade the voters they are a fit person to represent them in parliament. It does not necessarily mean they are going to be any use as ministers. Tristan Garel-Jones, who was a Conservative whip in the 1980s, recalls scanning a list of fifteen candidates for a junior ministerial job and thinking to himself, 'I wouldn't employ a single one of them.' The problem was that, if you include all the various ranks of ministers, 'You have to find maybe ninety people to form a government. You have perhaps 350 or so people to choose from. Once you've eliminated the bad, mad, drunk and over-the-hill, you've got rid of a hundred. You then have to pick ninety people out of a pool of 250. Is it any wonder the calibre is so low?' By the middle 1990s, things had got even worse. Not only had the overall number of Conservative MPs fallen, while the number of incompetents and has-beens had grown, there was also a much larger group who had already served in government and been worn out or found wanting by the process. Small wonder that it was so hard for John Major to give his administration an aura of either coherence or competence.

When Tony Blair succeeded the exhausted Conservatives, he implicitly acknowledged that having an ability to get yourself elected an MP was not necessarily the best qualification for running organizations which essentially needed inspired managers. Despite having no fewer than 419 MPs after the 1997 election he was, it seems, convinced that he did not have sufficient talent in the active sections of the Labour party to form an effective government. How else to explain his decision to involve so many people who had not bothered themselves with the inconvenience of getting elected? He sent his old friend Derry Irvine off to live in the lavish quarters Pugin had designed for the Lord Chancellor – a title which made him the grandest person in the land, after the royal family and the Archbishop of Canterbury. Blair's one-time flatmate Charlie Falconer was made Lord Falconer and brought into government, where he gleefully accepted the poisoned chalice of responsibility for the Millennium Dome, the greatest monument to his old friend's hubris. Larry Whitty was rewarded for years of service as General Secretary of the Labour party with another peerage and was soon travelling the country telling farmers what the government was not going to do to help them. Liz Symons, who had previously run the First Division Association, the trades union for senior civil servants, crossed the road to the House of Lords and was soon busy on foreign and defence policy. Patricia Scotland and Valery Amos were lured from the worlds of law and equal opportunities and likewise given jobs and peerages. There were many others.

The rash of appointments to public office of people the Prime Minister found congenial soon gave rise to the epithet 'Tony's Cronies'. It had a conveniently assonant sting to it, even if all Prime Ministers give peerages to their friends, and all governments have to find people to fill the raft of ministerial positions which the British constitution demands be occupied by people in the House of Lords.

(It is a duplication which could be abolished tomorrow, if parliament is ever properly reformed, making it possible for a minister to be made to explain himself in either place.) Among the appointees were a gaggle of businessmen. David Simon was lured away from running the oil company BP, given a peerage and made minister for European trade. Gus Macdonald passed 'Go' by parking his media career, collecting a peerage and becoming a minister. One of the richest men in Britain, David Sainsbury, took leave from his family supermarket empire to work in the Department of Trade. These people were not merely personally or politically congenial. They had been engaged in recognition of the fact that a career in a radical bookshop may not provide quite enough business acumen to perform well in government departments with budgets running into billions.

Hiring businessmen and women to carry out some of the functions of government recognizes that much of the administration's job is simply to deliver services. Most people's experience of government is that it demands money with menaces and offers to provide things – education, healthcare, personal security – in exchange. There is nothing very complicated about the transaction, and there is a superficial plausibility to the argument that the skills best suited to providing the service are entrepreneurial. But for businessmen and women enticed into government the experience is baffling and often bruising. For a start, there is the problem of discovering whether they are achieving anything. A chief executive of a company can set his staff targets. Whether they are met or not is usually measurable financially: successful companies increase their sales and their share price tends to rise. Simple. But there is no equivalent in the public sector. How to judge whether a defence minister has achieved anything, until the army is deployed and finds it has radios that will not work or tanks which cannot cope with the desert? How does a minister in charge of social security decide that he or she has accomplished something? One measure might be to see that more people are taking up the benefits they are entitled to, which would ensure that the overall bill rises – the precise opposite of what the ministers at the Treasury are trying to achieve.

But business people can also lack the antennae to sense how to survive in a political organization. If they join the government in the

House of Lords, their 'comrades' in the House of Commons will resent them if they become too successful. But if they attempt to give themselves democratic legitimacy, by being levered into a safe seat in the House of Commons, they have the unhappy example of John Davies as a cautionary tale. Previously head of the Confederation of British Industry, Davies was appointed to the cabinet in 1970 by Edward Heath, in the belief that a businessman might know how to run British industry. Heath later admitted that the decision was 'unfortunate' and 'not an inspired appointment'.[43] Davies began by proclaiming the government's refusal to bail out 'lame ducks' and then proceeded to do precisely that, on the ground that governments could not stand idly by when manufacturing concerns went to the wall and people lost their jobs. The wholesale retreat was not Davies's decision alone: it was a symptom of the collapse of an entire approach to policy. But it was up to Davies to sell the policy retreat to the House of Commons. Not having spent his life playing oratorical games, Davies was a hopeless speaker. Opposition MPs laughed and heckled. Worse, fellow Conservatives did nothing to help. He had done little to cultivate allies on the benches behind him and they sat there in silence, watching him drown. His fellow Conservative John Biffen, who in the later Thatcher government had the same job in cabinet, looked back later at Davies's unhappy career and explained, 'The cry had gone up "We need people with business brains in government," and they lured the poor chap into the Commons. And the moment he arrived, they resented him and they began to grease the steps he was supposed to ascend.'

The contrast is with the United States, where presidents may draw their cabinets from wherever they like. American Secretaries of State such as Dean Rusk, Henry Kissinger, Cyrus Vance and Colin Powell all came from outside the fevered world of elected politics. So the strength of the British system of government – the fact that it obliges each legislator to have a direct, accountable relationship to his constituency – can also be its weakness.

While the removal vans are shifting his possessions to Downing Street, the enormity of his responsibilities is borne in on the newly elected Prime Minister. In the first few hours, he will travel to Buckingham

Palace to be asked to form a government, be briefed by the Cabinet Secretary on the state of the country, appoint a cabinet, and then be presented with a scenario which assumes that he no longer exists. The Chief of the Defence Staff calls on the Prime Minister, to tell him how the country's Trident nuclear-missile submarines are deployed. The Cabinet Secretary then informs the Prime Minister that he must, personally, write a separate letter to each commander of the four submarines. It is to be written on the assumption that much or most of Britain has been annihilated, that communications have been destroyed, and that therefore no new orders can be given. The Prime Minister has a number of choices. He might choose to order retaliatory strikes against the enemy by flattening its capital and killing millions, or to tell the submarine commanders to find refuge somewhere in the southern hemisphere. A third option might be to order each commander to try to contact Washington and place himself under American control, or he might simply be told to use his own initiative.

The instructions – one sheet of paper for each of the four commanders – are to be written in the Prime Minister's own hand, sealed in an envelope without being disclosed to anyone, couriered under guard to the submarine base, and then kept inside the submarine's safe, to be opened if the captain concludes, from radio silence, that Britain has been hit by a nuclear attack and the Prime Minister incinerated, along with most of the rest of the citizenry. One of those present at the nuclear briefing after the 1997 election said that Tony Blair 'went white' when he heard what was involved.[44] When John Major was told in 1990, he cancelled a planned weekend at Chequers, the Prime Minister's official residence, to retreat to his home in Huntingdon, so that he would have a more 'human' frame of mind as he wrote these awesome instructions. He told me that it was the point at which the gravity of being Prime Minister was brought home to him.

In extreme times, the Prime Minister is the physical embodiment of the British state. Looking back over the holders of the office in the last hundred years it is striking what a diverse bunch they were. Most had to some degree the obsession with politics which characterized David Lloyd George ('He lived only for politics. He talked politics in his leisure hours – either the politics of the moment, or political reminiscence. Political history was his only serious reading,' according to the historian A.J.P. Taylor).[45] In recent years, all have been professionals and many have been astonishingly hardworking – few would be heard now repeating Stanley Baldwin's description of himself: 'I was born a gentleman. I am a lazy man. I am not such a fool as people think.'[46] Sometimes there seem superficial similarities between the vitriol heaped upon say, Sir Henry Campbell-Bannerman ('He has attained one of the greatest positions in the world without exhibiting any extraordinary talent or performing anything worthy of note,' according to a scathing contemporary)[47] and John Major ('this extraordinarily ordinary man . . . dependent on briefing cards for the most mundane of interviews and statements . . . the Tory party gave him everything, and he destroyed it,' in the words of a fellow Conservative).[48] But what could Clement Attlee ('the nearest approach to a saint we are likely to see in this place', according to Richard Crossman)[49] have in common with A.J. Balfour ('Humanity tired him, bored him, he was intolerant of men and women,' said Mary Gladstone)?[50]

Cometh the hour, cometh the man. One of the best advantages a politician can have is to have been born at the right time. In peaceful, prosperous times, the people care less for politics. Why should they? So little seems to be at stake, politics is no more than entertainment. The people will not accept an agitator when they need an organizer. In times of crisis, out goes Asquith or Chamberlain, in comes Lloyd George or Churchill. When the crisis abates, the public doesn't care for a Lloyd George or Churchill, it wants a Bonar Law or an Attlee. After the compromises of a Callaghan government, the call is for the simple clarity of a Thatcher, and when the public begins to chafe under her abrasiveness, it will even accept a Major, and when he is found bumbling, will applaud the missionary zeal of a Blair. Sometimes the public wants originality and sparks, other times it wants quiet consideration. The lucky politician is the one who finds a career trajectory matching that of the country in which he or she lives. Churchill had the good fortune to become eligible to vote in 1895, when Britain was the greatest country in the world, when what was decided at Westminster, by the greatest politicians in the world, mattered. A shrewd observer wrote that 'Winston could afford to take every shortcut to greatness himself, to break the social contract and climb on the dullards' backs because he and they all believed instinctively in the greatness they were part of.'[51] It gave him the self-belief to ride out the changes of public mood which periodically becalmed his political career and he lived long enough to see the wind change and give him another chance.

Originally, the Prime Minister was just that, the first minister of the government of the day. Nowadays the job is largely what the holder makes of it. The contrast between the two Labour landslides of the twentieth century could not be starker: The 1945 Labour administration, which brought about the greatest social reforms of the twentieth century, was a collective enterprise. Clement Attlee had to work on the assumption that, although he was theoretically the most important figure in government, it was his colleagues running government departments such as Health or the Board of Trade who had budgets to spend and therefore real executive power. Attlee refined the motif for such a style of government. 'He must remember that he's only the first among equals.'[52] He refused simply to appoint docile yes-men, and deliberately included people no one would ever have thought brilliant, to get a commonsense contribution. He decided that, if his government was going to work properly, he couldn't have much more than sixteen people sitting around the cabinet table. His style of chairmanship – 'You've said that already,' or 'Nothing more to say, I hope? Good' – was in utter contrast to Churchill's cabinets, which could go on for hours, at the end of which often enough nothing much had been decided. Attlee took no votes in cabinet – 'The job of the Prime Minister is to get the general feeling,' he said, and then to sum up what he believed to be the general view.[53]

The government which took power after the Labour landslide of 1997 was another beast altogether. Now there were over twenty people crammed around the cabinet table.[54] But bigger did not mean better: Tony Blair's cabinet was a shadow of the institution with which Attlee had run his government. The prussification of the party which had been necessary to recover from the long years in the wilderness meant that, once it was in office, the old conventions went out of the window. There were two towering figures in this government, the Chancellor of the Exchequer, Gordon Brown, and the Prime Minister himself. But the defining spirit was summed up in two words: 'Tony Wants'.[55] No other Labour government had ever been so concentrated in the person of one individual. Cabinet meetings still took place, with the ministers trooping up to 10 Downing Street every Thursday morning. The Prime Minister's spokesman still briefed reporters on what had been 'discussed' at the meeting. But the event itself had been stripped of any real moment. It frequently lasted not much longer than an edition of the television show *Ready, Steady, Cook*. Having set a pattern for short meetings, it was hard for a party so obsessed with its image in the newspapers to change: if cabinet gatherings started going on for long enough to have sensible discussions, the media might start talking about splits in the government. Blair was totally unapologetic. 'I remember Roy Jenkins telling me about the 1960s, when they would have Cabinet for two days. Can you imagine trying to conduct business today like that? The government would go into freefall,'[56] he claimed. Reading the diaries of that period, one can see why Blair would find the idea of old-fashioned cabinet government unappealing. Real political argument took place, and on at least one occasion, when he was unable to get his way, Harold Wilson had been reduced to a tantrum: if the cabinet wouldn't do what he wanted, well they could just get themselves another leader.[57] A very senior civil servant privately gave the real reason. 'It's not the fear of the press going on about splits that stops the Cabinet from discussing things. It's because the PM doesn't like argument. Cabinet these days is just a series of self-congratulatory remarks.'[58]

The fact that the cabinet no longer really discussed anything in any detail did have the merit of avoiding any open clash with the Chancellor of the Exchequer. Real discussion took place in separate meetings between the individuals concerned. But the frustrations in this style of government for merely mortal ministers were obvious: there was no effective way of gathering political support for an idea. It concentrated power in the hands of a lawyer who had never run anything in his life. Harold Wilson – like Heath, Callaghan and even Thatcher – had spent his political career in a world where cabinet mattered. Tony Blair came to power never having sat in a cabinet meeting in his life and with little apparent belief in the institution.

To be fair to Blair, the decline of government by a cabinet has been a gradual thing. In the Attlee government, cabinet met an average of eighty-seven times a year, and considered about 340 papers prepared for it. By the early 1970s the number of cabinet meetings had dropped by a third, to about sixty, at which they considered about 140 memoranda. By the early 1990s it had slumped to no more than forty meetings each year, in which fewer than twenty papers, on subjects such as the state of the economy and plans for forthcoming legislation, were chewed over. Contrary to the media myth that she was an autocrat who ignored the rest of her party, Margaret Thatcher took cabinet seriously – so seriously that she would organize small groups beforehand (in which she felt confident she would have a majority), to try to ensure it would approve formally things which had been agreed earlier. This had the obvious consequence of cutting out much genuine debate. Nonetheless, cabinets could still last for two or two and a half hours. The Chancellor of the Exchequer, Nigel Lawson, used to look forward to them as 'the most restful and relaxing event of the week',[59] and, 'apart from the summer holidays, the only real period of rest that I got in what was a very heavy job'.[60]

John Major had given Tony Blair a good example of why cabinet government was a dangerous thing. Aware that he owed his unexpected eminence to the fact that his predecessor had been dispatched by the very people now sharing the oval table with him, he felt obliged to listen. He was by temperament a man who preferred consensus to confrontation, which was fine when he was climbing the greasy pole, but was no help at all in trying to stay at the top of it: the secret of his rise, one bitter cabinet colleague said, had been to appear to agree with everyone. It made decision-taking a shambles. Furthermore, he was so worried by the possibility of being humiliated in Prime Minister's Questions on Thursday afternoons that the meetings, on Thursday mornings, were often cut short so that he could prepare himself for the ordeal. Worse, every time there was a disagreement in cabinet on a touchstone issue, such as Britain's relationship with the rest of Europe, someone or other briefed the papers. So leaky was Major's cabinet that they might as well have installed microphones and transmitted the thing on radio. When times are difficult, but not disastrous, cabinet meetings have the great merit of reminding members of a government that, in the end, they will all hang together. (It was, after all, her failure to carry the cabinet that eventually did for Margaret Thatcher.) But, with Major's government poised on the verge of disaster, it was *sauve qui peut*. Small wonder that Blair saw little to commend meaningful cabinet government.

There is nothing inherently wrong in ignoring the conventions of cabinet government. It is, after all, only a convention. But the old arguments in its favour are strong. Decision-taking is not easy: as John Kenneth Galbraith put it in a letter to President Kennedy, politics is largely about choosing between the disastrous and the unpalatable.[61] Somehow, the pressing demands of workers, patients, bosses, benefit claimants, commuters, doctors, soldiers, scientists, environmentalists and foreign allies have to be filtered into an order of priorities. The doctrine of collective responsibility, in which individuals were entitled to argue passionately for their particular cause, but then all agreed to accept and abide by the decision of cabinet, is both understandable and useful. But the justifications for turning the thing into an echo-chamber are all apparently plausible. A system of weekly cabinet meetings is said to be too slow and cumbersome for the speed with which decisions need to be taken in the modern world. If you invite everyone to contribute their views on a subject, too many people become involved for decisions to be taken effectively. It leaks: a controversial issue discussed among twenty-two people could well end up in the weekend newspapers. Hence the expression, heard at the topmost levels of government, that something is 'too sensitive to discuss in cabinet', which explains everything we need to know about the limits of collegiality. If British politics were played out in a more reflective, less hysterical atmosphere, it would matter a great deal less: you could argue that a cabinet which disagrees over nothing has found nothing worth while to discuss.

If decisions are no longer being taken in cabinet, where are they being taken? It is usually said that they happen in cabinet committees. But this is much less true than used to be the case, simply because it is so hard to convene a committee when its members are constantly being called away to meetings in Brussels or wherever. The answer to the conundrum of where decisions are made seems to be that they are increasingly taken away from both formal cabinets and cabinet committees, in meetings between the ministers involved and their staff. Most of all, they are taken by the Prime Minister.

The Prime Minister has always had a formidable range of powers at his disposal, both personally and constitutionally. He or she can firstly decide who gets appointed to one of the hundred-odd ministerial jobs. The Prime Minister is free to sack any of them at any time. He or she recommends people for honours. The patronage extends to the senior levels of the civil service, where the Prime Minister is entitled to approve appointments. Acting in the name of the Crown and without consulting parliament, the Prime Minister chooses judges, bishops, lords, the heads of Royal Commissions and the chairman of the BBC. A generation ago Lord Hailsham talked of 'elective dictatorship'.[62] Since then, the expression has become an even more accurate description of the actual power of the Prime Ministerial office. The status of the Prime Minister has risen, as the standing of the cabinet has plunged. The lesson, increasingly, is that for anything to happen in government it needs the personal backing of the party leader. Cabinet minister after cabinet minister has remarked, with a slightly despairing air, that 'It doesn't matter how devoted you are to a particular policy. It doesn't even matter if the whole party is crying out for a policy to be implemented. The only thing – the *only* thing – that determines whether the policy is acted upon is the passionate conviction of the party leader.'

Being almost the only significant figure at the centre of government means there are not enough hours in the day to give undivided attention to any issue. It almost defies belief that as recent a Prime Minister as Harold Macmillan should have boasted that he sat in Downing Street and read Trollope. Not only is there little time for fiction. There is scarcely time to think. So the job has been contracted out. Edward Heath's Central Policy Review Staff, or 'think tank', was designed to fill the void, as was Harold Wilson's Policy Unit. Margaret Thatcher drew ideas from a range of institutes set up to refine 'Thatcherism', and inserted her own favourite thinkers, such as her economic adviser Alan Walters, into the heart of the government machine. Tony Blair went further. Soon after getting elected he laid an Order in Council granting his key henchmen, Chief of Staff Jonathan Powell and Press Secretary Alastair Campbell, the authority to give orders to civil servants. Through the following years there followed an epidemic of 'tsars' and 'task forces' – more than there were tasks, it seemed – and so many politically congenial (and often unelected) figures appointed to the top jobs in government that 10 Downing Street had to issue an 'organogram' to try to explain how the Prime Minister's office worked. It revealed that all the key areas were commanded by political allies rather than civil servants. So much power had been consolidated that it amounted in all but name to a new and all-powerful department of government.

In the governments led by Tony Blair, these unelected advisers had more power than the great majority of MPs, including some members of the cabinet. Ed Balls, Gordon Brown's helpmate at the Treasury, promoted to the role of Chief Economic Adviser, was commonly referred to throughout Whitehall as the 'Deputy Chancellor'. Peter Hennessy, the best-informed analyst of Whitehall, was simply told, 'Ed Balls is not just a minister, he's a permanent secretary as well. The Chief Secretary to the Treasury [the cabinet-rank politician who is notionally second-in-command] is just a personnel officer.'[63] So pervasive was the influence of policy advisers, and so knocked about was the civil service, that by Blair's second term the man appointed to take over as Cabinet Secretary, Sir Andrew Turnbull, was conceding that his own background (Cambridge, followed by an entire career spent in public administration) was no longer appropriate: this once disinterested organization needed many more people like Ed Balls and his friends.[64]

Surrounded by his phalanx of policy advisers, and (apart from appearances at Prime Minister's Questions) venturing only rarely into the House of Commons, Tony Blair in the role of Prime Minister has become more presidential than anything else. Even his colleagues agree with this description. When Blair started holding routine news conferences inside Downing Street in the summer of 2002, the impression that he had been translated into a president was consolidated: during his time in Downing Street, Winston Churchill had given precisely none. The earlier concession, in the spring of 2002, that the Prime Minister would consent to answer for his government before a committee of select committee chairmen merely acknowledged how far the executive in Downing Street was now distinct from the legislature in the House of Commons. When the party ran for election, its manifesto contained seven photographs of the Leader and not one picture of the rest of the cabinet. His allies maintained that that was the only way a modern British leader could operate, yet they preferred not to mention the extent to which this supremely powerful figure was as free as a hobbled old mule. In the modern world, no British Prime Minister is truly free. The plain fact is that power has drained away – to Europe, to the assemblies in Scotland and Wales, to the law courts. For all the strutting on the world stage, the British economy is dependent upon international trade, British unemployment upon decisions taken in boardrooms in America, Japan or South Korea, much of foreign policy upon the laborious process of constructing some lowest-common-denominator form of words which would satisfy the rest of the European Union. Margaret Thatcher's decision to send soldiers, sailors and aircrew to the South Atlantic in 1982 was an independent action (although its success was still dependent upon American assistance). But Anthony Eden had learned the hard way, in the 1956 Suez Crisis, that Britain rarely had the freedom to act alone. Apart from the occasional small-scale intervention in a former colony, such as Sierra Leone, Tony Blair was free to send British troops into action, in Kosovo or Afghanistan, only if encouraged to do so by others, notably in Washington.

And no amount of presidential style can save a senior politician when the mood begins to turn against them. Arthur Balfour (known to his enemies as 'Pretty Fanny', 'Clara', 'Lucy', the 'palsied masher' or the 'perfumed popinjay') remarked, after a meeting of the Carlton Club had appointed Bonar Law leader in 1922, that 'It is not a principle of the Conservative Party to stab its leaders in the back, but I must confess that it often appears to be a practice.'[65] How readily Margaret Thatcher and John Major would agree. But what is striking to an outsider is how thoroughly unpleasant politicians are to one another in all parties. Attlee's comment that Herbert Morrison was 'his own worst enemy' was, famously, met with a mutter from Morrison's comrade in the crusade for a better world, Ernest Bevin, 'Not while I'm alive he ain't.' But it has also been said that Bevin was speaking of Aneurin Bevan, and his remark has been attributed to half-a-dozen other prominent Labour figures, precisely because it so perfectly captures the bitter rivalry which underlies fraternity. Only extremely rarely does it descend into real physical violence – as when George Brown attacked Richard Crossman in a House of Commons corridor because he didn't like something Crossman had written about him in a newspaper column.[66] The rest of the time, it is intrigue and gossip and sullen hostility, such as the victim of Brown's attack being known as 'Double Crossman' or Alan Clark hoping that his well-upholstered namesake Kenneth Clarke would go down with a heart attack. The tone was caught perfectly in the exchange I heard between two household-name politicians at one Labour party conference. It opened with 'Let me drop some poison in your ear.' Churchill dismissed Anthony Eden's speechifying by saying that it contained every cliché in the English language except 'Please adjust your clothing upon leaving' (the notice that used to adorn gentlemen's lavatories). Mo Mowlam, the most popular figure in the first Blair government, had her fate sealed when the party conference gave her a standing ovation in the middle of the Prime Minister's speech: no one could be allowed *that* much acclaim.

But, however hard they work to marginalize potential rivals, even the most hymned leaders accumulate odium, simply because they are leaders: in the days before the Falklands War, when Margaret Thatcher's unpopularity was running high, Young Conservatives held a poll to see who would be the most popular choice to take over from her if she were run down by a bus. The winner, who collected more points than all the other contenders put together, was the bus driver. Winston Churchill was so loathed by much of the Conservative party, who saw him as a traitor, that in the winter of 1938–9 secret plans were being made to persuade his Epping constituency to ditch him and find a truer, bluer replacement: his parliamentary career was saved by Hitler's sweep into eastern Europe. All leaders will make enemies, by passing over those who feel they deserve promotion or by endorsing some policies and blocking others. In any case, as David Lloyd George observed, 'There can be no friendship between the five top men in cabinet.'[67] But the *appearance* of collegiality must be preserved, especially at election times, when the leadership has to campaign together. 'One of the cruel absurdities of British politics', wrote the Labour leader Michael Foot, 'is that two men who hate each other's guts may be forced to stump the country handcuffed together.'[68]

And then there is the sheer, relentless opportunism of the Opposition. In 1996, as John Major was wrestling to keep his own party together, Thomas Hamilton, an unemployed single man who had once worked as a Scout leader, walked into a primary school in Dunblane armed with four handguns and carrying 743 rounds of ammunition. The unspeakable horror of what followed, in which sixteen young children and their teacher were shot to death and a further twelve injured, was the sort of event which puts the petty concerns of political advantage in their correct perspective. It was an act so unpredictable, so merciless, so incomprehensible, that no one could possibly have described it as a political act, or even the consequence of a political decision. Both the then Prime Minister and the Leader of the Opposition, Tony Blair, visited the town. Each was visibly distressed by what they saw and heard. The Conservatives believed that the two men had reached an understanding that this was an event neither party should try to exploit for political gain. An inquiry was set up to investigate what had happened and to try to ensure that nothing like it ever happened again. Six months later John Major turned on the television to see Blair with one of the grieving mothers from Dunblane at the Labour party conference in the Blackpool Winter Gardens. She was received with a standing ovation and heard in pin-drop silence. The woman translating the speech into sign language for the deaf stood on stage manipulating her fingers while tears rolled down her cheeks. At the end of the conference, Blair delivered a speech in which not only did he commit the Labour party to a 'total ban' on handguns, but many Conservatives felt he was almost making the government complicit in the tragedy. So much for not playing politics with grief.

The relentless interest of the media does not help either. The Prime Minister arrives in Truro on a Friday afternoon, where he visits a hospital, trailing half-a-dozen camera crews. Reporters accompanying the Prime Minister are telephoned by their newsdesks in London with the news that the Leader of the Opposition has said it is time to impose sanctions on a country in the South Pacific. As he emerges from the hospital, the questions are shouted, 'What are you going to do about sanctions on Nonga-Bonga?' The Prime Minister, who cannot quite recall where Nonga-Bonga is, has the choice, firstly, of telling the truth, which would involve admitting he does not know what the reporters are talking about. This runs the risk of headlines next morning proclaiming, 'I DON'T KNOW WHAT'S GOING ON, SAYS PM'. Alternatively, he can play for time, declaring that he is having the Foreign Office look into the matter, and it is being treated with the utmost urgency. This is only partly untrue, and at least gives no hostage to fortune. Thirdly, he promises action. This is much the most tempting option, because it seems to show him as a man of conviction and decision. It has the significant disadvantage, though, of being a response based upon profound ignorance. Even the reporting of a carefully prepared speech is not necessarily much better. The requirement for 'balance' means that, even if the television producers choose the most important part of the speech for inclusion in their report, it will almost certainly be followed by a section of videotape in which the relevant Opposition spokesman rejects the proposal, even though he may have neither heard nor read the speech. This may well be followed by spokesmen for minor parties who not only have neither heard nor read the speech, but do not even necessarily understand it.

As all these pressures crowd in on Prime Ministers, is it any wonder that they succumb to the chance to strut on a bigger stage, to speak at the United Nations, to be photographed with other leaders at conferences, to embark on personal odysseys to try to bring peace to some troubled corner of the world? At the very time that Tony Blair was being berated for faults in the National Health Service, education and public transport, he was a national hero in Kosovo and Sierra Leone. By the start of his second term in office, at the point at which voters were beginning to ask why, after the four years he had been in office, there had been so little improvement in public services, he was promising to sort out the misfortunes of Africa. A tour of the continent was hastily organized a few weeks later, although the officials responsible had no idea which countries to visit, or even what the trip was for. It would take a heart of stone to believe that striking an attitude on world poverty or racial hatred was more attractive than making hard practical choices about the quality of public services.

But, all the time, exhaustion is eating away at any sense of purpose.

A passage in Hugh Dalton's diary from 1930 captures the lassitude which can set in:

The Cabinet is full of overworked men [he writes], growing older; more tired and more timid with each passing week. Pressure from below and from without is utterly ineffectual. High hopes are falling like last autumn's leaves. There is a whisper of spring in the air, but none in the political air. One funks the public platform, and one wishes we had never come in. We have forgotten our Programme, or been bamboozled out of it by the officials. One almost longs for an early and crushing defeat.[69]

Thirty years later, when Britain's relative position in the world had sunk lower, Tony Benn was just as distressed. 'It is most depressing to have been born in a country at a time when things are going downhill so fast. One just wonders how far individuals can change this by their efforts, or whether one just has to accept the inevitable and sit back and administer a ruin.'[70] His cabinet colleague Richard Crossman was even more dejected. 'We're about as fantastic and sensational a failure as any government could be.'[71] The private papers of even a publicly unflappable figure such as Harold Macmillan reveal inner dejection time and again. 'The problems of the world grow more and more intense. Perhaps it really is now about to come to an end,'[72] he wrote to his confidante Lady Waverley, on another occasion remarking that 'there is a malaise which is beginning to show itself everywhere. The only thing is to look happy even if one is not.'[73] John Major became so dejected that he told Paddy Ashdown, 'I used to look at Italy and think we in Britain could never become so ungovernable – but now I am not so sure.' Ashdown felt that 'He seems in the most profound depths of inner despair.'[74]

Nothing proves the truth of Brutus' advice to Cassius that 'There is a tide in the affairs of men' as the fate of Prime Ministers. They both win and lose office as some invisible tide changes. Those who sense the waters going out on them and try to save themselves by decisive action are doomed to fail. Harold Macmillan's sacking of seven of his cabinet in the 'Night of the Long Knives' in 1962 did nothing to improve either his image or his popularity. John Major's attempt to draw the poison out of his administration by putting himself up for a leadership election was bold. But it did nothing to save his government from oblivion in the General Election two years later. In the end, the most powerful figure in the land ends up powerless.

8. The Price of Fame

It's been a long day. The Home Secretary opened his eyes at six-fifteen this morning, and his first act was to go to his fax machine. He pulled off half-a-dozen press cuttings sent overnight from the Home Office. They did not please him. Bill Morris, one of the country's most powerful trades union barons, leader of the Transport and General Workers Union and one of the Labour party's biggest moneybags, had gone into print with an all-out attack on the government's asylum and immigration policy. It was, he claimed, giving comfort to racists.

The Home Secretary was hurt. Immigration – along with a jumble sale of other things such as the police, drugs policy, responsibility for falling satellites, the Channel Islands and the swearing in of bishops – was his responsibility. He was not by any stretch of the imagination a racist. A substantial number of his constituents in Blackburn came from ethnic minorities, drawn to the town to work in one or other of its 130 cotton mills. (At one point Blackburn wove saris for export to India: now the mill in question was owned by an Indian immigrant making jeans for Britain.) Half the schoolchildren in the town were Asian.

After being hurt, he became angry. As he made a pot of tea and a bowl of porridge he thought about how to handle the claims. Then he showered and woke his wife, Alice, a career civil servant, to ask her advice about the tone he should adopt. At seven-forty, he called the BBC and was through to the *Today* programme on the ISDN line in his study. Although inwardly furious at being, as he saw it, stabbed in the back by a comrade, his tone in the interview was one of mild pain and incomprehension. Poor old Bill was a bit confused. He hadn't understood the regulations. When he did, he'd see they were anything but racist.

By eight, the Home Secretary had been delivered by his Special Branch driver to Euston station, for the three-hour rail journey to his constituency. In the first-class carriage, he ploughed through the papers in his two red despatch boxes and then wrote an article for one of the Sunday tabloids, defending himself. By midday, he was at his flat in Blackburn. From there he was driven to a conference on the future of the Fire Service, and after a couple of sandwiches was picked up and taken off to open a new IT company which had been set up in a refurbished mill. By six-thirty that evening, he had taken his second shave of the day and held two separate surgeries, at which he was available for local people to take up their grievances and problems with him.

And now it is seven-thirty and we are sitting in the back of his Ford people carrier, hurtling down the M6 towards the Mersey, where he is to be the guest speaker at a fellow Labour MP's constituency dinner. He has a Special Branch driver trained in defensive driving, head constantly swinging from side to side, as he checks the road in front and each of the rearview mirrors. A second bodyguard, in pinstripe suit and spit-and-polished shoes, sits in the front passenger seat. In the back is his constituency assistant, Anna. An unmarked police car in front is supplied by the local force. Jack Straw is sitting scribbling notes for his speech on a yellow pad and taking occasional swigs from a plastic bottle of water. It is over thirteen hours since he woke up and it will be another five before he gets to bed: the absolute prerequisite for a serious political career, before ideological commitment or anything else, is stamina.

The dinner itself, for which 160 members of the Wallasey constituency party have each paid £20, is a friendly affair. They are a predominantly late-middle-aged group of civic-minded people who, you sense, would all act well if a lunatic burst into the room waving a gun. There is a very noticeable absence of anyone under thirty-five. I am seated next to the head of the local team of occupational therapists, who gives me a lecture on vegetarianism. On the other side is the chair of the local police authority. Her hobby is collecting the autographs of chief constables. The menu is vegetable soup, lamb and apple pie, with cream which looks as if it has been sprayed from a shaving-foam dispenser. There will be a raffle of things like a bottle of whisky autographed by Tony Blair and an auction, at which a shirt signed by the Liverpool football team fetches over £300.

This is the third time that Jack Straw has spoken at a function in a fellow MP's constituency in the last six months. Why does he do it? He is honest enough to admit that he enjoys it – the welcome, the reassurance of being among friends, the sound of his own voice – and then adds that he feels 'a responsibility: I'm the only cabinet minister in the north-west of England and I've got to get out and tell the members what we're doing. There are council elections soon.' There are three motives here: pleasure, duty and party interest. More introspective people might question which of the impulses was stronger or nobler. But introspection is the enemy of political advancement.

At a day-to-day level, there is no more potentially stressful department to run than the Home Office. If someone breaks into Buckingham Palace in the middle of the night and is found sitting on the Queen's bed, it is the Home Secretary's responsibility. If a group of Afghans hijack an airliner and land it in Britain, it is the Home Secretary's problem. If the new computer at the Passport Office isn't up to the job and people can't go on holiday, that's his fault too. The joke in the Home Office is that it would all be a whole lot simpler if they changed their website address to *www.crisis.org* (too late – the name has already been taken by a twenty-four-hour telephone counselling organization in Minneapolis). I ask him where he acquired the necessary self-confidence, and he says he feels comfortable in the job, and 'When people say I'm useless, well maybe I am useless, but it's much easier to cope if you've got the confidence of the Prime Minister.' And in the meantime, here he is in Birkenhead on a Friday night.

Jack Straw's speech, 'the moment you've all been waiting for', in the words of the man from Radio Merseyside, is like falling off a log. Nearly four years into the first Labour government in two decades, the party leadership is beginning to recognize that one day the voters will feel sufficiently disenchanted to throw it out. His speech has a slightly defensive tone. The euphoria has passed, he admits: 'There is a point beyond which no politician can meet people's dreams.' But look on the bright side. Sticking to Conservative spending plans has at least meant the government has avoided the traditional sterling crisis which hits most new Labour governments. No one points this out as a Tory achievement. 'Now we can start to spend money on the NHS and on education.' It is a sensible, low-key, good-humoured speech, although Straw himself would doubtless concede that he is not the greatest orator. The call to arms for the forthcoming local elections ('No one ever left the party because they were asked to work too hard') is well taken: even here, with a majority of over 19,000, for every party member there are well over a hundred who don't belong. The two jokes, one of which involves an old lady fumbling around in a younger man's underwear, are met with polite laughter.

When she thanks Straw for attending, the Wallasey MP Angela Eagle touches upon one of the reasons people join, and stay with, political parties, even though they are forever being asked to stand on wet street corners, stuff envelopes or knock on an endless succession of front doors. 'The party', she says, 'is like a family.' And when she presents her long-standing election agent with a gift and a bunch of flowers, the recipient bursts into tears.

It is half an hour after midnight when, finally, Jack Straw falls into bed back home in Blackburn.

The next day, at eleven, he is squatting on the pavement in Blackburn town centre, plugging a couple of wires into a car battery and holding a microphone. It is a bright but cold spring morning, with a steam organ wheezing out tunes in aid of the Multiple Sclerosis flag day and a solitary Salvation Army officer rattling a can.

Straw's soapbox is the bench outside Marks and Spencer. 'One two three four five' comes reedily out of the megaphone, battling to be heard against the steam organ, before he persuades the operator to switch it off for an hour. Often, he has to pay the local busker and his dog five pounds for the same period of silence. He clambers on to the bench and begins. His audience consists of seven or eight party members and his election agent. Then a couple of curious shoppers stop to listen, then a few more.

'I'm going to talk for ten minutes, and then I'm going to tell you a joke. It's a good joke. You'll like it, sir. Even if your wife doesn't.' Telling people that your joke is funny before they've a chance to decide for themselves is a dangerous strategy, as any stand-up comedian could tell him. And, after the familiar recitation of the government's achievements, the joke falls pretty flat. It is, anyway, one of the two jokes he told at the dinner last night, although not the one about the old lady and the testicles. Another asset for a successful politician is not to get tired of the sound of his own voice. By now the crowd has grown to a couple of dozen. Then he invites questions.

A man in a wheelchair gives him a hard time about disability benefits and pensions.

'That's my old friend Jim, ladies and gentlemen,' says Straw through his megaphone, before he runs through a recitation of what the government has done and then, because he has a loudspeaker and Jim hasn't, drowns out Jim's supplementary remarks by asking for a question from someone else.

'Why is Blackburn so dirty, when we pay so much council tax?' asks an elderly lady.

'Because so many people drop litter,' says Jack and promises to take up her complaint if she will give her name and address to Anna, his assistant.

The crowd has swelled to ninety by the time a young mother takes him to task for tax changes which, she claims, set out to penalize 'traditional' families in which the mother stays at home to care for children. 'We can hardly make ends meet already,' she says forcefully.

'Give me your details, and I'll take it up with the Chancellor, Gordon Brown,' he says.

'He can't answer the question,' says a woman at the back of the crowd walking away in disgust.

Within half an hour, the crowd has dropped to sixty or seventy, and within another twenty minutes it has dwindled down to a couple of dozen. Despite the promises, he does not fully answer all the questions asked of him. But when an elderly man tells him that the Sellafield nuclear reprocessing plant should be shut, the Home Secretary can only confess that he can't quite recall where the government was on its plans for the place. A spotty Asian teenager wanders away muttering, 'It's all fookin' bollocks.' On and on the questions go, about the niggardliness of the rise in old-age pensions, tax changes which have made people worse off, why the street lighting is so poor. There is no question of who's in control. It is the man in the well-cut overcoat with the gloves and the microphone, not the sea of anoraks, leather jackets and car coats standing around him. But it must still be an inconvenience. And it is a way of practising politics which belongs to an earlier era, before radio and television. I wondered why the Home Secretary put himself through it.

'It's a great way of finding out what people are bothered about,' he says. It is one of the strengths of the British political system that it forces politicians to see their constituents face to face. Every second weekend (not always, but usually the weekends when Blackburn Rovers are playing at home), Straw is in the constituency, taking surgeries or holding his open-air meetings. Others may spend their weekends playing golf, shopping or grouting the tiles in their bathroom. This is what politicians do. And I got the very strong impression that he enjoyed the whole thing. But it comes at a price. The constant attendance at constituency parties flatters politicians' self-esteem as surely as the cheap wine rots their insides. To be asked to open another museum, to present the prizes at another speech day, or to propose the toast at another Burns Night Dinner does wonders for the ego. But to combine it with a requirement to be miles away in London, observing the obscure protocols of the Palace of Westminster and obeying the demands of the party whips, requires a kind of schizophrenia. Jack Straw – a professional politician almost since the days when he ran the National Union of Students – has the inner resources to carry it off. But not everyone has.

After several recent General Elections, many newly elected MPs have received a letter. It has come not from grateful constituents or party leader, but from north Wales.

'Congratulations on your recent success,' the letter begins. 'I trust you enjoy your new role.' Then it warns the recipients to remember that their children did not ask for the notoriety they now had to endure. Notoriety is not what the successful politician had courted, nor what he thought he'd achieved. But the letter is about the unintended consequences of success. The writer is the son of the former Labour MP for Bedford, Brian Parkyn. Although he represented the town for only four years, he had 'nursed' the constituency for a decade. The experience had clearly traumatized his son. Nicholas Parkyn claimed to have been expected to behave perfectly, so as not to jeopardize his father's ambitions. His letter 'begs' the newly elected politician to defy Labour orthodoxy, and to educate his or her children outside the constituency. Otherwise, their schooldays would be a nightmare, with their fellow pupils ganging up to torment them for being different. Unlike a politician who might have to endure a few aggressive hecklers at a meeting for an hour or so, before escaping back to the House of Commons, the child had to live with aggression day after day. The victimization was as bad from teachers as from other children. When stories about his father appeared in the local newspapers, or the government became unpopular, the playground taunt was 'My mum and dad say it's all Nicholas Parkyn's dad's fault.' When he stepped out of line, the school authorities punished him more harshly than others, because justice had to be seen to be done: there could be no suggestion that he was getting off lightly because his father was in parliament. The letter ends with the plea that newly elected MPs should consider the problem very carefully. Nicholas Parkyn was anxious that nobody else should have to put up with the misery he had experienced for thirty years. 'It has all but destroyed my family and I know I'm not the only one.'[1]

It is a heartfelt cry, and might to some degree be echoed by other children of famous people. But the children of politicians are a special case. Their parents prescribe to the rest of society how to behave. If their parents are Labour figures, they will come under a deal of pressure to educate their children in the community the politician represents, which will make them constantly available for victimization. But politicians often make the misery worse by their readiness to exploit their children for political advantage. Their families are a way for unusual people to demonstrate that they are, in fact, 'normal'. For both men and women, a posed picture on the election leaflet with husband or wife, children and doting dog is a way of saying, 'Hey, look, I'm just like you. I am fertile, upstanding and yet understanding. I know what real life is like. If you vote for me, you will get someone like you in parliament.' When he or she is triumphant on election night, the devoted spouse is there to reassure electors that they have sent to parliament a fully rounded human being. When he is threatened with disgrace, the family can be rolled out for reassuring photographs that all is well with the inner man. Few can resist the temptation to parade their family.

But it is a Faustian pact. When political decisions intrude into almost every area of life, almost every area of life becomes a legitimate subject of curiosity. As Prime Minister, Tony Blair objected vigorously to what his office claimed was 'intrusion' into the private life of his family. Yet proving that it was led by a man who belonged to 'Middle England' had been a critical part of Labour's attempt to make itself electable. Blair had been willing to be filmed helping his children with their homework for a propaganda film in the run-up to the 1997 election, had told the Labour conference in 1999, 'To our children we are irreplaceable. If anything happened to me, you'd soon find a new leader. But my kids wouldn't find a new dad.' He talked to magazines about whether he had smacked his children and of his worries about how much time they spent on the computer; he posed on the steps of Downing Street with his baby son. At Christmas, cards went out to an extraordinarily loose association of 'friends', adorned with a photograph of the secular Holy Family. Yet, still, the Blairs used the Downing Street machine to plead that they were entitled to 'privacy'. The argument might be accepted, in a worldly-wise sort of way, were it not for the fact that government spends so much of its time telling the rest of the citizens of Britain how they may or may not deal with their own children. The party expects parents to send their children to a local secondary school. Yet the Blairs' own son is educated miles across London. The youngest son is paraded for the television cameras, yet the parents refuse to say whether he has been given the combined mumps, measles and rubella vaccination which it asks every other baby be given.

No compassionate human being would wish to disadvantage their children for the sake of their own climb to the top of the tree. But the temptation to use the family for political advancement, particularly in a media-saturated age, is extreme. The Labour party knew full well that Blair's status as a family man was one of the factors that told against William Hague (who was not) in the 2001 election. Hague's successor, Iain Duncan Smith, has four children, but protested that he would never use them as political weapons: he claimed to find it offensive that the Prime Minister was 'ruthlessly' exploiting his family. 'I don't want my children to grow up like that,' he said.[2] But it is an unusual politician who survives without giving in.

In the days before the media became ubiquitous, the temptations (and the pressures) were fewer. Clement Attlee declared that he was able to spend more time at home with his family when he was Prime Minister than at any time either before or after entering Downing Street, because he lived on the job. But the family expects something in return. Three days after the 1945 election victory, a nephew serving in the RAF wrote to Attlee, telling him that he had to address the issue of service pensions. His sister was soon badgering him to sort out permission for the bells to be rehung in her parish church. Later, a daughter was on at him because she had had her traveller's cheques stolen in Denmark, and then a son was in touch, with a tale of how he had lost his wallet in Savannah – would his father get on to the local police? They are the sort of problems any parent might be asked to help with. But the resources of Downing Street encouraged friends and relatives to see Attlee as some sort of consumers' Seventh Cavalry. Within months of the end of the Second World War, a godson wrote about his model railway.

> My Dear Godfather
>   Its long past time you started the hornby Factores going again. Shoaly thay shood be started by now. I have j got to buy another pair of points by now. I Ride my little Poney Molly evry day, and I like it to. but remember the most important thing in this letter is start the horby Factores going again.
>   Love from
>   Paul P.T.O.
>   PS on october 8th I have My birthday, and I want a pair of points, and I cant have them unless the Factores are going. I do hope you will come and see me in Scotland soon.
>   xxxxx
>   ooooo[3]

The next folio in the Attlee archive is a terse memorandum from the PM's private secretary, who has obviously been dispatched to sort out the aforementioned Hornby factories: he failed, and Attlee had to send his godson a postal order instead.

Neglect of their children is a constant fear for any parent. Edward du Cann, a Conservative bigwig throughout the 1960s and 1970s (and, famously, a man with so many interests that he was said to have fingers in more pies than he had fingers), recalled his son claiming to have believed that his nanny was both his mother and his father until he was twelve years old. But, for politicians, there is something worse. It may be 'boring' to have a father or mother who runs a bank or a building company, but at least they are relatively anonymous. In politics, personal absence can be combined with public notoriety. It is a deadly combination. Winston Churchill's father Randolph was so busy pursuing his political career that he can scarcely be said to have had any proper personal relationship with his son. On top of that, Churchill suffered persecution at school because his father was a public figure. Oswald Mosley was told by the chairman of the Harrow Conservative Association that Churchill had been called out in front of the class by his form master, 'who invited his other pupils to look at the stupidest boy at Harrow who was the son of the cleverest man in England'.[4] Churchill's will to succeed was sufficiently strong for him to survive the persecution. But his own son – another Randolph – found the shadow of his father's greatness so vast that he never realized his promise and succumbed to drink and self-pity.

Sensitive children can develop a more or less permanent feeling that they simply don't matter enough to their politician parent. When the Liberal leader David Steel's son was in trouble his father went public. 'I was the classic absentee father. I've always felt guilty about that.'[5] Richard Crossman acknowledged the potential problems in his diary. He and his wife Anne were at the Labour party conference in Brighton on their son Patrick's ninth birthday. Crossman wrote, 'We telephoned him. Poor boy, he was born on the Friday of the Brighton Conference 1957 and the next time we came to Brighton was for the Conference five years later when Nanny brought the children. Here we are away again on his birthday. It's no fun to be the son of a politician.'[6] He spoke truer than he knew. Eight years later, at the age of seventeen, Patrick Crossman hanged himself with his judo belt in the kitchen of the family farmhouse in Oxfordshire.

The Crossman tragedy was neither the first nor the last to hit the children of political parents. Both Churchill and Macmillan had children with drink problems, Conservative and Labour cabinet ministers have had children with drug habits. All three major parties have had well-publicized cases of children who have killed or harmed themselves. Those who survive this peculiar upbringing have decided views on what it did to them. Even those politicians who develop armadillo hides themselves cannot stop their family being upset by the cruel things said about them. David Lloyd George's son Richard described how:

One day, when I was at school, I felt a violent blow in the small of my back. I gasped and turned in dismay to face one of the older school bullies. 'Dirty pro-Boer! Yah!' In the weeks that followed my father's political personality became an absolute nightmare figure that haunted me every moment I was at school. I understood little or nothing of what the aggressiveness was all about; all I knew was that I had become a sort of whipping-boy for my father's political crimes. There was a kind of hysteria. Small boys as well as large ones – children I had hardly exchanged a word with in the past – baited me, abused me or pursued me remorselessly to kick me in the bony places – boys have an instinctive anatomical knowledge about the more vulnerable places.[7]

Richard Lloyd George began to develop a ferocious hatred of what his father represented, which did not abate even with his death. His biography of his father, in which he laid out the details of some of his many affairs, is shot through with such bitterness that it is obvious he never emerged from the shadow in which he grew up.

The facts of Lloyd George's adultery are well known (so well known that he was nicknamed 'The Goat'). But his son's denunciation points up the jealousy of the hours his father lavished on politics. The tension between provincial family life and the metropolitan importance of parliament would be difficult enough for anyone to deal with. But it can lead to serious feelings of resentment among the children left at home. If he has satisfied his activists by setting up home in a constituency away from London, the MP will come home once a week, drop off his dirty laundry and perhaps do what he can to father another child (which his wife will later be expected to raise more or less single-handedly). He will be exhausted and probably irritable. Political colleagues may be in and out of the house all day with news of who's up and who's down, of struggles on the local council and of intrigues to secure the right motions and speakers at party conference. There may be phone calls at three in the morning from constituents complaining about their leaking roofs. And on top of all that, he will claim to have the moral high ground. Sarah Smith, daughter of the late Labour leader John Smith, recalls asking, 'Why can't you come to see me in the school play?' and being met with the response, 'Don't you know there are people in Airdrie without a roof over their heads?' The Labour party was trying to change the world. How could a children's play be more important than that? She emerged from the experience of growing up in a politician's family simply unable to understand why anybody with a similar background should ever contemplate a political career themselves.

There are other approaches. Tony Benn, who took less interest in constituency affairs, ran the family household on highly democratic lines, with votes being taken all the time, to decide the will of the majority. His son Hilary gave his first television interview, advocating the replacement of the Queen with an elected president, at the age of nine.[8] As an adult, Hilary followed his father into the House of Commons. There are legions of similar examples: as well as his unhappy son, Richard, Lloyd George had a daughter, Megan, who sat in parliament for both the Liberals and the Labour party, and a son, Gwilym, who became a Conservative Home Secretary.* Johnny Grimond, son of a later Liberal leader, cheerfully concedes that as well as the pressures of carrying a well-known name there is the advantage that it tends to open doors when you come to look for a job.

In a media-saturated age, though, the potential problems are worse. All teenagers rebel against their parents. But, as the sixteen-year-old Euan Blair discovered in the summer of 2000, if your father is Prime Minister and has just delivered himself of an unthought-out idea that young drunks be frog-marched to cash machines for on-the-spot fines, it does not make life easier when you are found drunk and

* It is Gwilym who is sometimes credited with the observation that 'Politicians are like monkeys: the higher they get up the tree, the more revolting are the parts they expose.'

incapable in the middle of Leicester Square. Nor is it particularly easy to deal with teenage drug use when your father is Home Secretary. There is, to put it mildly, a degree of *Schadenfreude* in the delight with which press and television fall upon the child of any policymaker who gets into trouble.

In 1991, a committee under the former Conservative Chief Whip Michael Jopling set out to investigate the effects of their working hours and conditions upon MPs. It heard a recitation of a 'trail of broken marriages, ruined health and exhausted irrationality', which meant that 'outside bodies usually know far more about impending legislation' than those who are supposed to debate it.[9] Intrigued by the findings, an occupational psychologist set out to try to discover more. Over the next ten years he tracked MPs (or the fifth or so of them who would respond to his inquiries). He found that they complained of being overworked, that three-quarters of them felt they spent too little time with their partners, that four out of five believed they saw too little of their children, that six out of ten had no time for a hobby, and that the vast majority could not switch off from the job when they went home. Plenty of them had trouble sleeping, drank and smoked too much, and felt exhausted.

What was, perhaps, most remarkable about his findings was that when the House of Commons accepted the recommendations of the Jopling Committee, and introduced apparently more friendly hours, neither the emotional nor the physical levels of strain among MPs fell. They *increased*. When the psychologist extended his investigation to politicians sitting in the Scottish parliament and the Welsh assembly, he was surprised to discover that the levels of pressure were much the same.[10] The conclusion seems inescapable that it is as much the nature of the people doing the job (or, at least, of those who confess their feelings to researchers) as the conditions in which they work which creates the pressure. Reading political diaries gives entirely different perspectives on how individuals see their responsibilities. But, whether they be snobs on the make or hair-shirted evangelists, the striking impression in many cases is how utterly lonely they seem.

At the very top of politics, the pressures are real: most human beings dislike making decisions, and Prime Ministers must make them every day. Few positions are as solitary. As Baldwin wrote to Asquith when he left the House of Commons, 'I don't think that anyone who has not been a Prime Minister can realise the essential and ultimate loneliness of that position, there is no veil between him and the human heart.'[11] But why should the pressures seem so acute for those who are nowhere near the top of the tree, and who could be amiably lying around in the shade of its branches? Providing they do enough to keep the party headquarters off their back, and sufficient to pacify the local party, their time is their own. How much effort they spend opening fêtes, holding surgeries or speaking at civic dinners in the constituency is largely a matter of choice. Perhaps the answer is that going into politics requires a certain drive, which for some people is simply incompatible with being content with their current status. They must advance. And if they cannot advance, they must whirl around being busy. It seems reasonable to conclude that, if the pressure was not there, some politicians would find a way to create it.

In the most extreme cases, this combination of frenetic public activity and intense personal loneliness can be fatal. John Heddle, the Conservative MP for Mid-Staffordshire, gassed himself in his Jaguar in 1989. Although money worries were said at the time to have been grinding him down, he was also disappointed not to have achieved more in politics. Jocelyn Cadbury, a Birmingham MP and member of the chocolate dynasty, shot himself in 1982; again he was said to have been ground down by the pressures of the job. Sometimes, being denied the approbation of public life can be fatal. In 1974, Desmond Donnelly, a former MP, went to a hotel near Heathrow Airport and took an overdose when he was unable to find a constituency association prepared to give him the chance of returning to parliament. In other cases, the viciousness of the intrigue involved in politics can do it: in 1997 Gordon McMaster, the young Paisley MP, suffocated himself in his garage. Renfrewshire is notorious for the viciousness of its politics, and he left a note blaming his own party comrades for a whispering campaign in which they had claimed he was a drunk, dying from AIDS, cohabiting with a Spanish waiter, on the verge of being exposed as a paedophile, and about to be deselected as an MP.

Scandalous or untrue allegations can hurt anyone. But if you are both a public figure and already personally vulnerable, they can tip you over the edge.

For most adults, protection from the world is the everyday reality of family life. But being a politician is not an ordinary job. Hence the need, in a mass-media age, to *simulate* normality. When Tony Blair appeared on the doorstep of 10 Downing Street clutching a mug of tea, when his voice became estuarial, when he deployed his 'ya knows' and his glottal stops, when he appeared in jeans and T-shirt, he was not being normal. He was acting normal. All these appearances had been choreographed to show that he was 'real'. In an age in which people seemed to be disengaging from party politics, the trick was to appear not to be a politician. William Hague's problem was not that he was abnormal – or little more so than many other career politicians – but that he found it hard to *appear* not to be abnormal. Blair may have gone to a public school, Hague to a comprehensive. But Blair's second-class degree at Oxford and the time he spent playing in a rock band were more commonplace experiences than Hague's first and his presidency of the Oxford Union.

Tony Blair's advisers had recognized that the combination of media saturation and consumer contentment made 'Me, I'm just an ordinary bloke' paradoxically appealing. The successful leader would be as like his followers as possible. Just before the 1997 election Blair came out with 'I'm very normal. I love my family. I have a lot of friends, a lot of whom aren't much to do with politics. When I close the door and get away from politics, I really can't be bothered to think about it a great deal.'[12] Four years later, after a term in Downing Street, he was saying the same thing. 'I am still very normal.'[13] But the person who protests their normality is not normal.

The image of Tony Blair may have been a triumph of marketing, but the cultivation of 'normality' goes back generations. Stanley Baldwin presented a largely artificial image as a countryman and declared, 'I am just a plain man of the common people. I understand the common people, and I believe that what I am thinking they are thinking.'[14] A week before Munich, Neville Chamberlain was writing to *The Times*, claiming to have spotted a grey wagtail in St James's Park; Winston Churchill liked to present himself as a painter, Edward

Heath as a musician and a sailor;* and John Major had a very public
love of cricket. For the Labour government which took office after
the 1997 election, the cloak of choice was soccer. The Labour party's
sainted Keir Hardie may have watched only one proper football
match, and been baffled by the 'unknown world' he saw on the
terraces. But by the 1960s the middle-class men who dominated the
party were swearing they had the game in their blood. Harold Wilson
boasted of his loyalty to Huddersfield Town, Tony Crosland of his to
Chelsea, Michael Foot to Plymouth Argyle. All these Oxford-
educated men had seen that the public protestation of supporting a
football club was the easiest way of passing themselves off as just
another Joe. In the Blair government, a football affectation became
almost as useful as a plausible television manner. Blair himself claimed
to follow Newcastle United, his Chancellor of the Exchequer, Gordon
Brown, was a Raith Rovers man, his Foreign Secretary, Jack Straw,
could be found in the stands at Blackburn, his Home Secretary, David
Blunkett, followed Sheffield United. A professed passion for football
not only transformed a politician into a human being, it gave the party
the appearance of a working-class identity when its radical roots had
been dug up years ago.

William Hague's attempts to simulate normality were calamitous.
This was a man whose childhood went from Action Man toys to
decorating his bedroom walls with pictures of Margaret Thatcher and
lists of MPs and their constituencies; who could recite the lists (and
the size of the MPs' majorities) by heart; who had delivered a speech
to the Conservative party conference at the age of sixteen; who had
told friends that one day he would be Prime Minister and that he
would not get engaged until he was a cabinet minister. Hague's
problem was not his talent or his intelligence. It was that he seemed
what he was. So he was repackaged. He appeared at the Notting Hill
carnival wearing a baseball cap. He allowed a television crew to follow
him around for a few days. (As his media advisers ought to have
predicted, this merely aggravated the distinction between the prodigy

* Owen Parker, who often sailed on Heath's racing yacht *Morning Cloud* as his
number two, reflected the gap between Heath's view of himself and the reality by
calling his memoir *Tack Now, Skipper* (London: Granada Publishing, 1979).

and his very good-natured family.) And he gave an interview to a men's magazine, sandwiched between advertisements for male cosmetics and articles about fast cars and faster women, in which he claimed to have been drinking fourteen pints of beer a day while working as a teenage deliveryman for his family's soft-drinks company.[15] But it was all in vain. Newspaper journalists contacted local publicans, who, the *Daily Telegraph* reported, reacted with exclamations about 'that lying little toad', said they couldn't recall him coming in even for a half of lager, and disclosed that he had been known locally as 'Billy Fizz' and 'Billy the Pop'. In the *Guardian*, the incredulous reactions of local people appeared alongside pictures of the Blair family on holiday in Tuscany, with the Prime Minister, in an expensive designer shirt, cradling the much more reliable accessory, the eleven-week-old Leo.

Until very recently, it was a truth almost universally acknowledged that a single man in possession of political ambition was in want of a wife. Even men congenitally unsuited to marriage felt the pressure. In 1951, at the age of forty-five, after a sexual career of heroic homosexual promiscuity, the Labour MP Tom Driberg felt compelled to take the plunge. None of his friends could quite understand why he had done it, not least the bride, who later wrote frankly to him, 'I don't know why you married me – you never told me.'[16] The marriage remained unconsummated. On being shown a photograph of Driberg's intended, Ena Binfield, Churchill is said to have sighed, 'Oh well, buggers can't be choosers!'

It is upon the political spouse that the burden falls of somehow keeping the family functioning. It is still, usually, a woman. The wife of a Conservative MP once described how she 'moves in four different orbits: in the constituency, in the home, in the House, and in the public eye'.[17] But it is a very particular sort of movement. She appears in public as the politician's loyal, silent support, gazing admiringly as she listens to the same old speech for the thirtieth time, moved by the familiar rhetoric, laughing at the tired jokes, or, if seated in the audience, leading the outbursts of spontaneous applause when he makes some particularly trenchant point. It is a pattern which bears less and less relationship to real life. The widow of the former Labour leader John Smith, Elizabeth, freely admits that she belonged to a previous generation of political spouses, 'where you followed what your husband did. The secret was to make the "other half" feel involved in the project: I simply couldn't imagine a successful political marriage in which the partners had different convictions. You worked as a team.' But in those days families tended to manage on a single income. Nowadays, much of family life is predicated upon the idea of two incomes. None of the parties, nor parliament, has come to terms with this enormous change in the way modern life is lived. The expectation that one member of the family will be in parliament while the other stays in the constituency opening flower shows simply won't work any longer.

The traditional role of the political wife could be spectacularly unappealing. Although George Brown met his wife through the local Labour party (they held their wedding reception at the Stepney Labour Club), once they were married her role became purely domestic. His biographer writes that 'George expected Sophie to organise his home life, act as his hostess, show off an image of domestic bliss to his constituents, listen to him rehearse his speeches, or wake up in the middle of the night to hear his account of his part in events – "Wake up and *listen*, what I'm telling you is history!" '[18] The relationship was more empty than even this anecdote suggests: Brown's biographer remarks that 'He always found it hard to resist a camera, a microphone, a quarrel, a drink, or a pretty woman.'[19] He once propositioned the wife of a visiting ambassador as they sat down to dinner: she could only fob him off with 'Pas avant la soupe, Mr Brown.'

Poor Mrs Brown confessed that she also learned – and taught their daughters – 'not to mention the [news]papers at all, good or bad, unless *he* wanted to discuss them. It became a habit, and one of the ways we'd learned to live together, but some of the sharing had gone.'[20] It got worse. In 1962, aged fifty, she was hit by a heart attack. She woke in the night, with a terrible pain that she described as 'tearing my chest apart'. George told her she had indigestion, and added, 'Try to go to sleep again. I've got a terribly important meeting in the House first thing, and then another in Belper [his constituency].'[21] It was left to her daughters to take their mother to hospital the next day. Sophie summed up her experience as a political wife with the words, 'I'd sat on a thousand platforms for his "public life", been alone for a thousand nights for it, packed a thousand suitcases, smiled when I felt like crying, kept silent when I felt like screaming . . .'[22] Those words might serve as an epitaph for the political spouse.

The way to avoid Sophie Brown's misfortune is to marry less of a monster. It certainly helps if the couple feel they are part of a shared mission. Tony Benn, who served in the Labour government with George Brown, and enjoyed a long and comparatively happy marriage, records in his diary that he celebrated his fortieth wedding anniversary at a socialist conference in Chesterfield, just as his wife and he had cut short their honeymoon to attend a socialist conference in Boston.[23] It is one of the few arguments in favour of starting a political career as young as possible that at least the MP's spouse knows what they are taking on: to discover that the constituency demands they abandon their identity as a software engineer or human rights activist to play the role of some human buttonhole can be a terrible shock.

Yet an overdeveloped sense of shared commitment is dangerous too. Had the cards fallen differently, Christine Holman could have been the one with a seat in the House of Commons, instead of ending up as the wife of Neil Hamilton, a man who will forever have the word 'disgraced' attached to him. Politics had, literally, brought them together: they met at a Young Conservatives' conference at Ripon. Then it was Christine who seemed the more ambitious one: when Gerald Nabarro came to talk to her Conservative group at York University she rearranged the seating plan so that she sat next to him at dinner. She obviously made an impression, because later the old bounder telephoned and asked if she would come to work for him. He tripled her salary and gave her use of a car (NAB 4).

Notionally, she was his personal assistant or secretary, although Nabarro had to hire a further secretary to cope with the typing and shorthand which she could not manage. Precisely what, I asked her, did she do for him for three years? 'I used to drive him around the place, hold his hand and generally look after him. I particularly remember standing in the dining room in the House of Commons, where he was having a pudding of tinned peaches. He was having the most awful time trying to open the cream container. That was the sort of thing I did for him.' This unswerving loyalty extended to her weeping on his shoulder when he was tried for dangerous driving.

After Nabarro's death in November 1973, she went to work for Michael Grylls, another Conservative MP at the too-smooth and sparkly end of the party. She remained friends with her old university pal Harvey Proctor, now a ferociously right-wing MP, author of *Billericay in Old Picture Postcards* (and later brought low by the unhappy exposure of a series of spanking incidents with rent-boys). But it was her boyfriend, Neil Hamilton, who was chosen as the candidate for the opulent acres of Cheshire, one of the most staunchly Conservative pieces of real estate in the land. They spent their honeymoon canvassing on the doorsteps. Nabarro, Proctor, Grylls, Hamilton: she obviously had an eye for the rococo. What was it that attracted her to them? 'Oh,' she gushes, 'wherever you went with Nab, people looked and stared and talked. It was just wonderful.'

After marriage she devoted herself to her husband's career representing the commuters and twinsets of Cheshire. There was even an agreement that they wouldn't have children, to leave more time for politics. There were consolations, though, like a sprawling former rectory, with beautiful lawns, gravel drive and rosebushes (with a cardboard cut-out of Margaret Thatcher seated on a chair inside the front door). There were endless invitations to this or that, and, inevitably, temptations. It was Christine with whom Neil Hamilton stayed in room 356 of the Ritz Hotel in 1987, where the two of them ran up a bill for extras alone of over £2,000, charged to the proprietor of Harrods, Mohamed al Fayed. Christine Hamilton liked to talk of her motto WDTT – We Do Things Together. But in the constituency they were already known as 'Mr and Mrs Cash-and-Carry'.

This taste for the high life was, famously, their nemesis. Neil Hamilton had been mired in allegations of sleaze for three years by the time, in May 1997, John Major finally called a General Election. Conservative headquarters had begged Hamilton not to stand for re-election, but in a gesture of overweening arrogance, he refused to go quietly. At that point, the Labour and Liberal Democrat candidates agreed to stand aside to allow the former war-reporter Martin Bell to run against Hamilton as an independent 'anti-sleaze' campaigner. The battle between the two immediately became one of the highlights of the election, drawing in reporters and camera crews from as far away as Australia and Japan. One of these reporters tipped off the Hamiltons that Martin Bell was due to hold a news conference later that morning on Knutsford Heath, a former racecourse. As Christine Hamilton recalls it, 'Neil said "Is he indeed! Well, I've got some questions to ask him."' The sitting MP went upstairs to change into a suit referred to ever afterwards as being in 'bounder check' or as 'the Terry Thomas outfit'. ('It's *so* unfair,' she says. 'It was a *perfectly normal* Prince of Wales check.') Yet it was not her husband who was to be the main attraction, but the extraordinary apparition at his side. Confronting the independent candidate, she boomed at him, 'Do you accept my husband is innocent?' again and again. Bell was embarrassed, confused and lost for words. Hers was the sort of performance which, one columnist commented later, displayed the valour of an early Christian martyr, making you wonder how Britain ever lost its empire.[24] But it was, in the end, to no avail. Neil Hamilton's defeat by Martin Bell was as comprehensive a humiliation as any politician has suffered in modern politics: it takes some astonishing public distaste to turn a Conservative majority of 22,000 votes into defeat by a margin of 11,000. Bell made a slightly prim speech at the count, while Hamilton simply said that he was 'devastated'.

Recalling the battle of Knutsford Heath later, Christine Hamilton could remember only that 'I just saw Martin Bell. He's so ghastly, so sanctimonious and smug in his white suit. I mean what sort of man wears a *white suit*? I just flipped. And then when I got home and saw it all on the news, I just broke down in floods of tears. I saw that Neil was being portrayed as a wimp. It's not fair. It's just that I'm the noisy one.' In the years after her husband's defeat, she loudly supported him in one vain attempt to 'clear his name' after another, defying the verdict of the parliamentary investigation which found 'compelling evidence' that he had taken money from al Fayed, endorsing the libel action Hamilton brought against the owner of Harrods – a verdict which led to the *Guardian* headline 'A greedy, corrupt liar' – encouraging him to take the case to the Court of Appeal, which again found against him. By the end of the legal process, a process which he need never have begun, the couple were left with debts of £3 million.

Yet within months of defeat Christine Hamilton had begun all over again. There was an entry into publishing with *Christine Hamilton's*

Bumper Book of British Battleaxes. There was a television cookery show, *Posh Nosh*. This was followed by *The Christine Hamilton Show*, a low-budget chat-show in which she trundled a vast scarlet sofa around the place. The most memorable edition involved two fellow Conservatives. The first, Piers Merchant MP, a member of Mensa, had been caught with a teenage girl. He had claimed to be employing her hitherto undiscovered literary talents 'researching a book'. The second, David Ashby, whose campaign literature had included the statements 'Married with a family and therefore understands the needs of families . . . a man of integrity who believes in traditional moral values', had been denounced as a homosexual by his pressure-cooker of a wife.

The Hamiltons appeared, smiling, on the front page of the *Daily Telegraph* property section when they put their house on the market to try to meet the massive lawyers' bills they had run up in their foolish libel case. They turned out for an Oxford University Conservative Association event described on the invitation as 'the most alcoholic dinner ever'. By the end of the evening, Hamilton was said to be swigging whisky from the bottle, while his wife smoked a cigar and threatened to take her clothes off. She then obliged a nineteen-year-old with what she subsequently dismissed as 'the briefest of kisses', but which seemed, from the photographs, to have been an attempt to suck his face off. It got worse. They appeared stark naked (with some discreetly placed ivy) in a men's magazine mock-up of Lucas Cranach's *Adam and Eve*. They collaborated in an intrusive television documentary, in the course of which they were questioned by police on trumped-up charges relating to an alleged orgy.

It is not all entirely freak-show. Most weeks, there is some suburban ladies' luncheon club to address, a party to attend. There is the occasional holiday jaunt to make a report for the BBC or someone. She occasionally performs at provincial theatres in *An Evening with Christine Hamilton*. But overall there is something of the Rector of Stiffkey★

★ The Rector from 1906 to 1932 was Harold Davidson. He was unfrocked after it was discovered that, instead of being in Norfolk ministering to his parishioners, he spent most of the week among the prostitutes of Soho, whistling back to his parish in time to preach on Sundays. After his exposure he took up a career with the circus. He died in the summer of 1937 after preaching to a group of holidaymakers at Skegness from inside a lion's cage. The lion disliked the text and ate him.

about this descent from constituency *grande dame* to pantomime dame. Why, you wonder, did she do it? She obviously had plenty to lose if her husband's case failed. But that doesn't explain the post-disgrace carousel. When we meet for lunch at a smart west London restaurant, heads turn and other diners whisper to one another, 'It's that woman.' She is immaculately, over-elaborately, dressed, although the strident reds and blues have been replaced by pink ('It's kinder to the older complexion'). But she still exudes the sort of sexual charge which used to send Conservative MPs weak at the knees in the presence of Margaret Thatcher. We drink a bottle of wine. Leaving the world of politics has been, she says, '150 per cent liberating . . . I've joined the 98 per cent of the population who don't give a damn about parliament. We switch off the radio whenever reports of what happened there come on.' And yet, of course, it is only because her husband was a member of the place that she has any value as an entertainer. She surely doesn't want to spend the rest of her life as 'wife of disgraced MP Neil Hamilton'?

'What should I do? I'm held up as something extraordinary. I don't see why. I married "for richer for poorer". Now I'm married to a bankrupt.' As a text, it doubtless goes down well with Conservative ladies' luncheon clubs, and there is something admirable about her loyalty. But her husband isn't just any old bankrupt who's had a bit of bad luck in his business. The courts have repeatedly found against him, the custodians of political morality have declared him dishonest. Why this perpetual shroud-waving? The reply is fierce. 'If he's a liar, I'm a liar. If he's corrupt, I'm corrupt.' Well, she said it. Perhaps the fact that they continued their legal fight for so long – after parliamentary investigations had failed them, after legal inquiries had gone against them – indicates that a terrible wrong was done. The only other explanation is that the self-confidence necessary for political success has, like some horrible disease, mutated into self-delusion and the belief that they can walk on water.

9. Feet of Clay

In 1997, Tony Blair walked into Downing Street on a carpet laid for him by people like Neil Hamilton. 'You need to rent an MP, like you rent a London taxi,' was said to be the philosophy of one of the several firms which had developed to lobby MPs for well-heeled clients. There were revelations of cash in brown envelopes being delivered to politicians. Tim Smith, a Vice Chairman of the Conservative party (who had defeated Tony Blair's first attempt to get into parliament), was forced to resign for taking payments. In a newspaper sting, two other Conservative MPs were caught offering to ask questions for cash. The smell of corruption made the Conservatives unelectable, and when Tony Blair came to power he promised – in a series of pledges set down in his own handwriting – to 'clean up' politics. He would, he said, 'eliminate sleaze and the causes of sleaze'.

It was a good drum to bang, but the truth is that, in any international comparison, Britain remains relatively untainted by serious venality. Hamilton's offences – taking money from businesses to promote their causes, lying to colleagues – were a stain upon parliament. But, in a parliament of over 650 MPs, they get nowhere near the starting gate in international terms. In Germany, for example, it is perfectly legal for a parliamentary deputy to be a lobbyist at the same time. The organization Transparency International,[1] which attempts to fight corruption, includes Britain among the fifteen least corrupt countries in the world, below Finland, Denmark and New Zealand, admittedly, but above the United States, Germany, Spain, Ireland and Italy. By comparison with countries at the bottom of the list – places like Nigeria, Indonesia and Azerbaijan – Britain is squeaky clean. In Japan, corruption of one sort or another is taken for granted in the political class.[2] The plain fact is that much of the rest of the world simply seems to have no idea of what is wrong with corruption, whether it be called bribery, backsheesh or guandao. Abusing public trust for private gain is simply a fact of life, from Beijing to Buenos Aires, Karachi to Kiev.

Even apparently sophisticated countries in the European Union are deeply tainted. (This is, after all, an organization whose entire college of commissioners was forced to resign in 1999 after allegations of sleaze.) The most remarkable thing about venality in Italy is that no one thinks it remarkable. 'Everyone knows. Everyone stays silent. Who will cast the first stone?' was the way the corrupt socialist leader Bettino Craxi put it before he ambled off to his mansion in Tunisia to escape investigation. When Silvio Berlusconi, the richest business-man in Italy, discovered that he was being investigated for corruption, he simply went into politics, became Prime Minister and changed the law to protect himself from examination. What is most shocking is that Italians voted him Prime Minister, despite knowing the allegations against him.

It is genuinely disturbing to discover the degree to which some other western European states accept corruption with no more than a knowing shrug of the shoulders. In 2001 the former German Chancellor Helmut Kohl admitted accepting \$1 million in donations for his party. In early 2002 the Bundeskriminalamt, the federal investigations agency, issued a report claiming that corruption now ran across 'nearly all sectors of public administration'. Revelations in France painted a similar picture of almost endemic corruption. It emerged that during his time as mayor of Paris President Chirac had allegedly been spending the equivalent of £400 of public money *a day* on feeding his family. He was also accused of using £240,000 from illegal sources to take friends and family on jaunts around the world from Mauritius to Japan. Chirac blithely explained that the money was perfectly legitimate, as he'd taken it from a secret government fund used to pay for anti-terrorist operations. After seven years of trying to discover the extent of Chirac's alleged wrongdoing, the investigating judge eventually resigned, saying that a 'mafia-like' code of silence and intimidation among politicians and their associates had made his work impossible. By then it had emerged that it was commonplace for French ministers to be given envelopes stuffed with cash at the end of the month, from a secret government fund which had been in existence since 1946. In May 2001, the former Foreign Minister Roland Dumas was convicted of taking bribes in an enormous scandal involving Elf-Aquitaine, a state-owned oil company. Dumas swapped his plush villa for prison.

Jean-Christophe Mitterrand, son of the former President, and the one-time Interior Minister Charles Pasqua were accused of involvement in a money-laundering and arms-dealing scandal but the case against them was quashed. The French people – who are notorious for their ingenuity in fiddling their tax returns – seem not to mind. By comparison, British politicians seem almost angelic.

But there is always sex, of course – the affairs with actresses or the 'moments of madness' on Clapham Common – for human nature is fallible. Here, British politicians can only look enviously across the Channel, or back to earlier, gentler times. In the 1930s Robert Boothby had begun a long affair with Harold Macmillan's wife, Dorothy, which was well known in political circles, but scarcely went beyond them. The Labour leader in the late 1950s and early 1960s, Hugh Gaitskell, had a long affair with Ann Fleming, wife of the James Bond author, but not a word of it appeared in the press, despite the existence of a photograph showing a drunken Gaitskell clinging to a lamppost, with Ann Fleming standing next to him. Another Labour MP of the period, Tom Driberg, had an encyclopaedic knowledge of gentlemen's lavatories, but somehow avoided public exposure.

Indeed, it is surprising how few gay scandals touched politicians, given the common estimate that one in ten of the population is gay, and that for most of the twentieth century homosexual acts were illegal. In 1941 the Conservative Sir Paul Latham was charged with 'improper conduct' with fellow members of the Royal Artillery. In 1953 a Labour member, William Field, was entrapped by policemen in a public lavatory. And in 1958 a Tory Foreign Office minister, Ian Harvey, picked up a soldier of the Household Cavalry (in uniform, apparently) on a November evening in St James's Park. The two were caught by a park ranger and a policeman, and although they were charged only with breaking park regulations, the scandal forced Harvey to resign both a promising ministerial career and his seat. He subsequently wrote a remarkably honest account of the conflict between his public and private lives, *To Fall Like Lucifer*.[3] Law reforms in the 1960s and since have made life a great deal easier for homosexuals, so that in Tony Blair's first government there were two openly gay cabinet ministers and two who were 'in the closet'. But it is absolutely certain that in the twenty-first century the picture of Gaitskell and his mistress would be printed somewhere.

Discretion began to die in the 1960s. Until then the popular mind had tended to accept at face value the Conservatives' self-proclaimed association with old-fashioned values based on the teachings of the Church. Hence the utter disbelief at the discovery, in 1963, that the Secretary for War, John Profumo, had been enjoying the company of nineteen-year-old Christine Keeler, who had also been sharing herself with a spy attached to the Russian embassy. The story is too well known to need retelling, but Profumo's resignation, for lying to the House of Commons, proved the catalyst for a new generation of reporters, editors and satirists, egged on by proprietors who knew that sex and scandal sell newspapers. The Thatcher government, which benefited from endorsement by some of these proprietors, took a relaxed view about sexual peccadilloes. It was still little more than twenty years since Anthony Eden had worried whether the fact that he was divorced might sink his political chances. But in that time society had changed hugely. Margaret Thatcher, married to a divorced man, had no such concerns. She was happy to have divorcees such as Nigel Lawson prominent in her government, and even to promote Cecil Parkinson, despite knowing that he was having an affair with his secretary.

Parkinson's spectacular fall from the cabinet came not because he was having an affair but because he was accused of behaving badly, in allegedly promising to marry his mistress and then changing his mind. The humiliation of politicians such as Parkinson (or David Mellor trysting with a minor actress, or Steve Norris with his girlfriends, or Stephen Milligan, who died during some bizarre auto-erotic experience, or others with mistresses, nightclub hostesses or clandestine children) is based on their hypocrisy. How dare they presume to control the rest of us when they can't control their own trousers? How the public exults at the revelation of their frailty! Yet this, too, is hypocrisy. We claim to want our politicians to be human. Yet when they are exposed for failing to keep their marriage vows, or for being greedy or just stupid, we castigate them for being no better than the rest of us.

The justification for exposing their human failings (it is not as if they've been planning murder) is a simple one: if they will cheat on their wives (and it is usually male politicians involved in this sort of thing) then might they not cheat on us? The argument has a persuasive simplicity to it. But of themselves the scandals are remarkably small beer. The contrast is, again, with France, where a worldly-wise Prime Minister once remarked that if he had to sack every member of his cabinet who had a mistress, then he would be left with just the women and the homosexuals. When you look back at the history of money scandals in recent British politics, the comparison with France is also instructive. In 1974, the Labour MP Joe Ashton wrote in *Labour Weekly*, 'The number of Labour MPs who can be hired can be counted on the fingers of one hand. And the rest of us know who they are.'[4] When he refused to name the guilty men, Ashton was forced to apologize to the House of Commons. But the message was more important than what his fellow politicians did to the messenger. Much the same thing has been said about Conservative MPs – that there may indeed be corrupt, or incipiently corrupt, figures in the House of Commons. But they are pretty few and far between. It is precisely because – whatever other faults they may have – most British politicians are comparatively clean that figures like Reginald Maudling, the Conservative former Chancellor of the Exchequer corrupted by the businessman John Poulson in the 1970s, stand out. Even when a later Conservative government was seen to be at its most rotten, before it went down to the most crushing defeat in modern political history, in 1997, the number of Tories who could be said to be personally corrupt – Jonathan Aitken, Tim Smith and Neil Hamilton being the most prominent – was a minuscule proportion of the party. When the *Sunday Times* set out to discover how easily MPs might be induced to ask a parliamentary question for money, it approached ten Labour and ten Conservative MPs. Eighteen rejected the bribe. Of the two relatively obscure MPs who fell into the trap, one subsequently returned the cheque. Of course it was two too many, but one wonders what might have happened in other parliaments in other countries.

That was not the way that the Labour party chose to present the issue. In his first speech in Downing Street Tony Blair repeated the promise to 'restore trust in politics in this country'. While his government did bring in laws to make it much harder for some of the unsavoury characters who had given money to the Conservative party – overseas arms-dealers and the like – to continue doing so, achieving an overall improvement in the image of politics was a great deal harder than he had claimed. During his first term in office he was plagued by a series of scandals which demonstrated that fallibility or dishonesty is not confined to any one party. As the years ticked by after the pledge to 'eliminate the causes of sleaze', there was one embarrassment after another. One MP borrows money to buy a house, another recommends someone for the honours list without disclosing the full nature of the relationship between them. A third is suspended from the House of Commons over relations with a corrupt businessman. All were abuses of trust, and all deserved to be punished. But they would scarcely have registered on the Richter Scale of political scandal as understood in much of the rest of the world.

They did not, however, add up to the government that Blair had promised would be 'purer than pure'. The much more profound problem is not so much the venality of individuals as the way in which the business of democracy is funded. British politicians may be comparatively honest. But running political parties and fighting elections are expensive activities. Neither of the biggest parties can survive on the subscriptions paid by members. Historically, the Conservative party has raised many millions of pounds from business, while the Labour party has had its bills paid by trades unions, but, though it is unimaginable that any of the great unions would ever endorse the Conservatives, the reverse is no longer true. Increasing numbers of business people came to believe Tony Blair when he claimed to have made his party safe for them. The fact that so many of his closest associates were so obviously smitten by the wealthy has made the conversion more plausible.

In theory, ever since the exposure of Lloyd George's practice of selling honours in exchange for donations to the Liberal party, it has been impossible for political leaders to barter knighthoods or peerages in exchange for party donations. The difference, though, is only one of degree. Lloyd George had done nothing that had not been done by other party leaders before him. His mistake was to be too flagrant, installing a conman, Maundy Gregory, as his intermediary in a magnificent office in Westminster (where he was estimated to be making £30,000 a year from commissions on the deals he brokered). When Lloyd George finally tried to send a man who had traded with Germany during the Great War to the House of Lords – in exchange for a substantial contribution to the Liberal party – the resulting scandal could be silenced only by a promise that in future all honours would be scrutinized by an independent committee.

So, eighty years later, if there is any correspondence between lists of donors to the political parties and lists of people sent to the House of Lords, it is purely coincidental. In the Thatcher years, it was businessmen like James Hanson and John King. When Tony Blair ran for the leadership of his party in 1994, money was raised from a collection of millionaires, at least three of whom – David Sainsbury, Melvyn Bragg and David Puttnam – were subsequently made life peers.[5] Michael Levy, the man who had unleashed Alvin Stardust, Chris Rea and Bad Manners on the world, was cultivated. Levy, an immensely wealthy man, raised millions for the party. He, too, went to the House of Lords. There he joined other Labour benefactors, like Swraj Paul.

Early in the second Blair term, opinion polls were showing that the public thought his administration, which had entered office with such noble ambitions, more 'sleazy and disreputable' than the Conservatives.[6] The change had begun less than six months after his 1997 triumph. Blair's government had taken office committed to a ban on tobacco companies sponsoring sporting events. Suddenly, it changed its mind, and made an exception for motor racing. Two days later the media reported that Bernie Ecclestone, the boss of Formula One, had given the Labour party £1 million before the 1997 election. The discovery that Blair had enjoyed the hospitality of the British Grand Prix the previous year was to lead to his becoming the first Prime Minister to be rebuked by the House of Commons Standards and Privileges Committee. There was more to come, like the uncomfortable sight of the Lord Chancellor, an old crony of the Prime Minister, but theoretically the independent head of an independent judiciary, playing host at a dinner for 120 lawyers at which, the guests were warned, they would be invited to make 'a significant contribution to party funds'. There were other policy decisions which left a bad taste in the mouth, such as the fact that Tony Blair had been prevailed upon to write a letter to the Romanian government to support an attempt by a 'British' company to buy a steel mill there. Not only did the company turn out not to be British (it had less than one-tenth of 1 per cent of its workforce employed in the UK and was registered in a tax haven in the Dutch Antilles) but its boss, Lakshmi Mittal, was seemingly not British either, as he was reported in the press to be Indian.[7] He had, however, given the Labour party £125,000. On another occasion, in early 2002, with the cry 'We hope to see businesses making much healthier profits in this field,' Blair's government trumpeted a relaxation of the laws on gambling. Betting, with its addictive qualities and the promise of reward for no effort, was an activity that many of the founders of the Labour party regarded as profoundly immoral. It came as no surprise to discover that the party had – quite separately – been given hundreds of thousands of pounds by casino and betting companies.

No doubt the government was made up entirely of honourable men and women. No doubt there would be no question of government policy being bent to please people who had given the party money. But there is an obvious contradiction. If a party leader says, in so many words, 'Whatever you give us, I will make sure that you don't benefit if we win the election,' then why should any rich and powerful person give the party anything?

Parties are vulnerable because they need money to function. The 'Americanization' of politics, in which image and personality are judged more important than ideology, has made all parties much more dependent upon research, analysis, advertising and other marketing techniques, all of which cost money. There are polling companies to be paid for the daily opinion surveys which tell the leadership what's playing well and where they ought to trim their sails. Millions more will pour out of party headquarters into the advertising agencies, billboard owners and transport companies. The problem is not unique to Britain: the same phenomenon is at work in the rest of Europe. Whether it is France, Germany, Italy or Britain, the first requirement of a political campaign is the same: money. It is the mother's milk of modern politics.

The alternative to soliciting money from donors is to force the taxpayer to foot the bill. The principle of state funding was conceded generations ago: the Leader of the Opposition has been paid a salary by the taxpayer since 1937, on the ground that it is in the interests of the state to have a properly functioning democracy. In the belief that democracy can function only through parties, since 1975 opposition parties have also been given public money to help with their performances in parliament. In 2002, the Electoral Commission gave grants of public money totalling £2 million a year to the parties represented in parliament, in the hope that they would enable them to work better. The question is whether the state ought now to be called in to replace possibly contaminated money with something relatively pure. There are many ways in which it could be done. On much of the European continent, the state gives money to parties in proportion to the votes they have won in elections or the number of seats they have gained in parliament. The system carries the significant risk of encouraging parties to become indifferent to their members, on whose subscriptions and donations they would otherwise rely. In North America, the state grants tax relief on donations from individuals. But that discriminates against people who do not pay tax. A third possibility might be to match state funding to the amount of money the parties could raise through individual membership subscriptions.

It is – and is likely to remain – an issue at the edges of public consciousness, because, by comparison with the sums of money involved in many other areas of government activity, the amounts are small. But there will be many taxpayers who would wonder why they should be compelled to give a government money in order that it can hand it on to other politicians, for them to give it to advertising agencies to insult our intelligence. And behind that lies a more philosophical objection. In the end, democratic politics is about the way a society reduces an abundance of individual hopes and fears, beliefs and prejudices to a coherent, collective system of government. The political parties are the means through which that process takes place, by organizing belief. But they are also a significant part of the sickness in British politics. If they are allowed to grow fat on taxpayers' money, they are unlikely to reform themselves. Democracy is about more than money.

10. Being History

The headquarters of the Cats Protection League are a nondescript redbrick semi-detached house on the outskirts of Horsham, Sussex. It is the sort of place that would not get a second glance, but for the two enormous trailers parked at the side of the building. They contain the League's travelling propaganda operation, for, this being Britain, the Cats Protection League is rather comfortably off. It has an annual budget of £15 million, much of it in the form of legacies from little old ladies. It employs 200 people. After the 1997 election, one of them was Derek Conway, whom we have already encountered in Chapter 6. For all its wealth, it is still not the sort of place you expect to find someone who once thought he could be Prime Minister.

Once upon a time, Derek Conway was a model Conservative. Literally. As a teenager he featured in a party political broadcast, walking through a council housing estate, talking in his Tyneside lilt about why he was a Tory. He had been chosen for the job precisely because, unlike most Conservative politicians, he was neither a landed toff nor a plummy, Home Counties professional. Like many who later became full-time politicians, his had been a political background. The local equivalent of the children's game of conkers was played with papier-mâché 'basters' painted in party colours. As a child he had been sent round the local streets, stuffing Labour leaflets through letterboxes, and then in the evening he had sat at the kitchen table filling in cards for voters to take to the voting stations to help his uncle become the mayor of Gateshead. But by the age of fifteen, while still at a tough secondary modern school, he was sufficiently unsure of his tribal loyalty to write off to all the political parties, to see what was on offer. The Communists were the quickest to respond, sending someone to knock on his door the very next day. But he decided (despite the fact that Conservative Central Office enclosed a bill with their literature) that, whatever his background, he was really a Tory. It was such an unusual trajectory that it flashed across the radar screens at

Conservative Central Office; the teenage Conway was invited to meet the party leader, Edward Heath, and then to appear in the propaganda film.

By twenty he had been selected as the Conservative candidate in Gateshead East, despite the fact that he would have been too young to sit in parliament had pigs flown and he had won. The following election, in October 1974, having now turned twenty-one, he fought Durham for the Conservatives, then stood for a seat in Newcastle at the 1979 election: it might have brought Margaret Thatcher to power, but the pigs had yet to grow wings.

Then, in what must have seemed an act of divine intervention, in 1982 Conway was chosen out of 263 contenders to fight Shrewsbury. It was the sort of place of which Conservative fantasies are made – the ancient capital of the kings of Powys, splattered with half-timbered houses, garnished with a famous public school. One hundred and sixty miles from Westminster, it was prosperous and naturally Tory. For the previous thirty-eight years it had been represented in parliament by Sir John Langford-Holt, the sort of MP for whom the expression 'knight of the shires' might have been invented. He had been chosen by the Conservatives of Shrewsbury in 1945, when he was said to have appeared before the selection committee as a young lieutenant in the Fleet Air Arm with a patch over one eye and an arm in a sling, having crashed his plane while flying down from Scotland on a holiday break the previous weekend. Charitably described as 'not exactly in the intellectual vanguard of the party', and listing his hobby in *Who's Who* as 'minding my own business', he never entirely shook off the habits of what was still known as the 'Silent Service'. When parliament attempted to improve the image of MPs by setting up a register of members' business interests, Langford-Holt simply refused to make an entry. His few political campaigns in nearly four decades included one to allow shops to open on Sundays, another to have dogs' collars stamped with a licence number, and a third to establish the number of nails bought and sold by the Ministry of Defence.

The Conservatives of Shrewsbury bore with their MP's singular interests until he decided to retire from campaigning and then they chose Derek Conway to succeed him. He was duly sent to Westminster at the 1983 General Election. Conway thought that, like his predecessor, he was there for life, or at least for as long as he fancied the job. His was hardly a stellar parliamentary career (except by comparison with his predecessor), but there was steady service on a succession of dull but worthy committees, the less than onerous burdens of the British–Moroccan Parliamentary Group and the usual round of receptions, parties, lunches and dinners. Eventually, in 1993, his loyalty to the party was repaid with a job as a junior whip. No office in government requires more self-abnegation than that of being a whip, and Conway submerged himself in his party and his constituency. If the Conservatives remained in office, he might have expected a junior ministerial job and, if he performed well, who knew what after that?

But the Conservatives did not win the next election. In 1997, they imploded. Conway found his Shrewsbury castle besieged not merely by Labour and Liberal Democrats but by single-issue anti-European candidates from the United Kingdom Independence party and the multimillionaire Sir James Goldsmith's Referendum Party. He also had a strong and uneasy sense that his own troops weren't bothered about leaving their quarters. By teatime on polling day, Conway knew his time was up. Astonishingly, Shrewsbury, a town which had remained the plaything of the landed gentry long after universal suffrage, was to be represented in the next parliament by a Labour MP. Conway claims that he took the blow philosophically. But pick at the scab and the poison is still bitter. The 1,800 votes taken by the two anti-European parties could have given him victory. 'Had it not been for James Goldsmith's intervention I'd have won. He died of pancreatic cancer,' he says, and then adds in the most chilling tone, 'I hear it's the most painful of deaths. I'm so pleased.'

Conway had known in advance that John Major would lose the 1997 election. 'I thought we were an awful government at the end. We deserved to lose. We were ready to go,' he says. But he had not included himself in the apocalypse. The sense of abandonment was profound. 'It was worst for my wife, Colette. She'd go into the supermarket and look around at people and think to herself, "My husband's been working seven days a week for you bunch of ingrates and you've betrayed him."' The country had abandoned the

Conservatives and Shrewsbury had abandoned Derek Conway. The family left Shrewsbury and moved to a flat in London. There was no income and no prospect of much. Children were withdrawn from 'pleasant little prep schools' and sent to inner-city primaries. For the first time in twenty-three years, Conway sat down and wrote out a CV.

When you come down to it, what does an ex-MP have to offer a possible employer? He has, obviously, plenty of self-confidence and, usually, plenty of energy. But what farmer wanting a working sheep-dog would buy a barking Doberman instead? He could sell lessons in public speaking (a speciality of the former Conservative member Hugo Summerson, once voted 'most romantic MP'). He can offer an understanding of how politics works. But that might as easily be bought from a lobbyist or a consultant, who is likely to have made particular efforts – unlike the politician – not to have made enemies along the way. A former MP may promise contacts in high places. But they may be good for a maximum of two or three years, and if his party has lost office they will be contacts only with the Opposition, and quite probably, therefore, counter-productive. There is, as someone once said, nothing so ex as an ex-MP. Once they leave the House of Commons, some will never have a proper job again: three years after he lost his seat in the 1997 election one MP was making ends meet by spending two days a week trying to sell cars imported from eastern Europe. Another was spending most of his time on an Open University degree, while David Ashby, who had lost both his wife and his seat in Leicestershire, after a ludicrous libel case, had been in therapy.

Conway was comparatively lucky. He hawked himself around firms of head-hunters and discovered that the Cats Protection League was looking for a new boss. Three months later, he was installed in the redbrick semi, on a salary package twice as big as when he had been an MP. There is something remarkably bathetic about exchanging a plan to save the country for one to rescue moggies. But the compensations, apart from the obvious financial improvement, were considerable. The most remarkable change that Derek Conway noticed was how much more time he had on his hands. 'It was amazing. When the House was sitting, I'd been used to getting to bed at two and getting up again at seven. Now I suddenly had all this extra time. It wasn't half as physically demanding. And I could see much more of my family.' This is a less than entirely rounded view: presumably the Cats Protection League operates for more than the equivalent of the thirty-two working weeks a year that parliament sits on average.

Most of us might have thought ourselves pretty fortunate to have turned public failure and humiliation into comfort. But, like all politicians, Conway had the worm eating inside him. No sooner had he got himself installed in a secure, well-paid job than he started trawling the country to find somewhere which would let him run for parliament again. This time, he was after a seat which would provide a meal ticket for life. He appeared before selection committees in Chelsea and Sutton Coldfield (just about the safest Conservative seat in the country) and a couple of others before, finally, he persuaded the committee in Old Bexley and Sidcup to let him succeed Sir Edward Heath. In the 2001 General Election he returned to parliament. Why on earth would anyone want to go back into parliament? There is a minority in politics who enjoy theorizing about how the country could be better run. But Conway was not one of them and never would be. And now he had decided to give up the security of the Cats Protection League for parliament. His explanation was simple.

'I miss the pressures. I love living on the edge.'

The price of living on the edge, as Conway had already discovered, was that sometimes you fall over it. When the end comes, it can arrive with breathtaking speed. Almost every cabinet minister remains in post only until the time when the Prime Minister decides to sack them, a decision which may have nothing at all to do with whether the minister concerned has been doing a good or bad job, but everything to do with placating different wings of the party, repaying a debt or trying to ingratiate himself with the public. Furthermore, they must try to continue doing their job while, in the run-up to any reshuffle, newspapers print story after story about who is going to survive and who is not long for this world. It must be hard enough to summon up the energy to go to work when every day you hear that someone else is about to get your job. But then there is the finality of it all. Compassionate employers, big or small, try to care for their staff. If they need to move someone on, they will try to let them down gently. 'Perhaps,' they suggest to a manager whose time has come, 'you should have a job that involves less travel, less administration or less pressure,' where they can eke out the days to their retirement. In politics, the end is sudden and devastating. The best that can be offered is a seat in the House of Lords, and a few years of gummy speechifying with no one listening. But no cabinet minister, told that his time is up, is in any doubt that his useful life is probably at an end. If he isn't being sent immediately to the knacker's yard, he is certainly being put out to grass.

As for those who walk away from office, the general rule of thumb is that anyone who resigns claiming they are doing it on principle was probably about to be fired. There are exceptions. Harold Wilson, famously, stormed out of the Labour government in 1951 because he could not stomach the Chancellor, Hugh Gaitskell's, plans to make people pay a fee for their false teeth and spectacles. At the time, this was presented as a gesture of left-wing principle. It turned out later that the thing had been planned in advance, and was probably not unconnected with the fact that there was an election in the offing and his own seat looked vulnerable. Hugh Dalton, to whom he confided his plan to resign, scribbled in his diary that 'He is a weak and conceited minister. He has no public face. But he is said to be frantically ambitious and desperately jealous of Hugh Gaitskell, thinking that *he* should have been Chancellor.'[1]

Or take the case of Michael Heseltine, who resigned the post of Defence Secretary in 'principled' protest at Margaret Thatcher's plans for the future of Westland, a small British helicopter company. Heseltine chose the most dramatic way possible for his exit, flouncing out of a cabinet meeting, and delivering himself of a twenty-two-minute statement explaining this 'spontaneous' decision shortly afterwards. Thatcher later remarked acidly that he and she were both ambitious, efficiency-conscious and single-minded, 'But whereas with me it is certain political principles that provide a reference point and inner strength, for Michael such things are unnecessary.'[2]

Because the guillotine falls so suddenly, senior politicians live their professional lives with their bags packed behind the office door. There is no notice period, no right of appeal, no trades union representation, no industrial tribunal, no compensation. It is another reason for the trade attracting the sort of people who like to take risks. Some Prime Ministers have tried to sugar the pill of demotion. While new ministers would be invited to walk up Downing Street in front of the mass of reporters and camera crews, Margaret Thatcher used to ask those she was sacking to come to the back door of Number 10. John Major even arranged for people to be hidden around the building, so that they didn't have to walk the gauntlet of reporters outside shouting, 'Have you been sacked?' There is no disguising the essential truth that you are being dispensed with because the Prime Minister thinks you're less good at your job than someone else might be. Few have been as brutally frank as Clement Attlee, though. He once got rid of a Scottish Secretary with the words, 'Good t'see you. I'm carrying through Government changes. Want your job for somebody else. Sake of the party, y'know. Write me the usual letter. Think of something as the excuse. Health, family, too much travelling, constituency calls. Anything will do. Good fellow. Thanks.' For a moment, the minister was stunned. Then it sank in. He was being slung out of the government. 'But why, Prime Minister? Why have you sacked me like this, without warning, with no complaints that I know of?' Attlee, who was already scribbling on the papers on his desk, looked up, removed the pipe from his mouth, and blurted out, ''Cos you don't measure up to yer job. That's why. Thanks for coming. Secretary will show you out.'[3]

It is odd how many ministers do not seem to realize that, just as one day they were elevated, so another day they will be jettisoned. So many seem to have believed they would go on for ever. But any government of any duration is going to run into choppy water, and the rougher it gets, the greater the temptation to start to throw people overboard. It may be the only way of keeping a tired administration looking fresh. Forty years on, the most notorious example is still the 'Night of the Long Knives' – Harold Macmillan's decision, after a series of by-election defeats, to jettison no fewer than seven members of his cabinet in July 1962. (Of which the Liberal politician Jeremy Thorpe remarked, 'Greater love hath no man than this, that he lay down his friends for his life.') When Charles Hill, the Minister of Housing, was summoned to have a knife stuck in his chest, he asked how long it would be before the purge became public. 'In an hour or so,' said Macmillan. Hill said it hardly gave him time to tell his family and friends, and that while he'd have been happy to step down before the election, presented like this it looked like a sacking. The Prime Minister is said to have replied, 'If I don't finish this now, the Government will fall,'[4] confiding to his diary that 'it was painful. But he is really *not* up to it.'[5] Another of those purged was a longstanding friend, fellow Guardsman and neighbour, his Lord Chancellor, Lord Kilmuir (formerly the Home Secretary David Maxwell Fyfe). It was he who had coined the phrase 'Loyalty is the Tories' secret weapon'. He discovered what this meant in practice when summoned to see Macmillan at 11.15 in the morning to be told that he was being sacrificed. Kilmuir had to go. He recalled, 'After my interview with the Prime Minister, I had seven hours of office left. In those last hours I had to entertain some distinguished American guests, and act as host at a cocktail party given to celebrate the centenary of the Land Registry.' Later, he drove with his wife to their country house in Sussex, where he heard on the radio who else had been ditched. 'And thus ended', he wrote, 'the great political adventure on which I had embarked as an undergraduate forty years ago.'[6]

There is no room for either friendship or gratitude at the top: when Macmillan heard that Kilmuir was claiming that he had been sacrificed because the Prime Minister had panicked, he just said, 'He was always a "beta minus"; the stupidest Lord Chancellor ever . . . hopeless in Cabinet – that's why I got rid of him.'[7] You wonder what he might have said if Kilmuir had been an enemy. But discovering what the Lord Chancellor was missing by losing office – entertaining visiting delegations, cocktail parties for the Land Registry – almost makes it seem desirable. At least losing your job means a break from ceaseless official functions at which you read out leaden speeches prepared by a functionary. And it gives the chance to tell the truth instead of the white lie or half-truth, no more standing up at Question Time for some smart alec to try to knock you down, no more evenings ruined ploughing through the documents the civil servants want you to sign by tomorrow morning.

There is, curiously, some comfort in a government losing an election: at least it means that everyone is in the same boat. To lose office by being sacked is such a terribly personal slight: it is you, and you specifically, who is unwanted. But the danger of preferring to lose office by losing an election is that you risk losing your own seat in parliament as well.

The pattern of recent British politics is that the voters simply get tired of hearing the same bunch of people spouting the same sentiments. Whatever they may claim in their manifestos and speeches, politicians cannot pave the streets of our cities with gold. They cannot even guarantee that the buses will run on time. And in the end the voters see through the promises. A wise political leader might recognize when he or she has run out of energy and quit the stage. That way there is less chance of their being found out. Instead, too many of them continue to plead with the electors to be given another chance. The longer governments stay in office, the more dangerous the arrogance of power. The consequence is that they always outstay their welcome. Or try to. And the nature of the political system means that a party must continue in government – and fight to stay in government – even well after the time when it has run out of useful things to do (and sometimes after it believes it should have lost office).

Once the electorate have made up their minds decisively, there is little or nothing a government can do to save itself. Jonathan Aitken faced the 1997 election from a safe Conservative seat on the Isle of Thanet in Kent: it had been Tory for twenty-three years. But as he went knocking on doors, he knew the game was up. It wasn't even his own behaviour which had done for him: many of his constituents seemed a remarkably forgiving lot. They were just sick to the back teeth of the Conservatives. He found himself in the pretty solidly Tory village of Worth.

The last house I canvassed was a Georgian six-bedroomed mansion [he knew a mansion when he saw one: he owned a nine-bedroom pile in Lord North Street, Westminster and another ten-bedroom place overlooking the sea at Sandwich Bay] whose owner I found watering the roses in his large garden. I knew him fairly well, having solved a problem for him when he had come to one of my weekly surgeries a year or so earlier. 'You've been a good MP but I'm afraid I'm definitely voting for Tony Blair,' he said. 'I'm just totally fed up with the Tories and so is my wife.' Like many other constituents, he was impervious to argument.[8]

Those who lose their seats must return to the House of Commons for the miserable business of emptying their offices. They come in three varieties. Some get to Westminster as soon as humanly possible after the election results have been published, race into their old offices, strip them, and disappear before there is any chance of their having to run into old colleagues, or, worse, their triumphant opponent. Others are so distressed that they arrive at the desk of the clerk in charge of offices looking for a shoulder to cry on. She helps them clear their rooms. The third category are so profoundly upset at being rejected that they cannot face going anywhere near Westminster. When the pressure from new MPs for offices becomes too intense, the Commons staff quietly parcel up their belongings in cardboard boxes and send them off to be collected from storage. (There are some former MPs who cannot even face going near their old seat, even when they decide to go of their own accord. Tim Eggar, MP for the London suburb of Enfield until he quit, one step ahead of the 1997 wipeout, found it impossible to revisit the constituency which no longer 'belonged' to him. 'I even feel slightly uncomfortable on the M25 when it goes near Enfield.')

For anyone with the slightest doubts about their purpose in life, political activity provides a justification for their existence and having it taken away can be devastating. When Leo Abse retired from the House of Commons after thirty years as a Welsh Labour MP, he was approached by various others who were also leaving Westminster. Several had tears in their eyes, some were totally bereft, as if there had been a death in the family. Keith Joseph, Abse's 'pair' on the Conservative benches and one of the most influential right-wing thinkers of the post-war years, was distraught. 'How will I manage?' he asked Abse, to which the Welshman replied, 'Well, you'll have a seat in the House of Lords.' But that was not enough. 'He looked at me, with tears in his eyes, and said, "But you've got your wife and family. I have nothing else."'

In practical terms, an entire life-support system disappears. Those who have been ministers suddenly lose the car, their driver, the office, the staff, the deference. If you lose your seat, there is a 'resettlement grant' of half a year's salary for an MP who has served ten years (and a full year's salary for those in their mid-fifties and older who have served fifteen years or more). But it comes as a heck of a shock to the system. When Tony Benn lost his seat in 1983, he suddenly found that for the first time in thirty years he had to provide his own stationery, because 'I have been using House of Commons letter-heading for thirty-three years and I haven't even got any with my name and address.' And there was no more free postage. 'The cost of stamps is astronomical; at this present rate, assuming I get 1000 letters a week, it would cost £120 on stamps alone.'[9]

A handful of former ministers may find a comfortable home and second career. But the spoils are not shared out evenly. John Wakeham, who served in Conservative cabinets through the 1980s and 1990s, was invited to run the Press Complaints Commission, chaired a Royal Commission into the future of the House of Lords, and picked up seats on the boards of half-a-dozen companies. Tony Newton, who rose from the presidency of the Oxford Union to serve fifteen years as a government minister, became chairman of Essex Mental Health Trust and 'director of professional standards' at the Institute of Directors. Harold Macmillan and Roy Jenkins both found a congenial billet as Chancellor of Oxford University. Rab Butler was offered the Mastership of Trinity College, Cambridge, a post in the gift of the Queen, on the recommendation of Harold Wilson. It gave him a happy second wind and enabled him to escape the fate which befalls so many one-time politicians of sitting in his club, or in the corner of his local saloon bar, talking about how he might have been a contender. As an old friend in the House of Commons wrote to him, 'My dear Rab, It's never possible to be absolutely unhappy looking out on Great Court.'[10] And so it turned out. Although David Lloyd George seriously thought he could become editor of *The Times*, he ended up pottering about as an amateur gardener, giving his name to a popular brand of raspberries, and turning up at eisteddfods dressed in druidical robes.

And then there are the memoirs. This largely dismal literature, in which the statesman's life unfolds as if he or she was God-ordained to rule from the moment they were a fertilized egg in their mother's womb, does not generally illuminate. It is characteristic of almost all political memoirs that, while they tell us a great deal about the achievements of the individual in piloting through parliament a bill to make the playing of loud music on Sunday afternoons an offence, they often say little or nothing about some of the most fascinating aspects of a politician. There will be more or less colourful depictions of childhood. But what is usually missing is any convincing sense of why the individual concerned decided to join the game in the first place. There will be ritual remarks about wanting to change the world or to be of service. They are rarely totally convincing. It often seems, in both autobiography and conversation, that the self-confidence required of a politician is the enemy of self-knowledge. They are not, by and large, a reflective breed.

Perhaps it is just that, from the dim-eyed perspective of the has-been, the youthful idealism which drove them cannot be recovered. But it also indicates the way in which the Game becomes more important than the reasons for which they started playing. This is why hardly any political memoirs contain charged accounts of what it was like to be selected as a prospective candidate, little about the feelings that churn through a candidate's heart as he or she watches the votes being stacked up, and nothing much, either, about what it is like to put politics behind you. Either these things do not matter any longer, or the wounds have been cauterized. There are honourable exceptions to this generalization. But they are few and far between. The titles express the tone: *The Time of my Life* (Denis Healey, rather good), *A Life at the Centre* (Roy Jenkins, also not bad), *The Path to Power* and *The Downing Street Years* (Margaret Thatcher, best-sellers), *Ministers Decide* (Norman Fowler, dire). An occasional foray, such as John Nott's *Here Today, Gone Tomorrow*, hints in passing at something more profound ('fame is an empty chalice . . . What is a throne? A bit of wood covered with velvet').[11]

The burden of the rest of them can be guessed at from the squeals of outrage in Reginald Bevins's well-named *The Greasy Pole*. Bevins, a rare working-class Tory in the days when the party was run by a 'magic circle' dominated by Old Etonians, sat in the cabinet as Post-master General. Years after leaving his job, Bevins was still smarting.

I recently read a rather unpleasant attack on me by Howard Thomas of ABC Television who said I did not maintain the vigorous and buoyant tradition of my predecessors. This really was plumbing the depths of distortion. I reckon we actually did more in my five years at the Post Office than all my post-war predecessors put together. At the risk of blowing my own trumpet and those of my advisers, we carried through, from start to finish, a major reform of commercial television, financially and otherwise; we started pay television; we authorised BBC2; we modernised most post offices and improved service; we started the micro-wave system with its centre at the huge GPO tower in London. But the most important of all was the vast expansion of the telephone system on an automated basis – easily the most rapid in Post Office history. These were solid achievements and they were not carried through without guts and drive.[12]

You can almost feel the outrage and pain. But who cares nowadays? If it had not been Bevins, who may well have had guts and drive, it would have been someone else: the expansion of television and the ubiquity of telephony were pushed by forces far stronger than any individual.

Even the most disgraced find things to crow about. Here is Jonathan Aitken reflecting on a trajectory that took him from Eton, via ministerial office, to prison.

What had I achieved during my 23 years in that palace of varieties? On balance, quite a lot. Few MPs contribute more than a thread or two to the tapestry of history, but I like to think that mine had been strong, positive, colourful strands of good public service. I could reasonably claim that I had represented my constituency well; changed a few lives for the better; championed the causes in which I believed without fear or favour; altered the perception of one or two key political issues; and exerted a modest amount of both power and influence for greater good. It would be tedious to list these achievements in specific form, but, looking back on my parliamentary life in the round, I felt much more fulfilment than disappointment.

All this from a man who, chastened by the discovery that he had knowingly conspired to lie in court, and suffused with humility, had entitled his memoirs *Pride and Perjury*.[13]

Twelve days after the 2001 election I went to the Palace of Westminster to talk to John Major. An appointment had been made, through his assistant, several weeks earlier. I arrived in the Central

Lobby of the House of Commons at five to ten. 'I've come to see John Major,' I told the doorkeeper in his tailcoat and white tie. He gave a look of decidedly superior bewilderment.

'It's OK,' I said, 'he's expecting me.' He looked unimpressed.

Finally, he spoke. 'He's not here any more,' he said. 'He retired at the election.'

'Oh God!' I said. 'So he did,' and wondered how I could have been so stupid as to make an appointment with a man in an institution to which he no longer belonged. Still, he would be bound to have an office somewhere round about. 'Do you have a phone number for him?'

'No,' he said, 'we just have numbers for members of the House of Commons and their staff.'

'But you *must* have a forwarding address for his mail.'

'No, we don't.'

How could this be? Five years before, Major had been the most important person in the country. Now, it was as if he didn't exist.

But the attendant wasn't being obstructive. A minute later he had an idea. 'I tell you what,' he said. 'One of his secretaries has gone to work for another MP.' He paused for a moment. 'The thing is, I can't remember his name.'

At this point, Andrew Mackinlay, the Labour MP for Thurrock, wandered by. 'What are you doing here?' he asked. I explained that I was looking for the former Prime Minister. He then helpfully called the switchboard, who also said they had no forwarding address or telephone number for Major.

Then Mackinlay said he thought that one of Major's secretaries had gone to work for the new MP for Huntingdon. Someone thought his name was Djanogly. We called his office. No reply.

Finally, the attendant rang Conservative Central Office, who eventually agreed to provide a number for Major's former constituency office in Huntingdon, where a kindly woman took pity on me and gave a number for the former Prime Minister's new office in London.

When, finally, I spoke on the telephone to John Major's assistant, she was mortified with embarrassment at having arranged for us to meet in a place where the former Prime Minister no longer had any status, let alone an office. It did not matter: the one thing the aborted meeting had demonstrated was the astonishing speed with which the waters close over political careers. One day you're running the country. The next, no one even has your telephone number. In the United States, former Presidents have libraries, mausoleums or universities built in their honour. In Britain, former Prime Ministers can simply vanish.

We met, eventually, at the Dorchester, on Park Lane. He ate sparsely and sensibly (minestrone soup, followed by a salad, although, sadly, no peas) and talked amiably about the difficulties of trying to get anything done in government, particularly with a small parliamentary majority. Halfway through our conversation, a man in a blazer crossed the bar.

'Mr Major, isn't it?'

Major flashed the sort of practised smile that comes from a thousand meetings with prime ministers of countries most people thought were just anagrams.

'I just wanted to say, I wish you were still Prime Minister.'

A weary look crossed Major's face. There was something about it which gave the impression that he might almost have believed that being president of Surrey Cricket Club was as vital a job as being Prime Minister. It was certainly more pleasant. Major shook the man's hand, and then, as he sat down again, muttered under his breath, 'Been there. Done that. Got the scars.'

Having presided over the most unhappy administration in recent British history, he gave the strong impression of being seriously relieved to be shot of the whole thing, as if he wasn't quite sure the journey from Coldharbour Lane to Park Lane had really been worth it.

All failure hurts, but the bitterest experience must be that of the person who has risen the highest. Unlike American Presidents, who can serve only two terms, British Prime Ministers can continue in office for as long as their party and the electorate will let them. They have no way of knowing when they are at their peak, and no inclination to walk away from a job which brings them status. There is no natural moment to leave with dignity: problems crowd in on every government, and the need to believe that things can only get better is understandable. But to try to defy nemesis is only to make it more certain. It really does end in tears.

Some of them try to put a brave face on it. Harold Macmillan claimed to feel that 'it has always seemed to me more artistic, when the curtain falls on the last performance, to accept the inevitable. "*E finita la commedia.*" It is tempting, perhaps, but unrewarding to hang about the greenroom after final retirement from the stage.'[14] Very few are as frankly sorry as John Major. 'I shall regret always that I rarely found my own authentic voice in politics,' he says of his unhappy government.

I was too conservative, too conventional. Too safe, too often. Too defensive. Too reactive. Later, too often on the back foot. I inherited a sick economy and passed on a sound one. But one abiding regret for me is that, in between, I did not have the resources to put in place the educational and social changes about which I cared so much; I made only a beginning, and it was not enough.[15]

Major's calamitous administration was only partly his own fault. But it will not do to seek comfort by wailing to the press that 'In thirty years' time, history will validate me.'[16]

As already noted, a former Prime Minister used to be sure of being offered an earldom and a seat in the House of Lords. Even so, as the great reporter James Margach noted in 1979, the year Margaret Thatcher took office, of all the previous twentieth-century Prime Ministers 'only two, Sir Alec Douglas-Home and Edward Heath, left No 10 Downing Street in as good shape as when they entered . . . the demands and exhaustions of power exacted a remorseless price. Lord Beaverbrook, as always, had the flair for telling the story in a single sentence: "In the moment of supreme triumph, decline begins to do its work."'[17]

In an age of all-pervasive media, we can see them change before our eyes. Tony Blair arrived in Downing Street in 1997 full of vim and vigour, with a full head of hair. By the time of the next election he was drawn and strained and his hair was falling out. Perhaps the physical change would have happened anyway: the middle-aged man or woman whose body does not begin to deteriorate has not yet been invented. But the physical strains are undeniable. The first Prime Minister of the twentieth century, Lord Salisbury, is said to have become so deaf, short-sighted and absent-minded that he once asked who the man was sitting alongside him at breakfast. It turned out to be W.H. Smith, who habitually sat opposite him across the cabinet table. Asquith was exhausted by the job of Prime Minister and was called 'Squiff' in the diaries and letters of the period because he needed so much alcohol to keep him going. Harold Wilson depended on brandy to get him through Prime Minister's Questions. Always vulnerable to exhaustion, after the Marconi scandal, in which he was accused of abusing public trust, David Lloyd George 'lost weight, lost vitality, fell ill again, and his black hair grew grey, the lines began to mark his face, and for the first time in public he was seen to use spectacles. A great life poised on the edge.'[18] Andrew Bonar Law smoked himself to death by throat cancer. Stanley Baldwin suffered depression ('My inside is a mess of cold rumbling fluidity; my brain is costive. Faith is dying; hope is dead').[19] Ramsay MacDonald was no happier: Harold Nicolson records in his diary a lunch at which the Prime Minister confessed that he was sleeping only a couple of hours a night, and found the business of government endlessly debilitating: 'The moment I disentangle my foot from one strand of barbed wire it becomes entangled in another.' The man was so ground down that he confessed, 'If God were to come to me and say, "Ramsay, would you rather be a country gentleman than a Prime Minister?", I should reply, "Please, God, a country gentleman." '[20] By the end, MacDonald was half-blind (he could read out official statements only by holding them a few inches from his eyes, while his enemies in the House of Commons laughed and jeered at him) and his mind was going.

Being forced out of office can add illness to unhappiness. Neville Chamberlain, who suffered from gout and sciatica, and never weighed more than ten stone, confessed to friends his deep depression after leaving Downing Street. At the end, his doctor said he had been powerless to save him because 'He did not want to live, and when a man says *that*, no doctor can save him.' When asked what was the cause of death, the doctor replied, 'He died of a broken heart.'[21] Churchill's hypochondria, his genuine heart problems and his enthusiasm for quack medicines are all well known. Defeat in the 1945 election had him swallowing 'reds' (barbiturates) to help him sleep, complaining incessantly about banging and whistling, and wishing out loud that 'It would have been better to have been killed in an aeroplane, or to have died like Roosevelt.'[22] In the year his apparently relaxed successor Clement Attlee lost power, he went down with a duodenal ulcer. Anthony Eden had the same problem, as well as a general lack of stamina and jaundice, had to have his gall bladder removed, and suffered from blocked bile passages. By the time of the Suez Crisis in 1956, which ended his Prime Ministership, he was often a wreck. A Labour MP described:

the Prime Minister sprawled on the front bench, head thrown back and mouth agape. His eyes, inflamed with sleeplessness, stared into vacancies beyond the roof except when they switched with meaningless intensity to the face of the clock, probed it for a few seconds, then rose again into vacancy. His hands twitched at his horn-rimmed spectacles or mopped themselves in a white handkerchief, but were never still. The face was grey except when black-ringed caverns surrounded the dying embers of his eyes. The whole personality, if not prostrated, seemed completely withdrawn.[23]

Harold Macmillan was prone to depression and hypochondria and eventually left office after prostate trouble. Several Prime Ministers, notably Asquith, Lloyd George, Baldwin, Churchill, Eden, Attlee and Macmillan, all found their health improved once they left office.

An ex-MP is just an ex-MP. The worst thing about being a former Prime Minister is to be the corporeal expression of an entire, generally discarded, world view. Ramsay MacDonald's achievement was to build the Labour party into a credible government, but he is remembered as a sell-out for joining a National Government with the Liberals and Tories: he will always be (Churchill's phrase) 'the boneless wonder'. Stanley Baldwin's pipe-smoking avuncularity is forever tainted by the knowledge of his cynicism. Harold Wilson came into office as a clear-eyed visionary and left it as a duplicitous schemer. The picture of Margaret Thatcher at the controls of a Challenger tank gives way to the ageing, red-eyed lady being driven away from Downing Street after losing the confidence of the party. The emollience of John Major looks like weakness, vacillation and scapegoating.

★

Some time after he had retired from politics to his beloved estate on the banks of the River Tweed, Sir Alec Douglas-Home fell into conversation with an elderly lady on the train to Berwick.

'My husband and I', said the woman, 'think it was a great tragedy that you were never Prime Minister.'

'As a matter of fact I was,' replied Home, adding wistfully, 'but only for a very short time.'[24]

How many former once-great men or women would answer with similar mild amusement? It helps to be an aristocrat, probably. For people whose existence has been devoted to standing out from the crowd, the sink into obscurity must be galling. But, with a few exceptions, it is the fate that awaits them. A few years after losing their seats, the only recognition that will be forthcoming is the occasional mildly perplexed second glance on the pavement from someone who wonders whether they didn't use to be that chap who was minister of something or other.

When he reflected on a political career which had seen him translated from 1930s Oxford don to 1960s Labour cabinet minister Richard Crossman concluded that the desire for power was just 'an old wives' tale', for having power necessarily involves a readiness to make hard choices. 'The vast majority of British politicians, like the rest of their fellow-creatures, desire success without too much effort and shudder if ever the moment comes when decision is unavoidable and power must be exercised ruthlessly.'[25] Fortunately for them, most politicians will spend most of their lives untouched by the whiff of real power. The best they can hope for is that some backbench piece of legislation will be named after them, or that a few grateful constituents may recall that it was the local MP who sorted out their housing or benefit problems. For the truth is that real power in government lies in the hands of a maximum of three or four people in government: the Prime Minister, the Chancellor of the Exchequer and perhaps a couple of trusted colleagues. The experience of the Thatcher and Blair governments is that what power there is is increasingly concentrated in the hands of the Prime Minister and his (largely unelected) staff. In the style of government developed by these two leaders, the days when cabinet meetings were gatherings of equals are long gone. Ministers no longer run individual departments of government as they see fit. They do as they're told.

But even Prime Ministers had better appreciate how limited their power is. If not, events will show them. The humiliations visited upon Prime Ministers since the Second World War follow a pattern. The Suez Crisis of 1956 (when troops were first dispatched to seize the canal, after Gamal Abdel Nasser had nationalized it, and were then, mortifyingly, brought home) demonstrated forcibly to Anthony Eden that Britain was no longer an independent military power. In 1963 President de Gaulle's veto of Britain's application to join the European Economic Community shattered Harold Macmillan's confidence in an alternative future within Europe. And then there have been the drearily repetitive attempts by one Prime Minister after another to behave like King Canute and to believe that the economy's fine because they say it's fine. Harold Wilson never recovered from being forced to devalue the pound in 1967. Edward Heath called an election in 1974 on the question of 'who governs Britain?' and discovered that whoever it was, it wasn't him. James Callaghan was forced to scurry off to the International Monetary Fund to be bailed out in 1976. And John Major's fate was sealed in 1992 when his government attempted to maintain the value of sterling and had it forcefully pointed out that it could not. These great crises of post-war British politics have been the moments when reality has crashed through the front window of 10 Downing Street and woken the Prime Minister from the dream that his powers are unlimited. There will be others: the best a Prime Minister can hope for is that it does not happen on his watch.

So it is a drama in which there will be few stars and many spear-carriers. Christopher Hollis, the Conservative MP who concluded that what brought someone to the top was 'that extra little ounce of ambition that is not quite sane', decided that, since most people realize that they would not wield power personally, three other motives must be at work: a sense of 'service', a love of the *trappings* of power and a hatred of others less distinguished getting on instead of them.[26] For the ambitious, life is corroded by the aching hope of advancement. It is a prescription for permanent dissatisfaction. Most simply refuse to live in the present: backbenchers want to be junior ministers, junior ministers want to gain the cabinet. Cabinet ministers want to be Prime Minister. Prime Ministers want to be on nodding terms with God. How can you be happy if you cannot enjoy the present?

One of the most astute assessments of the qualities necessary in a politician came from Humphry Berkeley. Claiming to belong to one of the three families in England able to trace their lineage back to before the Norman Conquest – the family castle was built in 759 – he might have seemed a natural member of the ruling class. (His great-aunt Amy used to indicate how *nouveau riche* she thought the royal family were by asking 'The royal family? What were they doing in 759?') In the days before the House of Commons was colonized by party machines, he could have served as an MP for years. Under the tyranny of the party system, his political career became more a voyage of discovery than one of conquest. First, he joined the Conservative party and sat as MP for Lancaster during the 1960s. Then he resigned from the party over its attitude to race. He rejoined a year later. He resigned again, to stand as a Labour candidate in the October 1974 General Election. Next he became a candidate for the short-lived Social Democratic party in 1987. Finally, he rejoined the Labour party. Along the way, he had played an active part in campaigning for speedy decolonization, homosexual law reform and the abolition of capital punishment. An eccentric at home nowhere, his experience of political life had two consequences. The first was that he was invited to stand for parliament to represent Hampstead by both the Conservatives and the Labour party, on the ground that 'You're exactly the sort of chap they want there.' Second, the odyssey left him with a greater self-knowledge than is available to the majority of people who decide to make a career in public life. He delivered this warts-and-all analysis of what it took.

Most politicians are rather odd people. Those, like Stanley Baldwin, who appear to be the most normal are in fact the oddest. Most politicians are simultaneously cynical and idealistic, self-centred and disinterested, candid and cunning. They are susceptible to the grossest flattery; they rival actors in their sustained ability to talk about themselves and ruthlessly to wrench any discussion into an examination of their own ego and its relationship to the matter being discussed. I recognise all these qualities in myself.

He had one piece of advice to anyone who wanted not to end up bitter and twisted. 'In many cases,' he wrote, 'they are jealous of their contemporaries. This feeling I have fought and overcome. Jealousy is poison. If you are embarked upon an enterprise where the stakes are as extreme as Downing Street or the gutter, you must rid your system of poison.'[27]

Most politicians will escape both the gutter and Downing Street and lead lives of modest achievement or semi-obscurity. If they don't have the hide of a rhinoceros (and a surprisingly large number, even including recent Prime Ministers such as John Major and Margaret Thatcher, do not), they must pretend they do. But those who rise highest have to recognize that the end, when it comes, can happen with astonishing ferocity. No one will recall their glory days, the times when they had been cheered to the rafters by their supporters, when anyone with ambition had tried to court them, when they had seemed to be the personal embodiment of the country as a whole. One old reporter,[28] who had watched their parties turn on Ramsay MacDonald and Anthony Eden, was reminded of crabs, which devour their own sick, wounded and dying.

In the recollections of Margot, Countess of Oxford, the formidable wife of the Liberal Prime Minister Herbert Henry Asquith, another image occurs. In his day, Asquith, with his dreams of a welfare state and attacks on the House of Lords, had been a heroic Liberal figure. But the quagmire of the First World War led to his eviction from Downing Street. On the couple's last night in Downing Street, late in 1916, Margot recalled the following conversation.

MARGOT: Why don't you go to bed, darling? Even last night when I came I found you translating Kipling into Greek. Surely that was an effort.
ASQUITH: Not at all; it was a relaxation.
MARGOT: What are you reading now?
ASQUITH: The Bible.
MARGOT: What part of the Bible?
ASQUITH: The Crucifixion.[29]

By then, his comrades had already cast lots for his clothing. When Margaret Thatcher 'resigned' the leadership of the Conservative party

– and the tenancy of 10 Downing Street – to John Major, she walked down from the Prime Ministerial flat to make one last check to see that she had left nothing in her study. She found that the key to the room had already been removed from her key-ring.

It takes a particular kind of inner strength to survive a very public humiliation like that sort of sacking, or the loss of an election. The wisest, like Neil Kinnock, who undertook to lead his party to the promised land and then found that he had lost them in the desert once again, come to recognize that losing an election is a long way short of the worst things that can happen in life. When I asked him what it felt like to be beaten, he shrugged his shoulders. 'Well,' he said. 'you've got to go on. It didn't come as a total surprise, after all. And anyway, it's not like losing a child. God knows how people cope with that.'

If a government loses an election, the prospect of opposition has little attraction to those who have wielded power. It is really only for the very ambitious and those who have never sat at the cabinet table. Once you have sat behind a ministerial desk, you know precisely the limited choice of policy options – none of them ideal and all fraught with disadvantages – open to the government. It makes it quite impossible for an honest man or woman to stand up in the House of Commons and call for something radically different. 'Once we lost the 1997 election,' one of the best-known Conservatives of the 1980s and 1990s told me, 'I knew it was over for me. What was the point of standing up in parliament and lambasting the Labour government, when I knew exactly how limited the options open to them were? It was all empty and pointless.'

But further down the dramatis personae, once they are on the stage, the proportion willing to leave it voluntarily is tiny. Even Martin Bell, who entered the House of Commons at the May 1997 election as Mr Clean, swearing to stay there for only one parliament, found the place irresistible and scurried down from Cheshire to Essex in (unsuccessful) search of a way of spending another five years as an MP. It takes a particular maturity (or jaundice) to see through the clubby self-importance of Westminster and recognize that there is another world out there.

Afterword

There is an old joke about a man emerging from a London taxi outside the Houses of Parliament. Throughout the journey, he has had the full benefit of the cabby's opinions on everything from world hunger to the price of fish. As he pays the fare, a thought strikes him with blinding clarity: why is it that the people who really know how to run the country are not inside parliament but driving taxis?

In a perfect world, of course, we wouldn't have politicians. Democracy is merely a mechanism for peacefully organizing ourselves without coming to blows. In a more harmonious world we should disagree less, and so could let the politicians get on with some harmless task, such as driving taxis. But the chances of being able to leave them to some intellectual basket-weaving in the foreseeable future are negligible. Even in a world where national parliaments have shrunk and ideological division has been replaced by consumer choice, society has to make decisions with which significant sections of the population may disagree. Politics matters. But we are increasingly disenchanted with it.

Disillusion is not unique to Britain. But there are problems specific to this country. The shrinking of British power has not helped. As one shrewd observer put it, 'Politicians were respected in the days when they could send a telegram to the Viceroy of India, touching a million lives, then stroll down to the club for a glass of sherry and a hand at whist.'[1] Nowadays, voters see – because the media show them – both that our politicians are now full-time professionals and how little they can do, even to ensure that the country has a reasonable library service. Power has been given away to Europe, taken away by our diminished status in the world and surrendered by international agreements. Judges are increasingly the ones who decide whether a citizen has been properly treated. Vast corporations, not individual governments, determine whether citizens will have jobs or not. The voter claims to want better public services, but objects to paying the taxes which would make them feasible. He or she also lives in a society in which standards of living have risen more or less steadily through-out their lives. With a few isolated examples – the Cuban missile crisis, the Falklands War, or the outrages of terrorism – Britain has been a peaceful place. When they are frightened, citizens look for leadership. When they are unthreatened, politics becomes a form of entertainment, in which all that matters is whether someone is up or down, with all the significance of the latest twists in the plot of a soap-opera. Peace is a corrupting thing.

Perhaps it is true that, as the public have come to think politics trivial, trivial people have become attracted to politics. Privately, senior party officials complain that the calibre of individuals hoping to become MPs is plummeting. But, for the most part, they are not scoundrels. Many have noble ideals and genuinely want to make the world a better place. With a few isolated exceptions, they are not corrupt, and for every minister who lies and every member who reeks of venality yet dances one step ahead of disgrace, there are more who work hard for their constituents. The disturbing anxiety is something else, the sense that too often they care less about what effect particular policies may have on the people of Britain than they care about their own part in events. It is like actors in a play not caring about whether it is any good or not, because all they really want is to be offered the chance to star in the next production. Sir John Hoskyns, who was called in by Margaret Thatcher to run her Policy Unit, had a close-up inside view of how politics worked. He was astonished by what he found. The politician was uninterested in 'method' – he or she saw the world as a canvas on which to paint a self-portrait, 'making his way in the world, until he holds one of the great offices of state, finally retiring full of honour and respectability. Political life is thus about the triumphs and disasters of personalities; living biography. The old legends fascinate them ... For most of them, questions of policy analysis and formulation are thus of secondary interest, until it is too late.'[2] One politician who made the rare decision to quit the game told me privately that 'On the whole, they would rather be on the stage losing, than off the stage winning,' going on to say that 'It is an awful life – risky, tough and psychologically damaging. Those who choose to play the game seem to consider themselves licensed to behave badly: there is a strong case for saying that political life encompasses the biggest dysfunctional family in the land.'

It would be stupid to pretend that politics was ever an entirely wholesome occupation. Nearly two centuries have passed since Disraeli wrote in his first novel that 'There is no act of treachery, or meanness, of which a political party is not capable; for in politics there is no honour.'[3] To some degree, politics has always been an illusionist's art, in which the performer must be seen as omniscient and his opponent as inept and untrustworthy. The qualities required to succeed, or even survive, are not the same as those necessary to triumph elsewhere. John Alderdice, the one-time leader of the Alliance party in Northern Ireland,[4] practised as a consultant psychotherapist. For a therapist, the experience of politics was salutary. Psychoanalysis is about solving internal conflict. Alderdice had wanted to try to help settle the conflict in Northern Ireland. But he found that 'Some people weren't interested in trying to find a way of reconciling different aspirations. More and more, politics is not so much about settling conflict as selling your voters illusions. The problem for all politicians is how to sell those illusions, when they know full well they *are* illusions. They can only do it if they go into denial. Businessmen have to live with reality. Politicians can deny reality.' The politics of Northern Ireland is of a particularly virulent kind, a matter, literally, of life and death. But the observation is true of the tribe as a whole.

Nearly thirty years ago, a psychologist tried to come to terms with why the British army had such an unhappy record of incompetent leadership.[5] He concluded that poor generals shared a number of characteristics. Among other things, they were fundamentally conservative and clung to outmoded traditions. They tended to reject or ignore information which didn't conform to their preconceptions. They underestimated the enemy, and had an obstinate persistence in a given task, even when they had ample evidence that it was doomed. They did not bother with proper reconnaissance or surprise, preferring frontal assaults and brute force. They tried to suppress or distort news from the front, usually on the ground that it was necessary for morale, and they had an unnatural attachment to mystical forces, such as fate or luck.

Most of these quirks could be applied to politicians. But it is a great deal harder to change a country's political class than it is to encourage military academies to reform the way they teach aspiring officers. The essential prerequisites of character if one wishes to become a politician – self-confidence, certitude, having a firmly held opinion on every subject – allow little room for free thought. Some politicians may, to borrow T.E. Lawrence's phrase, have 'too much body and too little head', but most of the main parties have plenty of intelligent, talented people sitting on their benches. Most are not stupid. The difficulty is that the arena in which they can deploy their skills has less and less to do with everyday life. Perhaps the parallel is with the military again. Alexis de Tocqueville observed that, when a country enjoys a long period of peace, the calibre of people entering its army falls. 'A circle of cause and consequence arises from which it is difficult to escape – the best part of the nation shuns the military because that profession is not honoured, and the profession is not honoured because the best part of the nation has ceased to follow it.'[6] Now, a similar malaise has overtaken the political class. Politics in Britain is held in low esteem because parties feel obliged to make unrealizable promises, while governments are seen as incapable of fixing things.

Shortly before the 2001 election, the Labour backbencher Austin Mitchell looked at the handful of journalists hoping to win election to the House of Commons, and wondered aloud why they were bothering. In the 1970s he had made the same transition himself. Now, he obviously regretted it. His word for those moving from media to politics was that they were 'barmy'. The days when a Nigel Lawson or a Michael Foot might make the transfer and succeed in both careers were gone. Journalists who had recently changed sides had failed in parliament. Furthermore, when it came to influence, they were simply trading down. 'Once, MPs set the agenda,' he said. 'Since then, the journalists have taken over the political arena . . . Once Parliament controlled the Executive. Today, the Government doesn't listen to us but to a fourth estate which obsesses it. Indeed, the Government devotes more time and energy to keeping *The Sun* on board than to the entire Parliamentary Labour Party. My job has been deskilled. All the interesting bits have been taken by journalists . . . What counts in journalism is ability, style, originality.

What counts in politics is the crawl up the ladder.'[7] There is something to this complaint of the child denied her pocket-money. '*It's not fair!*' It has a ring of truth about it.

He has a point about the media. At the start of the twentieth century, scrutiny of government policy was confined to a relatively small number of people. Although some of that scrutiny took place on the floor of the House of Commons, it was, by and large, dignified and discreet. In April 1925, for example, the then Chancellor of the Exchequer, Winston Churchill, announced that Britain was to return to the Gold Standard, whereby the value of sterling was guaranteed by allowing pounds to be exchanged for gold. This momentous (if ultimately unsuccessful) decision had been two months in preparation, involving heartfelt arguments on both sides of the debate. Yet not a word of it appeared in the newspapers. Indeed, it was hardly heard outside the confines of the Treasury. In contrast, when the pound toppled out of the European Exchange Rate Mechanism in September 1992, the entire humiliating process was broadcast on television, with the hapless Chancellor of the day, Norman Lamont, forced, blinking like a badger caught in the headlights, to announce the disaster not to a knowing coterie of fellow politicians, but, live, to the entire nation. The very public and very noisy scrutiny which has replaced private examination has obviously changed politics. The media can determine what is or is not an issue. And, since they also tend to behave as a herd, they can effectively set the terms of a debate. There are not only too many politicians. There are too many people reporting on what they say.

And as the media have become more boisterous, the voters have become more fickle. There was a time when Labour party politicians canvassing a heavy industrial area such as Port Glasgow would look at the surnames of the residents of tenements and know that if it was an Irish name they could count on their vote. Often, they didn't even bother to knock on the door, to waste time on someone whose support they could so confidently assume. But, as time has passed, the voters have become less tribal. Enabling tenants to buy their council houses created a class who began to look upon politics less as a matter of ancestral allegiance, while genteel Conservative certainties, spa towns such as Harrogate, Bath and Cheltenham, have fallen to the Liberal

Democrats. Yet in parliament the trend has been in the opposite direction: politicians seem to have become more tribal. Worse, whereas in
earlier times their loyalty might have been to a principle or a policy, it
is now judged almost entirely by fealty to a party.

We have reached the point where the general public is now ready
– almost eager – to believe the worst of politicians. But this is not the
same as saying that they have no interest in politics. The British are
not an apolitical people. So the gently sinking membership figures for
political parties do not reflect a disengagement from politics, merely
a lack of interest in the party system which has forced such a straitjacket
upon parliament. Ask members of the public what they care about,
and they will tell you that they feel passionately about the sort of
schools their children attend or the hospitals they rely upon when
sick. In the metropolis they have forgotten the words of the one-time
Speaker of the House of Representatives, Tip O'Neill, that, in the
end, 'All politics is local.' The most dramatic result of the 2001 election
was the entry into the House of Commons of an elderly retired doctor,
whose only policy was to stop the Kidderminster hospital being closed.
Richard Taylor's campaign was amateurish, but the more resources
Labour party headquarters threw into supporting their sitting MP,
the more his support grew. In their obsession with fighting national
elections, the political parties have lost touch with local communities.
To re-engage, they have to accept that in an unideological age people
are not making a lifetime commitment when they join: convictions
change as circumstances change. But you cannot rebuild trust between
politicians and voters by central diktat.

The British political system is stumbling and coughing its way into
the future. Unless some way is found to rejuvenate it, the chasm
between people and parliament will simply deepen. You might argue
that it doesn't matter. People are most engaged in the business of
politics when they want to change things. If they are not involved, it
may merely signify that they are relatively content. Disengagement
might also reflect a worldly recognition that there are strict limits to
what governments can do. Rome could never be built in a day.
Perhaps now it cannot be built at all. But governments *do* make a
difference.

Does it matter if people stop believing in politicians? In the short term, perhaps not much: the British people have always held them in healthily low regard. But a society which loses faith in how it governs itself is in danger of falling apart. For all its fogeyish love of ritual and protocol, there is no need for the British parliament to continue behaving in the way it carries on at present, nor for political life to stay the way it is. At the turn of the twentieth century, the Prime Minister was a marquess, the Labour party did not even formally exist, women were denied the vote, and most of the population would probably not have recognized their own member of parliament. There is no reason to suppose that at the turn of the next century the way we conduct politics now will seem any less quaint.

Outside the Palace of Westminster the world has changed. Most voters have opportunities, for education, for entertainment, for travel, that their parents or grandparents could only have dreamed of. With so many more people in higher education, so many alternative lifestyle leaders, such an abundance of mass-media outlets, the days of automatic respect for politicians and the process they represent are gone. If the citizens have become not so much apolitical as disenchanted with the Punch and Judy show at Westminster, the thing to do is to change how parliament behaves.

No one has yet begun to grapple properly with the implications of having devolved governments in Scotland and Wales, for one thing. Visitors to both Scottish and Welsh assemblies are stunned by the sheer tedium of the proceedings. But that is their point. The first Welsh Assembly had about it the aura of a not-very-dynamic local council with the extra frisson of proceedings being conducted in either English or Welsh, despite the fact that, while all sixty members of the first Assembly spoke English, only twenty-three were fluent in Welsh. There were, meanwhile, no fewer than thirty-five people employed as full-time translators. Within a couple of years, twelve of the Assembly members were learning Welsh, presumably in the knowledge that, if they ever lost their seats, there would always be work available translating from a language everyone understood into one intelligible only to a minority.

The institutions in Cardiff and Edinburgh – and the invention of directly elected mayors – may succeed in reconnecting the citizen with the politician by moving the whole process closer to the places where people actually live. As in natural evolution, so in any field of human activity: those who do not adapt sooner or later die. The British have always recognized their politicians' fallibility. But it is quite another thing to lose faith in the institutions themselves: put simply, why should anyone in Scotland bother to vote in elections for a parliament in London, when the things that matter most to them – schools, health or transport – are dealt with by the parliament in Edinburgh?

So the first challenge is to find a way of breathing life back into the House of Commons, which seems distant, opaque and disconnected from ordinary life. It is hardly holding the government of the day to account while the political process as a whole cannot answer adequately for the failure of the country's public services. The number of members of parliament could be reduced by one-third. Opponents will argue that it is already hard enough to find the hundred or so competent people needed to form a government. To which the answer is 'Then reduce the size of government.' Quite apart from the number of redundant jobs being performed by ministers, there is an obvious economy to be made by allowing the same ministers to answer questions in both the House of Commons and the House of Lords: at least the Lords would feel they were talking to the organ-grinder instead of the monkey. Prime Ministers have already developed the habit of padding out their government with congenial but unselected figures. Obliging these figures to appear before the House of Commons to justify themselves would at least put a little accountability back into government.

This implies the House of Commons reinventing itself as a place which holds the government of the day to account. It would necessitate changing the way it does business, so that there is less speechifying and more scrutiny, more thought and more cross-examination. It would involve having a sensible working pattern (in the parliamentary year which ran from 2000 to 2001 – and which was, admittedly, disrupted by an election – the House of Commons sat for only eighty-three days). It would involve giving select committees more power, and making sitting on a committee a worthwhile career choice. To give ambitious politicians an alternative career to rising through the government, chairmen of committees should be paid. In return, they would be expected to run the things as if they mattered. These are big changes. But if politicians cannot change the conditions in which they work, what can they change?

There is much that is terrific about British national politics. At the most important level, Britain *feels* like a democracy: an election takes place on a Thursday and the removal vans are in Downing Street on a Friday. The debate is lively: it sounds as if it matters. But what seems to be missing is passion. The public response to politicians need not be indifference or contempt. After all, if you can offer hope, you can inspire enchantment.

Acknowledgements

Attempting to list the very many people who helped write this book is a doomed exercise. We all talk about politics and politicians all the time, and after a while the ideas accumulate like a sediment. You forget who originally said what. But during the time that I was actively researching and writing I sought out dozens of people, to talk about specific subjects. Some were bought for the price of a lunch, many others were happy just to chat, because they had been turning similar questions over in their own minds. Several would only talk on condition they were neither quoted nor acknowledged, and so their names do not appear in the text.

I found most people, from former Prime Ministers to local councillors, keen to discuss what had gone wrong with politics in Britain. Among the minority who declined were Margaret Thatcher ('I would prefer to keep my reflections on these matters to myself at present'). I wrote to Tony Blair about his quoted acceptance that most political careers end in failure, but my letter wasn't even acknowledged. I got a similar lack of response from Denzil Davies, whose bizarre middle-of-the-night resignation from the post of shadow Defence Secretary was one of the great comic highlights of recent politics. The Speaker, Michael Martin, also didn't bother to reply to my letter about the way he runs the House of Commons, although his predecessor, Betty Boothroyd, had been glad to share a cup of tea for an hour or so. I wanted to ask another MP whether there was, by any chance, any connection between his receiving a knighthood and the fact that he had abandoned his longstanding opposition to particular aspects of government policy. He replied, 'I have found that answers or information I have given to the media have, almost invariably, been re-tailored to suit the preconceptions of the writer. So why bother?' Richard Body, the idiosyncratic Conservative, wrote that 'No story about me is ever true.' Another blank I drew was with an MP who turned out to be so depressed by the sheer pointlessness of what he was doing, or failing to do, that he simply couldn't face talking to anyone about it. I felt sorry for him and left it at that.

But these refusals were a tiny minority. Among those willing to discuss were Diane Abbott, Leo Abse, (Lord) John Alderdice, Douglas Alexander, Michael Ancram, Jeffrey Archer, Martin Bell, (Lord) John Biffen, Helen Brinton, Chris Bryant, Dale Campbell-Savours, the late (Baroness) Barbara Castle, Henry Clark, Charles Clarke, Derek Conway, Robin Cook, Sir Edward du Cann, Tim Eggar, David Faber, Michael Fabricant, (Lord) Charlie Falconer, Caroline Flint, Eric Forth, (Lord) Tristan Garel-Jones, Paul Goodman, Peter Hain, Michael Howard, Douglas Hurd, Jenny Jones, Neil Kinnock, Oliver Letwin, Andrew Mackinlay, John Major, Bob Marshall-Andrews, Jamie McGrigor, (Baroness) Doreen Miller, Frances Morrell, Archie Norman, Eric Pickles, John Redwood, Robert Rogers, David Ruffley, (Lord) Tom Sawyer, Dr Phyllis Starkey, Jack Straw, Dr Richard Taylor, (Lord) Norman Tebbit, Cyril Thornton, Carole Tongue, Andrew Tyrie, (Baroness) Shirley Williams, Michael Wills, Dr Tony Wright and Derek Wyatt.

Among those who work, live or study among politicians I am grateful to Priscilla Baines, Phil Bassett, Professor Vernon Bogdanor, William Bromley-Davenport, Bill Bush, Robin Butler, Ian Church, Professor Peter Clarke, Dr Stephen Coleman of the Hansard Society, Rhian Connell, Philip Cowley, Byron Criddle, the serjeant-at-arms, Michael Cummins, and his staff, notably Muir Morton, Judy Scott Thomson, Matthew Taylor and Henry Webber, Mark Garnet, Julian Glover, Johnny Grimond, Christine Hamilton, Michael Hammett of the British Brick Society, Robert Harris, Philip Hensher, Stephen Howe, Boris Johnson, the Right Reverend James Jones, Bishop of Liverpool, John Kampfner, Diana Macnab of Macnab, Mark Mardell, Professor David Marquand, Andrew Marr, John Martin-Robinson, Hugh Massingberd, Nick Menzies, Chris Moncrieff, (Lord) Philip Norton, Matthew Parris, Professor Ben Pimlott, Sarah Priddle and the House of Commons Information Office, Jane Rogerson, (Lord) Maurice Saatchi, Michael Sayer, Mark Seddon, Professor Patrick Seyd, Elizabeth Smith, Sarah Smith, the late Dr Anthony Storr, Dr Ashley Weinberg, Eileen Wise and, in Wales, Catherine Elliott, Owen Smith and David Williams.

The suggestion that I should tackle a book about politics came originally from Tom Weldon, at Penguin. He did not seem to blanch too visibly when the manuscript was not delivered until almost two years after the original deadline. It was a suggestion from Professor Anthony King that turned a more general book about politics into an examination of what it is like to be a politician. I was then hugely helped in filleting political memoirs by Alex von Tunzelmann, whom I found by advertising in the Oxford student paper *Cherwell*, of which, it turned out, she was the editor. My agent, Anthony Goff, kept me at it when I felt like giving up. Elizabeth Clough was meticulous and unsparing in her criticism. And Peter James has been an acute and industrious editor.

The misunderstandings, mistakes and errors of judgement which remain, despite their efforts, are all my own work.

Notes

Introduction

1. In the 2001 election, the total dropped slightly, to 3,318, including 427 UK Independence party candidates, 145 Greens, 98 Socialist Alliance candidates, 37 contenders from the Pro-Life Alliance and 33 from the British National party, as well as the usual smattering of New Millennium Bean party, Jam Wrestling party and the Rock 'N' Roll Loony party candidates.

2. It is true that there had been other 'independent' MPs in that time – such as Edward Milne (Independent Labour MP for Byth, 1974), Dick Taverne (Independent Democratic MP for Lincoln in 1973) and Sir John Robertson (Independent Conservative for Caithness and Sutherland, 1959), but they had all previously belonged to one of the mainstream parties.

3. Quoted in McDougall, *Westminster Women*, p. 30.

4. It was David Maxwell Fyfe, Conservative Home Secretary and (as Viscount Kilmuir) Lord Chancellor, whom he greeted at 11.15 one morning with the words 'David! Have *another* glass of port and a cigar.' (See Kilmuir, *Political Adventure*, p. 166.) Churchill wasn't the first Prime Minister with this attitude. Told that he had been so drunk in the House of Commons the night before that his breath had given one of the House of Commons clerks a headache, the younger Pitt said he didn't want to hear any more about it. 'It suited him very well: he had had the drink and the clerk had had the headache.' (Egremont, *Wyndham and Children First*, pp. 190–91.)

5. Fifteen years, one month, to be precise. The figure is based on an analysis of members of parliament since 1945 made by the respected co-author of the *Almanac of British Politics*, Byron Criddle, of Aberdeen University. I asked him to make the calculation after hearing Robin Cook (who had been charged by Tony Blair with reforming the way

the House of Commons operates) claim that the average career lasted nine years.

6. Powell, *Chamberlain*, p. 151.

1. Out of the Mouths of Babes and Sucklings . . .

1. Crick, *Heseltine*, p. 13, quoting *GQ*, February 1988.
2. Shepherd, *Powell*, p. 3.
3. Lloyd George, *Lloyd George*, p. 15.
4. Churchill, *My Early Life*, pp. 29–30: 'It was from these slender indications of scholarship that Mr Welldone [the headmaster] drew the conclusion that I was worthy to pass into Harrow. It is much to his credit. It showed a man capable of looking beneath the surface of things.'
5. Clark, *Diaries*, vol. 1, 15 February 1985, p. 106.
6. Cited in Crick, *Archer*, p. 47.
7. Cecil, *British Foreign Secretaries*, p. 280. See also Roberts, *Salisbury*, p. 9.
8. Gilmour, *Curzon*, pp. 7–8, quotes attributed to Curzon Papers 112/363, India Office Library.
9. Taylor, ed., *Lloyd George*, 22 November 1915, p. 77.
10. Lloyd George, *Lloyd George*, pp. 49–50.
11. Horne, *Macmillan*, vol. 1, p. 12.
12. Martin Jacques, *Sunday Times Magazine*, 17 July 1994.
13. Yorkshire Television, 18 November 1985.
14. Thatcher, *Downing Street Years*, p. 11.
15. Barnes, *Behind the Image*, pp. 144–5.
16. Kilmuir, *Political Adventure*, p. 325.
17. See, for example, Valentine, *British Establishment 1760–1784*, and Ellis Wasson, *Born to Rule*.
18. *New York Herald Tribune*, 8 September 1933.
19. Wasson, *Born to Rule*, p. 157.
20. Benn, *Office without Power*, 26 February 1970, p. 244. Benn himself was actually born on the site of Millbank Tower, 40 Millbank, the headquarters of new Labour. At the time, it was known as 40 Grosvenor Road.

21. Tim Rathbone, MP for Lewes from 1974 to 1997, had beaten him to that distinction.

22. James, *Chips*, 15 December 1947, p. 420.

23. The seat was in Southend, where, because Channon senior had married into the brewing dynasty, the advice was 'Have another Guinness!'

24. Chamberlain, cited in Longford, *Eleven at No 10*, p. 33.

25. Brown, *In My Way*, p. 25.

26. Harris, *The Prime Minister Talks to the Observer*, p. 1.

27. Hollis, *Jennie Lee*, p. 9.

28. Quoted in Rogers and Moyle, *Campbell-Bannerman*, p. 7.

29. Iremonger, *Fiery Chariot*.

30. Quoted in *ibid.*, p. 259.

31. *John Bull*, 4 September 1915.

32. MacDonald's diary, quoted in Marquand, *MacDonald*, p. 191.

33. Morgan, *Callaghan*, p. 10.

34. Major, *Autobiography*, p. 15.

35. Sigmund Freud, *The Collected Papers*, vol. 4 (London, 1952), quoted in Tucker, *Stalin as Revolutionary*, p. 76.

36. *Sunday Express*, 7 October 1984, quoted in Crick, *Archer*, p. 50.

37. Iremonger, *Fiery Chariot*, pp. 308–9.

38. Statistics from Englefield, Seaton and White, *Facts about the British Prime Ministers*, p. 373.

39. Quoted in Pimlott, *Wilson*, p. 18.

40. *Ibid.*

41. *Ibid.*, p. 20.

42. Castle, *Fighting All the Way*, p. 13. The first recorded written words of the future Foreign Secretary Robin Cook were his diary entry for 5 March 1953. They read, 'Today Joseph Stalin died. All the people of Russia will be very sad.'

43. Brivati, *Gaitskell*, pp. 6–7.

44. Brown, *Fighting Talk*, pp. 33, 35 and 36.

45. *Ibid.*, p. 29.

46. Major, *Autobiography*, p. 26.

47. Trollope, *Autobiography*, p. 230.

48. Ashdown, *Diaries*, vol. 1, 10 April 1992, p. 159.

49. Bevan, *In Place of Fear*, p. 21.

50. Thorpe, *Douglas-Home*, p. 43.

51. Quoted in Gilbert, *Churchill*, p. 80.

52. *Ibid.*, p. 88.

53. Churchill, *Savrola*, pp. 42–3.

54. Brendon, *Churchill*, p. 36.

55. Foot, *Loyalists and Loners*, p. 169. The latter quotation is from an essay by A.G. Gardiner for which Foot does not give either name or close reference.

56. Hollis, *Can Parliament Survive?*, p. 72.

57. Major, *Autobiography*, p. xvii.

2. Getting On

1. Unsigned article, *Isis*, no. 1691, 7 October 1976, p. 25.

2. Unsigned editorial, *Isis*, no. 807, 29 October 1930, p. 1.

3. Cited in Walter, *Oxford Union*, p. 124.

4. Adams, *Benn*, p. 44.

5. Jenkins, *Life at the Centre*, p. 26.

6. Crick, *Heseltine*, p. 38. Although he never became Prime Minister, Heseltine did eventually make it to be president of the Union, although only in the term *after* he finished his finals.

7. Heath, *Course of my Life*, p. 30.

8. St John Broderick, later Viscount Midleton, writing to Lord Curzon (who became president of the Union), 29 May 1878, Curzon Papers 111/9, India Office Library.

9. Waldegrave, in Blair, *History of OUCA*, p. 9.

10. Thorpe, quoted in Barnes, *Behind the Image*, p. 271.

11. The offer was not taken up. The Speaker wrote back suggesting that the matter be left in abeyance until the war was over, because it would be wrong to risk losing a second set of boxes.

12. Walter, *Oxford Union*, p. 117.

13. *Ibid.*, p. 11.

14. Critchley, *Westminster Blues*, pp. 15–16.

15. All quotations are from Conservative Central Office files held in the Bodleian Library, Oxford, cat. nos. CCO 506/17/3 and CCO 506/17/1.

16. *A New Jack the Giant Killer*, Bodleian Library, CCO 506/7/5.

17. Rentoul, *Blair*, pp. 33–4.
18. Thorpe, *Douglas-Home*, p. 31.
19. Attlee, *As It Happened*, p. 14.
20. Gaitskell, 'At Oxford in the Twenties', in Briggs and Saville, *Essays in Labour History*, pp. 6–7.
21. His tutor was Raphael Samuel. *Guardian*, 2 June 1992.
22. Foot, *Bevan*, p. 23.
23. Information from Leigh and Vulliamy, *Sleaze*, p. 52.
24. Clarke, *Question of Leadership*, p. 6.

3. Getting In

1. The hopeless-loser phenomenon applies to all parties, of course. In the Ladywood constituency in Birmingham, one of Labour's safest seats, held by Clare Short, the Conservative candidate in 2001 was 26-year-old Benjamin Prentice, a manager at a local employment agency. To say his organization was threadbare would be an insult to threads. It consisted of him and half-a-dozen mates. They had a total budget of £2,000, which is the sort of sum spent on sandwiches and coffee in some Labour seats. He was refreshingly realistic about his chances, telling me that he knew he wouldn't win, but that it was important people had a choice. He'd lived in the area since the age of eleven, and doubtless one day will reach the House of Commons. But not representing Birmingham Ladywood.
2. Johnson, *Friends, Voters, Countrymen*, pp. 15–16.
3. Fisher, *Macleod*, p. 55.
4. *Ibid.*, p. 66.
5. Cooper, *Old Men Forget*, p. 128.
6. Hailsham, *Sparrow's Flight*, pp. 122 and 115. Gilmour, *Curzon*, p. 58. Heath, *Course of my Life*, p. 119.
7. Heath, *Course of my Life*, p. 117.
8. Walden, *Lucky George*, p. 238.
9. Castle, *Fighting All the Way*, p. 122.
10. Fenner Brockway, quoted in Foot, *Loyalists and Loners*, p. 23.
11. From the *Finchley Press*, quoted in Young, *One of Us*, pp. 39–40.
12. When Michael Heseltine was trying to get the Conservative nomination

in Coventry in 1961, he played the son-in-law card to devastating effect, blowing into the hall late, with a young woman on his arm. He announced to the hall that she had just consented to become his wife. Hearts fluttered in Tory ladies' breasts. Heseltine got the nomination.

13. Peta Luscombe, 'Sometimes it's hard to be a Tory woman', *Spectator*, 1 September 2001.

14. Some 37 per cent of the members of the Scottish Parliament were women, and 42 per cent of the Welsh Assembly.

15. Douglas Smith, 'Soulless, selfish and smug – today's Tory candidates', *Daily Telegraph*, 18 June 2001.

16. Trollope, *Autobiography*, p. 230.

17. Quoted in Mullen, *Trollope*, p. 513.

18. Quoted in *ibid.*, p. 514.

19. *The Duke's Children*, quoted in *ibid.*, p. 516.

20. Letter to Anna Steele, quoted in Glendinning, *Trollope*, p. 390.

21. Churchill, *Great Contemporaries*, p. 17.

22. Cecil Roberts, *The Bright Twenties*, vol. 3, p. 168, cited in Boyle, *Poor, Dear Brendan*, p. 116.

23. Churchill, *My Early Life*, p. 235.

24. Wedgwood, *Testament to Democracy*, p. 17.

25. *Hailsham Gazette*, 25 April 2001.

26. Quoted in Barber, *The Prime Minister since 1945*, p. 53.

27. A friend who was alone with Churchill after the 1945 defeat found him bitter and distressed. 'What was it that enabled Stanley Baldwin to win elections, while I always lose them?' Churchill asked. His friend told him that Baldwin abided by three rules. He never imputed dishonourable motives to his opponents. He believed in understatement rather than overstatement. And he gave the impression that while the opposition were honourable chaps, they rather lacked the necessary experience and breadth of vision to run the country and deal with international affairs. (Lord Davidson, letter to Rab Butler, 20 April 1955, cited in James, *Memoirs of a Conservative*, p. 171.)

28. In the 2001 election, the Conservatives and Liberal Democrats printed about 100,000 copies of their manifestos apiece, the Labour party 60,000, with a further 1 million copies of an abbreviated version.

29. Thatcher, *What's Wrong with Politics?*, p. 6.

30. Jenkins, *Home Thoughts from Abroad*, p. 7.

31. Quoted in Rogers, *Political Quotes*, p. 26.

32. After these explosions, which had the effect of winding everyone up to a fury, Hogg would 'suddenly decide he'd been rather funny and stand there, his face wreathed in smiles'. Constituents found the performance so curious that they always wanted to meet his wife, asking themselves the question 'Who on earth is married to that man?' Barnes, *Behind the Image*, p. 139.

4. New Boys and Girls

1. Until very recently, the cry 'I spy strangers!' was the way that MPs held up proceedings in the House of Commons: officials would then be obliged to empty the chamber of everyone who was not a member of parliament.

2. De Montfort's parliament of barons, knights, clergy and burgesses was one of the key events in the struggle to resist the autocratic rule of the monarch. He was considered such a pernicious influence that, after defeat in the Battle of Evesham, his head, hands, feet and testicles were hacked off. What remained was entombed in Evesham Abbey, which rapidly became a shrine.

3. Major, *Autobiography*, p. 66.

4. From Lloyd George's diary, 12 November 1881, quoted in George, *My Brother and I*, p. 155.

5. Bevan, *In Place of Fear*, p. 25.

6. *Ibid.*, p. 26.

7. Major, *Autobiography*, p. 70.

8. Kilmuir, *Political Adventure*, pp. 42–3 and 326.

9. Shepherd, *Powell*, p. 98.

10. Hansard, 5th series, vol. 393, col. 403, 28 October 1943.

11. *Ibid.*, cols. 403–4.

12. *Ibid.*, col. 437.

13. Robert Lutyens, 'The New House of Commons', *Country Life*, 20 October 1950.

14. Adams, *Benn*, p. 72.

15. Critchley, *Westminster Blues*, p. 79.

16. *Ibid.*, p. 84.

17. By comparison with politicians elsewhere in the European Union, in salary terms British members of parliament are not overpaid. That honour belongs to the Italians, where a record of incompetence has done nothing to dull a sense that they are entitled to handsome rewards. In September 2001 they were paying themselves 10,643 euros a month, which was over three times the salary Spanish politicians had given themselves and twice the rate of Danish, Dutch, Swedish or Irish parliamentary pay. British MPs' salaries, at the equivalent of 6,566 euros, were similar to those of German or French politicians.

18. Boothroyd, Foreword to *Houses of Parliament*, p. 1.

19. Letter, 24 July 1965, cited in Thorpe, *Douglas-Home*, p. 377.

20. Berkeley, *Crossing the Floor*, p. 27.

21. Quoted in Byron Criddle, 'MPs and Candidates', in Butler and Kavanagh, *The British General Election of 2001*, p. 186.

22. See *ibid.*, and *The British General Election, 1997*, to which I am much indebted, and Butler and Butler, *Twentieth Century British Political Facts*, pp. 189–90.

23. When the place was rebuilt after the Second World War, female MPs were promised an increase in the number of lavatories. They did not get an adequate supply. Their predicament wasn't helped by the fact that the men's lavatories were simply labelled 'Members Only', as if female members did not exist.

24. Quoted in McDougall, *Westminster Women*, p. 39.

25. *Ibid*. If Starkey ever read the diaries of Chips Channon, the Conservative MP for Southend, she would have her unhappy impressions confirmed. 'The first week I was shy but flattered, then I had a fortnight of doubt, and of boredom, but ever since I have loved every minute of it. I like the male society. It reminds me of Oxford or perhaps of the private school to which I never went.' (James, *Chips*, 4 May 1936, p. 59.)

26. Harold Nicolson, *Spectator*, 2 June 1939.

27. Nicolson, *Long Life*, p. 147.

28. Hollis, *Can Parliament Survive?*, p. 31.

29. Hoggart, *Back on the House*, p. 9.

30. Bevan, *In Place of Fear*, p. 27.

31. Grant, *Random Recollections*, pp. 77–9. Partially cited in Asquith, *Fifty Years of Parliament*, vol. 2, pp. 176–7.

32. *National Review*, March and April 1888.

5. *Look at Me!*

1. Simon Hoggart, quoted in Waller and Criddle, *Almanac of British Politics*, p. 502.

2. Driberg, *Best of Both Worlds*, 25 June 1952, pp. 185–6.

3. Hollis, *Lee*, p. 37.

4. Austin Mitchell, *Westminster Man*, quoted in Norton and Wood, *Back from Westminster*, p. 40, and Power, *Under Pressure*, p. 23.

5. History of Parliament Trust, *History of the House of Commons, 1715–1754*, p. 126.

6. 86 per cent of them, according to a survey for *The House* magazine quoted in Power, *Under Pressure*, p. 23.

7. Some of them were also expected to honour 'contracts' with the party, promising to get in touch with 100 voters each week, so that by the projected date of the next election they would have built up contacts in 26,000 households. For this Stakhanovite industry, they would be rewarded by having their constituency designated a 'key seat'.

8. Norton and Wood, *Back from Westminster*, p. 40.

9. *Ibid.*, p. 41.

10. *Ibid.*, p. 43.

11. Power, *Under Pressure*, p. 24.

12. Matthew Parris, 'Troublesome class of '95 gets a taste of Forth form discipline', *The Times*, 22 February 1995, quoted in Roth, *Parliamentary Profiles*, p. 760.

13. Quoted in Hoggart, *On the House*, p. 13.

14. Quoted in Jenkins, *Churchill*, p. 531.

15. Burke, *Speech to the Electors of Bristol*, 3 November 1774.

16. Walden, *Lucky George*, p. 238.

17. Orwell, *Politics and the English Language*, pp. 6–7.

18. *Ibid.*, p. 9.

19. David Maxwell Fyfe, *Report on the Party Organisation*, 1949.

20. Attlee, *Labour Party in Perspective*, p. 78.

6. *Busy Doing Nothing*

1. Nicolson, *People and Parliament*, pp. 64–5.
2. *Ibid.*, p. 12.
3. Hansard, 5th series, vol. 360, cols. 1075–82, 7 May 1940.
4. *Ibid.*, col. 1093.
5. *Ibid.*, cols. 1250–83.
6. Churchill, Foreword to Keyes's own *Adventures Ashore and Afloat*.
7. Hansard, 5th series, vol. 360, 1940, col. 1125.
8. *Ibid.*, col. 1362.
9. Hollis, *Can Parliament Survive?*, pp. 69–70.
10. Thatcher, *Downing Street Years*, p. 829.
11. *Ibid.*, p. 855.
12. Crossman, *Charm of Politics*, p. x.
13. 'War is not a matter of conscience', *Mail on Sunday*, 21 October 2001.
14. Tess Kingham, 'New MPs beware: if you think you can express an opinion, forget it', *Independent on Sunday*, 10 June 2001.
15. Jefferson, letter to Tench Coxe, Monticello, 21 May 1799, in Ford, Paul Leicester, ed. *The Writings of Thomas Jefferson*, vol. 7. New York/London: 1896, pp. 380–81.
16. Hansard, 6th series, vol. 373, col. 1118, 2 November 2001.
17. Crossman, *Diaries*, vol. 1, 24 August 1966, p. 628.
18. Andrew Rawnsley, 'Lame ducks play chicken', *Observer*, 31 October 1993.
19. Hansard, 6th series, vol. 322, col. 1158, 17 December 1998.
20. Lindsay, *Parliament from the Press Gallery*, p. 157.
21. Chandos, *Memoirs*, pp. 167–8.
22. Ashdown, *Diaries*, vol. 1, 3 June 1992, p. 168.
23. Crossman, *Diaries*, vol. 2, 17 November 1966, p. 130.
24. *Ibid*, pp. 130–31.

7. *Power at Last*

1. Healey, *Time of my Life*, p. 253.
2. Eden, *Facing the Dictators*, p. 316.

3. Jenkins, *Nine Men of Power*, p. 64.

4. Fisher, *Macleod*, pp. 85–6.

5. James, *Chips*, 26 February–4 March 1938, pp. 184–6.

6. *Ibid.*, 8 July 1938, p. 201.

7. Quoted in Kilmuir, *Political Adventure*, p. 145.

8. Clement Attlee to Tom Attlee, 10 June 1935, Bodleian Library, Ms Eng c 4792, f. 69.

9. Crossman, *Diaries*, vol. 1, 22 October 1964, p. 29.

10. Benn, *Out of the Wilderness*, 21 October 1964, p. 168.

11. *Ibid.*, pp. 168–9.

12. Crossman, *Diaries*, vol. 1, 22 October 1964, p. 29.

13. Castle, *Diaries 1964–70*, p. xii.

14. Ashdown, *Diaries*, vol. 1, 7 February 1989, p. 26.

15. Castle, *Diaries 1974–76*, 11 October 1975, p. 518.

16. Crossman, *Diaries*, vol. 1, 13 December 1964, p. 99.

17. Kaufman, *How to be a Minister*, p. 10.

18. *New Republic*, 8 April 1985.

19. By 1939 there were between 3 and 4 million people paying income tax, a figure which rose to 12 million by the end of the war. By the early 1980s, the total number of victims had increased to 25 million.

20. Figures from the House of Commons Library.

21. Gould, *Goodbye to All That*, p. 115.

22. Watkins, *Brief Lives*, p. 35.

23. Bridges, *Portrait of a Profession*, p. 8.

24. *Ibid.*, p. 28.

25. Private letter from Beaverbrook, reproduced in Martin Gilbert, 'Horace Wilson: Man of Munich?', in *History Today*, vol. 32, October 1982, p. 9. Churchill couldn't stand the man, and, after taking over as Prime Minister said that if Wilson showed his face in Downing Street again, 'I'll make him Governor of Greenland!' (Hennessy, *Whitehall*, p. 86.)

26. Campbell, *Nye Bevan*, p. 153.

27. Kaufman, *How to be a Minister*, p. 23.

28. Lloyd George, *Lloyd George*, p. 115.

29. Haines, *Politics of Power*, p. 34.

30. It is indicative of the civil service idea of the pecking order that the Cabinet Secretary, Sir John Hunt, acting 'without political instructions', tried to prevent the diaries being serialized in the *Sunday Times*.

31. Crossman, *Inside View*, p. 74.

32. Castle, *Diaries 1964–70*, 29 May 1967, p. 259.

33. Benn, cited in Young and Sloman, *No, Minister*, pp. 19–20.

34. Benn, *Out of the Wilderness*, 25 January 1965, p. 209.

35. *Ibid.*, 25 February 1965, p. 226.

36. *Ibid.*, 10 March 1965, p. 232.

37. *Ibid.*, 29 June 1965, pp. 281–2.

38. Benn, cited in Young and Sloman, *No, Minister*, pp. 29–30.

39. Dell, *Diaries*, 4 June 1974, Bodleian Library, MS Eng c 4828, ff. 37–8.

40. Barnes, *Behind the Image*, pp. 159–60.

41. Edward Stourton, 'How firebrand Milburn became a model manager', *Guardian*, 7 May 2001.

42. By the RAC.

43. Heath, *Course of my Life*, pp. 320–21.

44. Hennessy, *Secret State*, p. 191.

45. Taylor, Lloyd George Lecture, in *Lloyd George: Rise and Fall*. Cambridge University Press, 1961, p. 4.

46. Three phrases he used to repeat from time to time at Chequers, quoted in Waterhouse, *Private and Official*, p. 273.

47. Quoted in Rodgers and Moyle, *Campbell-Bannerman*, p. 12.

48. Williams, *Guilty Men*, p. 1.

49. Crossman, *Charm of Politics*, p. 69.

50. Gladstone Papers, 46270, ff. 275–6.

51. Green, *Children of the Sun*, p. 82.

52. Cited in Williams, *A Prime Minister Remembers*, p. 83.

53. See *ibid.*, pp. 81 and 84.

54. Since 1980, the cabinet has had twenty-two members.

55. The title of Professor Peter Hennessy's Gresham College lecture, 7 November 2001, to which I am indebted.

56. Anne Applebaum, 'I am still normal', *Sunday Telegraph*, 18 March 2001.

57. Benn, *Office without Power*, 17 June 1969, p. 187.

58. Unnamed Whitehall source, quoted in Hennessy, '*Tony Wants*', Royal Historical Society/Gresham College Colin Matthew Lecture, 7 November 2001, p. 3.

59. Lawson, *View from No. 11*, p. 125.

60. Lawson memoirs, quoted in Butler, *Cabinet Government*, p. 8, from whence also come the statistics on frequency of cabinet meetings.

61. 'Politics is not the art of the possible. It consists in choosing between the disastrous and the unpalatable.' Letter to JFK, 2 March 1962, quoted in Galbraith, *Ambassador's Journal*, p. 312.

62. The title of his Dimbleby Lecture, 19 October 1976.

63. Hennessy, '*Tony Wants*'.

64. Interview, *The Times*, 1 May 2002.

65. Balfour, cited in Watkins, *Road to Number 10*, p. 7.

66. Crossman had merely suggested that Brown might not be the ideal man for the Defence portfolio. The fight ended with Crossman knocking Brown to the ground and then sitting on him. Brown also loathed Harold Wilson, with what Crossman called 'a pestilential hatred and contempt'.

67. Cited in Sampson, *Anatomy of Britain*, p. 132.

68. Foot, *Loyalists and Loners*, p. 84.

69. Pimlott, *Dalton Political Diary*, 3–9 March 1930, p. 96.

70. Benn, *Out of the Wilderness*, 23 November 1964, pp. 191–2.

71. Crossman, *Diaries*, vol. 2, 21 November 1966, p. 134.

72. Macmillan to Lady Waverley, 17 January 1960, MS Eng c 4778, f. 59.

73. *Ibid.*, 7 May 1961, MS Eng c 4778, ff. 91–2.

74. Ashdown, *Diaries*, vol. 1, 24 March 1994, pp. 256–8.

8. *The Price of Fame*

1. 'The Special Difficulties of Education and MPs' Children', letter to many MPs, 22 May 1997. Mr Parkyn did not reply to my letters to him.

2. Interview, *Wanstead and Woodford Guardian*, quoted in *The Times*, 22 March 2002.

3. Undated letter to Attlee, received 10 September 1945. Bodleian Library, MS Attlee dep. 142, f. 44.

4. Mosley, *My Life*, p. 29.

5. 'Sins of the sons (and daughters)', *Guardian*, 8 April 1999.

6. Crossman, *Diaries*, vol. 2, 5 October 1966, p. 65.

7. Lloyd George, *Lloyd George*, p. 73.

8. Benn, *Out of the Wilderness*, 31 July 1963, p. 45.

9. Quoted in Ashley Weinberg, 'Stress and the Politician', in Power (ed.), *Under Pressure*, p. 32.

10. *Ibid.*, pp. 34–5.

11. Margach, *Anatomy of Power*, pp. 23–4.

12. Anne Applebaum, 'I am still normal', *Sunday Telegraph*, 18 March 2001.

13. *Ibid.*

14. Speech, Worcester, 24 November 1923, quoted in Williamson, *Baldwin*, p. 207.

15. The interview appeared in *GQ* magazine, September 2000.

16. Undated letter, quoted in Wheen, *Driberg*, p. 247.

17. Iremonger, *And his Charming Lady*, p. 13.

18. Paterson, *Tired and Emotional*, pp. 31–2.

19. *Ibid.*, p. 2.

20. Sophie Brown cited in Joan Reeder, 'My Cinderella Life', *Woman*, December 1968–January 1969. Here in Paterson, *Tired and Emotional*, p. 33.

21. Paterson, *Tired and Emotional*, p. 35.

22. Sophie Brown cited in Joan Reeder, 'My Cinderella Life', *Woman*, December 1968–January 1969. Here in Paterson, *Tired and Emotional*, p. 43.

23. Benn, *The End of an Era*, 17 June 1989, p. 569.

24. Linda Lee-Potter, *Daily Mail*, 9 April 1997.

9. *Feet of Clay*

1. Transparency International, Otto-Suhr-Allee 97/99, 10585, Berlin, Germany.

2. So much so that in March 2002, the country's best-known anti-corruption campaigner, Kiyomi Tsujimoto, was forced to resign after it emerged that she was using public money improperly. By the standards of the gerontocracy which runs the parliament her offence was puny – using funds which ought to have been paid to an aide to fund her office – but it did nothing to enhance the public standing of politicians.

3. In it he discloses, among much else, that he had lost his father as a child, that he had known he had a taste for young working-class men in uniform for many years, that he had never had sex with a woman before he married, which he did because 'I knew that politically it was both helpful and desirable to be married.' He described the experience of losing a role in public life as like 'falling off a mountain'. A young man who had devoted his life to riding asked him at a dinner party if he

missed political life. Harvey told him the man would understand how he felt if he lost both his legs.

4. Quoted in Baston, *Sleaze*, p. 35.
5. See Rentoul, *Blair*, pp. 359–60.
6. 'Labour now sleazier than Tories, says new poll', *Sunday Times*, 17 February 2002.
7. 'Blair and Romania deal: the questions and some of the answers', *Guardian*, 14 February 2002.

10. Being History

1. Pimlott, *Political Diary of Hugh Dalton*, p. 518. See also Pimlott, *Wilson*, pp. 163–4.
2. Thatcher, *Downing Street Years*, p. 423.
3. Margach, *Anatomy of Power*, pp. 25–6.
4. Bevins, *Greasy Pole*, p. 135.
5. Harold Macmillan, Diary, 14 July 1962, quoted in Horne, *Macmillan*, vol. 2, p. 345.
6. Kilmuir, *Political Adventure*, pp. 324–5.
7. Macmillan, interview, quoted in Horne, *Macmillan*, vol. 2, p. 346.
8. Aitken, *Pride and Perjury*, p. 195.
9. Benn, *End of an Era*, 13 June 1983, p. 298.
10. Butler, *Art of the Possible*, p. 262.
11. Nott, *Here Today, Gone Tomorrow*, p. 380.
12. Bevins, *Greasy Pole*, pp. 71–2.
13. Aitken, *Pride and Perjury*, p. 198.
14. Macmillan, *At the End of the Day*, p. 520. Quoted in Fisher, *Macmillan*, p. 348.
15. Major, *Autobiography*, p. xxi.
16. Jasper Gerard, *Observer*, 17 October 1999.
17. Margach, *Anatomy of Power*, pp. 41–2. The quote is from Aitken, *Decline and Fall of Lloyd George*.
18. Owen, *Tempestuous Journey*, p. 236.
19. Cited in L'Etang, *Fit to Lead?*, p. 33.
20. Nicolson, *Diaries and Letters 1930–1939*, Diary, 5 October 1930, p. 57.
21. Asquith, *Off the Record*, p. 81.

22. Moran, *Churchill*, p. 289.
23. *New Statesman*, 10 November 1956, p. 576.
24. Thorpe, *Douglas-Home*, p. 8. From Thorpe's private information.
25. Crossman, *Charm of Politics*, p. 3.
26. Hollis, *Can Parliament Survive?*, p. 72.
27. Berkeley, *Crossing the Floor*, pp. 144–5.
28. Margach.
29. Asquith, *Off the Record*, p. 33. A comparison with Jesus Christ may be immodest, but it is far from unique: believing they have been especially chosen makes political leaders more than ready to reach for it. When his comrades turned on him, Keir Hardie remarked that 'I understand what Christ suffered in Gethsemane as well as any man living' (quoted in Benn, *Keir Hardie*, p. 18).

Afterword

1. Mark Garnett, 'Ministerial wannabees need not apply', *New Statesman*, 9 October 1998, pp. 5–6.
2. Sir John Hoskyns, 'Conservatism is not enough', Institute of Directors Annual Lecture, 1983, quoted in Hennessy, *Whitehall*, pp. 328–9.
3. Disraeli, *Vivian Gray*, IV, 1. The book was published when Disraeli was only twenty-two, and he was later so embarrassed by it and by its utterly unprincipled hero that he tried unsuccessfully to suppress it.
4. And subsequently Speaker in the devolved assembly which followed the Good Friday Agreement.
5. Dixon, *On the Psychology of Military Incompetence*.
6. Alexis de Tocqueville, *Democracy in America*, p. 280, quoted in *ibid.*, p. 20.
7. Austin Mitchell, 'Don't be an MP', *The Times*, 11 May 2001.

Bibliography

Books

Adams, Jad. *Tony Benn*. London: Macmillan, 1992

Adams, R.J.Q. *Bonar Law*. London: John Murray, 1999

Aitken, Jonathan. *Pride and Perjury*. London: HarperCollins, 2000

Aitken, W. Francis. *The Marquess of Salisbury, KG*. London: S.W. Partridge & Co., 1901

Aitken, William M., Baron Beaverbrook. *Men and Power*. London: Hutchinson, 1956

——*The Decline and Fall of Lloyd George: And Great was the Fall Thereof*. London: Collins, 1963

Alexander, Andrew and Watkins, Alan. *The Making of the Prime Minister 1970*. London: Macdonald Unit 75, 1970

Ali, Tariq, ed. *The Thoughts of Chairman Harold*. London: The Gnome Press, 1967

Amery, L.S. *My Political Life*, vol. 1: *England before the Storm, 1896–1914*. London: Hutchinson, 1953

——*My Political Life*, vol. 2: *War and Peace, 1914–1929*. London: Hutchinson, 1953

——*My Political Life*, vol. 3: *The Unforgiving Years, 1929–1940*. London: Hutchinson, 1955

Ashdown, Paddy. *The Ashdown Diaries*. 2 vols, London: Allen Lane, The Penguin Press, 2000–2001

Ashley, Jackie. *I Spy Strangers: Improving Access to Parliament*. London: Hansard Society, 2000

Aspinall-Oglander, Cecil. *Roger Keyes*. London: The Hogarth Press, 1951

Asquith, H.H., Earl of Oxford. *Fifty Years of Parliament*. 2 vols., London: Cassell & Co., 1926

Asquith, Margot, Countess of Oxford and Asquith. *Off the Record*. London: Frederick Muller, 1943

Attlee, C.R. *The Labour Party in Perspective*. London: Victor Gollancz, 1949

——*As It Happened*. London: William Heinemann, 1954

Baker, Kenneth. *The Prime Ministers: An Irreverent Political History in Cartoons*. London: Thames & Hudson, 1995

Baldwin, A.W. *My Father: The True Story*. London: George Allen & Unwin, 1955

Barber, James David. *The Presidential Character: Predicting Performance in the White House*. Englewood Cliffs: Prentice-Hall, 1972

Barnes, Susan. *Behind the Image*. London: Jonathan Cape, 1974

Baston, Lewis. *Sleaze: The State of Britain*. London: Channel Four Books, 2000

Begbie, E.H. (writing anonymously as 'A Gentleman with a Duster'). *The Mirrors of Downing Street: Some Political Reflections*. London: Mills & Boon, 1920

——*The Conservative Mind*. London: Mills & Boon, 1925

Bell, Martin. *An Accidental MP*. London: Viking, 2000

Bell, Steve and Hoggart, Simon. *Live Briefs: A Political Sketch Book*. London: Methuen, 1996

Belloc, Hilaire and Chesterton, Cecil. *The Party System*. London: Stephen Swift, 1911

Benn, Caroline. *Keir Hardie*. London: Hutchinson, 1992

Benn, Tony. *Out of the Wilderness: Diaries 1963–67*. 1987; London: Arrow Books, 1988

——*Office without Power: Diaries 1968–72*. 1988; London: Arrow Books, 1989

——*The End of an Era: Diaries 1980–90*. 1992; London: Arrow Books, 1994

Berkeley, Humphry. *Crossing the Floor*. London: George Allen & Unwin, 1972

Bevan, Aneurin. *In Place of Fear*. With an introduction by Jennie Lee. London: MacGibbon & Kee, 1961

Bevins, Reginald. *The Greasy Pole: A Personal Account of the Realities of British Politics*. London: Hodder & Stoughton, 1965

Bierce, Ambrose. *The Devil's Dictionary*. New York: Sagamore Press, 1957 [written as a partwork, 1881–1906]

Bigham, Hon. Clive. *The Prime Ministers of Britain 1721–1921*. London: John Murray, 1922

Blair, David. *The History of the Oxford University Conservative Association*. Oxford: Andrew Page [self-published], 1995

Boothroyd, Betty. *The Autobiography*. London: Century, 2001

Boyd-Carpenter, John. *Way of Life: The Memoirs of John Boyd-Carpenter*. London: Sidgwick & Jackson, 1980

Boyle, Andrew. *Poor, Dear Brendan: The Quest for Brendan Bracken*. London: Hutchinson, 1974

Brazier, Rodney. *Ministers of the Crown*. Oxford: Clarendon Press, 1997

Brendon, Piers. *Winston Churchill: A Brief Life*. London: Secker & Warburg, 1984

Bridges, Sir Edward. *Portrait of a Profession: The Civil Service Tradition. The Rede Lecture, 1950*. Cambridge: Cambridge University Press, 1950

Briggs, Asa and Saville, John, eds. *Essays in Labour History*. London: Macmillan, 1960

Brivati, Brian. *Hugh Gaitskell*. London: Richard Cohen Books, 1996

Brown, Colin. *Fighting Talk: The Biography of John Prescott*. London: Simon & Schuster, 1997

Brown, George. *In my Way: The Political Memoirs of Lord George-Brown*. London: Victor Gollancz, 1971

Bryson, Bill. *Down Under*. London: Doubleday, 2000

Bullock, Alan. *The Life and Times of Ernest Bevin*. 3 vols., London: William Heinemann, 1960–83

Butler, David and Butler, Gareth. *Twentieth-Century British Political Facts, 1900–2000*. London: Macmillan, 2000

——and Kavanagh, Dennis. *The British General Election of 2001*. London: Palgrave, 2002

Butler, Richard Austen, Lord. *The Art of the Possible: The Memoirs of Lord Butler K.G., C.H.* London: Hamish Hamilton, 1971

——*The Art of Memory: Friends in Perspective*. London: Hodder & Stoughton, 1982

Butler, Robin (Lord Butler of Brockwell). *Cabinet Government*. The Attlee Foundation Lecture, Mansion House, London, 18 February 1999

Campbell, John. *Nye Bevan: A Biography*. London: Richard Cohen Books, 1997; first published as *Nye Bevan and the Mirage of British Socialism*. London: Weidenfeld & Nicolson, 1987

——*Margaret Thatcher*, vol. 1: *The Grocer's Daughter*. London: Jonathan Cape, 2000

Carlton, David. *Anthony Eden: A Biography*. London: Allen & Unwin, 1986; originally London: Allen Lane, 1981

Carrington, Lord. *Reflect on Things Past*. London: Collins, 1988

Carvel, John. *Turn Again Livingstone*. London: Profile Books, 1999

Castle, Barbara. *The Castle Diaries 1964–70*. London: Weidenfeld & Nicolson, 1984

——*The Castle Diaries 1974–76*. London: Weidenfeld and Nicolson, 1980

——*Fighting All the Way*. London: Macmillan, 1993

'Cato' (F. Owen, M. Foot and P. Howard). *Guilty Men*. London: Victor Gollancz, 1940

Cecil, Algernon. *British Foreign Secretaries 1807–1916: Studies in Personality and Policy*. London: G. Bell & Sons, 1927

Chandos, Oliver Lyttelton, Viscount. *The Memoirs of Lord Chandos*. London: The Bodley Head, 1962

Child, Susan. *Politico's Guide to Parliament*. London: Politico's, 1999

Churchill, Winston Spencer. *Savrola: A Tale of the Revolution in Laurania*. London: Longmans, Green & Co., 1900

——*My Early Life: A Roving Commission*. London: Thornton Butterworth, 1930

——*Great Contemporaries*. London: Thomas Butterworth, 1937

Clark, Alan. *Diaries*. 2 vols., London: Weidenfeld & Nicolson, 1993, 2000

——*The Tories*. London: Weidenfeld & Nicolson, 1998

Clarke, Peter. *A Question of Leadership*. London: Hamish Hamilton, 1991

——*The Cripps Version*. London: Allen Lane, The Penguin Press, 2002

Cockerell, Michael, Hennessy, Peter and Walker, David. *Sources Close to the Prime Minister: Inside the Hidden World of the News Manipulators*. London: Macmillan, 1984

Coleman, Stephen, Taylor, John and Donk, Wim van de, eds. *Parliament in the Age of the Internet*. Oxford: Oxford University Press, 1999

Cooper, Diana. *The Light of Common Day*. London: Rupert Hart-Davis, 1959

Cooper, Duff, Viscount Norwich. *Old Men Forget*. London: Rupert Hart-Davis, 1953

Craig, F.W.S., ed. *British General Election Manifestos 1900–1974*. London: Macmillan, 1975

——*British General Election Manifestos 1959–1987*. Aldershot: Parliamentary Research Service, 1990

Crick, Michael. *Jeffrey Archer: Stranger than Fiction*. Revised edn, London: Penguin Books, 1996

——*Michael Heseltine: A Biography*. London: Hamish Hamilton, 1997

Critchley, Julian. *Westminster Blues*. London: Elm Tree Books, 1985

——*A Bag of Boiled Sweets*. London: Faber & Faber, 1994

——and Halcrow, Morrison. *Collapse of Stout Party*. London: Victor Gollancz, 1997

Crosland, Susan (née Barnes). *Looking Out, Looking In: Profiles of Others and Myself*. London: Weidenfeld & Nicolson, 1987

Crossman, Richard. *The Charm of Politics: And Other Essays in Political Criticism*. London: Hamish Hamilton, 1958

——*Inside View: The Godkin Lectures at Harvard University, 1970*. London: Jonathan Cape, 1972

——*The Diaries of a Cabinet Minister*, vol. 1: *Minister of Housing 1964–66*. London: Hamish Hamilton and Jonathan Cape, 1975

——*The Diaries of a Cabinet Minister*, vol. 2: *Lord President of the Council and Leader of the House of Commons 1966–68*. London: Hamish Hamilton and Jonathan Cape, 1976

Crozier, W.P. *Off the Record: Political Interviews 1933–1943*, ed. A.J.P. Taylor. London: Hutchinson, 1973

Cudlipp, Hugh. *Walking on the Water*. London: The Bodley Head, 1976

Curtis, Sarah, ed. *The Journals of Woodrow Wyatt*, vol. 1. London: Macmillan, 1998

Curzon of Kedleston, Marchioness. *Reminiscences*. London: Hutchinson, 1955

Dalton, Hugh. *The Fateful Years: Memoirs 1931–1945*. London: Frederick Muller, 1957

Davies, A.F. *Skills, Outlooks and Passions: A Psychoanalytic Contribution to the Study of Politics*. Cambridge: Cambridge University Press, 1980

Day, Robin, *Grand Inquisitor*. London: Weidenfeld & Nicolson, 1989

De-la-Noy, Michael. *The Honours System*. London: Virgin, 1992

Dell, Edmund. *The Chancellors*. London: HarperCollins, 1997

——*A Strange Eventful History*. London: HarperCollins, 2000

Denham, Andrew and Garnett, Mark. *Keith Joseph*. Chesham: Acumen, 2001

Dilks, David, ed. *The Diaries of Sir Alexander Cadogan, O.M., 1938–1945*. London: Cassell, 1971

Dimbleby, Jonathan. *The Last Governor: Chris Patten and the Handover of Hong Kong*. 1997; London: Warner Books, 1998

Dionne, E.J. *Why Americans Hate Politics*. New York: Touchstone Books, 1992

Disraeli, Benjamin. *Vivian Gray*. London, 1826

——*Lothair*. London, 1870

Dixon, Norman. *On the Psychology of Military Incompetence*. London: Jonathan Cape, 1976

Douglas-Home, William, ed., written and researched by Jennifer Browne. *The Prime Ministers: Stories and Anecdotes from Number 10*. London: W.H. Allen, 1987

Driberg, Tom. *The Best of Both Worlds: A Personal Diary*. London: Phoenix House, 1953

——*Ruling Passions*. 1977; London: Quartet Books, 1978

Dunn, John. *The Cunning of Unreason*. London: HarperCollins, 2000

Eden, Anthony, Earl of Avon. *The Memoirs of Sir Anthony Eden: Full Circle*. London: Cassell, 1960

——*The Memoirs of Sir Anthony Eden: Facing the Dictators*. London: Cassell, 1962

——*The Memoirs of Sir Anthony Eden: The Reckoning*. London: Cassell, 1965

Egremont, John Wyndham, Lord. *Wyndham and Children First*. London: Macmillan, 1968

Einzig, Paul. *In the Centre of Things*. London: Hutchinson, 1960

Englefield, Dermot, Seaton, Janet, and White, Isobel. *Facts about the British Prime Ministers*. London: Mansell Publishing, 1995

Etang, Hugh L'. *Fit to Lead?* London: William Heinemann Medical Books, 1980

Evans, Harold. *Downing Street Diary: The Macmillan Years 1957–1963*. London: Hodder & Stoughton, 1981

Feely, Terence. *Number 10: The Private Lives of Six Prime Ministers*. London: Sidgwick & Jackson, 1981

Fenno, Richard F. *Home Style: House Members in their Districts*. Boston: Little, Brown & Co., 1978

Fisher, Nigel. *Iain Macleod*. London: André Deutsch, 1973

——*The Tory Leaders: Their Struggle for Power*. London: Weidenfeld & Nicolson, 1977

——*Harold Macmillan*. London: Weidenfeld & Nicolson, 1982

Flynn, Paul. *Dragons Led by Poodles*. London, Politico's, 1999

Foot, Michael. *Aneurin Bevan, 1897–1960*, ed. Brian Brivati. 1997; London: Indigo, 1999

——*Loyalists and Loners*. London: Collins, 1987. Originally London: Collins, 1986

Galbraith, John Kenneth. *Ambassador's Journal: A Personal Account of the Kennedy Years*. London: Hamish Hamilton, 1969

George, William. *My Brother and I*. London: Eyre & Spottiswoode, 1958

Gilbert, Martin. *Churchill: A Life*. London: William Heinemann, 1991

Gilmour, David. *Curzon*. 1994; London: Papermac, 1995

Glendinning, Victoria, *Trollope*. London: Hutchinson, 1992

Gordon Walker, Patrick. *The Cabinet*. London: Jonathan Cape, 1970

Gould, Bryan. *Goodbye to All That*. London: Macmillan, 1995

Gove, Michael. *Michael Portillo: The Future of the Right*. London: Fourth Estate, 1995

Grant, James, writing as 'One of No Party'. *Random Recollections of the House of Commons: From the Year 1830 to the Close of 1835, Including Personal Sketches of the Leading Members of All Parties*. London: Smith, Elder & Co., 1836

Green, Jonathon. *The Book of Political Quotes*. London: Angus & Robertson Publishers, 1982

Green, Martin. *Children of the Sun: A Narrative of 'Decadence' in England after 1918*. 1976; London: Pimlico, 1992

Hailsham of St Marylebone, Quintin Hogg, Lord. *A Sparrow's Flight*. London: Collins, 1990

Haines, Joe. *The Politics of Power*. London: Jonathan Cape, 1977

Harding, Luke, Leigh, David and Pallister, David. *The Liar: The Fall of Jonathan Aitken*. Updated edn: London: The Guardian/Fourth Estate, 1999

Harris, Kenneth. *The Prime Minister Talks to the Observer*. London: Observer Publications, 1979

Harvey, Ian. *To Fall Like Lucifer*. London: Sidgwick & Jackson, 1971

Healey, Denis. *The Time of my Life*. London: Michael Joseph, 1989

Heath, Edward. *The Course of my Life*. London: Hodder & Stoughton, 1998

Hellicar, Eileen. *Prime Ministers of Britain*. London: David & Charles, 1978

Hennessy, Peter. *Cabinet*. London: Basil Blackwell, 1986

———*The Great and the Good: An Inquiry into the British Establishment*. London: Policy Studies Institute, 1986

———*Whitehall*. London: Secker & Warburg, 1989

———*The Prime Minister: The Office and its Holders since 1945*. London: Penguin, 2000

———*'Tony Wants': The First Blair Premiership in Historical Perspective*. The Colin Matthew Memorial Lecture for the Understanding of History, Gresham College, 2001

———*The Secret State: Whitehall and the Cold War*. London: Allen Lane, The Penguin Press, 2002

———and Seldon, Anthony, eds. *Ruling Performance: British Governments from Attlee to Thatcher*. Oxford: Basil Blackwell, 1987

———and Coates, Simon. *Little Grey Cells: Think Tanks, Governments and Policy-Making*. Glasgow: Strathclyde Papers on Government and Politics, 1991

———and Smith, Frank. *Teething the Watchdogs: Parliament, Government and Accountability*. Glasgow: Strathclyde Papers on Government and Politics, 1992

———and Anstey, Caroline. *Politics, Politicians and the English Language*. Glasgow: Strathclyde Papers on Government and Politics, 1992

Hoggart, Simon. *On the House*. London: Robson Books, 1981

———*Back on the House*. London: Robson Books, 1982

Hollis, Christopher. *Can Parliament Survive?* London: Hollis & Carter, 1949

Hollis, Patricia. *Jennie Lee: A Life*. Oxford: Oxford University Press, 1997

Horne, Alistair. *Macmillan*. London: Macmillan, 1988, 1989

Howard, Anthony. *Crossman: The Pursuit of Power*. London: Jonathan Cape, 1990

———and West, Richard. *The Making of the Prime Minister*. London: Jonathan Cape, 1965

Howe, Geoffrey. *Conflict of Loyalty*. London: Macmillan, 1994

Iremonger, Lucille. *And his Charming Lady*. London: Secker & Warburg, 1961

———*The Fiery Chariot: A Study of British Prime Ministers and the Search for Love*. London: Secker & Warburg, 1970.

James, Robert Rhodes, *Anthony Eden*. London: Weidenfeld & Nicolson, 1986

———*Bob Boothby: A Portrait*. London: Hodder & Stoughton, 1991

———, ed. *Chips: The Diaries of Sir Henry Channon*. London: Weidenfeld & Nicolson, 1967

———ed. *Memoirs of a Conservative: J.C.C. Davidson's Memoirs and Papers, 1910–37*. London: Weidenfeld & Nicolson, 1969

Jay, Douglas. *Change and Fortune: A Political Record*. London: Hutchinson, 1980

Jenkins, Roy. *Nine Men of Power*. London: Hamish Hamilton, 1974

———*Home Thoughts from Abroad: The Richard Dimbleby Lecture*. London: BBC, 1979

———*European Diary 1977–1981*. London: Collins, 1989

———*A Life at the Centre*. 1991; London: Papermac, 1994

———*Portraits and Miniatures*. 1993; London: Papermac, 1994

———*Baldwin*. 1987; corrected edn, London: Papermac, 1995

———*Churchill*. London: Macmillan, 2001

Jenkins, Simon. *Accountable to None: The Tory Nationalization of Britain*. 1995; London: Penguin Books, 1996

Jennings, George Henry. *An Anecdotal History of the British Parliament from the Earliest Periods: With Notes of Eminent Parliamentary Men and Examples of their Oratory*. Fourth edn, London: Horace Cox, 1899

Johnson, Boris. *Friends, Voters, Countrymen*. London: HarperCollins, 2001

Jones, G.W. *The Prime Minister's Aides*. Hull: University of Hull, 1980

Jones, Mervyn. *Michael Foot*. London: Victor Gollancz, 1994

Kampfner, John. *Robin Cook*. London: Victor Gollancz, 1998

Kaufman, Gerald. *How to be a Minister*. 1980; London: Faber & Faber, 1997

Kavanagh, Dennis and Seldon, Anthony. *The Powers behind the Prime Minister*. London: HarperCollins, 1999

Keyes, Sir Roger. *Adventures Ashore and Afloat*. London: Harrap, 1939

Kilmuir, David Maxwell Fyfe, Lord. *Political Adventure: The Memoirs of the Earl of Kilmuir*. London: Weidenfeld & Nicolson, 1964

Lamont, Norman. *In Office*. London: Little, Brown, 1999

Lasswell, Harold D. *Psychopathology and Politics*. Illinois: University of Chicago Press, 1930

———*Politics: Who Gets What, When, How*. London: McGraw-Hill Book Company, 1936

———*Power and Personality*. New York: W.W. Norton & Company, 1948.

———*World Politics and Personal Insecurity*. 1935; revised edn, London: Collier-Macmillan, 1965

Lawson, Nigel. *The View from No. 11: Memoirs of a Tory Radical*. London: Bantam Press, 1992

Lee, Jennie. *My Life with Nye*. London: Jonathan Cape, 1980

Leigh, David and Vulliamy, Ed. *Sleaze: The Corruption of Parliament*. London: Fourth Estate, 1997

Lester, Anthony, Mackie, Lindsay and Renshall, Michael. *What Price Hansard?* London: The Hansard Society for Parliamentary Government, 1994

Lindsay, T.F. *Parliament from the Press Gallery*. London: Macmillan, 1967

Lippmann, Walter. *The Phantom Public*. New York: Harcourt Brace & Co, 1925

Lloyd George, Richard (Earl Lloyd George of Dwyfor). *Dame Margaret: The Life Story of his Mother*. London: George Allen & Unwin, 1947

——*Lloyd George*. London: Frederick Muller, 1960

Longford, Frank Pakenham, Earl of. *Five Lives*. London: Hutchinson, 1964

——*Eleven at No. 10*. London: Harrap, 1984

Lyman, Richard W. *The First Labour Government 1924*. London: Chapman & Hall, 1957

McDougall, Linda. *Westminster Women*. London: Vintage, 1998

——*Cherie: The Perfect Life of Mrs Blair*. London: Politico's, 2001

Macleod, Iain. *Neville Chamberlain*. London: Frederick Muller, 1961

Major, John. *The Autobiography*. London: HarperCollins, 1999

Margach, James. *The Abuse of Power: The War between Downing Street and the Media from Lloyd George to Callaghan*. London: W.H. Allen, 1978

——*The Anatomy of Power: An Enquiry into the Personality of Leadership*. London: W.H. Allen, 1979

Marquand, David. *Ramsay MacDonald*. London: Jonathan Cape, 1997

Merriam, Charles E. *Political Power*. London: Collier-Macmillan, 1964

Mikardo, Ian. *Back-Bencher*. London: Weidenfeld & Nicolson, 1988

Miller, J.D.B. *The Nature of Politics*. London: Gerald Duckworth, 1962

Montague Browne, Anthony. *Long Sunset: Memoirs of Winston Churchill's Last Private Secretary*. London: Cassell, 1995

Moran, Charles Wilson, Lord. *Winston Churchill: The Struggle for Survival 1940–1965*. London: Constable, 1966

Morgan, Kenneth O. *Callaghan: A Life*. Oxford: Oxford University Press, 1997

Morris, Dick. *The New Prince*. Los Angeles: Renaissance Books, 1999

Morrison, Herbert. *Government and Parliament: A Survey from the Inside.* London: Oxford University Press, 1954

Mosley, Sir Oswald. *My Life.* London: Thomas Nelson, 1968

Mowlam, Mo. *Momentum.* London: Hodder & Stoughton, 2002

Mullen, Richard. *Anthony Trollope.* London: Duckworth, 1990

Naughtie, James. *The Rivals.* London: Fourth Estate, 2001

Nel, Elizabeth. *Mr. Churchill's Secretary.* New York: Conrad-McCann, 1958

Nicolson, Harold. *Diaries and Letters 1930–1939.* London: Collins, 1966

——*Diaries and Letters 1939–1945.* London: Collins, 1967

——*Diaries and Letters 1945–1962.* London: Collins, 1968

Nicolson, Nigel. *People and Parliament.* London: Weidenfeld & Nicolson, 1958

——*Long Life.* London: Weidenfeld & Nicolson, 1997

Norton, Philip. *The Commons in Perspective.* Oxford: Martin Robertson, 1981

——and Wood, David. *Back from Westminster: Backbench Members of Parliament and their Constituents.* Lexington, Kentucky: Kentucky University Press, 1993

Nott, John. *Here Today, Gone Tomorrow: Recollections of an Errant Politician.* London: Politico's, 2002

Orwell, George. *Politics and the English Language.* London: The News of the World, no date [pamphlet]

Owen, Frank. *Tempestuous Journey: Lloyd George: His Life and Times.* London: Hutchinson, 1954

Parsons, Wayne. *Public Policy: An Introduction to the Theory and Practice of Policy Analysis.* Aldershot: Edward Elgar Publishing, 1995

Paterson, Peter. *Tired and Emotional: The Life of Lord George-Brown.* London: Chatto & Windus, 1993

Pelling, Henry. *Winston Churchill.* London: Macmillan, 1989; first edn 1974

Petrie, Sir Charles. *The Powers behind the Prime Ministers.* London: MacGibbon & Kee, 1958

——*The Carlton Club.* London: White Lion Publishers, 1972

Pimlott, Ben. *Hugh Dalton.* London: Jonathan Cape, 1985

——, ed. *The Political Diary of Hugh Dalton 1918–40, 1945–60.* London: Jonathan Cape, 1986

——, ed. *The Second World War Diary of Hugh Dalton 1940–45.* London: Jonathan Cape, 1986

——*Harold Wilson.* London: HarperCollins, 1992

Pincher, Chapman. *Inside Story: A Documentary of the Pursuit of Power*. London: Sidgwick & Jackson, 1978

Powell, Enoch. *Joseph Chamberlain*. London: Thames & Hudson, 1977

——*Wrestling with the Angel*. London: Sheldon Press, 1977

Power, Greg, ed. *Under Pressure: Are We Getting the Most from our MPs?* London: Hansard Society, 2000

Prior, Jim. *A Balance of Power*. London: Hamish Hamilton, 1986

Rentoul, John. *Tony Blair*. Revised and updated edn, London: Warner Books, 1996

Riddell, Peter. *Honest Opportunism*. London: Hamish Hamilton, 1993

Roberts, Andrew. *Salisbury: Victorian Titan*. London: Weidenfeld & Nicolson, 1999

Robson, John M. *What Did He Say? Editing Nineteenth-Century Speeches from Hansard and the Newspapers*. Lethbridge: University of Lethbridge Press, 1987

Rodgers, Edward and Moyle, Edmund J. *Sir Henry Campbell-Bannerman: His Career and Capers*. London: G. Mitton, 1906

Rogers, Michael. *Political Quotes*. London: Sphere Books, 1982

Rose, Kenneth. *Kings, Queens and Courtiers*. London: Weidenfeld & Nicolson, 1985

Rose, Richard. *The Prime Minister in a Shrinking World*. Cambridge: Polity Press, 2001

Ross, J.F.S. *Elections and Electors: Studies in Democratic Representation*. London: Eyre & Spottiswoode, 1955

Roth, Andrew and Criddle, Byron. *Parliamentary Profiles*. Various eds. 4 vols.

Rubinstein, W.D. *The Harvester Biographical Dictionary of Life Peers*. Hemel Hempstead: Harvester Wheatsheaf, 1991

Salter, Arthur. *Personality in Politics: Studies of Contemporary Statesmen*. London: Faber & Faber, 1947

Sampson, Anthony. *Anatomy of Britain*. London: Hodder & Stoughton, 1962

——*The New Anatomy of Britain*. London: Hodder & Stoughton, 1971

Santayana, George. *Soliloquies in England, and Later Soliloquies*. London: Constable & Company, 1922

Searing, Donald. *Westminster's World – Understanding Political Roles*. Cambridge, Mass.: Harvard University Press, 1994

Sedgwick, Romney, *The House of Commons 1715–1754*. Published for the

History of Parliament Trust by Her Majesty's Stationery Office. 2 vols. London, 1970.

Seldon, Anthony, with Baston, Lewis. *Major: A Political Life*. 1997; London: Phoenix, 1998

Shepherd, Robert. *Enoch Powell: A Biography*. 1996; London: Pimlico, 1997

Shuckburgh, Evelyn. *Descent to Suez: Diaries 1951–56*. London: Weidenfeld & Nicolson, 1986

Simon, Viscount. *Retrospect: The Memoirs of the Rt. Hon. Viscount Simon, G.C.S.I., G.C.V.O.* London: Hutchinson, 1952

Sopel, Jon. *Tony Blair: The Moderniser*. London: Bantam Books, 1995

Spender, J.A., and Asquith, Cyril. *Life of Herbert Henry Asquith, Lord Oxford and Asquith*. 2 vols., London: Hutchinson & Co., 1932

Stone, William F. *The Psychology of Politics*. London: Collier-Macmillan, 1974

Storr, Anthony. *Feet of Clay: A Study of Gurus*. London: HarperCollins, 1996

Stuart of Findhorn, James, Viscount. *Within the Fringe: An Autobiography*. London: The Bodley Head, 1967

Sweeney, John. *Purple Homicide*. London: Bloomsbury, 1997

Taylor, A.J.P. *Lloyd George: Rise and Fall*. The Leslie Stephen Lecture. Cambridge: Cambridge University Press, 1961

——, ed. *Lloyd George: A Diary by Frances Stevenson*. London: Hutchinson, 1971

——and others. *Churchill: Four Faces and the Man*. London: Allen Lane, 1969

Taylor, G.R. Stirling. *Modern English Statesmen*. London: George Allen & Unwin, 1920

Templewood, Samuel Hoare, Viscount. *Nine Troubled Years*. London: Collins, 1954

Thal, Herbert van. *The Prime Ministers*. 2 vols., London: George Allen & Unwin, 1974, 1975

Thatcher, Margaret. *What's Wrong with Politics?* London: Conservative Political Centre, 1968

——*The Downing Street Years*. London: HarperCollins, 1993

——*The Path to Power*. London: HarperCollins, 1995

Thorpe, D.R. *Alec Douglas-Home*. London: Sinclair-Stevenson, 1996

Thorpe, Jeremy. *In my own Time*. London, Politico's, 1999

Tiratsoo, Nick, ed. *From Blitz to Blair: A New History of Britain since 1939*. 1997; London: Phoenix, 1998

Trewin, J.C. and King, E.M. *Printer to the House: The Story of Hansard*. London: Methuen & Co, 1952

Trollope, Anthony. *The Way We Live Now*. London, 1875

——*An Autobiography*. London, 1883

Tucker, Robert C. *Stalin as Revolutionary 1879–1929*. New York: W.W. Norton, 1973

Tunstall, Jeremy. *The Lobby Correspondents*. London: Routledge & Kegan Paul, 1970

Valentine, Alan. *The British Establishment, 1760–1784: An Eighteenth-Century Biographical Dictionary*. Norman: University of Oklahoma Press, 1970

Various authors. *Brendan Bracken 1901–1958: Portraits and Appreciations*. London: Eyre & Spottiswoode, 1958

Walden, George. *Lucky George: Memoirs of an Anti-Politician*. London: Allen Lane, 1999

Waller, Robert and Criddle, Byron. *The Almanac of British Politics*. Seventh edn, London: Routledge, 2002

Walter, David. *The Oxford Union: Playground of Power*. London: Macdonald, 1984

Wasson, Ellis. *Born to Rule: British Political Elites*. Stroud: Sutton Publishing, 2000

'Watchman'. *Right Honourable Gentlemen*. London: Hamish Hamilton, 1939

Waterhouse, Nourah. *Private and Official*. London: Jonathan Cape, 1940. [The copy I have looked at was one of six advance copies. Various changes were made by the Law Officers of the Crown to the eventual published version. The original is more interesting.]

Watkins, Alan. *Brief Lives, with Some Memoirs*. London: Hamish Hamilton, 1982

——*A Slight Case of Libel: Meacher v Trelford and Others*. London: Duckworth, 1990

——*The Road to Number 10: From Bonar Law to Tony Blair*. London: Duckworth, 1998

Wedgwood, Lord. *Testament to Democracy*. London: Hutchinson, 1942

Wheen, Francis. *Tom Driberg: His Life and Indiscretions*. London: Chatto & Windus, 1990

Whitehead, Phillip. *The Writing on the Wall: Britain in the Seventies*. London: Michael Joseph in association with Channel 4, 1985

Wilding, Norman and Laundy, Philip. *An Encyclopaedia of Parliament.* Fourth edn, London: Cassell, 1971

Williams, Francis, ed. *A Prime Minister Remembers: The War and Post-War Memoirs of the Rt Hon. Earl Attlee, K.G., P.C., O.M., C.H. Based on his Private Papers and on a Series of Recorded Conversations.* London: William Heinemann, 1961

——*A Pattern of Rulers.* London: Longmans, 1965

Williams, Hywel. *Guilty Men: Conservative Decline and Fall, 1992–1997.* London: Aurum Press, 1998

Williams, Marcia. *Inside Number 10.* London: Weidenfeld & Nicolson, 1972

Williamson, Philip. *Stanley Baldwin.* Cambridge: Cambridge University Press, 1999

Wilson, Des. *So You Want to be Prime Minister: An Introduction to British Politics Today.* London: Peacock Books, 1979

Wilson, Harold. *A Prime Minister on Prime Ministers.* London: Weidenfeld & Nicolson and Michael Joseph, 1977

——*Memoirs: The Making of a Prime Minister 1916–64.* London: Weidenfeld & Nicolson and Michael Joseph, 1986

Wilson, John. *CB: A Life of Sir Henry Campbell-Bannerman.* London: Constable, 1973

Wright, Tony, ed. *The British Political Process.* London: Routledge, 2000

Young, Hugo. *One of Us.* 1989; London: Pan Books, 1990

——*This Blessed Plot: Britain and Europe from Churchill to Blair.* 1998; London: Papermac, 1999

——and Sloman, Anne. *No, Minister.* London: BBC, 1982.

Young, Kenneth. *Arthur James Balfour: The Happy Life of the Politician, Prime Minister, Statesman and Philosopher.* London: G. Bell and Sons, 1963

Periodicals, series and articles

Boothroyd, Betty. Foreword to *The Houses of Parliament.* Norwich: Jarrold, 1999

Gerrard, Nicci. 'Grey Major will be remembered in colour, oh yes'. *Observer,* 17 October 1999

Gordon Walker, Patrick. 'On Being a Cabinet Minister'. *Encounter,* April 1956

Hansard (various references as cited in the Notes)

Isis (the Oxford University Magazine, 1892–). Various articles, including (all Anon.): 'Isis Idol: John Boyd-Carpenter', No. 805, 15 October 1930; 'Union Notes', No. 806, 22 October 1930; 'Editorial', No. 807, 29 October 1930; 'Michael Foot Joins Labour', No. 914, 27 February 1935; 'The Oxford Union Debating Society', No. 1691, 7 October 1976

Kingston, Peter. 'Learning Curve: Julian Critchley'. *Guardian*, Education Section, 12 October 1999

Norton, Philip. 'The Individual Member in the British House of Commons: Facing Both Ways and Marching Forward'. In Longley, Lawrence D., and Hazan, Reuven Y., eds., *The Uneasy Relationships between Parliamentary Members and Leaders*. London: Frank Cass, 2000

Rogow, Arnold A. 'Towards a Psychiatry of Politics'. In Rogow, Arnold A., ed., *Politics, Personality and Society Science in the Twentieth Century: Essays in Honour of Harold D. Lasswell*. London: University of Chicago Press, 1969

Stewart, Louis H. 'Birth Order and Political Leadership'. In Hermann, Margaret G., ed., with Milburn, Thomas W., *A Psychological Examination of Political Leaders*. London: Collier-Macmillan, 1977

Various eds. *The Times House of Commons* 1910–1966. Continued as *The Times Guide to the House of Commons* 1970–1997. London: Times Books

Weinberg, Ashley. 'Stress and the Politician'. In Power, Greg, ed., *Under Pressure: Are We Getting the Most from our MPs?* London: Hansard Society, 2000

——Cooper, Cary and Weinberg, Anne. 'Workload, Stress and Family Life in British Members of Parliament and the Psychological Impact of Reforms to their Working Hours'. *Stress Medicine*, 15, 79–87, 1999

Index

Index